THE URBAN EXPERIENCE
Second Edition

Claude S. Fischer

University of California, Berkeley

Under the General Editorship of
Robert K. Merton
Columbia University

HARCOURT BRACE JOVANOVICH, PUBLISHERS
San Diego   New York   Chicago   Washington, D.C.   Atlanta
London   Sydney   Toronto

ISBN: 0-15-593498-8

Library of Congress Catalog Card Number: 83-82508

Printed in the United States of America

Cover credit: © 1984, Bela Kalman, Stock, Boston.

Photo credits: Facing Chapter 1, HBJ Photo; p. 12, © 1980, Hazel Hankin; p. 42, © 1983, Harvey Stein; p. 74, © 1982, Hazel Hankin; p. 112, HBJ Photo by Jim Theologos; p. 142, HBJ Photo by Robin Forbes; p. 172, Zephyr Photo, © 1983, Melanie Kaestner; p. 200, © 1982, Hazel Hankin; p. 236, Courtesy Schwinn Bicycles; p. 270, HBJ Collection.

Figure credits:

Figure 1   Fischer, C. S. 1975b. "Toward a subcultural theory of urbanism." *American Journal of Sociology* 80: 1319–1341.

Figure 2   Adapted from Ford, A. B. 1976. *Urban Health in America.* New York: Oxford University Press.

Figure 4   Keyes, F. 1958. "The correlation of social phenomena with community size." *Social Forces* 36: 311–315.

Figure 9   Fischer, C. S. 1982a. Chapter 10 in *To Dwell among Friends: Personal Networks in Town and City.* Chicago: University of Chicago Press.

Figure 10   Srole, L. 1978. "The city vs. town and country: new evidence on an ancient bias," p. 481 in L. Srole and A. K. Fischer (eds.) *Mental Health in the Metropolis.* Rev. ed., 1978. New York: New York University Press.

To Annie

PREFACE to the SECOND EDITION

This Second Edition of *The Urban Experience* resembles the first in structure and perspective. But it differs considerably from the first in several other ways. The book has been heavily revised to include research appearing in the last seven years and studies overlooked in the first edition, spanning sociology, history, psychology, anthropology, and allied fields. (The bibliography is about 75 percent longer than before.) The book has been updated to present the latest available data and to address the latest controversies. It has been expanded to deal with new topics, such as "return migration" to rural areas and urban "gentrification," as well as to extend the discussion of previous topics, such as crime and neighborhood organizations. And the book has been thoroughly rewritten and edited, line by line, for greater clarity and easier reading.

A selection from the preface to the first edition, which provides an overview of the book's perspective and organization, is reprinted after this preface.

Several people have helped produce this Second Edition. Reviewers and other readers of the first edition alerted me to its problems. Judith Rothschild and Linda Fuller helped scour the libraries. Avery Guest of the University of Washington, Albert Hunter of Northwestern University, and Harvey Molotch of the University of California, Santa Barbara, carefully reviewed the initial draft of this edition. Their suggestions were helpful, but because I did not accept all of them, those eminent urban scholars are innocent of complicity in any remaining errors. Berkeley's Institute of Urban and Regional Development, directed by Melvin M. Webber and managed by Kathy Crum, provided the needed clerical assistance of Dorothy Heydt, Tawnya Pickett, Linda Reichman-Garcia, Maureen Jurkowski, and Eric Billitzer. Eric Brown and Louise Jezierski proofed the text and constructed the index.

General Editor Robert K. Merton continues to be an inspiration. I would also like to thank the editors at Harcourt Brace Jovanovich who, over the years, managed this project: Judith Greissman, Peter Dougherty, Gary Burke, Suzanne Wedow, and Marcus Boggs. Larry Platt edited the manuscript excellently. Thanks are also due to Bill Shaw, Helen Faye, Lynn Edwards, and Cate Safranek of the HBJ staff.

Ann Swidler, who between the first edition and this one moved from "significant other" to wife, continues to be my prime motivator and more than earns the dedication of this book every day. Finally, Abraham (Avi) Fischer did not, in his first year of life, help produce this book, but he deserves mention because he could have done so much more to prevent it and because he made the year of its writing so much more fun.

C. S. F.

From the PREFACE to the FIRST EDITION

The purpose of this book is to summarize our knowledge of the social and psychological consequences of urban life. Does living in a densely populated community rather than in a small town or village cause any differences in a person's social relationships, psychological state, or life experience? If so, what are the differences and how can they be explained? Speculation about these questions has abounded as long as cities have existed—more than 5,000 years—and will continue to flourish as long as cities continue to exist. But it is only recently, especially in the last two decades, that the social sciences have accumulated enough facts about urban life to permit an informed stock-taking.

The Urban Experience examines many areas of urban life: Chapters 1 and 2 are devoted to the historical background of cities and the three main sociological theories of urbanism that are the foundation of the subsequent discussion; Chapters 3 and 4 consider the physical and social settings of urban life and their impact on the city dweller; Chapters 5 and 6 discuss the nature of such social groups as the neighborhood and the family in the urban environment; Chapters 7 and 8 deal with the psychology of urban individuals and their typical styles of belief and behavior; Chapter 9 examines the *sub*urban experience; and Chapter 10 summarizes and draws conclusions, indulges in speculations about the urban future, and sets out the moral of the story.

The presentation is organized around a confrontation between three different theories of urban life: first, the most popular theory—that urbanism weakens social cohesion, subjects city dwellers to stress, and culminates in alienation and disorder; then, the opposing theory—that urbanism has little impact on social groups and individuals, certainly far less than the effects of social class, age, and ethnicity; and, finally, a theory that synthesizes these two views, arguing that urbanism does not debilitate social groups, but, instead, that it helps to create them. The predictions of these three theories are evaluated against our best estimate of the facts, across many realms of social life.

This book is intended primarily for students of urban life— most specifically of urban sociology, but also for students of psychology, economics, political science, and urban anthropology. And the topics discussed are certainly of interest to students of urban design, urban architecture, and urban planning. The book presupposes no sociological training; thus the discussion has been kept simple, with little or no intricate analysis, and a conscientious attempt has been made to explain the significance of what might seem to be academic obsessions—for example, the importance of analyzing definitions. But my hope is that the book will also interest professionals in the social sciences and urban studies who are seeking a comprehensive review and analysis of the field. Primarily for them, the notes at the end of the text provide extensive references and some extended discussions of complex or technical issues. For both students and professionals, the result, I hope, is an easily read but also fully documented text.

The Urban Experience began in the form of lectures to a few hundred undergraduates at the University of California, Berkeley. Their responses, positive and negative, have improved it for those who follow them. Discussions with graduate students who have worked with me—especially Mark Baldassare, Kathleen Gerson, Robert Jackson, Lynne Jones, and Ann Stueve—contributed to several of the analyses. Melvin M. Webber lent encouragement and the support of the Institute of Urban and Regional Development at Berkeley. Ann Swidler provided key sociological ideas and strong moral support. Gerald Suttles' comments on the initial draft gave helpful direction in the writing. Charles Tilly's many specific suggestions on various drafts were invariably insightful and markedly improved the book. And Robert K. Merton more than lived up to his fame as a dedicated and peerless editor; working with him has been an altogether edifying experience.

C. S. F.

CONTENTS

1

Introduction
An Overview

Over the centuries millions of people have left their hamlets and villages to seek a new life in cities. Each of them—a midwestern farm boy toting a shabby valise through the streets of Chicago, a displaced peasant building his shanty on a steep hillside overlooking Rio de Janeiro, or a free-spirited girl in West Africa catching a ride on a mammy-wagon to Accra—must have wondered: What will life be like in the city? What will the city do to me? What sort of person will I become?

This book is about such questions. It deals with the social psychology of urban life—the experiences of people living in cities; how their social relationships are influenced by the urban scene; and how their attitudes and actions change by being city dwellers.

This topic, the consequences of living in cities, has generated a large and ancient body of popular opinion and scholarly speculation. The predominant school of thought and popular opinion both hold that residing in cities, in and of itself, tends to alter people's minds and social lives, largely for the worse. Another view holds that city life does not have such effects. To the extent that differences between ways of life in city and country exist, they result from different types of people coming to live in each place, or from different economic circumstances in the communities, not from the urban or rural qualities themselves. One objective of this book is to pit these two arguments against each other, and to extract a third theory from the clash of ideas and facts. This third theory is a synthesis of seemingly opposed ideas. It emphasizes the difference between the kinds of people and institutions found in the city and the countryside, but argues that the urbanism of the community— essentially, its population concentration—itself does have significant consequences for these people.

A larger purpose of this book is to present and integrate current knowledge about the consequences of urban life to the person. What does the intensive research of the last few decades teach us about what cities do to people? Just as important, what do we *not* know? This book provides both a compendium of our knowledge and a specification of our ignorance about the experience of living in cities.

In reviewing the book's various topics—housing, crime, social attitudes, and so forth—we will engage in two related but distinct logical tasks: description and explanation. In each instance, we will first *describe* the differences, if any, between city-dwellers and country residents, and then we will consider various *explanations* for those differences, including the explanation that something about cities *as cities* caused those differences.

Urban social psychology is a familiar and inevitably important topic for everyone concerned with urban problems, whether the problems are those currently plaguing the central cities of modern nations or the crises accompanying rapid urbanization in the less-developed countries. How many of these difficulties, observers have often wondered, result from urbanism itself? Does population concentration per se disrupt "natural" ways of life? Although these questions have often been raised, they have rarely been answered with more than guesses and anecdotes. Within the limitations of contemporary social science, this book is intended to provide more substantial answers.

CITIES AND THE HUMAN EXPERIENCE

The crises of the contemporary city are distractingly dramatic, but they should not deter us from viewing the urban experience within a historical context. For millennia, people have had to adjust to city life. According to most estimates, the first cities arose in Mesopotamia about 5,500 years ago, followed by similar developments in the Nile, Indus, and Yellow River valleys; around the Mediterranean Sea; in West Africa, Central America, and the Andes. From those earliest urban centers—cities that rarely housed more than 30,000 souls—to metropolises of the modern day, urban civilizations have risen and fallen. But cities and ideas about city life have endured as part of our common experience.

In human terms, six millennia is a very long time. But from the perspective of natural history, our experience with cities is still short and slight. People have lived in permanent settlements of any kind for only the last 2 percent of our history (about 10,000 years), and the urban era covers only about one-half of that. Most societies have been completely rural; those that were urbanized at all only occasionally had cities exceeding 30,000 people, and rarely had any that reached 100,000 (the population of Cedar Rapids, Iowa in 1980). Even in great ancient civilizations, less than 10 percent of the populace actually lived within the capital city.

The great urbanization of *homo sapiens* occurred almost yesterday. Demographer Kingsley Davis has estimated that as late as 1850 only 2 percent of the world's population lived in cities of more than 100,000 persons. But today about a one-fourth do. And the pace of urban growth is accelerating, so that by the end of the century perhaps 40 percent of all people will live in such large cities (Davis, 1955, 1966, 1972). Our urban experience in the last three to five generations, then, is much more intense than in any preceding time.[1]

This "urban revolution" makes understanding the social consequences of city life imperative. From wandering hunters and gatherers, human beings have "suddenly" become city-dwellers. Some writers and theorists worry that the human organism cannot adjust from its original nomadic makeup to that of an urban office-worker. Popular books have argued that cities are unnatural (one author calls them "human zoos") and that their crowding breeds pathological symptoms and behaviors.[2] Of more serious concern is the possibility that human cultures may be slow to adapt to cities because peoples' fundamental values and beliefs were formed during pastoral eras. To what extent, for example, might our picture of the ideal childhood—lived on a farm, complete with dog and intimate neighbors—interfere with raising children successfully in a large city? For these reasons, it is both timely and important to take stock of the social psychology of urban life.

It is important for other reasons. For sociologists, understanding the consequences of urbanism provides insights into the general development of modern society. Urbanization has been highly significant in modernization, and the two processes, different as they are, contain parallel features, especially in the matter of size or scale (see Fischer, 1975a). Cities compared with villages and modern societies compared with primitive ones are immensely large. What happens to social order and to individual psyches with such increases in scale is of widespread concern. For all students of communities, the subject is important because urbanism is a major dimension of commmunities. No single settlement can be understood unless it is put within the context of the entire range of settlements (see Reiss, 1959a; Arensberg, 1965). Other interests also lead us to study the urban experience: understanding the interaction of people with their environments, the professional task of planning new communities, and concern about urban problems, for example.

But better than any of these "good" reasons for studying the social psychology of living in cities is our own curiosity about ourselves. Does urban life alter the way we think and act? If so, how? For better or for worse? And what is the explanation of those alterations?

THE PLAN OF THIS BOOK

This section briefly explains the strategic decisions I have made in studying the urban experience, since these form the basis of my approach in this book.

The very use of the word "experience" in the book's title reflects an important decision. In truth, there are many urban experiences, as many as there are urban individuals. A millionaire being driven down Park Avenue in his limousine and a junkie huddling in a burned-out tenement in the South Bronx are both New Yorkers, yet their experiences are scarcely the same. Nevertheless, as we shall see, similarities exist even between such seeming opposites, because of the significant similarities in the individual experiences urban people have and the ways they react to them. The social-science procedure for uncovering such similarities is to collect "objective" indicators of people's experiences, using techniques that are sufficiently reliable and valid for different investigators to arrive independently at the same conclusion.

The word "urban" in the title of this book also requires some comment. The obviously related terms "urban" and "urbanism" both refer—in this book—to the population of a place of settlement; the greater the number of people residing in and around a place, the more urban it is and the more urban are the experiences of its residents. Thus, urbanism is a gradation, a matter of degree (Wirth, 1956). "Urban" is a confusing word (see Chapter 2), but I use this simple definition. I will also often use the contrasting terms "urban" versus "rural" or "city" versus "countryside," but I do not mean to imply any sharp dichotomy. Such labels usually refer in simple terms to the relationship between a phenomenon and the degree of urbanism. For example, the statement "there is more crime in the city than the countryside" translates into "rates of crime increase as urbanism increases."[3]

Another term will come up, particularly in discussing American communities: "metropolitan." The U.S. Census Bureau defines a "Standard Metropolitan Statistical Area" (SMSA) as, roughly, a county with a city of at least 50,000 people, plus adjacent counties if they are heavily built up, plus other counties if many of their residents commute to work in the center city. Because this definition depends on the political boundaries of counties, many SMSAs include more area than would a sociologically defined urban community. But an SMSA is approximately a city and its suburbs. In 1980, 75 percent of Americans lived in such designated metropolitan areas.

These definitions turn a study of "the urban experience" into an inquiry concerning whether and how the size of the community affects people's lives, as those effects are manifested in behavior and measured by social science research. The method of our inquiry involves reviewing research that compares residents in communities of varying urbanism on many social psychological dimensions: their beliefs, styles of interaction, relationships with friends and relatives, types of deviant behavior, and so on. My aim is to survey all the important social-psychological phenomena, and to establish the correlation of each with urbanism. More ambitious still, I hope to explain these correlations.

The strategy of comparing communities and persons of varying degrees of urbanism requires emphasis. Both the popular and sociological literature often describe some condition within a single urban setting and label it "urban," thereby implying that its urban character caused the condition, as in "urban poverty" or "urban alienation." But this is not logically sound. An event or situation cannot be explained by its urban nature unless it has been systematically compared with similar events in places that are more urban and places that are less urban (see Wirth, 1956).

As unremarkably simple as this principle is, it is more often breached than observed. When we read passages such as following (which will reappear in the Chapter 6 discussion of friendship), "the awful fact is that modern urban society, as a whole, has found no way of sustaining intimate contacts" [Alexander, 1967: 243]," we must ask the following questions: Does the author mean to say that this sad condition is not true of modern rural society? If so, is he suggesting that urbanism itself—that is, population size—is the cause of the "awful fact"? If so, has he actually compared urban and rural places with respect to the relative intimacy of their inhabitants' social ties? And has his comparison resulted in evidence that is more objective than his personal impressions? These are the burdens that the comparative method places on assertions about urban matters. (In this example the answers to the questions would seem to be yes, yes, no, and no.)

In comparing urban and rural places and persons, we should not expect to uncover many large or dramatic social-psychological differences. Substantial variations in personality and social relationships are related to the more intimate attributes of individuals: physical constitution, sex, age, education, and so on. It is unlikely, for example, that urban–rural differences in feelings of despair would be greater than differences in such feelings between rich and poor, black and white, or young and old. Compared to attributes like these, community size forms only a general, crude, and distant context for people. That is why the contrasts between urban and rural persons are generally modest—far too modest to completely explain social-psychological variations, but still meaningful enough to help us understand the urban experience.

Having established what urban–rural differences exist—or do not exist, as the particular case may be—we must then explain them. If, to pursue the earlier examples, farm boys newly arrived in Chicago are on the average more traditional and less intellectual then city boys, or if the young women from the African bush are friendlier but less sophisticated than the market women in Accra, how do we account for these differences? Again, one important school of thought holds that something intrinsic to cities alters people. Another view contends that differences between urban and rural individuals can be largely explained by the personal circumstances of the people being compared—their age, ethnic heritage, job, and so on—and not by the fact that they live in the city or the countryside. In the next chapter, I will set out in detail the major theoretical approaches to this issue, and will then refer to them throughout the book.

In pursuing the theoretical controversy, I return repeatedly to the question whether behavior and attitudes associated with urbanism result from the urbanism itself. Does the concentration of population per se, all else equal, create unique experiences and ways of life? Put another way, would moving people from small communities to large ones, and that alone, change their lives and personalities?[4] When we can answer this question, we will use two general techniques. One technique examines characteristics of cities in different societies and historical eras. This enables us to study instances in which cities exist but in which characteristics inevitably associated with them in modern society (mass media and industrialization, for example) do not. If we find certain experiences common to the people in these various cities, we can at least assert that they result from urbanism itself. A second technique involves statistical analyses of data on communities and their residents. The statistical tools permit us to control complicating factors, and thereby to simulate a situation in which everything except the population concentration of the communities is "held constant." The following chapters draw upon a large number of studies employing such procedures.

MAINTAINING A PERSPECTIVE

The aim of this book, to understand the social psychology of urban life across the entire range of human experience, is unabashedly vast. But its actual scope is more modest because of the limitations of contemporary social science and of the author. I will deal mainly with urbanism in the twentieth century, and that largely in the United States.[5] But this constraint upon the available empirical data need not stunt our imagination or foreshorten our perspective. Throughout the book we must bear in mind that many specific features of contemporary cities casually assumed to be inherent to urban life are actually quite different in the cities of other nations and years. This relativistic perspective not only permits greater accuracy in our understanding, but also places in bold relief those aspects of the urban experience that do consistently occur across space and time.

The variety of cities is immense, including precolonial West African settlements built of grass houses; a city like Aztec Teotihuacan, with its boulevards carefully laid out in geometric patterns; ancient cities in Mesopotamia, with their clay houses built upon the remains of earlier civilizations; and so on up to modern Los Angeles, virtually a country of its own, most of its residents living on freeways and in back yards. This diversity can hardly be encompassed in a short space, so I shall concentrate only on an illustrative contrast between contemporary American cities and the sort of city—for example, Damascus or Cairo—that existed in the Mediterranean area during the Middle Ages.[6]

The first and most dramatic contrast between these cities is size—size of area and population. A feudal city such as Damascus could be easily strolled from one side to another in a morning, but the large metropolises of our period can barely be driven across in the same time. The populations of all but a few of the greatest medieval cities could be dropped into our modern urban centers and make scarcely a ripple. The Los Angeles metropolis was in 1980 over 150 times greater in area and about 14 times greater in population than Cairo at its most glorious around 1500. Yet each was the most urban place of its own time and region, and thus equally a subject for our study.

The streets of modern cities are virtually uniform: two or four lanes of asphalt belong to automobiles, with a yard or two of pavement border conceded to pedestrians. The ambiance of the average noncommercial street in a modern metropolis tends to be rather peaceful. A low city hum in the background may be punctuated by an occasional baby's cry or motorcycle roar. In some neighborhoods, particularly suburban ones, a pedestrian may be only an occasional sight.

Vastly different were the streets of feudal cities such as Damascus or Cairo. They were and many still are very narrow, unpaved or at best laid with stones, often scarcely wide enough for a cart, hemmed in and loomed over by overarching and unstable buildings, cluttered with stalls and benches, and usually following some rambling path understandable only by a long-deceased goat. Most of the city's social life—and more—was packed into the streets. It was as if the urban institutions of today had emptied their contents into dark and narrow alleys—the hospitals their ill and lame; the schools their teachers and pupils; the prisons their inmates and guards; the stores their merchants, customers, and goods; as if the nursing homes had deposited their charges to beg in the streets, the laundries had done their work at public wells, the animals had escaped from the zoos, and sewers ran through the middle of it all. It was a kaleidoscope to the eye, a stench to the nose, and a din to the ear.

Even as late as 1896, a doctor in New York City could complain of

> the useless postman's whistle, the shouting pedlars and hucksters, the yelling "rags and bottles" man, the horn-blowing scissor-grinder and four-in-hand driver, with scores of other noise-makers too numerous to mention, who keep up a continuous din of distracting, nerve-wracking sounds in our residential streets [Girdner, 1896].

In medieval cities these noises would die down at night, as would everything else. The inhabitants had little to do and little light by which to do it. Adequate street lighting did not reach London until 1736 (George, 1964: 101), whereas most cities had to suffer much longer with a darkness broken only by an occasional smoky taper. In fact, in the dark of the night, many of these cities were completely shut down, and the gates to their various quarters locked. "Bright lights" indeed!

Anxiety over violent crime pervades modern American city life, yet the contemporary problem of crime is far less serious than it was in many earlier periods in urban history (see Chapter 4). For instance, fourteenth-century Damascus was "a world where no man was truly safe except among his kin," and in eighteenth-century London, certain quarters were openly ruled by criminal gangs (Lapidus, 1966: 85; Tobias, 1972). Similar reports of organized guilds of gangsters come from the Chinese city of Hangchow, 500 years earlier (Gernet, 1962: 99).

The economic activities supporting urban populations also vary greatly from era to era and city to city. Commonalities exist, of course: administration, specialized crafts, the arts, and supportive services. But the emphases differ. Ancient Peking, for example, was organized around a national bureaucracy. European feudal cities were largely commercial centers facilitating long-distance trade, and some large communities in West Africa were based on agriculture. The cities most familiar to us subsisted first on industry and trade, and now subsist increasingly on communications and organizational services.

In modern American cities the social use of urban land is vastly different from what it was through most of urban history. We casually assume that employed persons work in a district devoted to business and reside in a different and perhaps quite distant neighborhood, commuting regularly between the two places; that they choose their residences largely on the criteria of space, convenience, and cost; that who their neighbors are is determined by who can afford and wishes to live there (with certain exceptions, because of such practices as racial discrimination). In most of the cities most of the time, people lived in or next to the places where they worked. People lived in neighborhoods partly according to their general class—the rich at the center, the poor pressed against the walls—but, more specifically, on the basis of their occupations, with streets set aside for silversmiths, potters, and so forth; foreigners and ethnic and religious minorities were strictly segregated in special quarters. These "ghettos" were often more than just a result of taste or custom; in many cases they were often a matter of law, enforced by walls and gates padlocked at sunset.

These comments barely suggest the great diversity among cities of the past and present. The American metropolis is distinct in many ways from most of these other cities. We have considered size, layout, street activity, safety, economic enterprise, and residential segregation, but the full list is much greater. Rural life, too, has varied greatly over historical memory. For millennia, nomadic tribesmen hunted or herded across barren plains and deserts; peasants huddled with their animals in windowless, dirt-floored shacks, in small hamlets connected by long walks on faint footpaths. More recently, in places like America, settlers have lived in isolated farmhouses, distant not only from town but also from the nearest neighbor. And most recently, the rural community is often a development of expensive retirement homes perched along a rushing stream and an interstate highway, just a half-hour from a sizeable town. This complex picture of the "country" we need also to remember. The social psychology of urban life presented in this book is, by necessity, largely based on modern American urban and rural life. When evidence at hand makes it possible, we will extend the analysis to cover other places, whether ancient Athens, medieval Damascus, or modern Accra. But throughout, it is important to maintain a cross-cultural and historical perspective that places contemporary facts within the context of the greater urban experience.[7]

chapter 2

IMAGES of City Life
Popular Views and Sociological Theories

Cities are viewed as the seed of corruption and duplicity, and New York is the biggest city.—Senator Joseph Biden, explaining the resistance of the U.S. Congress to a request for financial assistance from New York, as quoted in the *New York Times,* 25 May 1975.

Public opinions of urban life have practical consequences. Such opinions motivate people to choose or avoid cities, suggest how visitors and migrants should act in cities, and fuel political battles between urban and rural interests. They also affect the *study* of urbanism. On the one side, social scientists, just like other people, tend to accept stereotypes about the city and countryside; on the other, stereotypes often have a proverbial germ of truth. Both possibilities, being misled and being well-led by folk views, must be considered in the sociological study of city life.

URBANISM IN WESTERN CULTURE

Citizens of the West are heirs to millennia of legend, literature, and art about cities and city life. The messages conveyed by those cultural expressions have not always been consistent or uniform, but the themes that repeat are largely negative.

The image of the sacred city appears in the Bible, of course—Jerusalem, City of Peace, is the residence of God—but the image of the sinful city predominates. Sodom and Gomorrah, heretical and vice-ridden, rather than Jerusalem, are the predominant symbols of the city. Virtue and justice are distinctly pastoral. (On traditional views of the Near East, see Gulick, 1980.) The ancient classical cultures expressed similar themes. In spite of having founded the fabled *polis* in the relatively small city-state of Athens, the Greeks saw country life as altogether more wholesome and virtuous than urban life; they feared large cities (Baroja, 1963). Roman philosophers and poets presented similar ideas. The poet Juvenal, for example, complained that there was "no place in the city . . . for an honest man," that Rome was run by the moneyed and ill bred, that it produced ulcers and insomnia, and that it subjected the unfortunate resident to larcenous landlords and brash burglars (Juvenal, 1958).[1] In the East, too, in traditional China, the city was seen as a place of corruption, the countryside as the site of simple virtue and the good life (Murphey, 1972).

More recent times have seen little change in these opinions. Great European writers since the Renaissance have shown some ambivalence; they often depict the city as the site of civilization, literacy, and the arts; in contrast to the "savagery" and "idiocy" of peasant life. Nevertheless, the prevalent image is the city as the *mise-en-scène* of vice and human degradation. The novels of Balzac and Dickens are characteristic. Romantic philosophers, such as Rousseau, emphasized the greater nobility an virtue of rural man (Schorske, 1963; Howe, 1971). The pastoral and even the modern poets of England have typically yearned for a simpler, more innocent, younger England in reaction to the harsh modernity of its pulsing metropolises (Williams, 1973).

The new American culture of the eighteenth and nineteenth centuries adopted the negative themes about urban life but underplayed the positive "civilization" motif found in much European thought. Combined with the heroic figure of the frontiersman, these notions gave American thought and letters a powerful antiurban bite. "I view great American cities," wrote Thomas Jefferson, "as pestilential to the morals, health, and the liberties of man," and he saw a then-raging yellow-fever epidemic as a potential blessing if it would reduce the size of the cities. Democracy, in the Jeffersonian tradition, flourishes in the countryside and grows ill in urban quarters. Political figures from Andrew Jackson, Abraham Lincoln, and

William Jennings Bryan to recent presidential candidates have often founded claims of virtue on their rural origins. Conversely, cities have been specifically associated with the "shame" of political machines, the danger of foreign hordes, and, in its time, the triple threat of "Rum, Romanism, and Rebellion." Especially during the period of heavy immigration, cities represented to many middle-class Americans: "social upheaval, moral collapse, and an undifferentiated, omnipresent menace. Beneath their showy facade lay traps ever ready to ensnare the unsuspecting; in their unholy glare, village innocence withered [Boyer, 1978: 72; see, also, White and White, 1962; Rourke, 1964]."

American literature also presents a predominantly negative opinion of city life. "Cities," wrote Emerson, "make men talkative and entertaining, but they make them artificial." And his friend Thoreau went off to Walden Pond to rediscover his soul. Of course, there have been exceptions and qualifications to such critiques. Carl Sandburg (1926: 30), for example, even as he admits to Chicago ("Hog Butcher for the World") that "they tell me you are wicked, and I believe them, for I/have seen your painted women under the gas lamps/luring the farm boys," extols its power and vitality:

> Laughing the stormy, husky brawling laughter of
>   Youth, half-naked, sweating, proud to be Hog
>   Butcher, Tool Maker, Stacker of Wheat, Player
>   with Railroads and Freight Handler to the Nation.

Even so, the major motif in American letters was and remains anti-urban (Walker, 1962; Goist, 1977).

Today's America carries on this tradition, as reflected, for example, in its popular songs. For every city thrill there are many more urban laments and rural yearnings. Science fiction, a form of prophecy and parable for our time, is replete with plots about heroes struggling to escape from mammoth, sterile, and dehumanizing cities of the future to the salvation of the countryside (e.g., see Elwood, 1974). One of the most vigorous social movements of the 1970s, environmentalism, carried the banner of proruralism among its leading standards. Modern American society, like an earlier America, sees urban life as a dubious enterprise.

Of all the urban exemplars, perhaps the most mighty is New York City. The prolific traveler John Gunther described it as "the incomparable, the brilliant star city of cities . . . a law unto itself, the

Cyclopean paradox, the inferno with no out-of-bounds, the supreme expression of both the miseries and splendors of contemporary civilization [cited by Strauss, 1961: 18]." This, of course, is hyperbole; but if the reality of New York does not conform to such hyperbole, the *idea* of New York does. As suggested by the remark of Senator Biden quoted earlier, New York is the quintessence of "the City" in the public mind. Expressions of that idea form a montage of mixed and clashing elements, yet each is electric in itself: New York as the place of senseless, brutal crime; of personal freedom and boundless hopes; of variety, choice, excitement; of callous and uncaring people; of social groups diverse enough to satisfy each individual's unique needs; of crass and crushing materialism; of experiment, innovation, and creativity; of anxious days and frightful nights. New York, concluded British author Anthony Burgess after sojourning there, is "the big growling human condition, complete with baroque music and 50 varieties of sour cream [A. Burgess, 1972: 39]."[2]

In this kaleidoscope of images, I can see four basic polarities that organize Western views of city life: 1) nature versus art; 2) familiarity versus strangeness; 3) community versus individualism; and 4) tradition versus change.[3] Each pair presents a characteristic associated in Western culture with rural life and its opposite associated with urban life. Neither pole is universally regarded as "better" or "worse" than the other; instead, they pose dilemmas of personal choice. Depending on which horn of the dilemma they have grasped, philosophers and poets have become either pro urbanists or (as is usually the case) antiurbanists.

Nature Versus Art

The city is art, artifact, a construction of people. To inhabit it is to live in an "artificial" environment, albeit an artistic and intellectual one. Rural life is "natural," closer to nature, "organic." Subthemes deriving from this polarity include instinct versus rationality, body versus mind, outdoors versus indoors, disarray versus order, frankness versus guile, and crudity versus sophistication. A major element is "civilization." People associate it with the city, but in potentially contrary ways. Civilization can mean great sculpture, painting, literature—building a school over a swamp. It can also mean imposing social regulation—the binding collar of propriety—over natural will; constructing a fast-food outlet where an orange grove once grew. All these examples form part of the general polarity between what are seen as rural nature and urban art (see Thrupp, 1963).

Familiarity Versus Strangeness

The countryside is associated with familiar things and familiar persons, with "home." Literary critic Raymond Williams (1973: 297) pointed out that "often an idea of the country is an idea of childhood: not only the local memories, or the ideally shared communal memory, but the feel of childhood . . . those successive and endlessly recessive 'happy Englands of my boyhood.'" But the city is new, different, full of unexpected things and often incomprehensible people. This theme also has its correlatives. One is the notion of the stranger (Simmel, 1950). The city is composed of unknown and often odd-looking, oddly-acting people. Concern over such strangeness expresses itself in xenophobic anxieties about "outlanders," particularly about immigrants clustering in large cities. Yet it is also celebrated as cultural diversity. E. B. White once wrote: "The city is like poetry: it compresses all life, all races and breeds, into a small island and adds music and the accompaniment of internal engines [White, 1949: 229; see Lofland, 1973]." A second aspect of the theme concerns the variety of opportunities provided by the city—activities, sights, and people to meet. Seen by many as a blessing, it is seen by others as temptation: "The city has many attractions/But think of the vices and sins/When once in the vortex of fashion/How soon the course downward begins [Alden, 1887: 34]." In modern days, the moral word "temptation" has been replaced by psychological terms such as "complexity" and "rat race." The essential meaning is the same that the opportunities of the city can entrap. Third, there is the subtheme of "excitement." The city provides thrilling sights, sounds, and adventures; the country is routine and deadly dull. Yet the same observations lead others to say that rural life is humanely paced while urban life is garish, overwhelming, and frenetic.

Community Versus Individualism

A major concern of recent Western thought is the tension between "community," in the sense of intimate and enveloping social groups, and "individualism," in the sense of freedom from social shackles. In its prorural form, this motif presents country-dwellers as ensconced in warm, humanly rich, and supportive social relations: the family, neighborhood, town. Meanwhile, city-dwellers are strangers to all, including themselves. They are lonely, not emotionally touching or being touched by others and consequently are set psychically adrift. This theme has deeply concerned American writers. A student of urban literature notes: "City fiction has portrayed man searching for a complete self in an urban world where personal integration or completeness seems to have become impossible. . . . The characters in urban fiction typically feel that they are strangers moving in an alien world [Gelfant, 1954: 23]." This description fits the English poets as well; Wordsworth, for example:

How often in the overflowing Streets
Have I gone forward with the Crowd, and said
Unto myself, the face of everyone
That passes by me is a mystery.

In its prourban form, the same motif presents the country-dweller as stifled by conventionality, repressed by the intrusion and social control of narrow-minded kin, neighbors, and townsmen, while the city resident is free—free to develop individual abilities, express personal styles, and satisfy private needs. (e.g., see Midwestern American novelists' "exposés" of small-town life.) From both perspectives, community is identified with rural life, and individualism with urban life.

Tradition Versus Change

The countryside is the past: the treasury of fundamental values and traditional ways of life, of morality, religion, neighborliness, and patriotism. The city is the future: where the challenging, the untested, the tradition-shattering, and the deviant flourish. From the prorural perspective, the city is a "den of iniquity," the breeding ground for sin—dishonesty, blasphemy, venality, and every sort of crime. From the prourban perspective, this same theme should be read as creativity: The city produces original ideas, startling inventions, and modern styles of dress, behavior, and thought.

This distinction is so imbedded in American political rhetoric we hardly notice that it is rhetorical. But when politicians or journalists want to praise the "values that built America," they go to a small town. When they want to point with alarm—or with pride—about new trends in American life, the scene is a major metropolis.

These four themes, or ones like them, appear throughout Western statements about urban and rural life. They summarize the prevailing ambivalence toward the city. Each pair can be interpreted in favor of the city, and the choice made accordingly for "art, excitement, freedom, and progress." But each can also be interpreted the opposite way, with the city to be avoided as "contrived, grotesque, lonely, and deviant." Both interpretations are of the same image; the difference is in the attitude of the interpreter. By and large, Western authors—particularly Americans—have judged against the city.

This intellectual heritage, accurate or not, directs our views of city and country: what we look for, how we interpret what we see, what we feel, and what we might do. Yet, more profoundly, the city-versus-country dichotomy is one of the major ways Westerners interpret their societies and social change around them—what the good life is, how the world is changing, what makes people what they are. The mythic categories of city and country help us understand (or misunderstand) much of social life.[4]

PUBLIC OPINION

The images and judgments discussed in the preceding section were those of men and women of letters; in this section, the judgments will be those of the general public, as expressed in attitude surveys. These polls generally are good indicators of the adult population's opinions, but are regrettably limited to only recent decades and largely to American samples. Nevertheless, they compare the images and attitudes of urban life as expressed by the literati with those of "people in the street."

Many surveys have asked people to pick the type of community in which they would ideally prefer to live. The response, at least among Americans today, is loud and clear: the smaller the better. People tend to prefer their own community. But when they wish they were elsewhere, that elsewhere is usually a smaller place. A 1972 survey found the following contrast between where Americans lived and where they said they wanted to live (Commission on Population Growth, 1972: 36).

	Where Americans now live	Where Americans prefer to live
Country	10%	34%
Small town or city	30	33
Medium town or city	28	22
Large city or suburb	27	14

A 1977 survey used different categories but came up with the same basic finding (Louis Harris Assoc., 1979: 91).

	Where Americans now live	Where Americans prefer to live
Town and rural	8%	48%
Suburb	46	26
City	47	24

Note: Because of rounding errors, columns in both tables may not total 100%.

If Americans moved in accord with their tastes, a tremendous shift from the city to the countryside would occur.[5] Even among those currently living in cities, many—in some surveys, majorities—prefer smaller communities. For example, a 1978 Gallup survey found that of the residents of cities over 50,000 one-third would move away if they could.[6] These negative attitudes toward cities increased sharply during the 1960s and 1970s. In 1966, 22 percent preferred cities; ten years later, only 13 percent; preferences for rural places went up from 18 percent to 37 percent (Zuiches, 1981). Apparently, the real "urban crises" have had their effects in this realm as in many others.

Americans prefer small communities. What of attitudes in other nations? Data are available for only a few, but they suggest that northern Europeans similarly lean toward the rural—at least the British and Dutch do (Mann, 1964; *Polls,* 1967). But, people in other nations appear to be more divided on this topic, the French, for instance, seeming to prefer medium-sized towns over the countryside (Girard, Bastide, and Pourcher, 1966: 138), and Latin cultures esteeming the urban life (M. Harris, 1956: 279–289).[7]

We have little systematic information from the world's less-developed nations on this matter, only hints from anthropologists and from popular sayings and stories indicating that the benefits of city life outweigh its drawbacks—"He who hasn't been to Koumassi (a city of 380,000 in Ghana) won't go to Paradise [Hanna and Hanna, 1971: 32–47; Little, 1973]."

The clearly prorural consensus in America shows up not only in residential preferences but also in evaluations of actual communities. When asked a question such as "Would you say that you are satisfied or dissatisfied with the quality of life in your community?," most Americans respond "satisfied." Consistently, however, the proportion that does so drops off as the size of the community goes up. In a 1974 poll, for example, 83 percent of residents in places of under 2,500 responded "satisfied"; 71 percent of residents in metropolises of over a million did the same [Gallup Opinion Index (hereinafter cited as GOI), 1974, #110: 12; see also Louis Harris Assoc., 1979; Marans and Rodgers, 1975; Fischer, 1973b]. Americans' opinions also appear in their desires to and expectations of moving. In a 1980 Gallup Poll, more than one-third of those living in cities larger than 100,000 people wanted to move from their cities if they had the chance; of those living in smaller places, the figure was only 15 percent.[8]

Why do Americans feel this way about their cities? Increases in antipathy over the last generation point to some topical complaints: the high urban cost of living (Rodgers, 1980), poor schools (Louis Harris Assoc., 1979: 134), and, especially, *crime*. Crime was the major reason urban Americans in 1980 gave for wanting to leave town. And crime is so connected with cities in popular opinion that people even tend to judge how "urban" a place is by its crime rate.[9] At a deeper level, Americans typically believe that cities are worse than small towns in terms of congestion, order, friendliness, mental health, and the proper environment for raising children. In the eyes of most people, these basic drawbacks of city life far outweigh its advantages in economic opportunities and entertainment.[10]

But these views represent only the most general consensus among Americans. Certain groups are less antiurban than others.

"City lovers" tend to be more highly educated than most other people, either in professional and white-collar occupations or un-employed, quite young or quite elderly, single or married without children, black, interested in "high culture"—and already living in cities.[11]

Another way of assessing people's preferences is to watch what they do, not listen to what they say. When we examine what people actually do—how they "vote with their feet"—we have to qualify our conclusions substantially. Men and women have moved and continue to move overwhelmingly *toward* urban, especially large urban, areas. Throughout recorded history and in all societies, migration has almost always been from countryside to city (Davis, 1966). But in the 1970s, the United States experienced something new: More Americans moved out of metropolitan areas than moved into them from the countryside. In Chapter 4 we will examine this "turn-around." For the moment we should note two points: First, an average rural American is still more likely to move toward the city than is an average urban American to move to the country. And second, migration toward the city has been the overwhelming his-torical and world-wide pattern. Why is there this contrast, then, between people's—or at least, Americans'—preferences for the country and their moving to the city?

The most important reason is evidently economic. In some instances, rural people have been pushed off the land by drought, expropriation, or plain hard times (as in the case of the "Okies" during the Dust Bowl days). More commonly, young country men and women have been attracted away from the land by the city's beckoning opportunities. It has been historically true and continues dramatically so in most nations that cities provide more oppor-tunities for economic advancement than rural areas do. In the United States the differences are not as great as in less-developed nations, and they continue to narrow here—urban residents having slightly higher standards of living, on the average, than people outside the city, higher costs notwithstanding (see Chapter 4). Some ex-ruralites living and working in cities wax nostalgic about the "green, green grass of home," but few want to return to the country other than to retire or to be buried there (e.g., see, Perlman, 1975; Hanna and Hanna, 1971).

These facts about actual behavior in regard to cities need not belie people's spoken opinions. Instead, the explanation for the one helps to explain the other. Most people (or, at least, most Americans) see residence in cities as a necessary evil—necessary to achieve a desired standard of living, but not desirable in its own right. As long as it is a necessary evil, they are reluctant urbanites.[12] With new economic opportunities developing in rural areas, Americans are less constrained by these considerations than they used to be, but a taste for country living, by itself, does not move them to the country (Carpenter, 1977a; Blackwood and Carpenter, 1978; DeJong and Sell, 1977).

The suburb appears to be one escape from this reluctant urbanism. The suburb has long been seen as combining the virtues of country and city, having the economic and recreational opportunities or urban life together with the wholesomeness of rural life. This hope has motivated surburban expansion and has been part of the sales pitch used by suburban developers (Donaldson, 1969; Warner, 1962; Tarr, 1973). The aspiration is explicit, for example, in the bucolic names chosen for suburban developments: Park Forest, Sleepy Hollow, Mountain View. The wish to have the best of both worlds also finds expression in responses to surveys. In one poll, when people expressing a preference for living in rural areas were then asked whether they wanted their rustic home to be far from a city or near it (within 30 miles), the majority (74 percent) answered "near" (Fuguitt and Zuiches, 1973; Carpenter, 1977). Now, a village or small town within 30 miles of a large city is usually a suburb. That seems to be where most Americans are moving. Metropolitan areas (using 1970 definitions) in the United State grew about 13 percent in population between 1960 and 1980; *all* of that growth and more was in the suburbs. In the past decade, the suburbs continued to grow, albeit more slowly, but the center cities actually lost population—over four million people [U.S. Department of Commerce. Bureau of the Census, 1982a: 16 (hereinafter cited as BOC)].

In summary, soundings of general public opinion echo the literary voices of Western (and especially American) culture: The theme is predominantly antiurban. In part, this popular view reflects concern about the choices examined in the previous section—strangeness, change, and the like. In part, it expresses discontent with other features of urban life, which will be discussed in the next two chapters: noise, pollution, crowds, crime, and so on. Nevertheless, migration *to* the city continues to be the worldwide norm, mainly because of the economic opportunities the city provides.

This discrepancy between the yearning for small-town life and the desire for urban advantages creates among many an unfulfilled desire to leave the city; and it creates among many a fulfilled desire for the best of rural and urban, which they see represented by suburbia.

Much like the heritage of our culture, these public attitudes are based partly on certain assumptions about the nature of urban life. One purpose of this book is to test those assumptions.

SOCIOLOGICAL APPROACHES

Having described cultural values and popular attitudes, we begin our inquiry into the urban experience by considering social science theories about the consequences of urbanism. The purpose of developing such theories before looking at the "real world" is to provide investigators with the concepts needed to organize their perceptions of what would otherwise be a bewildering complexity. Properly developed, these concepts concentrate our attention on the most critical features of the "real world." To begin a major study without a good theory or theories is like being dropped into a dark jungle with neither map nor compass.

But before reviewing those theories, we must consider, once again and more exactly, the problem of defining "urban." It turns out that some of the disagreement and confusion about the urban experience stems from differences in interpreting the terms "urban" and "city."[13] Four broad types of definitions are: demographic, institutional, cultural, and behavioral.

Demographic definitions stress the size and density of population (e.g., Tisdale, 1942). This is the sort of definition we shall use. The greater the concentration of population in and around a place, the more "urban" it is. (The word *around* is important. From a sociological perspective, the influence of population concentration does not end at the municipal boundary, but extends far beyond. So, the critical space is not the legal city, but the general area, often defined, like SMSAs, to encompass the daily commuting range.) A "city," in this sense, is a settlement marked by high population concentration.[14] (We use this general definition until Chapter 9 when, in discussing suburbs, we further delimit the meaning of "city.")

Institutional definitions reserve the term "city" for communities with certain specific institutions. For example, to be a city, a community must have its own autonomous political elite; or, it must have specific economic institutions, such as a marketplace. *Cultural* definitions require that a community possess particular cultural features, such as a group of literate people. And *behavioral* definitions require certain distinctive and typical behavioral styles among the people of a community—for example, an impersonal style of social interaction—before the community is labeled a "city."

The demographic definition has at least three advantages: One, the numerical criterion is common to virtually all definitions of "urban" or "city"; even those dealing with other variables employ size as well. Two, the purely demographic definition does not beg the question about whether any other community trait—institutional, cultural, or behavioral—is necessarily associated with size; that remains open for research. And three, the demographic definition implies that "urban" and "city" refer to matters of degree; they are not all-or-nothing characteristics.[15]

What theories concern the social-psychological consequences of urbanism? Here and throughout the rest of the book, we shall center on three major theoretical stances toward urbanism, two of which confront each other directly, and a third which attempts their synthesis.

1. DETERMINIST THEORY (also called *Wirthian* theory or the *theory of urban anomie*) argues that urbanism (i.e., population concentration) directly alters people's social lives and personalities, mostly for the worse.

2. COMPOSITIONAL (or *nonecological*) THEORIES deny such effects of urbanism; they attribute differences between urban and rural behavior to the social characteristics of the different populations living in city and country, or to their economic circumstances. Urbanism itself has no effects.

3. SUBCULTURAL THEORY—the one I shall propose—adopts the basic orientation of the compositional school (that social characteristics are most important), but holds that ur-

banism *does* have certain effects on people, with consequences much like the ones determinists see as evidence
of social disorganization.

Before considering each theory in detail, we should review the
history of social thought from which they all emerged.

The most influential and historically significant theory of urbanism received its fullest exposition in a 1938 paper by Louis
Wirth (thus the term "Wirthian") entitled "Urbanism as a Way of
Life" (1938). This essay, one of the most often quoted, reprinted, and
cited in all sociological literature, needs to be examined carefully. It
is heir to a long tradition of sociological theory.

The events of most concern to social philosophers during the
nineteenth and early twentieth centuries have been termed the
"Great Transformation" (Polanyi, 1944). Western society was undergoing vast and dramatic changes as a result of the Industrial
Revolution and its accompanying urbanization, nationalization,
and bureaucratization. The early social scientists (Karl Marx, Emile
Durkheim, Max Weber, Georg Simmel, Ferdinand Tönnies, and
others) sought to understand the forms of social life and the
psychological character of the emerging civilization—our civilization.

Their analyses greatly emphasized the matter of *scale*. Innovations in transportation and communication, together with rapid
increases in population, meant that many more individuals than
ever before were able to interact and trade with each other. Instead
of a person's daily life being touched at most by only the few
hundred people of one village, an individual in modern society is
potentially in direct contact with thousands, and in indirect contact
with millions.

This "dynamic density," to use Durkheim's term, in turn produces social differentiation, or diversification, the most significant
aspect of which is an increased division of labor. In the preindustrial
society, most workers engaged in similar activities; in modern society, they have very different and specialized occupations. In a small,
undifferentiated population, where people know each other, perform the same sort of work, and have the same interests—where
they look, act, and think alike—maintaining a consensus on proper
values and appropriate behavior is relatively easy. But in a large

differentiated society, where people differ in their work and do not know each other personally, they have divergent interests, views, and styles. A pipe fitter and a ballet dancer have little in common. And so, little moral consensus or cohesion exists in a modern society; the social order is therefore precarious. Further ramifications of social differentiation, it was thought, included the development of formal institutions, such as legal systems and bureaucracies, to try to keep order; the rise of rational, scientific methods of understanding the world; an increase in individual freedom—but at the cost of interpersonal estrangement; and more deviant behavior and social disorganization.[16]

The essence of this classical analysis connects the structural characteristics of society, particularly its scale, to the quality of its "moral order." That turns out, not coincidentally, to parallel the interest of urban sociology: the association between structural features of communities—particularly their scale—and their moral orders (Fischer, 1975a). In fact, the city has long played a significant role in classical sociological theories. The city was seen as modern society in microcosm, so that the ways of life in urban places were viewed as harbingers of life in the emerging civilization.[17] At the same time, the classical theories have significantly influenced the study of cities; the determinist approach borrowed from them liberally.

The development of urban theory moved from Europe to the University of Chicago during the first third of this century. There, the Department of Sociology, under the leadership of Robert Ezra Park, a former journalist and student of the classical German sociologist Georg Simmel, produced a vast and seminal array of theoretical and empirical studies of urban life, research conducted chiefly in Chicago. In an influential essay published in 1916, Park followed the lead of the classical theorists by arguing that urbanism produced new ways of life and new types of people, and that sociologists should venture out to explore these new forms in their own cities, much in the style of anthropologists studying primitive tribes (Park, 1916). Another strong motive for such research was the social turmoil then accompanying the rapid growth and industrialization of Western cities, a realm of civic activity in which Chicago about 1916 was probably a leader. The serious social problems accompanying these developments demanded understanding.

The studies of Chicago resulted in a remarkable series of descriptions of urban ways of life. The "natural histories" depicted many different groups and areas: taxi-hall dancers, hobos, Polish–Americans, juvenile gangs, the Jewish ghetto, pickpockets, police, and so on (see Short, 1971; E. Burgess and Bogue, 1964; Hunter, 1980). A theme running through the findings of these various studies was that the groups, whether "normal" or "deviant," formed their own "social worlds." That is, the groups tended to be specialized social units in which the members associated mainly with each other, held their own rather distinctive set of beliefs and values, spoke in a distinctive argot, and displayed characteristic styles of behavior. Together these studies described a city that was, to quote Park's famous phrase, "a mosaic of social worlds which touch but do not interpenetrate." As we shall see, the explanation for the urban phenomena observed by Chicago's sociologists was drawn largely from the classical theories about modern society.

Determinist Theory

The determinist theory of urbanism can be found in Park's 1916 paper, but its fullest exposition was achieved in Wirth's essay 22 years later.[18] Wirth begins by defining the city as "a relatively large, dense, and permanent settlement of socially heterogeneous individuals"—essentially, a demographic definition. He then seeks to demonstrate how these inherent, essential features of urbanism produce social disorganization and personality disorders—the dramatic aspects of the city scene that fascinated the Chicago School. Essentially, Wirth's analysis operates on two levels, one a psychological argument, the other an argument about social structure.[19]

The psychological analysis draws heavily on a 1905 paper by Georg Simmel, a teacher of both Park and Wirth. In "The Metropolis and Mental Life," Simmel suggested ways that the city altered individuals' psyches and personalities. The key, he thought, lay in the sensations that life in the city produces: "The psychological basis of the metropolitan type of individuality consists in the *intensification of nervous stimulation* which results from the swift and uninterrupted change of inner and outer stimuli [Simmel, 1905: 48;

italics in the original]." The city's most profound effects, Simmel maintained, are its profusion of sensory stimuli—sights, sounds, smells, actions of others, their demands and interferences. The onslaught is stressful; individuals must protect themselves, they must adapt. And their basic mode of adaptation is to react with their heads instead of their hearts. This means that urban dwellers tend to become intellectual, rationally calculating, and emotionally distant from one another. On the positive side, these changes promote individual freedom for self-development and creativity (see Levine, Carter, and Gorman, 1976). Sixty-five years later, social psychologist Stanley Milgram translated Simmel's analysis into modern language drawn from information theory. The threat of city life is "psychic overload," which must be met by diverting "inputs." But the argument is essentially the same (Milgram, 1970; Geller, 1980; see, also, Meier, 1962; Deutsch, 1961).[20]

Wirth's treatment follows Simmel's and begins with the assumption that the large, dense, and heterogeneous environment of the city assaults the hapless city dweller with profuse stimuli. Horns blare, signs flash, solicitors tug at coattails, poll-takers telephone, newspaper headlines try to catch the eye, strange-looking and strange-behaving persons distract attention—all these features of the urban milieu claim a different response from the individual. Adaptations to maintain mental equilibrium are necessary and they appear. These adaptations liberate urbanites from the claims being pressed upon them. They also insulate them from other people, so that city-dwellers become aloof, brusque, impersonal in their dealings with others, emotionally buffered in their human relationships. Even these protective devices are not enough; inevitably, psychic overload exacts at least a partial toll in irritation, anxiety, and nervous strain.

The interpersonal estrangement that follows from urbanites' adaptations produces further consequences. The bonds connecting people to one another are loosened—even sundered—and without them people are left both unsupported and unrestrained. At the worst, they must suffer through material and emotional crises without assistance. Being alone, they are more likely to fail, to suffer physical deterioration or mental illness, or both. The typical picture is one of an elderly pensioner living in a seedy hotel without friends or kin, suffering loneliness, illness, and pain. This same estrangement also permits people to spin out and act on their wildest fancies—whether the acts be feats of genius or deeds of depravity. The typical picture here is of a small-town boy suddenly unshackled from conventional constraints and given unlimited options—including a life of creative art or a life of crime. Ultimately, interpersonal estrangement weakens community cohesion and dissipates residents' "sense of community." All these psychological changes, Wirth argued, follow from increases in urbanism.

In his analysis of social structure, Wirth reached essentially the same conclusion as he did in his psychological analysis, but he posited different processes. The size, density, and heterogeneity of the population accelerate economic competition. This competition, in turn, produces many differences of the community, manifested most significantly in the division of labor, but in other ways as well: in the diversity of locales—business districts, residential neighborhoods, "bright-lights" areas, and so on; in places of activity, with work conducted in one location, family life in another, recreation in yet a third; in people's social circles, with one group of associates being coworkers, another group neighbors, another friends, and still another kin; in institutions, with the alphabet-soup diversity of governmental agencies, specialized schools, and media catering to every taste. Importantly, this community differentiation is reflected in individuals' activities. Their time and attention come to be divided among different and disconnected places and people. For example, a business executive might move from breakfast with her family, to discussions with coworkers, to lunch with business people, to a conference with clients, to golf with friends from the club, and finally to dinner with neighbors.

This differentiation of social structure and of people's lives within that structure weakens social bonds in two ways. At the community level, people differ so much from each other in such things as their jobs, neighborhoods, and life-styles that moral consensus becomes difficult. With divergent interests, habits, and views of life, groups in the city cannot agree on values or beliefs, on ends or on means. As community-wide cohesion weakens, so does the cohesion of the small, intimate, "primary" groups of society, such as families, friends, and neighbors—the ones on which social order and individual balance depend. The unravelling of social life at each level quickens the other. Primary groups are weakened because, as a result of the differentiation of urban life, each encompasses less of an individual's time or needs. For instance, people work outside the family and increasingly play outside the family, so that the family becomes less significant in their lives. Similarly, they can leave the neighborhood for shopping or recreation, so that the neighbors become less important. Claiming less of people's attention, controlling less of their lives, the primary groups become debilitated. Thus, by dividing the community and by weakening its primary groups, differentiation produces a general loosening of social ties.

This loosening in turn causes anomie, a social condition in which the norms—the rules and conventions of proper and permissible behavior—are feeble. Because people do not agree about the norms, they tend to challenge or ignore them. Yet some degree of social order must be, indeed is, maintained even in the largest cities. The personal means of providing order have been undermined, so other means must be used. These other means that arise to prevent or to moderate anomie[21] are called formal integration: bureaucratic procedures based on universal and impersonal rules, often involving specialists in social control. For example, instead of controlling the behavior of unruly teenagers by talking to them or their parents personally, neighbors call in the police. Instead of settling a community problem through friendly discussions, people organize lobbying groups and formal elections.[22]

This sort of formal integration avoids chaos and can even maintain a well-functioning social order. But according to the classical theories, such an order can never fully replace communal harmony based on consensus and the moral strength of small, primary groups. Consequently, anomie must develop more in urban than in nonurban places.

The behavioral consequences of anomie and of shredded social ties are similar to those eventually resulting from overstimulation. Indeed, weakened social cohesion makes it harder for people to avoid psychic stress. People are left unsupported to suffer their difficulties alone; and they are unrestrained by social bonds or rules from committing all sorts of acts, from simply "odd" acts to dangerously criminal ones.

These, then, are the arguments Wirth and his associates used to explain what seemed to the Chicago School to be peculiarly urban phenomena—stress, estrangement, individualism, and, especially, social disorganization. On the psychological level, urbanism generates threats to the nervous system that then lead people to separate themselves from each other. On the level of social structure, urbanism induces differentiation, which also isolates people. A society with weak social relations frees people, but it also suffers a debilitated moral order, a weakness that permits social disruption and promotes personality problems.

Critiques: Compositional and Similar Perspectives

The determinist approach has been criticized long and strenuously from several alternate positions. These various analyses share the contention that urbanism itself—that is, population concentration—does *not* cause particular ways of life or personalities. If behavioral differences occur between residents of cities and those of villages, the differences are explained by something else, some social features of the communities or of the people themselves, not by population concentration per se.

The most common and significant challenge to determinist theory I will call "compositional theory." It is perhaps best represented by the work of Herbert Gans (1962a, 1962b, 1967; see also Lewis, 1952; Reiss, 1955). Its position has been summarized by another exponent, anthropologist Oscar Lewis.

> Social life is not a mass phenomenon. It occurs for the most part in small groups, within the family, within neighborhoods, within the church, formal and informal groups, and so on. . . . [Consequently,] the variables of number, density and heterogeneity . . . are not crucial determinants of social life or personality [1965: 497].

Compositionalists emerged from the same Chicago School tradition as the determinists, but they derived their inspiration largely from that part of the school that describes the city as a "mosaic of social worlds." These "worlds" are intimate social circles based on kinship, ethnicity, neighborhood, occupation, lifestyle, or similar social attributes. They are exemplified by enclaves such as immigrant neighborhoods ("Little Italy") and upper-class colonies ("Nob Hill"). Wirth himself described such an enclave in his book on Chicago's Jewish ghetto (Wirth, 1928). The crux of the compositional argument is that these private worlds endure even in the most urban of environments.

But social scientists such as Gans and Lewis believe that small, primary groups persist undiminished in the city: not that people are torn apart because they must live simultaneously in different social worlds, but instead that people are enveloped and protected by their social worlds. This point of view denies that ecology—particularly the size, density, and heterogeneity of the wider community—has any serious, direct consequence for personal social worlds.[23] In this view, it matters little to the average kith-and-kin group whether there are 100 people in the town or 100,000; in either case the basic dynamics of that group's social relationships and personalities are unaffected. Instead of "lost community" in the modern urban world, community is "saved" (see Wellman, 1979).

In compositionalist terms, the dynamics of social life depend largely on the nonecological factors of social class, ethnicity, and stage in the life cycle. People's behaviors are determined by their economic position, cultural characteristics, and by their marital and family status. The same attributes also determine their associates and the social worlds they inhabit. These attributes—and not the size of the community or density—shape social and psychological experience.

Compositionalists agree that urbanism might have social psychological consequences, but they argue that any direct effects on people and indirect effects on social worlds are trivial. If community size does have any consequences, these theorists stipulate, the consequences appear because size indirectly affects people's economic situations—which ethnic groups move where, and which age groups live where. For example, large communities may attract industries that in turn provide high-paying jobs, and those jobs will in turn change the lives of the people who obtain them. But that ultimate effect results from the jobs, not the urban experience. Or a city may, because of its industry, disproportionately attract males, so that many men cannot find wives. The shortage of spouses will certainly affect the men's behavior, but not because of any urban anomie. Or having a large percentage of some kinds of people in a community will influence others near them—for example, where many residents are young, the older residents may become interested in youthful pastimes. But this "contextual" effect is produced by population composition, not population concentration. Thus, the compositional approach acknowledges urban–rural social–psychological differences, yet accounts for them by class, ethnicity, or life cycle. Compositional theory contends that such differences are not directly created by the psychological experience of city life, nor by a change in social cohesion caused by numbers.

Other critiques of the Chicago School typically incorporate the compositional analysis, but also make additional claims. Marxist political economists contend that the earlier approach errs in treating individual communities as separate and distinct environments. Instead, towns and cities should be seen as specialized subparts of a national and international *economic system*. In this system, large cities are essentially places for accumulating and mobilizing "surplus" wealth. Because communities have such specialized economic roles—for example, San Francisco, California, handles financial matters, and Tracy, California, processes agricultural goods—they will necessarily differ in kinds of residents and kinds of activities. Perhaps those social differences vary with the size of the communities, but that connection is coincidental. The key considerations are two: How people act depends on their economic or class circumstances, not on where they live; and the social variations we might see among communities reflect the economic structure of the towns and the wider society. In particular, much of what the Chicago School thought was an *urban* way of life is actually a *capitalist* way of life. In other economic systems, these social contrasts between town and country would not appear.[24]

Other scholars besides political economists also contend that the sorts of urban–rural cultural contrasts described by Park et al. are unique to certain societies or historical periods. For example, some have questioned whether this European-bred theoretical tradition can be applied to the United States at all. Rural Europe was largely composed of peasant villages with centuries-old traditions and of small towns held under rigid political control (see M. Walker, 1971; Redfield and Singer, 1954). The rural United States, on the other hand, is largely composed of isolated farm houses and boom-or-bust frontier towns. America may never have had the sort of tightly knit country villages that typify rural "community."[25] This argument challenges determinist theory by implying that it is not ruralism itself that promotes a village's integration, but age-old stability and isolation. Another implication is that the contrasts between city and village found in the classic theories never existed here and exist no longer even in Europe. For example, some argue that the urban disorder identified by the Chicago School was unique to that specific period of rapid urbanization a few generations ago; it had not occurred before nor has it since. A similar but more common argument contends that city and country ways of life *did* differ, in Europe and even in the United States, and indeed perhaps because of urbanism itself, but they differ *no longer.* In societies with radio, television, telephones, cars, nationwide organizations, and the like, "urban–nonurban differences are differences that have ceased to make a difference" (Palen, 1979: 155).

The various criticisms of determinist theory have led some to conclude that it is no longer taken seriously. That is a premature conclusion. The general public takes it seriously, best-selling books proclaim versions of it (e.g., Sale, 1980; Sennett, 1977; D. Morris, 1969), official commissions use it [e.g., *Le Comité d'Etudes* (Lech and Labrousse, 1977)], and as we shall see, urban scholars find considerable evidence in support of it. It remains a major theoretical perspective on the urban experience.

The basic contrast between the determinist and compositional approaches is this: Both emphasize the importance of social worlds in forming the experiences and behavior of people, but they disagree sharply on whether urbanism directly alters those personal milieus. Determinist theory maintains that urbanism weakens the coherence of such groups, with serious consequences for individuals. Compositional theories maintain that these social worlds, although shaped by economics, ethnicity, and so on, are largely impervious to population concentration, and that urbanism thus has no serious *direct* effects on groups or individuals.

Synthesis: Subcultural Theory

The third approach, the author's *subcultural theory* (Fischer, 1975b), contends that urbanism does shape social life—*not,* however, by *destroying* social groups as determinism suggests, but instead by *strengthening* them. The most significant social effect of community size is to promote diverse subcultures (culturally distinctive groups, such as musicians, college students, or Chinese–Americans). Like compositional theory, subcultural theory maintains that intimate social circles persist in the urban environment. But, like determinism, it maintains that ecology significantly changes communities, precisely by supporting the emergence and vitality of distinctive subcultures.

As the Chicago School held in some of its works and as compositionalists argue, the subcultural position holds that people in cities live in meaningful social worlds. These worlds are inhabited by others who share a particular trait (like ethnicity or occupation), who tend to interact disproportionately with one another, and who manifest relatively distinct beliefs and behavior. Social worlds and subcultures are roughly synonymous.[26] Obvious examples of subcultures include ones like those described by the Chicago School: the country club set in Grosse Pointe, Michigan; the Chicano community in East Los Angeles; and the "singles" set in young-adult apartment complexes. There are more intricate subcultures as well. For example, on the south side of Chicago is an area heavily populated by workers in the nearby steel mills. These workers form a residential and occupational subculture, with particular habits, interests, and attitudes. But they are further divided into even more specific subcultures by ethnicity and neighborhood; thus, for example, the recently immigrated Serbo–Croatian steelworkers live in one area and the earlier generation live elsewhere, each group somewhat different from the other (Kornblum, 1974). In both subcultural and compositional theory, these subcultures persist as meaningful environments for urban residents.

But unlike compositional analysis, which discounts any effects of urbanism, subcultural theory argues that these groups *are* affected directly by urbanism, particularly by "critical mass": That number of people great enough to permit what would otherwise be only a small group of people to become a vital, active subculture. Increasing scale creates new subcultures, modifies existing ones, and brings them into contact with each other. Urbanism has unique consequences, including the production of "deviance," not because it destroys social worlds—as determinism argues—but because it creates them.

The subcultural theory holds, first, that urbanism produces Park's "mosaic of little worlds which touch but do not interpenetrate" in two ways: 1) Large communities attract migrants from wider areas than do small towns—migrants who bring with them a great variety of cultural backgrounds and thus contribute to the formation of a diverse set of social worlds. And 2), population concentration produces the structural differentiation stressed by the determinists—occupational specialization, distinctive neighborhoods, specialized institutions, and special interest groups. To each of these structural units are usually attached subcultures. For example, police, doctors, and longshoremen tend to form their own milieus—as do students, or people with political interests or hobbies in common. In these ways, urbanism generates a variety of social worlds.

But urbanism does more: It *intensifies* subcultures. Again, two processes are involved. One is based on our notion of critical mass: Sufficient numbers allow them to have a visible and affirmed identity, to act together in their own behalf, and to interact extensively with each other. For example, let us suppose that one in every 1,000 persons is intensely interested in modern dance. In a small town of 5,000 that means there would be, on the average, five such persons, enough to do little else than engage in conversation about dance. But a city of one million would have 1,000—enough to support studios, occasional ballet performances, local meeting places, and a special social milieu. Their activity would probably draw other people beyond the original 1,000 into the subculture (those quintets of dance lovers migrating from the small towns). The same general process of critical mass operates for artists, academics, bohemians, corporate executives, criminals, computer programers—as well as for ethnic and racial minorities.

This intensification process will tend to make the greatest difference for small subcultures or would-be subcultures, such as the dance afficionados. Urban concentration would make less difference for those types of people who are relatively common in most places, such as, say, the fans of Hollywood movies.

The other intensification process results from contacts among these subcultures. People in different social worlds often do "touch," in Park's language. But in doing so, they sometimes rub against and irritate one another. Whether the encounter is between blacks and Irish, hard-hats and radicals, or town and gown, people from one subculture often find people in another subculture threatening, offensive, or both. A common reaction is to embrace one's own social world all the more firmly, thus contributing to its further intensification.

Unlike the process of attaining critical mass, the process of cultural reaction tends to affect members of large groups more than those of small minorities. The minorities—for example, Jews or the physically handicapped—tend to sense their distinctiveness both in small town and large city. But in the urban centers, by virtue of the minority group's concentration, majority group members tend to become especially aware of them. (Smaller groups have the particularly urban experience of encountering one another—for example, Vietnamese refugees and Palestinian grocery-store owners in San Francisco, bluegrass-music fans and opera fans around Carnegie Hall in New York.)

This description of tension and conflict does not deny that positive contacts often occur between groups. They do occur; and a good deal of mutual influence as well—for example, young construction workers growing beards popularized by college "hippies," or middle-class whites using black slang. The diffusion of cultural elements across group lines and the opportunities urbanites have to participate in a few subcultures, thereby acting as personal bridges among them, weaken the distinctiveness and cohesion of urban social worlds. (This process highlights the importance of relative group size in addition to absolute size. Which subculture influences which other, and how much, depends in part on their proportions in the population.) But many—in some instances, most—intergroup contacts involve some tension and estrangement. This contrast and recoil helps define and intensify subcultures.

Among the subcultures spawned or intensified by urbanism are those usually considered to be either downright "deviant" by the larger society—such as delinquents, professional criminals, and homosexuals; or to be at least "odd"—such as artists, missionaries of new religious sects, and intellectuals; or to be breakers of tradition—such as life-style experimenters, radicals, and scientists.[27] These flourishing subcultures, together with the conflict that arises between them and mainstream subcultures, are both effects of urbanism, and they both produce what the Chicago School thought of as social disorganization. According to subcultural theory, the signs of disorganization appear, not because social worlds break down and people break down with them, but quite the reverse—because social worlds are formed and nurtured.

Subcultural theory is thus a synthesis of the determinist and compositional theories: Like the compositional approach, it argues that urbanism does *not* produce mental collapse, anomie, or interpersonal estrangment; that urbanites at least as much as ruralites are integrated into vigorous social worlds. But like the determinist approach, subcultural theory also argues that urbanism itself—population concentration—*does* affect social groups and individuals. And it argues that the differences between rural and urban persons' lifestyles and personalities have causes other than the economic, ethnic, or other circumstances of those persons. Figure 1 summarizes the subcultural argument.

SUMMARY

The intent of this chapter is twofold: to describe the popular views of urban life that variously color any study of the city, and to list the three key sociological approaches to understanding the urban experience. We have noted a few reasons why contemporary public opinion, particularly in America, is largely antiurban; other reasons will be considered in the next chapter. But one source of these views is the image of the city projected in Western thought since ancient times. We noted four major themes in that cultural heritage: nature versus art, familiarity versus strangeness, community versus individualism, and tradition versus change. Each of these can be interpreted as being for or against city life, and most have been interpreted against the city. The classical determinist theory of urbanism draws on many of the same ideas, in a sense arguing that the strangeness and complexity of urban life creates a pervasive individualism that in turn leads to deleterious consequences for the individual and the society. Against this determinist position, compositional theory argues that urbanism has no major social–psychological effects. Subcultural theory, a third and synthesizing

Figure 1
A SCHEMATIC PRESENTATION OF THE SUBCULTURAL THEORY

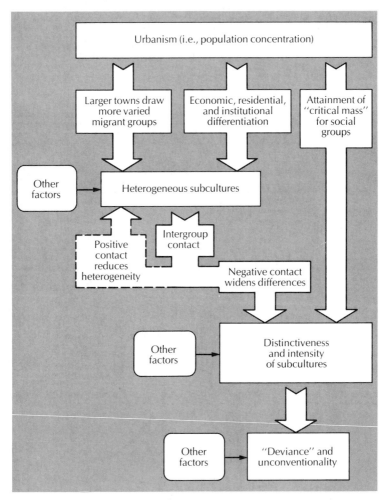

Source: Adapted from Fischer (1975b: Figure 1).

approach, argues that these effects do occur—not because social groups break down, but rather because they are created.

These conceptions, popular and sociological, state the question of this book with some force: What are the major social–psychological consequences of urban life? In the next chapter we begin to discover the answers.

CHAPTER 3

URbAN LifE: ThE PhysicAl SETTiNG

The visitor's first impressions of a city are of its physical nature. I confess that I never fail to be awed by Manhattan—left gaping at its buildings grazing the clouds; swept up by its massive crowds; dazed by its cacophony of horns, truck brakes, and construction machines; alarmed by how quickly its soot gathers under my collar; and, not least, rendered wide-eyed by the exotic and beautiful objects found in its galleries and stores. All the great cities—London, Paris, and the few others in their league—leave impressions much like this, though each is spiced in its own way.

How is the urbanism of a community related to its physical features? And what are the effects of these physical dimensions on individuals? The debate between the determinist and compositional theorists begins here, on the issue of whether the physical context of the urban experience affects psychological states.

THE ECOLOGICAL VARIETY IN CITIES[1]

The urban visitor soon learns that the city is not physically uniform; its various subareas often differ radically from each other. For example, a tourist in San Francisco driving on Geary Street from its downtown intersection with Market Street all the way across the northern part of the peninsula to Geary's western terminus at the Pacific Ocean sees, in rapid succession: a financial district of modern glass-and-girder office buildings; an older area of fancy shops and large department stores; a small theater and night-life district; a seedy strip of bars and hotels for transients; an area of recently constructed high-rise luxury apartment buildings mixed in with low-rise public housing projects; a hospital district; and a long stretch of small stores surrounded by residential neighborhoods of well-kept duplexes and triplexes.

This variety within cities is familiar; it is also important because the physical differences in the various locales of a city are accompanied by social differences in the people who live and work in these locales and the activities that take place in them. Together, the various kinds of differences mean that *the urban experience is plural.* People living in the same metropolis will be affected in very different ways by the place in which they live—sprawling suburb, inner-city ghetto, penthouse—and by their work place—downtown office or a factory on the city's outskirts. These internal variations are not random. They occur in systematic patterns common to many cities. Although, as we have seen in Chapter 1, great diversity exists in the types of cities throughout urban history, we can usefully distinguish between preindustrial cities (or cities mostly established before industrialization) on the one hand, and modern cities on the other. Each type tends to have its own pattern (Sjoberg, 1960).

Preindustrial cities tended to be small, and densest near the center. At the center were usually the main market, the temple, and the homes of the rulers. Other members of the elite lived nearby. Around them resided well-to-do merchants, small shopkeepers, artisans, and craftsmen. The further out from the center, the lower the quality of the dwellings and the social rank of the residents, until near the city wall and beyond were the laborers and the poor. The pattern was not simply circular; it was significantly "cellular" in spatial structure. Various streets or sections ("quarters") of the city held the residences of particular ethnic groups (a form of segregation that continues today) and of particular occupations, such as the "street of the leatherworkers." In the preindustrial city, occupation and ethnicity usually overlapped a good deal. Usually, the lines between sections were not sharp, but sometimes the quarters were walled apart, with gates locked at night (as, for instance, in the Jewish ghetto). Often, settlements were just outside the walls and linked to the city, such as the residences of the long-distance trad-

ers. Many of these preindust
the developing world and in

Cities of the industrial W
different structures over the las
historians describe this evolution
were "walking cities," compact
walking distance and residences,
cally mixed together. By 1900, th
"streetcar cities," grown into starlir
following streetcar lines radiating fron
was increasingly specialized in business
(excepting the poor) moved to homes a   end of
the trolley lines. By mid-twentieth century   ad "automobile cities." The area of what are now   ropolises expanded
tremendously, the land between the fingers of streetcar development were built up, and many subcenters of commerce and industry
appeared around the metropolitan region (e.g., see D. Ward, 1971;
Warner, 1962; Guest, 1972b; see, also, discussion in Chapter 9).

We now have a modern layout that differs from preindustrial
ones in at least three major ways.

1. Home and work place are now separate. Silversmiths or
   merchants of earlier days worked and lived at the same
   location; today they live at one place and work at another perhaps many miles away. We have therefore two
   systems of land-use distinctions: variations in business
   locations—the warehouse, financial, and entertainment
   districts, for example—and variations in residences—
   the apartment house, high society, and tenement districts, for example.
2. Social classes have probably become more separated. Although residential segregation existed in preindustrial
   cities, it seems not to have been based primarily on
   income. Rich and poor artisans lived near one another
   (albeit in dwellings of different quality); the rich and
   poor members of an ethnic community shared a common quarter. In modern cities, the major differences
   between residential areas depend largely on what the
   inhabitants can afford to pay. Age groups—singles,
   families, and elderly—have probably also become more
   segregated.

between centrality and social rank has been reversed. Whereas residents' status used to decline the farther they lived from the city center, it now tends to increase, if it varies with distance at all.

In most Western nations these preindustrial-to-industrial changes occurred from the mid-nineteenth century through the first few decades of the twentieth—a period when the economic bases, social composition, and technologies or urban social structures were in rapid flux. Whatever the various forces that produced the physical layout of modern cities, the changes could not have occurred without the invention and spread of cheap and efficient means for short-distance transportation. Beginning with horse-drawn buses on cobbled streets through individual automobiles on paved highways, getting around the city became immensely easier for people who could afford it. In Boston during the 1870s and 1880s, trolley lines extending west from the compact center city opened up large strips of land for profitable home building. These areas have since become suburbs such as Cambridge, Belmont, Watertown, and Brookline (Warner, 1962; Guest, 1972b). Within 30 years, trolley lines in Cairo, Egypt had similarly opened up land for settlement—in this case, in the desert to the east of the city (Abu-Lughod, 1971: Chapter 9).

These changes in transportation made it possible for many people to obtain spacious dwellings in attractive surroundings while not overextending the household budget or the breadwinner's commuting time. And the middle class could now separate its residences and its children from the "dangerous classes" (e.g., see Schneider, 1980). These options were meaningful, of course, only to those who could afford them (Chudacoff, 1975: 67ff).[3]

The ecological form of the modern city is most clearly seen and best known in the United States. And generally, the larger the city, the more accentuated the distinctions in land use. A concentric-circle pattern serves as a crudely accurate description (unlike the cellular pattern of the preindustrial city). In the center circle are usually found bureaucratic enterprises (financial institutions, corporate headquarters) and specialized retail stores. The next ring usually includes manufacturing and warehouse districts. Around these business areas are deteriorated neighborhoods housing low-income families and transients. Unlike the preindustrial city, in modern cities with a few exceptions, residential areas tend to be higher in quality the farther they are from the center. And the farther out, the less dense the neighborhood, the smaller the proportion of minority residents, and the higher the proportion of children in the population.

This circular pattern is only a gross simplification. Many physical and social considerations modify any simple pattern of concentric circles: topographical features such as hills and lakes; cultural values that preserve old neighborhoods; political forces influencing availability and use of land; historical inertia (exemplified by former industrial towns that have become engulfed in the suburban expansion of large cities), and the direct effects of transportation lines. This last factor is especially important, for social groups tend to move outward along roads and rail lines, creating pie-shaped wedges of class or ethnic enclaves. The confluence of these various forces complicates the circular pattern: Luxury apartment buildings appear near city centers, for example, and office structures in outlying areas.

A noteworthy instance of such a specialized subarea, mentioned in the last chapter, is the steel-working community of South Chicago. The district is unique in the city: steel mills were built along a stretch of the Calumet River, and over the years workers moved in to be near their jobs. The local neighborhoods are shaped partly by the plants themselves—the mills, railroads, and slag heaps slice up the community. The neighborhoods are also marked by the history of immigration to Chicago and its steel mills. As different waves of migrants reached South Chicago, they moved to newly built sectors of the community, or often replaced one another in older neighborhoods. For example, "Slag Valley," once largely South Slavic, became increasingly Mexican (Kornblum, 1974: Chapter 1).

I have described these urban patterns largely in terms of physical features and economic activities. Other patterns of spatial differentiation follow the social characteristics of city residents. Studies of North American cities indicate that urban neighborhoods typically differ from one another along three such social characteristics.

1. ECONOMIC STATUS—residential areas differ by the cost of living in them, which is also a good indicator of the

residents' educational attainments and occupational status. As we have seen, the social rank of residents tends to increase with distance from the city center, and even more definitely, classes are segregated by sector (for example, the Lakeshore Drive stretch of Chicago and the northwest section of the Los Angeles basin are especially affluent districts).

2. FAMILY STAGE—unmarried people and childless couples tend to congregate in city-center apartment neighborhoods; and families with children also typically live in their own neighborhoods, usually areas of detached dwellings in outlying districts (Guest, 1972a).

3. RACE AND ETHNICITY—The segregation of blacks from whites is most obvious, but in many cities other groups are also concentrated—the Spanish-speaking or the Italian, for example. Differences in social rank tend to show up in wedges of cities and age differences in rings of cities, but ethnic concentrations tend to be spotted around the metropolis.[4]

How did these patterns of spatial variation by business use and by type of resident evolve? Urban growth itself may be a cause: The larger the community, the more its subparts are distinguised (Janson, 1980; Berry and Kasarda, 1977). But how those subareas are distinguished—the centralization of certain industries, the outward dispersion of families, and so on—depends on several additional processes. One is the competition for land among buyers who have different abilities to pay. For example, businesses generally prefer central locations to reduce transportation costs, which makes such locations expensive. Businesses that can use each square foot more profitably, such as insurance companies, can outbid those who use it less efficiently, such as used-car lots, and thus the former tend to be more centralized. With regard to residences, people—Americans, at least—have a strong taste for large, detached dwellings, which leads them to buy where land is cheaper, on the outskirts. In a region with good transportation from the periphery to the center and many affluent buyers and a free market in land, the well-to-do will purchase large sites away from downtown; and the less well-off must settle for being "stacked" near downtown [stacked in order to pay the high per-acre cost of central space; see Alonso (1964)].

Technology is also important. Transportation technology partly determines how near to their jobs people must live, how much benefit a firm will realize from being centrally located, and the kind of trade-off of land versus commuting time that home buyers must make. Building technology affects the profitability of land and decisions about locations. The elevator, for instance, made it possible to use downtown space far more intensively than it could be used when people had to walk all those flights of stairs.

Simple history is critical, too, in at least two senses. One is aging: As buildings and neighborhoods get older, they usually deteriorate and are sold by more affluent users to less affluent ones in a continuing process that often results in total abandonment. This helps explain the tendency for residents' incomes to be greater on the outskirts. That is where the space for new construction is. A second effect of the past is the straitjacket it places on the future. Once certain streets, land uses, and structures are in place, old patterns persist because altering them would be so expensive—for example, to replace the New York subway system. This kind of heritage partly explains why, for example, a San Diego or a Houston is often more attractive for business expansion than a Boston or a Cleveland.

These considerations can all be incorporated into a general economic explanation of the urban ecology. But noneconomic social considerations are also important. Cultural values, such as the prestige of specific neighborhoods (Firey, 1945) or the traditions of residents (e.g., Gans, 1962b; Barton, 1975) affect land-use development. So do conflicts between ethnic groups (e.g., Schneider, 1980). For example, some groups have been more resistant than others to allowing blacks into "their" neighborhoods (e.g., see Glazer and Moynihan, 1970). The exercise of political influence by vested interests has, of course, always been important, especially the influence of real estate owners and dealers on local officials (e.g., see Form, 1954; Molotch, 1976; Gottdeiner, 1977; Shlay and Rossi, 1981). Political attacks by citizen groups against vested interests and against one another—for instance, over where to put a highway or new public housing—also help determine the ecology of the city (Suttles, 1972; Castells, 1978).

As this discussion suggests, the internal structure of cities is in flux. Neighborhoods usually change over time, sometimes going through regular stages of decline and resurgence (see Hunter, 1974; cf. Guest, 1974). In the 1980s one of the more visible kinds of changes is the "upgrading" or "gentrification" of decaying central-city neighborhoods. We will consider this development in detail in Chapter 9.

We know a good deal more about North American ecological patterns than about those in other regions. Studies of cities abroad have yielded complex results. Social rank seems always to differentiate neighborhoods. Occasionally, family stage is also important. Ethnicity or race is less commonly a differentiator (in some cases because of great ethnic homogeneity, and perhaps in others because of government policies that integrate housing). Unique features of nations or cities often produce distinct neighborhoods. In British cities, for example, because government projects form such a large segment of home construction, many areas are distinguished basically by whether they are public housing developments or private estates (Rees, 1972). Metropolises outside North America tend to exhibit many features of the preindustrial city, but they also appear to be changing toward the modern form. For example, their social class segregation is increasing (Hoyt, 1969; Schnore, 1965; Goldstein, 1962).

The *degree* of spatial differentiation that we see in American cities seems to exceed that in most modern societies. In European metropolises, such as Stockholm and London, there is some (but less) sprawl, less residential separation among social groups, less exclusive-use areas (such as downtowns without any residences). One reason for this difference points to yet another process in land use: governmental planning. The United States is quite unusual in how little it has. "[L]and is treated as a private possession in the U.S., the use and disposition of which rest largely with the owner, while in Europe it is a public resource, the use and disposition of which are determined in part by government [Popeneo, 1980; cf. Hall, 1977]." Thus, the internal variations in the American cities is relatively highly influenced by the buying, selling, and profit-making of the marketplace.

Because of all the internal variations discussed here, the experience of the city is not the same for all; for the resident of an elegant townhouse in Manhattan, say, as it is for the owner of a small frame house in Brooklyn. Let us remember this plurality of the urban experience even as we search for sweeping generalizations.

CROWDS

Putting up with crowds, their jostling, their noise, their heat, and their abrasion, seems to be an integral part of urban life. Manhattan sidewalks at lunch hour, Los Angeles freeways at rush hour—these are indelible images of urbanism. Common experience tells us bluntly that the larger a community, the more its residents and visitors must put up with crowds. The problem for the social scientist is that we do not know just how true this is. Lacking any specific studies on the matter, we do not know how much of an average urbanite's life is spent in a crowd, nor how that experience differs from small-town experiences. Before we dismiss these questions as being trivially obvious, several points should be considered.

If we could find those mythical figures, the average urbanites, we would probably see that they spend only brief periods of their typical day in crowds, most notably as they commute to and from work. Other than that, they live in relatively uncrowded homes and probably work in relatively uncrowded offices. Even the work trip may be only mildly crowded, in the sense that an automobile provides a sheltered and private space. [In virtually every large city, only a minority of workers commute by mass transit, and their number has been declining (Schnore, 1963; Blumenfeld, 1971).] Even after the gasoline crises of the 1970s, only about 6 percent of U.S. workers used mass transit in 1980 (Hebers, 1983c). The overall "crowding" of industrial cities has been declining since 1900. Even as cities have been growing in population size, they have been declining in population density—in objective crowding. For example, urbanized areas in the United States averaged 5,411 persons per square mile in 1950; they averaged 3,539 persons per square mile in 1970, a reduction of 35 percent in 20 years. This growth in numbers combined with a drop in density means of course that homes have spread out; and it means that the destinations of the residents have also spread out. Work and shopping places are less concentrated in the center, more dispersed in outlying areas (Zimmer, 1975; Kasarda, 1976). Since 1970, with fewer people in the center cities and more in rural America, the dispersion has accelerated. As a result, relatively fewer people may be going in the same direction or to the same places at the same time, all of which implies less crowding.

Our images of daytime crowding may be exaggerated; we do not really know the hard facts. We do know some facts about nighttime crowding—that is, statistics on the number of persons per room and the number of persons per dwelling unit. The statistics indicate that, if anything, urban residences are less crowded than nonurban ones. For example, in 1970 American housing units outside metropolitan areas were overcrowded (having more than one person per room) in 9.3 percent of the cases. Central-city units were overcrowded in 8.5 percent of the cases, and suburban units in 7.1 percent (BOC, 1971a; Carnahan, Gove, and Galle, 1974). Recent years have seen some narrowing of this gap,[5] but household crowding still cannot be called an "urban" problem—and this is especially so overseas.[6] These statistics, like most others reported in this book, refer to averages that can conceal enormous variations—there are city-dwellers who are severely cramped and rural persons who live in spacious houses. Nevertheless, on the average, household crowding is *not* intrinsic to the urban experience, even if public crowding may be more common in cities.

PHYSICAL ENVIRONMENT

Modern cities are the bane of the environmentalist. They suck the earth of energy sources and then contaminate the air with the remains; they draw off riverfuls of water and send it back befouled to the bays. Trees give way to concrete, animals are run off by cars, and silence succumbs to traffic noise. And in the end, the citizen of the city is physically sickened by it all. Ghastly as these aspects of the modern city seem, the city of today is as pure as an alpine meadow when compared to the cities and even the villages of earlier times. Preindustrial cities may not have consumed the amount of natural resources that modern cities do, but they were vastly fouler environments.

Cities as glorious as Athens and as grand as Rome were by modern standards horrifying. Their narrow stone alleys were used not only as pathways for foot and carriage traffic and as places of business for sidewalk merchants and hawkers, but also as troughs for animal and human wastes. The most polluted cities were the early industrial ones that relied on coal energy. Although cities have become less soot-covered since, substantial improvements occurred only in the twentieth century. As late as 1866, the streets of New York City were cleaned by letting hogs run wild. At the turn of the century, horses left a daily average of over 3 tons of manure, 150 gallons of urine, and 40 carcasses between the sidewalks of New York (Tarr, 1971). Noise was loud and constant. When the technology permitted, multistory buildings rose along these narrow alleys, casting them and the buildings' inhabitants into constant gloom. The air was full of odors, fumes, and the ashes of fires—some intended, and some not, as when London burned in 1666 and Chicago in 1871. The density of buildings and of the people within them, combined with little sanitation and the presence of chickens, goats, and other animals as boarders, made epidemics a regular event.[7]

Rural villages of the Western past—and of the Eastern present—were no arcadias either. In the typical nineteenth century French village, "[h]amlets and villages were wrapped in suffocating stinks, their streets turned into cesspools by great rills of foul stuff fed by liquid manure from stables, in which one had to flounder and be mired [Weber, 1976: 147]." Peasants also typically shared their homes with their most valued possessions, their animals.

Some preindustrial cities and some quarters of others were more pleasant than these descriptions imply. Yet it is not an unfair portrait. The change wrought by modern sanitation was revolutionary. In Cairo the construction of a sewage system alone saved 5 of every 1,000 lives each year (Abu-Lughod, 1971: 123–131). Compared to their pasts, most cities today could be advertised as health spas.[8]

Heat

But modern cities are scarcely pure, natural environments. For example, they bring about artificial changes in the weather. Cities tend to produce "heat islands," a result of several urban characteristics. Many people active in a restricted area produce heat. Buildings pressed close together reflect and trap sunlight and warmth, while simultaneously retarding cooling winds. Their construction materials absorb and conduct heat, radiating it back at night. One byproduct is increased rain, including "acid rain." All cities produce these effects, but modern cities add on heat from industry, home furnaces, and, especially, automobiles. Pollution particles in the air then help contain the heat within the city. In general, cities are notably warmer than their surrounding countrysides, although great variations can occur, sometimes as much as 20°, between various neighborhoods within a city.

The consequences for city residents are mixed. Winters are milder, but summers are more uncomfortable. Probably, in some cases of already sickly city-dwellers, the extra heat has meant a losing margin between life and death (Lowry, 1967, 1979; Bryson and Ross, 1972; Bach, 1972).

Noise

Noise levels can be safely assumed to increase with the size of community (Elgin, Thomas, and Losothetti et al., 1974; GOI, 1974, #110: 11). But, we should note two qualifications. First, noise levels differ greatly within urban areas. Indeed, noise is not so much a problem of metropolitan life as it is of life in the center city and near major traffic arteries (Beranek, 1966). Second, the technology exists to significantly reduce the level of noise in our cities by, for instance, the better muffling of automobiles and construction machinery (Stevenson, 1972), given a decision to spend money on it. But even then, noise will be to some extent an inevitable concomitant of urban life.

The major source of noise and public irritation with noise is transportation, especially automobiles and trucks. They contribute the most to the ambient noise level and the most to people's complaints. Two other major sources are construction activity and the pandemonium of playing children (Stevenson, 1972; Goldsmith and Jonsson, 1973).

Studies of the consequences of living in a noisy environment indicate that some loss in hearing sensitivity is common, and that psychosomatic symptoms such as headaches and nervousness can also result. Noise may even increase mental hospital admission (U.S. Environmental Protection Agency, 1971; Beranek, 1966; Goldsmith and Jonsson, 1973). A study of school children living in a high-rise building near a busy highway indicated the closer the children were to the road, the more their hearing was weakened, and the lower their reading ability (S. Cohen, Glass, and Singer, 1973; see also Michelson and Roberts, 1979). A series of experimental studies subjecting college students to various kinds and levels of noise revealed that the type of noise especially damaging is unpredictable and uncontrollable noise (such as the persistent crying of a neighbor's baby or the roar of motorcycles without mufflers). Predictable noise, unless quite loud, can often be adapted to (Glass and Singer, 1972).

Because urbanism probably increases ambient noise levels, and because noise tends to reduce hearing sensitivity, it should follow that the larger the community, the higher the incidence of hearing impairment. But that does not seem to be true. Tests given to more than 7,000 6-to-11-year-old children revealed only a tiny, insignificant superiority in the hearing sensitivity of small-town children compared with that of city children [U.S. National Center for Health Statistics, 1972 (hereinafter cited as NCHS)]. A U.S. Census Bureau survey of more than 250,000 adults revealed that the proportion whose hearing was so poor as to impair their regular activities tended actually to be lower in metropolitan than in nonmetropolitan areas (NCHS, 1969a). These findings suggest that the connection between urbanism and severe noise is real but may not have measurable health effects. Nevertheless, noise tends to be a city-dweller's complaint (Louis Harris Assoc., 1979: 119; Lansing, 1966; see Table 1, p. 56). And if residents (such as the apartment-house children) are directly exposed to high noise levels, it does cause serious damage.

Filth

A third environmental issue is pollution—less decorously, dirt and filth. Cities produce enormous amounts of pollutants, and our brief description of the preindustrial city indicates that the problem of waste disposal has plagued cities (literally and figuratively) for many centuries. To the usual wastes, modern cities have added cellophane wrappers, nonreturnable bottles, and Sunday newspapers. In 1977, 62 percent of American city residents said that dirty streets were a problem; in suburbs and smaller places the figure was under 40 percent (Louis Harris Assoc., 1979: 118; see, also, Table 1). Even so, a brief look at the evidence indicates that, today, cities probably fare better with regard to sanitation than do rural areas, which often

Table 1

PROPORTION OF HOUSING UNITS WHOSE RESIDENTS SAID THAT THEIR
NEIGHBORHOODS HAD PROBLEMS OF SPECIFIED TYPES

Complaint	RESIDENTS			
	In Nonmetropolitan Housing Units	In Center City Units	In Suburban Units	All Residents
Street Noise	28%	36%	29%	33%
Heavy Traffic	28	34	26	30
Rundown Houses	9	14	8	11
Odor, Smoke, or Gas	8	10	8	9
Trash in the Streets	15	21	13	16
Crime	9	26	17	21

Source: BOC (1977b: Table A-4).

lack organized garbage collection and sewage treatment plants, and whose housing units are more likely than metropolitan units to lack indoor plumbing—even in the United States as late as 1979 (BOC, 1982a: 700).

But the pollution of the air is an obvious urban problem. Animal fumes, grain dust, peat-fire smog, and the like plague rural areas, but the things floating in city air are even more serious matters. A study commissioned by the National Academy of Sciences reported that air pollution was 15 times greater in large cities than in rural areas (*Los Angeles Times,* 11 September 1972). This, too, is not a new problem: "Hell," wrote the poet Shelley, "is a city much like London, a populous and smoky city." But instead of the coke and peat smoke of an earlier London, modern cities have chemical smogs, complete with high levels of dangerous lead and micro-organisms (Chilsom, 1971; McDermott, 1961).

The effects of air pollution are costly in terms of cleaning bills, corroded materials, and employee illnesses—estimated at over six billion dollars a year for residents of large U.S. cities. There is some debate over whether air pollution accounts for the higher rates of cancer among urban Americans as compared to nonurban ones (see next section); by itself it seems not to. But lead poisoning, bronchitis, emphysema, and other respiratory diseases have been attributed to smog, especially diseases among people living near highways. And air pollution during heat inversions has been blamed for mass deaths, including 170 in New York City in 1953 (Revelle, 1970; McDermott, 1961).[9]

PHYSICAL HEALTH

What price must the city dweller pay in life and health for this heat, noise, and dirt? Historically, urban life has seemed hazardous to human health. Poor sanitation combined with high population densities constantly bred epidemics, so that death was more common in cities than birth. But with advances in diet, sanitation, and medicine in the modern age, this urban–rural difference in mortality seems to have disappeared, even perhaps reversed in favor of the city-dweller (see Kleinman, 1981; Sauer, 1980; Preston, 1977; Ford, 1976; Cassel, 1972).

Figure 2 summarizes death rates by their major causes for the United States circa 1960.[10] The total is the same for metropolitan and nonmetropolitan populations, but the two major killers, cancer and coronary heart disease, are high in the more urban places.

Evaluating health differences from such official statistics is not easy. For one thing, sick rural people often go to cities for treatment, sometimes to die there. And, in general, diagnosing the causes of death tends to be more accurate and sophisticated in larger than in smaller communities.[11] Nevertheless, we can combine such information with other data—such as the health surveys conducted periodically by the U.S. Public Health Service. In all, contemporary statistics suggest that the once clear-cut rural advantage no longer exists; that the health benefits to people of the salubrious environment of small communities are offset by the benefits to urban people of access to medical care.

The U.S. health surveys indicate, for example, that people in metropolitan areas are somewhat *less* likely than residents of non-metropolitan areas to suffer impairment of their regular activities because of a chronic condition, whatever the condition—whether heart trouble, mental or nervous tension, arthritis, back strain, hypertension, or the like. At the same time, the surveys indicate that living in a large community somewhat *increases* the likelihood that residents will contract temporary acute illnesses restricting activity or requiring medical care, particularly upper respiratory conditions

Figure 2

U.S. AGE-ADJUSTED DEATH RATES (DEATHS PER 100,000 PEOPLE, 1969–1971, BY MAJOR CAUSES

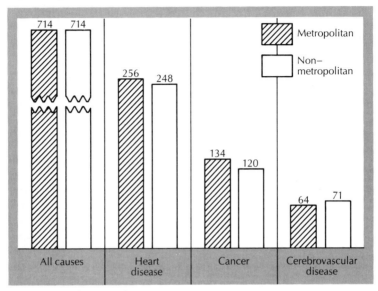

Source: Adapted from Ford (1976).

(colds, flu, pneumonia, and so on), and also increases slightly the probability of being injured in a traffic accident—but *not* killed in it; that is a more rural phenomenon (DHHS, 1981: Table 27; NCHS, 1967a, 1969a, 1971; Ford, 1976; Rosenblatt, 1981). British mortality statistics indicate similar patterns (Mann, 1964).

The same American surveys show that urban residents are substantially more likely to visit doctors and health centers, to visit more specialized ones, and to receive preventive health care than are people living outside cities. This may partly reflect urbanites' greater susceptibility to colds and the like, but it mostly indicates the greater opportunity they have for the diagnosis and treatment of potentially chronic conditions. Even among those in failing health, urbanites make more frequent visits to doctors than do ruralites. Simply put, urban people get better care (Kleinman, 1981).

When we take an historical and cross-cultural perspective, the same distinction between illness and mortality needs to be made.

Rural people in Western societies tended to be in worse physical condition than urban people (e.g., see Weber, 1976: 154), to a great extent because of inferior diet. That is still true in the less developed nations (e.g., see Gugler and Flanagan, 1978: 59). But in early eras, the contagion and contamination of cities would periodically strike down large portions of the population so that their death rate was higher. Today those epidemics are largely gone. In the poorer nations, the net outcome is a better health situation in the cities. In the richer nations, the health problems and health advantages of city and countryside roughly balance.

HOUSING

Of the many harrowing urban scenes playing in the public mind, one of the most depressing is the tenement: four or five creaky flights high, dark and dense both with people and rats, tilting and tearing at the seams, its denizens turned miserable and malevolent by their surroundings. The history of cities reveals that this vision may be more reality than caricature, for the housing situation of city-dwellers, while often concretely better than that of their rural cousins, must have seemed worse because the hovels pressed together so densely, and open space was insufficient to provide relief. Perhaps the worst recent period of urban housing was the late nineteenth century. Cities were engulfed by unprecedented and unanticipated tidal waves of rural immigrants. The newcomers, whose cheap labor fueled modernization, crammed into whatever makeshift housing was available. While a rising middle class first discovered the pleasures of suburban life, the poor and laboring classes lived in conditions such as those of some New York City "cellar dwellers" in the 1840s.

> Typical of overcrowded cellars was a house in Pike Street which contained a cellar ten feet square and seven feet high, with one small window and an old-fashioned inclined cellar door; here lived two families consisting of ten persons of all ages. The occupants of these basements led miserable lives as troglodytes amid darkness, dampness, and poor ventilation. Rain water leaked through cracks in the walls and floors and frequently flooded the cellars; refuse filtered down from the upper stories and mingled with the seepage from outdoor

privies. From such an abode emerged the "whitened and cadaverous countenance" of the cellar dweller [Ernst, 1949: 266].[12]

As the statistics will indicate, much of this squalor has ended, though a suffering minority in center-city ghettos must still contend with abominable conditions. Nevertheless, the popular image plays on, revised perhaps into a picture of high-rise concrete "bunkers," cramped, sterile, and lifeless, save for the occasional mugger stalking the halls. In this section we will examine the reality of urban housing. Let us begin with some basic statistics.

Figure 3 compares metropolitan to nonmetropolitan housing, and within metropolitan areas, center-city to outer-city (mostly suburban) housing. The warning about statistical averages deserves repetition: Averages mask much internal variation. For instance, to say that there are 5.1 rooms in the median metropolitan dwelling unit glosses over the fact that some metropolitan areas average higher or lower than that within metropolises, center cities average 4.8 rooms and suburbs 5.3. Similarly, within center cities, some neighborhoods average far above 4.8 rooms and some far below. We continue to use averages, because they are the best way to summarize great masses of data; but we should also remember that they summarize much diversity. Figure 3 demonstrates that:

1. Metropolitan housing more often consists of apartment and rental housing than does nonmetropolitan housing. The difference results particularly to center cities, where half the units are apartments and rentals.
2. The number of rooms per unit and of persons in these units do not differ much between metropolitan and nonmetropolitan locations. They do differ between city and suburb, center cities being disproportionately the locale of small households residing in small housing units. In fact, center cities are especially likely to have people living alone. Twenty-eight percent of the units in center cities were single-occupancy in 1977. If we were to exclude elderly people living alone—who disproportionately live in nonmetropolitan places—the differences would be even sharper.

Figure 3
HOUSING STATISTICS FOR THE UNITED STATES BY PLACE OF RESIDENCE,
1977–1979

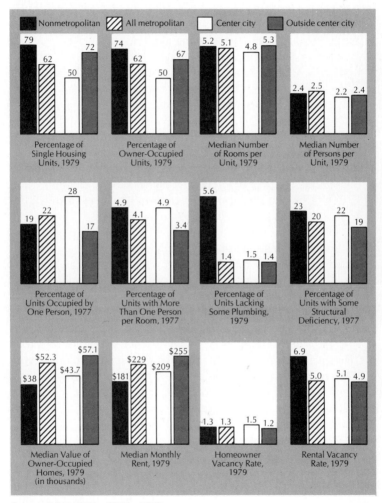

Source: BOC (1977a, 1977b, 1980).

3. As noted earlier, one is more likely to find over-crowded units—defined as homes with more people than rooms—in nonmetropolitan areas than in metropolitan areas partly because of the distribution of single-occupancy units. Rural areas improved greatly in this regard since 1970, losing about 600,000 over-crowded homes and gaining about five million uncrowded ones.

4. Metropolitan housing units appear to be in slightly better physical condition than nonmetropolitan units, more often with plumbing, slightly less often with structural problems, and selling and renting at higher prices— although on all these counts, nonmetropolitan regions have experienced large positive changes since 1970. While the higher urban housing costs are no doubt partly the result of the generally higher cost of city living and city land, they probably reflect differences in quality as well (as suggested by the vacancy rates).

These statistics cannot completely reveal the quality of life provided by urban housing, but they should cast doubt on the tenement image. They suggest that the quality of metropolitan housing is—*on the average*—as high as, sometimes higher, than of nonmetropolitan housing. Nevertheless, urban Americans tend to be more dissatisfied with their housing than do rural Americans. For instance, in a 1969 Gallup poll, 84 percent of the interviewees who lived in small communities reported being satisfied with their housing. The proportion of satisfied people dropped off with increasing community size until, in metropolitan areas of over one million, only 60 percent reported being satisfied with their housing (Fischer, 1973b; cf. Louis Harris Assoc., 1979: 105).

Although no studies have yet explained this difference in satisfaction, it is unlikely to be simply a result of differences in housing quality, given the statistics just presented. Instead, the differences probably represent a spillover of the general dislike for city living (Marans and Rodgers, 1974; Fischer, 1973b), and, more specifically, of the dislike North American and Northwestern European people have for apartment living. (Other Europeans like or do not mind apartment living.) They overwhelmingly prefer the spacious, single-family house, as demonstrated by responses to surveys and buying patterns. At best, Americans see apartments as acceptable temporary quarters for young singles or as convenient arrangements for elderly widows and widowers.[13]

Given that the single-family house is almost a universal ideal, what are the consequences—besides some discontent—of apartment living? Estimating such consequences is complicated by two general difficulties: First, North Americans who live in apartments bring to them attitudes and characteristics different from those of house-dwellers. The apartment residents are more likely to be either young adults or quite elderly, unmarried, childless, of low income, and minority group members. Moreover, the buildings they inhabit are usually in less affluent neighborhoods. So, neighborhoods of apartments more often have problems (high rates of crime and ill health, for example) than do neighborhoods of detached dwellings. And apartment residents more often suffer personal problems than house-dwellers. But this does not demonstrate that apartment living *caused* the problems. Residents typically bring those problems with them. Demonstrating a causal relationship requires a far more complex analysis in which we take into account the prior traits of residents.

The second difficulty is that owning a house is the ideal in North America, so that apartment dwellers may be chronically upset simply because they lack one of life's "good things." One study of residents in a cooperative, low-rise apartment development concludes: "the primary problem of multi-family housing is that most residents aspire to live in a single-family house. The more a housing environment deviates from this norm, the less happy will be the inhabitants with their lot [Cooper, 1972: 141]."[14]

Yet several studies do permit us to draw some conclusions. One conclusion is that housing conditions in general have little direct effect on social life or psychological states. While moving from an extremely poor dwelling unit to an adequate one is likely to improve health, other changes—such as more rooms—are unlikely to have significant consequences (Schorr, n.d., Michelson, 1970).

A similar conclusion emerges from specific studies of apartment living: few, if any, significant effects. There is evidence that living on higher floors may interfere with managing children. Either the children are downstairs and out of sight—something parents object to, although we do not know whether the children object—or they get under foot, producing some parent–child conflict and anxiety (R. Mitchell, 1971; Cooper, 1972; Michelson, 1970: 161,

Michelson and Roberts, 1979). But in general, there is little support for the contention that apartment living per se, ruling out serious overcrowding and the personal characteristics of the residents, notably alters personality, the family, or social life.[15]

Two consequences in particular are often thought to result from apartment living: higher crime rates and personal isolation. It seems that building design can affect crime by either sheltering or revealing the illicit act to neighbors and passers-by. High-rise buildings more often include hidden areas not easily kept under surveillance, such as elevators, stairwells, and blind corridors, which can harbor muggers, rapists, and drug addicts. But if so, the high-rises do not *cause* their residents to commit crime; rather, their designs may *allow* residents or nonresidents to asault inhabitants in public places (Newman, 1973, 1980: 91–93; cf. Mawby, 1977; Gillis, 1974). And, residents of high-rise buildings designed for tight security or located in affluent neighborhoods do not often suffer these attacks.

The belief that apartment-dwellers are lonely souls is deeply embedded in American folk wisdom. Research suggests that the notion is in part true and in part false. Generally, apartment residents are less likely to know, interact with, or be close to their neighbors than persons living in detached homes (e.g., see Gates, Stevens, and Wellman, 1973; Korte, 1978; McCarthy and Saegert, 1978; see also Chapter 5). Yet this does *not* mean that they are isolated and friendless, only that their friends tend not to live nearby. A careful study conducted in Toronto by William Michelson (1973a, 1977) compared people moving into apartments to those moving into detached dwellings and found that the apartment residents had less contact with their neighbors than the house residents did. But this was not a result of the buildings, but, rather, a result of the characteristics that the individuals brought to those buildings. In particular, families with working wives tended to rent apartments, and such families are precisely those that have relatively little contact with their neighbors: The wife is not at home during the day, and the couples are very active. Yet the apartment-dwellers had as many social ties as the house-dwellers, only their friends and relatives were more geographically dispersed.

North Americans have some shared expectations about apartment life that may discourage neighboring—norms that we should not intrude on others, that apartment residence is just temporary, and so on (Michelson, 1977; Silverman, 1983). Where these expectations do not exist, neighborliness is more common [in, for instance, societies where living in apartments is typical (Ginsberg and Churchman, 1981)]. Apartment buildings may or may not discourage social interaction among residents—that is probably a function of other conditions, such as how similar those residents are—but we have little evidence yet to believe that the buildings estrange and isolate their inhabitants.[16]

Even if we have little evidence that apartment living is physically or socially harmful, there is still much evidence that it is more annoying and generally less satisfying (at least for North Americans) than living in a house. People living in multiple-family units more often report being bothered by noise from their neighbors, feeling inhibited in their behavior, noticing a lack of privacy, and generally feeling that their housing desires are unfulfilled (Lansing and Hendricks, 1967; Marans and Rodgers, 1975; Michelson, 1977; Silverman, 1983).

In recent years, Americans have had increasingly to swallow their distaste for apartment life because of rapidly rising housing costs. As a result of several factors—the baby-boom generation entering the family-formation stage, the increase in young and old singles living alone, land use and growth controls, inflation, speculation, and high interest rates—affording a house in the late 1970s became increasingly difficult. In 1970, the average family would have paid about 2½ times its annual income for the average house on the market; by 1980, the ratio was approaching 3½ times (Arensen, 1981; Frieden, 1977). This crunch especially catches people seeking their first homes and is acute in large metropolitan areas. Besides creating a great deal of strain, the housing "crisis" is also reshaping the physical character of urban America by encouraging more townhouse and apartment construction and altering the physical character of rural America by encouraging more mobile home parks [up 83% between 1970 and 1977 (BOC, 1977a: 1)]. And it is probably slowing down residential mobility.[17]

FACILITIES AND SERVICES

In one of its frequent introspective examinations of the quality of life in the "Big Apple," the *New York Times* published an article by a refugee New Yorker living in Vermont. The author said that on a visit back to New York,

> I kept hearing this tempting ad for a Czechoslovakian restau-
> rant. . . . When the ad went on to say that this particular place
> had been chosen by the critic of the Times out of all the Czech
> restaurants in New York as the very best, I could have broken
> down and cried. We hardly get a choice of doughnut stands in
> Vermont; New Yorkers idly pick and choose among Czech
> restaurants [30 January 1972].

This is the same city that provides a unique official service, reported by the *Wall Street Journal,* as follows: "How do you get rid of a dead elephant? Move it to New York: City's offal truck will take expired rhinoceroses, yaks or mules offal your hands [Kleinfeld, 1972]." The point is obvious: the immense variety of facilities and services that a great city can provide.

The fact that cities offer arrays of services unavailable in smaller communities is important. It forms part of the theme of strangeness discussed in Chapter 2. And it is one of the images of urban life that turns out to be resoundingly true. Figure 4 presents the results of a survey conducted in the 1930s of the services and facilities available in cities of different sizes. It shows approximately how large a city must be before it almost certainly has a given service. For example, 95 percent or more of cities above 100,000 had bookstores in 1930; the smaller the city below that figure, the less likely it was that a bookstore could be found. These data demonstrate the positive association between community size and services.

More recent but less complete studies indicate the same. Whatever the service—retail stores, specialty goods, religious denominations—the more urban a place, the greater number and variety of services, particularly specialized ones (Berry, 1967). Economists have estimated that a population of about 200,000 to 250,000 is necessary for a community to provide a "comprehensive range" of services (H. Richardson, 1973: 131).[18]

Some of the services and facilities absent in small communi-ties are luxuries (such as symphonic orchestras) or are very spe-cialized [such as "gay bars" (Harry, 1974)], but many of them are fundamental. The dearth of doctors and medical centers in rural areas, for example, forms one of the crises of country life—even in modern America. Such health services tend to be generally lacking wherever poor people live—in big-city ghettos, for instance—but nonurban places are especially disadvantaged (J. W. Foley, 1977;

Figure 4
CITY SIZE NECESSARY FOR THE CERTAIN PRESENCE OF SPECIFIED SERVICES, CA. 1930

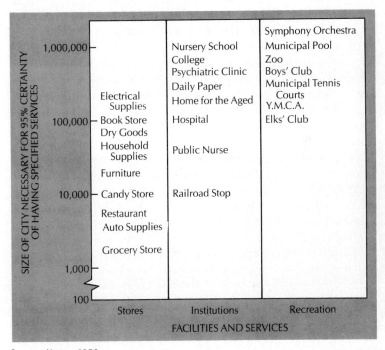

Source: Keyes, 1958.

Reskin and Campbell, 1974; Marden, 1966). Rural areas also lack public transportation, thus forcing many people to use or hire cars (Youmans, 1977; Saltzman and Newlin, 1981). Although residents of smaller communities are generally more content with their towns than are those living in larger places (see above), the paucity of specific services is a chronic complaint (BOC, 1977b: 16–17; Louis Harris Assoc., 1979: 100–117).

This lack seems to have actually worsened in recent decades, as private provisioners relocated to the cities where they could draw on a larger, auto-driving clientele (Johansen and Fuguitt, 1973). Despite the growth in rural population over the last decade, for example, the "doctor gap" between city and country does not seem to have shrunk (Rosenblatt, 1981). And in the 1970s, more than

1,800 nonmetropolitan communities lost bus service, so that by 1978, only 11 percent of places with fewer than 2,500 residents had bus connections (Saltzman and Newlin, 1981). Recent deregulation of the transportation industry has allowed companies to drop even more of the unprofitable connections to small towns, further isolating those places.[19]

Though informative, studies of service availability do not demonstrate that rural people actually have less *access* to services than urban people. After all, a hardware store or a veterinarian may be available in a neighboring village only a short drive away. But there are indications that residents of small communities *do* suffer from limited access to at least some services. The National Health Survey cited earlier queried respondents on their frequency of visits to and from doctors. From 1963 to 1964, families in metropolitan areas averaged 17 contacts a year with doctors; nonmetropolitan, nonfarm families averaged 15; farm families averaged 13. More dramatic were the differences in visits to specialists. Metropolitan families reported about twice as many visits as did nonmetropolitan nonfarm families with pediatricians, dermatologists, gynecologists, and the like. For farm families the ratio was about 3 and 4 to 1 (NCHS, 1969b). More recent statistics show similar differences (Ford, 1976: 103; Rosenblatt, 1981). Our evidence on physical health suggests that metropolitan residents do not *need* medical care that much more frequently than rural persons, so their greater frequency is not caused by greater illness. In fact, rural people are actually a bit likelier to be hospitalized (Ford, 1976: 103–105). Affluence and the health insurance more typically held by urbanites is part of the reason they see doctors more, but the experts seem to agree that the differences are probably a result largely of availability in the community. (Unfortunately, this supposition has never been definitely tested.) Rural families go to general practitioners if they see doctors at all; urban families go to specialists.

The phrase "only a short drive away," is bitterly ironic for rural residents who are without cars, or money to pay for transit, or for those who are generally immobile. Such people are disadvantaged in almost every community, but their handicaps are compounded in isolated towns with few local services. The elderly often suffer from all these constraints. Studies indicate that the smaller the elderly's community, the less frequently they are able to use stores and general facilities (Riley and Foner, 1968: 127; Youmans, 1977).

The best explanation for the positive association between urbanism and facilities is probably based on the notion of "critical mass" introduced in Chapter 2. For any service, facility, or institution to exist—whether it is a store, fraternal association, theater, or church—it must have a sufficient number of customers or members. The point is simple enough: An exotic restaurant could not usually thrive in an isolated hamlet of 300, nor a YMCA in a town with only 20 young men. For a service to be established and maintained, it must have a certain minimum number of users; the larger the community, the more easily is that minimum attained.

The importance of community size increases the more a service is special or occasional. Virtually everyone shops in a grocery store and needs a general practitioner, so they are found even in small communities [fewer than 400 persons will suffice (Yeates and Garner, 1971: 165)]. But only a minority cares much for symphonic music, and few people have need for plastic surgeons, so services such as these are concentrated in large cities where it is possible to find a sufficient and regular clientele. The rarer and more unusual the want or need, the greater the necessity for a large community to support the institutions satisfying those wants and needs.

The rule of the larger the community, the greater the variety of services, has exceptions—exceptions that prove (i.e., test) the rule by demonstrating the effects of critical mass. Prostitution, for example, is a commercial service disproportionately concentrated in cities. Yet the small town of Hurley, Wisconsin—"the city that brought sin to Wisconsin"—once had an estimated 400 prostitutes when its population was only 3,400, a ratio of 1 prostitute for every 8 residents. The reason for this curious statistic was the iron mines outside the town, which employed many young, single males. Such a mass of customers for the services of so many prostitutes can usually be found only in cities. But in this unique case they were concentrated in a rural area (Reiss, 1955: 51). Another more common exception is services for students, such as book stores and inexpensive coffee houses. They can often be found in a small college town or a state university town in a rural area, because campuses contain an unusually large number of young adults. Otherwise, these services are found in more urban communities.

Exceptions like these, the result of a concentration of particular populations, appear in many small communities. But it is principally in the larger communities that such distinctive clienteles—

single male laborers, college students, Italian-Americans, symphony fans, dog-breeders, adherents of mystical sects, and so forth—are usually found, and all found *together*. Consequently, it is in the larger communities that facilities and services, from the very general to the very specialized, are also found.

In this sense, access to services is an intrinsic part of urban life. This does not imply that all cities always have more of all services than smaller places do. We have noted exceptions; moreover, many other factors beside population size determine access to facilities; for example, the wealth of the population. Nevertheless, as a general rule, the larger a community, the greater the availability of services, particularly specialized ones.[20]

What consequences does this plenty of services and facilities have for the individual? Hard conclusions are not available, but speculations are. One hypothesis, drawn from Simmel's analysis examined in the last chapter, suggests that all these services provide a multitude of options and choices, which in turn require decisions by city-dwellers. This profusion of decisions is taxing for human beings and leads to stress, strain, tension, and irritation. Having to choose among many stores, restaurants, movies, and so on becomes a psychic burden, but having little or no choice is relaxing (Milgram, 1970; Meier, 1962). This may be so. But perhaps people do not suffer from making decisions, especially when it involves deciding among attractive alternatives; perhaps boredom is a greater threat. Having to choose one of Baskin-Robbins' 31 flavors of ice cream may perhaps create strain, but having to settle for vanilla every day might be experienced as worse still. Or it may be that urbanites, no less than ruralites, are creatures of habit. Instead of agonizing over choices, they return to the same places (and same flavors) as a matter of routine. In that case as well, freedom of choice would not be psychologically enslaving.

One tidbit supports the last suggestion: CBS radio conducted a survey of radio listeners in different markets to find out how many stations they listened to in an average week. People in the biggest cities, with as many as 42 stations to choose from, typically listened to 2.6 of them; people in smaller cities with about 10 stations typically listened to 2.0 of them. Thus, people facing a wealth of choices pick slightly more of those choices, but basically "most people have two or three favorite stations and stick to them, ignoring all the others most of the time," rather than turning into frantic dial-twirlers.[21]

Another hypothesis is that these facilities and services create feelings of "relative deprivation." In store windows, fancy restaurants, and on fashionable streets, people see objects and life-styles they do not have but, having seen them, wish they did (Durkheim, 1897; Merton, 1938a, 1964; Pettigrew, 1967). In smaller communities, with fewer and less visible signs of affluence, people are less often confronted by unattainable objects of yearning. In that sense, ignorance is bliss. For example, one city planner has suggested that the reason large cities seem so expensive is not because their costs of living overreach their pay scales, but because they offer so many nice ways to spend money, far more than anyone could hope to satisfy (Alonso, 1971). Though the thesis that urban services evoke a sense of relative deprivation is intriguing and plausible, no more than the barest indications support it (Fischer, 1973b).

A third hypothesis is that specialized services and facilities nourish and sustain a variety of special social worlds. For example, the availability of art museums, art stores, and art schools makes a flourishing art community more likely. Or the existence of synagogues, Hebrew schools, delicatessens, and Jewish newspapers makes a vigorous Jewish community more likely. Obviously, the causality runs both ways: A critical mass of the artistically inclined is necessary for the art institutions to develop; and a critical mass of Jews is needed for the Jewish institutions to develop. But, these services—newspapers, clubs, stores, and the like—help turn what is only a mass, just numbers, into a meaningful and robust social group. Artists become an art community; Jews, a Jewish community.

Clear evidence that urban facilities produce such consequences does not exist (Fischer, 1982a), but research on immigrant groups in cities indicates that the development of ethnic services is an important ingredient in maintaining group identity and cohesion. A study of immigrants to Montreal found that groups with the greatest number of ethnic churches, newspapers, and organizations maintained the most cohesive social ties [Breton (1964); see, also, Barton (1975) and the discussion of ethnicity in Chapter 6].

Fourth and finally, perhaps the greater the number of facilities and services in a community, the happier its people. Maybe, not much evidence exists to support this. Persons bereft of services may complain, but there is little evidence that this deficit haunts the lives of most ruralites in any major way.[22]

One or more (or none) of these speculations about the results of the availability of services in urban places may be true—they are as yet unproved. What does seem clear now is that residents of large communities have easier access to a greater and more specialized variety of services and facilities than do those in smaller places. This fact forms part of the physical context of urban life, and must somehow affect the individual urban experience.

A closing note on this topic: We have reiterated that cities are internally diverse, and we should do so again here. Although metropolitan areas as wholes are advantaged in services, some districts within them—usually the quarters of people who are of low income, or minority groups, or both—are almost as barren of stores, doctors, bus stops, and so on as any rural hamlet. Although the residents may be physically nearer to facilities than are the rural isolated, and urbanites though they be, they are often trapped on an island of scarcity within an ocean of plenty.

SUMMARY

This chapter has described the ways living environments differ by size of community. We have also considered their consequences. The physical setting of urban life produces somewhat more encounters with crowds, but probably an extreme amount for only a relatively few. It provides a moderately noisier and dirtier environment, features that make urban areas undesirable places to live for most persons. But, as far as we know, these aspects of the urban environment do not impair the physical health of modern urbanites relative to that of ruralites. On the whole, today's metropolitans appear as healthy, if not more so, than nonmetropolitans. There is one psychological effect of city pollutants—annoyance—that for some people is a prime reason for not living in the city.

Urban areas, particularly their center cities, are characterized by high-density housing, notably apartment buildings. Urban dwellings are probably of slightly better average quality than nonurban housing. And there is little scientific reason to endorse the popular suspicion that apartment living has negative social or psychological effects. Nevertheless, people—particularly North Americans— generally dislike apartment life. Whatever this distaste is based on—whether myths about apartment living, or a desire for outdoor space, home ownership, a secure playing area for young children, freedom from noisy or intrusive neighbors, or any other reason—it probably helps explain city dwellers' dissatisfaction with urban housing. But urban areas do have a clear advantage in one regard: the larger the community, the greater the availability and diversity of services and facilities.

With respect to all these dimensions of the physical scene, we should remember that the urban experience is plural. Metropolises are internally very heterogeneous, so that any generalization must always be specified. Some sectors of an urban area are more crowded, or noisy; some are dirtier than others. Some have high housing density; some, even in center cities, have spacious houses. Some neighborhoods have a wealth of services and facilities easily at hand; others suffer a dearth of services. The internal physical variety should not be overlooked, as it both reflects and generates internal social variety. It is to that social context we turn next.

CHAPTER **4**

Urban Life: The Social Setting

*Every day the people sleep and the city dies; every day the
people shake loose, awake and build the city again.*
                                                —Carl Sandburg

Once having assimilated impressions of the city's physical features,
the visitor soon begins to notice the special features of its people.
Particularly at a busy intersection, the visitor is probably bemused
by the variety of humanity he or she observes. Compared to almost
any small town, the city appears to be a Noah's Ark of colors,
languages, physiognomies, costumes, styles, and activities. A statistically inclined observer might soon remark on the relatively high
proportion of certain types, such as young adults, racial minorities,
people carrying briefcases. All of these are the human bricks and
mortar from which the city is built.

The urban-dwellers and what they do collectively form much
of the urban experience for each individual among them. To describe the nature of that experience, we must therefore describe the
social setting of urban life.

The social setting must also be considered in order to explain
the urban experience. Compositional theories of urbanism argue
that any social–psychological differences between city and country
result from the different personal and social traits of the residents of
each place. So if urbanites are, say, more "offbeat" than ruralites, it

is because urbanites tend to be younger, and young people are generally more unconventional than their elders.[1] Determinist theory concentrates on features of the social context other than personal traits—for example, the psychological strain of novel experiences. And subcultural theory directs attention to the social setting by examining contacts between people from different social worlds and the effects of those encounters on cultural identity. To evaluate any of these arguments, we must clearly understand how the social composition of urban and rural places differs: We need to know who the urbanites are and what they do.

SOCIAL COMPOSITION: WHO ARE THE URBANITES?

The differences between urban and rural populations in gender, age, economic status, and ethnicity have several implications. They *cause* a distinct urban social psychology. That is, certain beliefs or behaviors may result from living in the city, not because of the city itself, but because of the other people who live there. For example, on average city-dwellers might be especially "sophisticated," because they deal with more highly educated people than do country people. Compositional differences can also be *consequences* of urban life. For example, something about being in the city may delay marriages, or it may make people wealthier. Either consideration, cause or effect, makes these sociodemographic differences important. This section examines the various compositional differences in some detail.

Gender

No generalization can be made about urban–rural differences in sexual composition that is valid internationally. Instead, a distinction must be drawn between the developing nations of Africa and Asia and the Western nations, particularly the economically advanced nations. In Africa and Asia, cities are typically full of men who have moved there to fill strenuous jobs. Calcutta, for example, 20 years ago had 3 males for every 2 females (Bose, 1965), and similar male–female proportions existed in West African cities (Little, 1973). This ratio leaves at least one-third of the males without local mates. But Western societies have less extreme imbalances of the other kind, with some having more females than males living in the cities (Jones, 1966).

Several factors contribute to these patterns: land-inheritance rules that push younger sons off the land, for instance, and labor laws, such as those in white-ruled South Africa that compel young black men to move to mining towns but restrict the movement of women (Hanna and Hanna, 1971; Little, 1973). In general, the international differences in urban sexual ratios appear to result from differing demands for labor. Like Western nations a century ago, cities in industrializing societies need strong manual laborers; young men migrate to fill those jobs, leaving the elderly and the women behind in the villages. In cities of economically developed countries, the demand is for light, clerical labor. Young women, especially those willing to take low wages, are regarded as ideal (McGee, 1975).

This heavy imbalance in the sexual ratio can have dramatic effects. One is the expenditure of effort and wealth by deprived urbanites to find a mate. In many parts of Africa, an urban worker will labor to accumulate enough resources to permit him to bring a wife back from his home village. Immigrants to nineteenth-century American cities frequently did the same, going or sending home for a wife, even when their home villages were thousands of miles away.

Second, being unmarried tends to promote footlooseness and weaken social commitments. Young unmarried singles form a somewhat detached mass in the city. Perhaps it was their notable presence in Chicago—as boarders in rooming houses (Zorbaugh, 1929)—that led the Chicago School to think that urbanism itself produced isolation.

A third consequence is that young singles, especially men, tend to act in unconventional ways and are likely to patronize and enrich unconventional institutions such as prostitution and "swinging-singles" bars. They are also the ones most likely to commit crime. The imbalance in the sexual ratio thus variously influences a city's ongoing activities.

Age and Stage in the Life Cycle

In all countries, urban adults tend to be younger than nonurban adults. But even at the same age, urban adults are also less likely to be married; or, if they are married, to have children; or, if they have children, to have many of them. This disproportionate number of youthful and unencumbered residents forms an urban "surplus" of people between 15 and 45. During that wide range of years many people move from farms and villages to the cities, leaving the children and the elderly behind. The contrasts are most dramatic in the developing nations of the world, where the great waves of rural-to-urban migration continue to roll. But even in the United States in 1980, the difference persisted. In metropolitan areas, 14.8 percent of the adults were 65 or over, in nonmetropolitan areas the figure was 18.4 percent (BOC, 1982b: 356–357; the metropolitan elderly were disproportionately in the center city). And in many nations, the urban–rural difference in age is much sharper.[2] The social order of a society is much affected by the age structure of its population, so that even a slight difference can have serious impli- cations for economics, politics, and life-styles.

We have seen that urbanites are less likely to have ever been married than have ruralites; they are also more likely to be divorced (for divorce rates in the United States, see Plateris, 1978: Table 6). Thus, the city-dweller tends more often to live alone (see pp. 30–31) or, increasingly during the 1970s in the United States, to live out of wedlock with another person (Reinhold, 1979). One study found that the larger the metropolitan area, the less likely women were to have ever gotten married, partly but not wholly because the larger places provided better job opportunities (Preston and Richards, 1975).

Historically, in the West at least, urbanites have had fewer children than people in the countryside, although the gap has varied a great deal.[3] It seems to have shrunk in the United States over the last few generations, but then widened or stabilized recently (Rindfuss and Sweet, 1977: Chapter 7). A study of the Washington area, for example, found that in the 1970s, 97 percent of the increase in households comprised singles or childless couples (*New York Times,* 15 June 1980). (But the housing crunch of the early 1980s is making the single-person household less feasible.[4])

Figure 5 summarizes some of the life-cycle differences found in the United States in 1980. Metropolitan places had relatively more people in the young adult and middle years; nonmetropolitan places had more children and elderly. Marriage was more common outside the metropolises, but nonfamily households were more common inside. Note carefully that these charts *understate* the

Figure 5

LIFE-CYCLE AND HOUSEHOLD CHARACTERISTICS OF METROPOLITAN AND
NONMETROPOLITAN POPULATIONS IN THE UNITED STATES, 1980

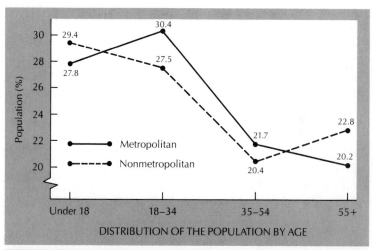

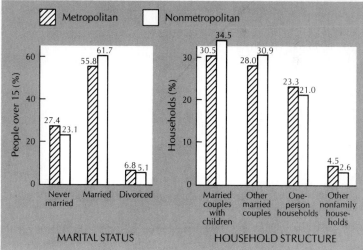

Source: BOC (1982b: 4–5).

connection between the city and the life-cycle in at least three ways. One, *among* metropolitan areas—which range from New York with 9 million people to Sarasota, Florida, with 202,000—the larger the area, the more "metropolitan" it is; that is, the greater the concentration of the young, unmarried, and so on. Two, *within* metropolitan areas, the more central the neighborhood, again the greater the concentration of nonfamily households (see Chapter 9). Three, in earlier eras and less developed countries, the differences were or are usually greater.

Urban–rural differences in stages of the life cycle result largely from migration. Young, unmarried, or childless persons have greater freedom from the obligations that restrain others from moving. They are more likely to have the physical or technical skills needed to fill the urban jobs. Often, city life is for them only a brief sojourn to accumulate capital before retiring in affluence to the village. Finally, young persons are the ones most attracted to the "bright lights" and the lively congregation of their kind (see Jacoby, 1974).

The consequences of urban–rural differences in age and life-cycle stage are substantial. First, because of their larger families and older citizens, rural places are more burdened with economically unproductive residents. In nonmetropolitan areas of the United States in 1980, each 100 persons between the ages of 18 and 64 had to support 74 persons below 18 or over 64. But in metropolitan areas, the burden was 63 people (calculated from BOC, 1982b: 356–357; see Taeuber, 1972: 103–105). This difference is modest by world standards. Second, the disproportionate presence of young people without families to support means that the activities and behavior to which they are especially prone—including support for public entertainment such as movies, liberal opinions on social questions, avant-garde life-styles, and criminal activity—will be particularly evident in urban areas. These activities then become part of the urban context, helping to shape the experience of every resident in the city.

Ethnicity, Religion, and Race

The more populous a community in almost any country, the higher the proportion of minorities (racial, religious, and national groups that include less than a plurality of a nation's populace—e.g., Catholics in the United States). Put another way, the minority groups of any society will tend to be concentrated in the cities. In the United States in 1970, 8 percent of the rural population, 11 percent of the small-town population, but 20 percent of the metropolitan population was foreign-born or of foreign-born parentage. For example, 93 percent of all Americans who were born or whose parents were born in Greece lived in metropolitan areas, but only 70 percent of the general population did (Weber and Burt, 1972: Table 108). There are some exceptions. In the Southwest, the Mexican–American population is disproportionately nonmetropolitan. But the general pattern is of urban heterogeneity. Similar though less sharp patterns exist in this country with regard to religion and race (Bradburn et al., 1970: Chapter 6). Kenya provides another example. In 1964, only 3 percent of its total population was non-African, but the figure was 42 percent for the population of the city of Nairobi (Hanna and Hanna, 1971: 109). Nations and historical periods vary in the degree to which minority urbanization occurs, but it remains typical.[5]

Two basic processes probably explain the correlation between community size and ethnic variety. First, the larger an urban settlement, the more central it is to transportation. As a direct consequence, minorities engaged in trade concentrate in cities. For example, in West Africa, Hausa tribesmen form minority enclaves in many cities along old caravan routes, from which they conduct long-distance trade (Cohen, 1969). The position of cities on these transit lines also means that the cities are ports of entry for immigrants. Many of the newcomers choose—or as with some Irish immigrants in Boston, were compelled—to remain at those disembarkation points (Handlin, 1969). New York City is a classic example of such a port of entry; Buenos Aires is another, with over two-thirds of its population between 1869 and 1930 being foreign born (Germani, 1966: 2).

Second, even for cities that do not bestride long-distance transportation routes, size provides a wide and diverse hinterland from which to draw migrants. On the average, the larger a community, the larger and more culturally diverse the region it influences, and, therefore, the more heterogeneous its incoming population. Further, the larger a minority group becomes, the more it attracts still additional migrants to the city.

Such ethnoreligious variety plays a major role in theories of urbanism. According to the compositional theory, urban minorities explain much of the behavioral differences between rural and urban communities. According to Wirth's determinist analysis, the cultural heterogeneity of cities is one source of psychological and social strain. The threat of dealing with people who differ in customs and beliefs leads people to withdraw and communities to develop formal institutions to preserve social order.

We could argue, on the other hand, that especially in large cities people can live almost entirely within the bounds of their own ethnic group, have only rare encounters with members of other groups, and thus develop an urban parochialism. They may actually have *less* contact with people differing from themselves than do residents of smaller communities.[6] An Italian–American in a large city, for instance, could grow up within the confines of parish and parochial school, almost never encountering non-Italians. In American cities without aggressive integration programs, schools are typically homogeneous in social class and ethnicity; but in small towns without aggressive segregation programs, the one or two schools probably tend to have more of a cross-section of the community. In this way, the consequences of urban concentration for members of the majority may be different from those for minority persons. In the small community, the former may hardly be aware of the few members of a minority; but in the city the latter may be much more concentrated, and active, and be more striking to the majority person.

The consequences of ethnic heterogeneity for the community as a whole would seem to be competition and conflict arising from the presence of groups with disparate values and interests (e.g., Hanna, 1982). Consensus over community ends and means becomes harder to achieve; deep cleavages are more likely to develop. This expectation derives from both Wirthian and subcultural theories, and appears to be borne out. For example, the likelihood and severity of racial conflict in the United States increases with the size of community (Morgan and Clark, 1973). This problem of intergroup relations will be taken up again later; it is an important feature of urban variety.

Social Standing

Two kinds of urban–rural comparisons are relevant in examining social standing: one, the contrast between urban and rural communities in the average *rank* of their residents—in educational achievement, occupational prestige, and income level; two, the relative extent of *differentiation* in large and small communities— the number of substantially distinct strata.

In general, the larger the community, the higher the average education, occupational prestige, and income of its residents. Cities contain proportionately fewer people at the low end of these scales and proportionately more at the high end. For example, Figure 6 presents the 1979 distribution of *household* incomes in the United States for residents of large- (over 1 million population), small-, and nonmetropolitan areas. The graph shows that the more urban the area, the greater the proportion of households whose joint incomes exceeded $20,000; the smaller the community, the greater the proportion who fell below $12,500. [The differences are slightly understated because urban households more often include just one adult; see, also, Seniger and Smeeding (1981).] There is, to be sure, a major contrast *within* metropolitan areas: Residents of center cities make less than suburbanites (see Chapter 9). But in the United States and generally elsewhere, urbanites are more affluent than ruralites. Education and occupational prestige follow similarly (Weber and Burt, 1972: Table 110; BOC, 1977a: 5–6; Blau and Duncan, 1967).

Note two qualifications about these figures: One, they represent summary statistics that veil a great deal of internal variation. Some small towns are quite affluent, others are miserably poor; urban neighborhoods vary likewise. We are reporting *averages*. Two, these comparisons refer to percentages; in absolute numbers, a large community will of course contain many more rich *and* many more poor families than a small one.

This advantage in rank of urbanites persists in contemporary America, even after the recent years of catching up by smaller communities. During the 1970s, median family income in the most rural counties went from 58 percent of that in the most urban counties to 67 percent of it (Long and DeAre, 1982b: Table 7; Zuiches and Brown, 1978). In earlier historical eras there were, and in developing countries today there still are, much sharper contrasts between the social positions and affluence of city-dwellers—even in the lower classes— and those of country people; the kinds of contrasts, in fact, that often led nineteenth-century observers to describe backwoods residents as animals (e.g., see, Weber, 1976). The socioeconomic differences continue even in societies that have

Figure 6
U.S. DISTRIBUTION OF MONEY INCOME FOR LARGE-, SMALL-, AND
NONMETROPOLITAN AREA AND NONMETROPOLITAN HOUSEHOLDS, 1979

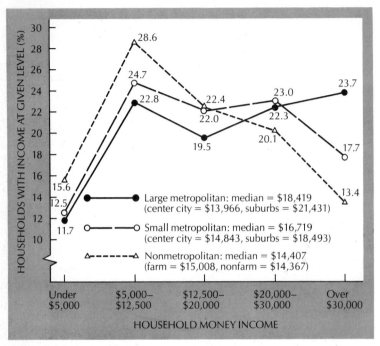

Source: BOC (1980: Table 8).

explicitly tried to narrow the gaps, notably, the Peoples' Republic of
China (e.g., see, Frolic, 1978; Murphey, 1976; Gardner, 1971).

This urban advantage in income can be explained in various
ways. It may be spurious, not a product of urbanism, but instead a
product of the high cost of living in cities or of city-dwellers' youth
and the tendency for young adults, being well-educated, to have
high-paying jobs. These form part of the explanation, but not the
whole. Employed ruralites tend to make notably less money than do
urbanites in the same industry (Long and DeAre, 1982b: Tables 7,
A4). Even when such differences as jobs and living costs are taken
into account, residents of larger communities tend to earn more
money (Danzinger, 1976; Bibb and Form, 1977; Hoch, 1976).

One explanation is that cities expropriate and concentrate the "surplus" wealth extracted from the countryside. In the simplest form, a rapacious ancient despot heavily taxes the peasants and then spends the booty on urban artisans, traders, and servants (see Mumford, 1961). In a modern form, capitalist institutions—industry, commerce, and especially, finance—accumulate capital from the wider society into the largest centers, where some of it trickles down to the urban workers (e.g., see, Harvey, 1973: 216–239). Neoclassical economists, on the other hand, try to explain wage differentials in terms of free-market processes. A few have argued that the higher income of city-dwellers is a "bribe" the market pays workers for putting up with pollution, crime, and urban life in general (e.g., Hoch, 1972, 1976; but see Alonso, 1975). The most likely explanation seems to be that population concentration provides higher efficiency, economies of scale, occupational and industrial specialization—all of which interact to upgrade the urban economy and ultimately increase the affluence of the urban population (Alonso, 1971; H. L. Richardson, 1973).[7]

Urban–rural differences in education, occupation, and income have important practical and theoretical consequences. From the practical point of view, if sociology has demonstrated any fact of social life, it is that the social standing of an individual is a critical determinant of the opportunities, experiences, beliefs, and behavior of that individual. One consequence, therefore, is that city-dwellers, because of their higher positions, generally have slightly greater access to the good things in life than do rural people. Another is that most urbanites inhabit a social setting composed of more affluent neighbors than do otherwise comparable rural people. In many ways, the metropolis seems largely constructed for the affluent, in for example, sprawling suburban developments, the locations and designs of which presume ownership of a car. In a sense, the urban environment is the affluent environment.

From the theoretical point of view, the status difference underlines the importance of distinguishing the effects of urbanism from the effects of social rank. If urban-dwellers differ from ruralites in experience or behavior, our first question must be whether the differences can be explained by status rather than by residence in the city. Only when the former is ruled out might the latter be accepted.

As well as differences between city and county in socio-economic rank, differences exist in socioeconomic diversity. The concentration of people stimulates differentiation in economic activities, with a proliferation of specialized lines of work (such as neurosurgeons, Persian rug salesmen, concert pianists). With the greater array of occupational types, especially white-collar and professional ones, finer gradations within social ranks become possible and real. Thus, people in larger communities can distinguish a greater variety of socioeconomic levels than can those in smaller towns.[8]

But there are large settlements with little economic and class differentiation—for example, precolonial African towns populated largely by farmers (Krapf-Askari, 1969; Hull, 1976; Bascom, 1963). But descriptions of these cases suggest that smaller villages in the hinterlands are even less differentiated, so that the generalization still holds. A description of ancient India illustrates what is probably an almost universal pattern: "The distinguishing mark of a town or city in the ancient texts was that *only* there did one find all the castes resident. It was in the city alone that the more specialized castes, the learned Brahmins and astrologers, as well as the artisans producing luxury goods, could be maintained" (Rowe, 1973: 213). Occupational differentiation seems to be a consequence inherent in urbanism.

The potential effects of economic heterogeneity parallel those of ethnic heterogeneity: either urban confusion over values, or urban insularity. In either case, as we will discuss in Chapter 5, greater chances for class conflict occur in larger communities.

Migrants to the City[9]

People have moved toward the city throughout recorded history. Much movement has occurred to and fro, but net migration has been consistently from rural to urban places (with recent interesting changes; see next section). Lewis Mumford, the noted urban critic, put it forcefully.

> The chronic miscarriages of life in the city might well have led to a wholesale renunciation of city life and all its ambivalent gifts, but for one fact: the constant recruitment of new life, fresh

> and unsophisticated, from rural regions, full of crude muscular strength, sexual vitality, procreative zeal, animal faith. These rural folk replenished the city with their blood, and still more with their hopes [1961: 54].

Although perhaps not quite right (see Sharlin, 1978, 1981), Mumford points to a critical urban fact: The population of cities is composed heavily of people from rural regions.[10]

Why do migrants come to the city? Although there are many national and personal variations, the motive is overwhelmingly economic: a desire for a better job, higher wages, better schooling, a materially better life; or conversely, a need to escape rural famine, disorder, or expulsion. Supplementary motivations exist as well for those who freely migrate: to see the bright lights of the city, to reunite with kin, and to escape constricting families. But the essential lure is economic improvement.[11]

Who are the migrants? What distinguishes them from the people they left behind and the ones they have come to join? Before we can draw a composite picture of the migrants, we must make two crucial distinctions. First, some migrants to the city arrive alone but others arrive in families. During eras of industrialization, the former are usually male; sometimes they are attached to a work cadre. Many Italian, Greek, and black immigrants to American cities followed this pattern; the Irish, Jews, and Poles tended to come in families (e.g., see Bodnar et al., 1979). Single migrants are usually transitory (though occasionally they pioneer a later family migration); sojourners in the city, they intend to return to the village and usually do, often seasonally. The single migrants are also unlikely to be integrated into city life (e.g., see Findlay, 1969) and are likely to experience loneliness, instability, and deviance. The second important distinction is that some migrants have associates in the city to which they are moving, but others do not. The majority do, but those who do not have such contacts will more often be isolated, move on, and become drifters (see Thernstrom, 1968, 1973).

With these distinctions in mind, we can make some general statements about the characteristics of migrants. They are principally young adults, largely accounting for the age distribution discussed earlier. Migrants are generally distinct from the people left behind—they are sometimes less capable, sometimes more capable, but either way, different. In some cases, migrants are unemployed, unemployable, social outcasts, misfits, even psychologically disturbed. Their failure is a reason to move. But in more cases, migrants are better educated, smarter, more highly motivated than the people who stay behind. Reaching for an opportunity is also a reason to move.[12]

A Peruvian study compared 50 pairs of brothers; in each pair, one brother had stayed in (or returned to) the home village, and the other had moved to the city for good. In most pairs, the brothers agreed that the one who had migrated was harder working in school and was more daring, independent, and intelligent (Bradfield, 1973). Many anthropologists have studied the rural migrants who build shantytowns on hillsides overlooking Latin American cities. The researchers' impression is that these migrants are relatively resourceful, innovative, and enterprising, compared both to those who stayed behind and to the native urbanites (e.g., see Mangin, 1967; Perlman, 1975).

Misfits move to cities for obvious reasons (they are often pushed out), and for less obvious ones (they can find a compatible group among the urban multitudes). The talented, who may also be outcasts, move to cities partly because their skills can pay off in city jobs, partly because they have that extra measure of drive that permits them to sunder old ties and take new risks, and partly because they are frustrated in environments of limited opportunity. Over time, it appears, such "creaming off" tends to decline as even the less informed and able in a village are drawn to the city (Cardona and Simmons, 1975). But selective migration is the general pattern, and it has clear consequences: Cities receive some portion of the rural misfits, but they also receive probably a much greater portion of rural talent, leaving the villages to suffer brain drains and youth drains (e.g., see Butterworth and Chance, 1981: 81–90; Romanos, 1979).

What happens to the migrants when they arrive has been intensively investigated over the last two or three decades. The predominant viewpoint, related to urban anomie theory, used to be that rural migrants suffered great social and psychological strains, adjustment traumas, alienation, and disorganization, which led to deviant behavior. The migrants became an unstable and volatile mass, a potential mob. This thinking was reflected, for example, in the McCone Commission Report on the 1965 racial disturbances in Watts (Los Angeles). The Commission attributed the violence to unassimilated black migrants from the rural South (Governor's Commission, California, 1965).

But the empirical evidence tends *not* to support this theory. Instead, research done on several continents supports the view that, especially after the first year or two, migrants to cities are at least as adjusted, satisfied, and integrated as the city-born. They are also generally uninterested in returning to the village, except to retire or to be buried. Adjustment tends to be successful, because, as just noted, migrants are often resourceful types; they typically have tested urban life in visits or by living in smaller cities, and they have, as we shall see, supportive associates in the city. (In the American racial disturbances of the 1960s, later research demonstrated that, in fact, *city-reared* blacks more often participated in riots than the rural newcomers.)[13]

A critical reason for the inadequacy of disorganization theory is that the popular image of the migrant to the city—a lonely soul, just off the train, friendless and overwhelmed in the great metropolis—is highly inaccurate. Many such experiences existed, of course. And many occurred during the nineteenth century—young men and women who came to the big city and moved into boarding houses—when Americans worried about the social problem of "roomers" (Boyer, 1978). Harvey Zorbaugh (1929: 76–81), a member of the Chicago School in the 1920s, recounted the story of a "charity-girl" who disobeyed her father and left Emporia, Kansas, to pursue a musical career in Chicago.

> Never shall I forget the time of the night that I arrived at the Northwestern Station, my purse clutched tightly in one hand, and my bag in the other, shaking my head at redcaps, confused and dazzled by the glare of the lights—but my heart singing, my ambition aflame, it was the gate to the promised land.

She lives in the YMCA and boarding houses, and takes odd jobs to support her music lessons. But finally, she realizes she will not achieve her ambition, her family has cut her off, and she is alone.

> The city is like that. In all my work there had been the same lack of any personal touch. In all this city of three million souls I knew no one, cared for no one, was cared for by no one. . . .

> Of course, there were two ways out: I might slip into the lake, there, and end it all. But somehow I didn't think seriously of that. Or I might do as some of the girls in the house, become a "gold digger," play life for what there was in it, pay with what there was in me. The idea half-sickened me, yet I played with it for a while—for so long that I drew up startled at the unknown possibilities that lurked within me, cold at the thought that there was neither person nor thing to hold me back.

And she becomes someone's mistress, eventually to be jilted.

But *this story is not typical*—certainly not now, nor probably even in the 1920s or earlier. In a much more common story, the girl would have come to stay with a cousin or old friend, would have found a stable job, would have married and settled down, or failing all these, gone back to Emporia. Only a minority of newcomers arrive without their families and without associates in the city. All the others have decided where to move largely because someone already there has drawn them in. Those associates—kin, friends, or friends of friends—provide shelter, orientation to the city, and connections to obtain a job. Even more, these people provide a network of ties in a social world composed of those much like the migrant. In this compatible milieu, the migrant finds social support to aid satisfactory adjustment to the urban experience. As migrants settle in they may often drop some of these home-town connections, but usually because they have formed successful new relations in the city (Kemper, 1975; Skeldon, 1976). Moreover, most migrants maintain ties to the home village through visits and third parties.[14]

A study conducted in the *favelas* (shantytowns) of Rio de Janeiro demonstrates the general point. Of interviewees who had migrated to Rio, all but 3 percent either knew someone already there or had traveled there with someone. (In an earlier generation, when urbanization was newer, more migrants had come alone, but even then single migrants were atypical.) And 6 of every 7 migrants had obtained a job within 3 months of arrival, usually through a friend (Perlman, 1975; see Lomintz, 1977; Nelson, 1981: 75).

The move to the city is frequently an unhappy one. Many migrants do not "make it." They quickly return to their villages. But the ones who remain do not form an unintegrated and anomic mass. Instead, more often than not, they tend to be skilled, determined, and involved in supportive social worlds.

This research on migrants has led some theorists to suggest a hypothesis directly opposed to the previously prevailing ideas: Cities do not change migrants; migrants change cities. They "ruralize" the city by converting sections of it into versions of rural villages. The city becomes infused with the values and life-styles of the countryside. The chickens, goats, and cows roaming third-world shantytowns today and that roamed American cities of the last century are vivid illustrations of the "country in the city." This compositional thesis, for which some evidence can be found in urban ethnographies, turns the determinist theory on its head (Halpern, 1965; Cornelius, 1971). Whether or not such a reversal is appropriate, the basic point remains: Part of the setting of city life is the company of migrants from other places, and most notably, from smaller towns.

Migrants *from* the City[15]

In the 1970s and 1980s, the United States experienced a new development in migration: More people moved *from* metropolitan areas to nonmetropolitan areas than the other way around (between 1975 and 1980, 1.3 million more). This city-to-countryside migration appears to be a radical development in modern history. The media were quick to highlight the trend and to publish stories about young city-dwellers escaping urban decay and finding "community" in small towns. What has happened? Why? And to what effect?

In understanding this phenomenon, we must recognize a few critical points. First, as noted in the previous section, migration back and forth between metropolis and hinterland has always existed. Now the net result has tilted toward the rural areas, as migration out of the smallest places dropped, and migration out of the largest places increased. Second, this is not a uniquely American experience. A similar pattern has emerged in several developed nations (Vining and Kontuly, 1978; Berry, 1976a, 1976b) and may emerge in yet others [such as Canada; Bourne (1977–1978)]. Third, this is *not* a movement back to the farm. Americans are moving into the countryside, but most probably into the "suburbs" of small towns rather than onto isolated homesteads and hardly any are becoming full-time farmers (Long and DeAre, 1982a, 1982b). Ironically, such moves actually increase the number of urban places and the breadth of metropolitan areas in the United States (Long and DeAre, 1980).

Fourth, and especially important for our analysis, the chances that an individual will move one direction versus the other have *not* reversed. A nonurban person is still *more* likely to move toward the city than an urban person is to move toward the countryside. The chances a nonmetropolitan resident in 1975 had of ending up in a metropolitan area in 1980 were about 10 out of 100; the chances an urbanite had of going the other way were about 5 out of 100.[16] And this difference was even greater for young adults (Tucker, 1976; Alonso, 1978). The reason for this apparent contradiction between the total flow and the probabilities is simply that so many Americans live in metropolitan areas—over two-thirds of the population—that even the small percentage who move out will outnumber the larger percentage of nonmetropolitan people who move in. Part of the migration change, here and in other nations, occurs simply because more urbanites and fewer ruralites are available to move. Nevertheless, the propensity to move has *also* changed. For almost all age groups, the probability of moving *to* urban areas has declined in recent years, and the probability of moving *away* has increased (Tucker, 1976).[17]

Several explanations have been offered for the changes in American urbanites' and ruralites' propensities to cross the metropolitan divide, and different explanations apply more strongly in different regions (see Brown and Beale, 1981). One is simply definitional: As urban development grows past the county lines that define SMSAs, the new residents appear in the statistics to be moving to "rural" areas. This "spill over" accounts for a sizeable chunk of the apparent turnaround migration, but it is not the key, because the outward move has been reaching even the most remote places and has also occurred in Europe, where the statistics are less misleading. Another major explanation is retirement (Beale, 1978). By one estimate, twice as many of the migrants to nonmetropolitan areas are *returning* to a place they had left than are moving there for the first time (Zuiches, 1981); many of these are retirees or near-retirees.

There is also a major economic contribution to reverse migration. With the growth of retirement towns—and the recreational towns, too, near water or near ski slopes—the opportunities for commercial and service jobs have grown: real estate, fast-food operations, hotels, and the like. The energy crunch invigorated coal mining in various places (at least for a while). And in other regions, a more substantial growth in manufacturing has created many potentially permanent blue-collar jobs (Beale, 1980; Till, 1981; Wardwell, 1980). Amidst the general stagnation of American and other Western economies, the largest economic gains of the 1970s were in the nonmetropolitan regions. (Likewise, the last time urban growth in the United States stalled was during the Great Depression.)[18]

The most publicized aspect of the turnaround—the desire of young, middle-class families to escape urban hassles—is real (e.g., Swanson, 1983), but it accounts for little of what has recently happened. Many people do want to move to smaller places for those places' rural character. But only some are willing to make economic sacrifices to do so, and fewer still actually make such moves.[19] This explanation is also hindered by several other facts: Although antipathy to city life has increased in the last generation, Americans have always preferred country living (see Chapter 2), even when they flocked to the big cities. And other major cities in the world, such as Oslo, Paris, Tokyo, and Amsterdam, have also lost population; this cannot be explained by the American urban crisis. Finally, among the youngish, educated, supposedly "back-to-the-country" population, the migration flow is relatively— perhaps even absolutely—greater *toward* the metropolitan areas. That is, metropolitan communities are actually gaining at least as many—and probably more—well-educated young adults from the countryside as they are losing to it (Wardwell and Brown, 1980; Zuiches and Brown, 1978; Alonso, 1978).

The critical change seems not to be the yearning for small-town life but the cost of attaining it. Pension checks, highways, and modern amenities such as sewers make it easier now for people to retire to places like the Ozarks or Sierra Nevada mountains. Rapid transportation and communication, combined with cheap non-union labor, encourages factories to open in areas such as the rural South (Till, 1981), thereby keeping native sons home. And both trends in turn create jobs for professionals and white-collar workers. These kinds of *structural* changes may account for the international pattern (see Wardwell, 1980).

Whether the changes of the 1970s will continue is a matter of speculation. Certainly, in a heavily urbanized society, more people will always be available to move out of the metropolises than to move in. But the individual *probabilities* of moving—still, we recall, heavily favoring metropolitan areas—depend in part on what will happen to Western economies, whether there will be a burst of development that will tend to advantage the cities. It will also depend in part on further technological developments in work patterns and on whether there comes a real "urban renaissance" (see Chapter 9). It does seem likely, with families moving to the countryside, that nonmetropolitan areas will grow faster in absolute numbers than metropolitan areas, even while the individual probability of moving will be greater in the urban direction.

The consequences of this turnaround are several. But none are new; they are simply larger in scale. Many small communities must now face rapid population growth, increases in congestion and school crowding, and reductions in their rustic flavor. Although the earlier residents welcome some changes, they object to others, resulting in fights over zoning, sewer construction, road building, and so on. Many residents complain that their country towns will no longer be country. [On the general topic, see Baldassare (1982b).][20] Many rural regions are developing enclaves of city residents. A section of the Ozarks has so many retirees from upstate Illinois that it is called "Little Chicago" (Dailey and Campbell, 1980). These exurbanites often contribute significantly to their new towns—as doctors, editors, investors, for example—but they often also demand a great deal of expensive public services and bring new ways of life that disturb older residents. Newcomer–oldtimer conflict is common (Ploch, 1980; Dailey and Campbell, 1980).

Another expected effect of this turnaround migration is to reduce some urban–rural differences. As we have seen, economic contrasts between town and country seems to have narrowed. Yet demographic differences may actually have widened, because young adults are now even more concentrated in cities. And we have little evidence yet that migration outward has substantially altered the cultural contrasts between metropolis and hinterland (see Chapter 8).

The urban migrant in the village is not a new figure. There have always been city-dwellers who vacationed at or retired to country estates, migrants who circulated back and forth from the city until they could secure land in the countryside, and others who simply moved to the hinterland. What is unusual about the 1970s and 1980s is the proportion moving out of the city compared to those moving in.

Strangers

The stranger is one of the most dramatic figures in the urban literature. The resident of a small town is depicted as living in a world of friends and family, but the urbanite is often portrayed as cast adrift in a world of strangers.

> The city, whatever else it may be, is a world peopled in large measure by strangers. It is a place where people are continually brought together who do not, and, in most cases will never, know one another *at all*. It is a place where, on its sidewalks and in its parks, on its buses and subways, in its restaurants and bars and libraries and elevators, in its depots and terminals, people are surrounded by persons whom they do not know and with whom their only basis for relationship is that they happen to occupy the same territory at the same time (Lofland, 1972: 93–94).

The precise meaning of the term *stranger* is somewhat elusive. In the sociological tradition founded by Simmel (1950), a stranger is an outsider visiting or residing temporarily in a community (see Levine, 1975). We will discuss this kind of stranger in Chapter 6. The meaning of *stranger* in the passage just quoted is different: It refers to the person whom the observer does not know personally, who is *unfamiliar*. Later in this section, we will consider yet another meaning: The stranger is the person who appears *unusual* or "odd" to the observer.

As a general rule, the larger a community, the more often are people among persons they do not personally know. This absence of familiarity among residents of the community is one of the key elements in the popular understanding of city life (see Chapter 2). And speculations about the consequences of living among strangers are at the heart of the urban theories of social scientists such as Simmel, Wirth, and Milgram. The presumed consequences can be divided into two categories: direct consequences and adaptations to those direct consequences. The first category includes cosmopolitanism and sophistication that presumably come from encountering exotic strangers, a breakdown in normative expectations caused by misunderstandings and disagreements between individuals of different cultures, psychic overload from encounters with unfamiliar and odd persons, and what one author calls "the urban unease"—a general anxiety about the threatening styles of strangers (Wilson, 1968; Fischer, 1981a; but see Eisinger, 1973; Foster, 1974).

In the second category, adaptations to conflict, unease, and so on are some of the anomic consequences predicted by determinist theory: isolation, impersonality with strangers, an emphasis on status symbols, and distrust. Critically, these adaptive styles supposedly permeate people's entire lives, including their relationships with people they do know. The question of whether adaptations such as these occur in dealing with *strangers* is partly trivial—by definition we can hardly have a personal relationship with a stranger. It is also partly serious, though yet to be researched: Are urban people colder to strangers than are rural people? This question will be posed again in Chapter 8. The matter of whether such adaptations alter city-dwellers' conduct of their *personal* lives will be dealt with in Chapters 6 and 7.

Much of the literature on the stranger seems to confuse the two meanings of the term we have distinguished—the person not personally known to another and the one who appears unusual to another. A stranger can be both simultaneously, but the distinction is important. The native Americans who met the first Europeans to disembark in the Western Hemisphere encountered strangers in both senses. But the critical factor in the natives' reactions was not that the white men were personally unfamiliar to them, but that the explorers were strange, odd, unusual, bizarre.

Urban life no doubt involves more frequent experiences with people who are simply *unknown* than does rural life (though we do not know the degree to which this is so). But the importance of this difference remains unclear. Perhaps being among people who are unknown but *look* familiar has little effect. Unknown people fade into the background, or urbanites learn a polite etiquette to deal exclusively with them. Lyn Lofland, in a study of encounters among strangers in public places, concludes that city-dwellers maintain their usual personal styles of behavior with their friends; but they also learn special styles for public encounters with unknown people (Lofland, 1973).

More important is the probability that urban life involves more frequent encounters than rural life with people who are *unusual* (because of the heterogeneity discussed in this chapter). Strangers, in this sense, are individuals who are often clearly identifiable as members of a particular ethnic, class, age, or life-style group. Edward Bruner's observations about the adjustment of rural Indonesians to life in the big city make the point. The essence of becoming urban, he suggests, is learning to distinguish among unusual strangers, to learn which ones are members of which distinct groups, and what that implies for dealing with them (Bruner, 1973b); Lofland calls this distinction "categoric knowing." An American example underlines the dictinction between the unusual and the simply unfamiliar: When a stranger in an affluent white suburb is white and well dressed, little will happen around him; but if the stranger is black and shabbily dressed, a great deal will happen—perhaps including the arrival of the police. I suggest that the presence of distinctively different "others" is a more significant aspect of the urban experience than is the presence of unknown others.

The consequences that can follow from life among visibly distinct others are the consequences of different social worlds, or subcultures, touching each other. For one, urbanites systematically avoid and ignore fellow citizens who seem odd. Residential segregation encourages that outcome, and even in mixed neighborhoods, people usually go their own separate ways (Molotch, 1969; Suttles, 1968; Merry, 1981). Beyond that, contrasts, competition, and conflicts between "us" and "them" can be expected (see Chapters 5 and 6). At the same time, ironically, a positive contact also occurs, including adoption of one another's dress styles, foods, and political attitudes. Put grossly, part of the urban experience involves being both offended by and influenced by "odd" people. This interpretation of urban strangeness leads us directly to a subcultural interpretation of urbanism.

The role of the stranger in urban life partly involves being personally unknown, but it more significantly involves being "categorically known"—known to be a member of a group that is different, "foreign," and perhaps threatening. An apt illustration is San Francisco's Number 30 bus:

nobody looks out the window to sightsee. Instead, the regulars sightsee each other—colorful South of Market types, recipro-cally sightseeing exotic Orientals, Italians, bohemians and immaculate Marina dowagers an endless wonder, each to each.

And especially wondrous to all the regulars are the irregulars—the train riders up from the mysterious Peninsula for lunch at the Palace, and the pickpockets who ride the short Sutter Street segment, from W. and J. Sloane's to the Stockton Tunnel turnoff, where they drop their incriminating emptied billfolds in the sidewalk planter, and hike briskly back for another ride [Wallace, 1975].

Activities

Urbanites are surrounded by a social environment that includes the activities in which residents engage—their leisure and work.

Rural people in America, especially farmers, appear to have slightly less leisure time than do others. This may be a result of their lower incomes, their greater number of children, or both (Reiss, 1959b; Leevey, 1950). In recent years the use of leisure time, by Americans at least, does not appear to differ much between resi-dents of large and small communities (Brail and Chapin, 1973). One reason is that watching television is the favorite pastime of about one-half of the population, rural to urban. The small variations in leisure are the sorts one might have anticipated: Residents of smaller places incline toward at-home pursuits such as gardening, but members of urban communities are more commonly away from home (BOC, 1973), often pursuing public entertainments such as dining out or seeing movies (De Grazia, 1962: 461; Swedner, 1960; GOI, 1974, #105: 12–13).

Urbanites tend to engage in a wider range of social activities, in part simply because more are available (Fischer, 1982a: Chapter 5). In fact, the absence of leisure facilities—theatres, stores for window-shopping, restaurants, and so on—in small communities is often a major complaint (Louis Harris Assoc., 1979: 100, 118), especially for young people—and not only in the United States. For example, a group of schoolchildren in a Russian village wrote to a government newspaper in 1972:

> Dear Editor: Advise us how to occupy ourselves. It is dull and uninteresting in our village, especially in the summer. The river

is far from [here]. There are no sports facilities. The club has only dances and films for adults. Even when he is sober, the projectionist does not consider us an audience [*New York Times*, 20 April 1976].

Small-town residents and city-dwellers seem also to differ in their favorite pastimes, the former involved in popular outdoor activities, group sports, and crafts, the latter leaning toward specialized pursuits such as following or participating in the arts (Fischer, 1982a). Urbanites are also apparently more often "into" the lastest leisure fads. For example, a 1978 survey found that Americans in different types of places were about equally likely to say they exercised regularly, but city residents more often specifically reported jogging and long-distance running (GOI, 1978, #151).

Small communities vary greatly in their predominant work. There are manufacturing towns, mining towns, college towns, and military towns. There are villages where residents reap wheat and villages that reap tourists (see Berry, 1972). Large communities, on the other hand, tend to be economically diversified and thus more similar to one another. But *within* a large community, plenty of variety exists in its various districts: business, wholesale, theater, and so on (e.g., see Herbert, 1972). In spite of all this variability, some broad statements can be made. In very general terms, rural communities specialize in "primary" industry, medium-sized communities in "secondary" industry, and large communities in "tertiary" industry.

Traditionally, residents of small villages tend to specialize in working natural resources: farming, fishing, mining, and lumbering. Not all village residents work at such jobs. Some—storekeepers, bankers, barbers, and the like—provide basic services to the primary workers. In small cities, manufacturing (secondary) industries become more prominent, as well as somewhat more specialized (tertiary) services—hospitals, colleges, government agencies, and so forth—for the people in the hinterland. Large cities are notable for such tertiary work, their residents performing both blue- and white-collar services for entire regions. In addition to manufacturing plants, large cities contain the major financial and governmental institutions, corporation headquarters, centers of mass communication media, and transportation centers. Finally, in the few "super-cities," such as New York, Paris, and Tokyo, are specialized services for the whole world: the centers and suppliers of art, science, and knowledge. As we saw in the last chapter, the more specialized a service, the more centralized it is in large cities (Schnore, 1967; W. R. Thompson, 1965; Berry, 1967).

In recent years in the United States, these differences in industrial activity have declined somewhat. The growth of nonmetropolitan areas has involved, not so much a return to primary industry like farming, as the growth of manufacturing and of some service jobs in sectors such as recreation, real estate, and medicine (e.g., see Menchik, 1981). Indeed, in 1980 American workers in nonmetropolitan counties were slightly *more* likely to be employed in manufacturing jobs than were those living in metropolitan counties (Long and DeAre, 1982b: 11). Still, the distinctions drawn here remain valid for most of the nations of the world and, in moderated form, for the United States, too.

In simplified terms, the shift from primary through secondary to tertiary industry means a shift from land- to machine- to paperwork. These three kinds of industry shape the immediate social environment by determining the jobs that are available and the kinds of people who form the population. Thus, urbanites face a complex and specialized work setting, which may include greater opportunity for advancement, more interesting jobs, or perhaps narrower, more alienating jobs than the simpler rural work setting provides.

THE FEAR AND REALITY OF CRIME

One threat thoroughly colors life in American cities today: crime. In *Little Murders,* his horrific play about New York, Jules Feiffer has his protagonist say:

> You know how I get through the day? . . . in planned segments. I get up in the morning and I think, O.K., a sniper didn't get me for breakfast, let's see if I can go for a walk without being mugged.
>
> O.K., I finished my walk, let's see if I can make it back home without having a brick dropped on my head from the top of a building. O.K., I'm safe in the lobby, let's see if I can go up in the elevator without getting a knife in my ribs.

O.K., I made it to the front door, let's see if I can open it without finding burglars in the hall. O.K., I made it to the hall, let's see if I can walk into the living room and not find the rest of my family dead.

This goddamned city! [1968: 88].

Once again, New York City serves as the quintessential symbol of the city. Exaggerated as it is, Feiffer's image symbolizes a stark American reality: the seriousness of urban crime, the notable risk of being a victim, and the reasonable fears of city-dwellers.[21] Crime is so strongly linked to urbanism in Americans' minds (Louis Harris Assoc., 1979) that, to some extent, people actually judge whether a place is a city or not by its perceived crime rate (Silverman, 1982).

In this section, we will review the connection between city life and crime, specifically examining popular anxiety about being victimized and the real chances of being victimized. Both form part of the social context of the city. In Chapter 8, we will consider alternate explanations for the link between cities and crime, asking whether urbanism might actually cause criminal behavior.

Public concern about crime is a curious matter. During the late 1970s, about 20,000 Americans a year were murdered, but about 50,000 a year died in auto accidents, perhaps one-half because of drunken drivers. Yet the public has until recently worried relatively little about the latter crime. White-collar and corporation crimes such as price-fixing probably cost the average family considerably more money than do burglaries and robberies. Yet Americans clearly want a crackdown on "street crime." These latter crimes inflict, in addition to pain and loss, "a whole range of injuries, insults, and intrusions on an individual's sense of self and his world," and, as "primarily random and unpredictable actions by strangers," are particularly frightening (Merry, 1981: 143, 223). They are crimes of uniquely social and deeply psychological character.

The more urban the community Americans live in, the more likely they are to fear crime. Public opinion polls regularly show that the larger the place, the more often respondents report feeling unsafe in their neighborhoods and complain about crime. And this cannot be explained by who city-dwellers are; it is a feature of the cities themselves.[22]

In a 1983 poll, 33 percent of Americans living in nonmetropolitan communities said that there was an area near their home that they were afraid to walk in alone at night; 45 percent of suburbanites said the same; and 61 percent of residents in center cities reported this fear. For daytime, the percentages were nonmetropolitan, 8; suburban, 12; and center city, 22 percent afraid.[23] When the population is divided according to the size of their town or city, polls show that greater fear comes with greater size—in answer to these and to similar other questions (e.g., Marans and Rodgers, 1975: Table 18). Put simply, part of the American urban experience is to feel anxious about crime.

American urbanites are not the only ones worried about crime. In a 1976 French survey, about half the rural respondents reported that there was some area near their homes they were reluctant to walk alone in at night; that was so for about two-thirds of the big-city people. And the latter were more likely to be taking or planning security precautions (Lech and Labrousse, 1977).

But this association of danger and city life has not always existed, at least in America. In 1948, for example, only 3 percent of city residents said that crime was their communities' worst problem; within 20 years that had jumped to 21 percent of city residents (GOI, 1973, #91).[24] What changed? One thing that changed was the actual *experience* of crime, and to understand that we need briefly to consider the history of crime.

The kinds of criminal activities in today's newspaper headlines are not new. An 1889 Horatio Alger novel describes Seventh Avenue in New York in terms of its "unenviable notoriety as the promenade of gangs" that attacked passersby (*New York Times*, 28 January 1973). Towns and cities of seventeenth- and eighteenth-century England, notably London, routinely included criminal quarters. Citizens were beset by roving gangs of criminals in almost purposeless attacks, and Dickensian schools for the training of child criminals flourished (Tobias, 1972). The people of medieval Damascus suffered from the "Zu'ar"—organized youth gangs who dressed distinctively, and who controlled their own neighborhoods as criminals, assassins, looters, and, occasionally, mercenaries. In general, they resembled a melange of Hell's Angels, Mafiosos, soldiers of fortune, and Robin Hoods, all rolled into one (Lapidus, 1966).

The best estimate of historical patterns in crime—usually

based on tracking homicides because they are recorded most accurately—is that people in modern societies are *safer* from crime than were people in most earlier societies. At least, from the early nineteenth century to the middle of our century, a general decline in crime seems to have occurred, particularly violent crime, in the United States and other Western societies.[25] But if this is so, how is it that we have such a distinct impression of increasing crime? One answer is that crime *has,* in fact, gone *back* up since World War II and has risen especially rapidly since 1960. Why this happened is a matter of considerable debate, [26] but the reality of the recent and rapid increase has colored our historical view. Moreover, the rise has occurred first and fastest in the largest cities (Fischer, 1980), thereby linking urbanism and crime quite firmly in public perception.

Thus, not only has the society's overall crime level fluctuated historically, so has the extent to which crime is associated with cities. In the 1940s, America's biggest cities were no more crime-ridden than its medium-sized ones, but a generation later, they were considerably more so (Skogan, 1977). During the 1960s, the crime "gap" between rural and urban America widened, although there were signs of it narrowing again in the mid-1970s (Fischer, 1980).

Can we make some general sense out of these historical ups and downs? We can begin by looking at the crime picture for contemporary America, as shown in Figure 7. It presents the rates of various crimes in 1980, by size of city, expressed as *ratios* of rural rates. (The size categories are further divided by metropolitan versus nonmetropolitan county. So the smaller sizes in the metropolitan group represent suburban municipalities, and the larger ones in the group are generally center cities.) The figure indicates, for example, that the rate of violent crimes per person was about eight times greater in the largest cities than in the most rural places, and that the murder rate, though in small cities only two-thirds the rural rate, was about three times greater in large cities than in rural places. Other crimes not shown here, such as drug abuse, prostitution, and gambling, also increase with urbanism. There are a few exceptions—rates of fraud, family neglect, and drunk driving—where countryside incidence is higher than urban incidence. Still, the risk of suffering serious crime was, and still is, substantially higher in large communities than in small ones.

Figure 7   U.S. CRIME RATES BY CITY SIZE AS RATIO OF RURAL RATES, 1979

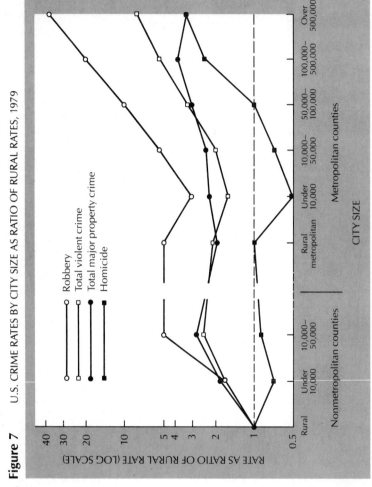

Source: Webster (1981).

One problem with using these figures is the fact that the United States is so extremely violence-ridden compared to other wealthy societies. The U.S. homicide rate is about 8 to 12 times greater than that of societies like England, the Netherlands, and Japan.[27] For another view, then, Figure 8 provides comparable statistics for Canada in 1978. They are arranged in a similar way: All the crime rates are shown as ratios of the rates for the smallest communities. (But remember that the *absolute* rates for serious violence are generally lower in Canada than the United States: homicide about one-third the U.S. rate and robbery about two-fifths. Total violent crime rates—which includes fist-fights—and total property crime rates are about the same.[28]) This graph shows that in Canada in 1978 the rates of total violent crime and of homicide did *not* increase with increases in city size. Rates of total property crime, robbery, and prostitution certainly *did* go up with urbanism.

We must keep in mind that these official statistics have numerous dificiencies. For instance, because people do not report most crimes, the actual rates are usually two or more times greater than those indicated in the figures. Police sometimes "misfile" crime reports ("Burying Crime in Chicago," *Newsweek,* 16 May 1983: 63). But independent studies support the central conclusion that urban crime rates are substantially higher than rural ones. For example, a Gallup poll conducted in 1972 asked a sample of Americans whether they had been victims of crime in the previous twelve months. Thirteen percent of central-city residents reported having their homes broken into, 6 percent of suburbanites, and only 3 percent of residents in small communities. The proportions of households experiencing one or more serious crimes were 33 percent, 19 percent, and 13 percent, respectively (GOI, 1973, #91). More recent surveys by Gallup and the U.S. Census Bureau show that differences are narrowing, but in all of them reporting victimization was most common in cities and least common in small towns or rural areas.[29] Thus, as weak as official statistics may be,[30] they do seem to reflect a real urban–rural difference in crime—a reality that partly explains the fear of crime.

How does this pattern of urban criminality in modern North America compare with those of other historical eras and other nations? We must immediately note the tremendous variation in

Figure 8
CANADIAN CRIME RATES BY CITY SIZE EXPRESSED AS RATIO OF SMALL-TOWN RATES, 1978

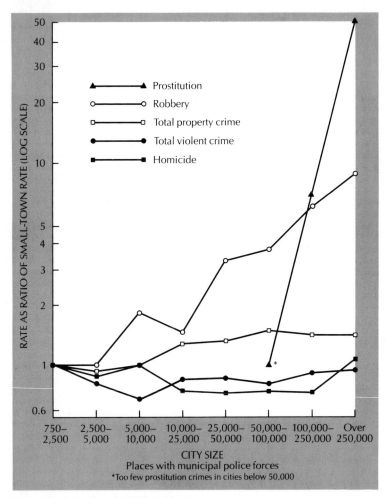

Source: Statistics Canada (1980: Table 2).

urban crime from country to country and from time to time. Some of the world's largest cities, such as Tokyo, Hong Kong, Buenos Aires, and Rome, have crime rates—especially for crimes of violence—that fall *below* those of small towns in America.[31] In some periods of European history, cities were homes for mayhem and misdeed, and in other periods, cities were ruthlessly cleansed of the "criminal element," leaving them far safer than the surrounding countryside (Mulvihill and Tumin, 1969: 707). (Sherlock Holmes reputedly once remarked: "It is my belief, Watson, founded upon my experience, that the lowest and vilest alleys of London do not present a more dreadful record of sin than does the smiling and beautiful countryside.")

In spite of these great historical swings, a general pattern exists: Almost everywhere and all times, rates of *property* crime increase with the size of the community.[32] In some cases, thievery of various kinds increases sharply with increases in urbanism, and in others not, but I know of no society where the opposite has been reported. One possibly anomalous case—the greater banditry in the countryside of premodern societies—may turn out under closer examination to be city-linked: Bandits in the English countryside, for example, did not roam too far from the urban centers, because that was where they sold their loot (Given, 1977: Chapter 6). In contemporary record-keeping, robbery is listed as a violent crime together with homicide, rape, and assault; but if we think of robbery as a crime for material gain, we see that it and the standard property crimes most strongly accompany city life (see Figures 7 and 8; also, e.g., Worden, in press).

Rates of victimless crime, or *vice*, such as gambling, prostitution, sexual deviance, and the like, certainly increase sharply with urbanism. In a society as far from modern North America as twelfth-century China, it was in the cities that the vice trade, such as male prostitution, thrived (Gernet, 1962).

But the story for crimes against persons, *violent* crime, is more complex. European and American statistics for the nineteenth century and earlier indicate that homicide—the most accurately recorded, and, of course, most serious violent crime—was definitely more common in *rural* than in urban areas. In the twentieth century, particularly the late twentieth, homicide and violence are often greater in cities, although even this is not consistently so. The 1978

Canadian data, for example, show that, aside from robbery, violent crimes were *not* especially linked with urbanism.[33] It seems safe to say that city life is regularly accompanied by property crime and vice, but it seems best to conclude that *there is no general* correlation between urbanism and *violent* crime.

This summary will begin our explanation of the crime-ridden character of city life to be taken up in Chapter 8.

These realities of crime help us understand why the fear of crime is part of the urban experience, especially in the contemporary United States. But the actual incidence of victimization is not the only, and may not be the major, contributor to anxiety. There are other sources. One is probably the newspaper and television publicity given crimes, which tends to frighten people throughout a city—even if they live far from the actual scene. By way of contrast, it is possible that in the Soviet Union, where news of crimes is suppressed, people are less scared than they perhaps "should" be (Shipler, 1978).

Crime stories are popular in both big-city and small-town media, but anxiety-creating sources are particularly common in urban centers. One force is the conflict between classes, ethnicities, and other social groups, which is more common in cities than the countryside (see Chapter 5). Social unrest—be it a student demonstration or a heated labor dispute—is often perceived as generally "dangerous" by the mainstream members of a community and contributes to a general crime anxiety (Gurr, 1977).[34] Another urban source is the encounter with strangers described earlier in this chapter. Not only is being among unknown people often unnerving, being among unknown people who act strangely is especially scary, even if the strange behavior is not obviously criminal. Sally Engle Merry studied a crime-ridden housing project in a big city and found that the sense of danger people had was only partly the product of their actual experiences. It was more clearly linked to how unfamiliar the residents—black, white, and Chinese—were with people from other racial groups. Although becoming a victim was a real threat, Merry concludes that "fear of the stranger, of the morally repugnant, of the culturally unfamiliar, and of the disorderly blend into an undifferentiated sense of danger, which has been given the rubric 'fear of crime' [1980: 14]."[35] Intergroup conflict and public encounters with strangers would likely create greater fear of crime in cities than in small towns, even if the reality of crime was *not* any greater there.

Whatever the various sources of such fear, it is great in urban America today. And the fear itself has consequences. Some signs indicate that fear of crime takes a psychological toll on urbanites and that it poisons the public atmosphere of city life, making people less trustful of and helpful toward their fellow citizens who are strangers (Fischer, 1981a, 1982a; House and Wolf, 1978; Korte, 1978). Journalists have provided many accounts suggesting that fear of crime keeps people, especially the elderly, locked indoors at night and sometimes in the day, too. Some survey data suggest that fear of crime is propelling middle-class people out of America's big cities.[36] Crime anxiety probably contributes to residents' reluctance to further invest in their homes (Taub and Taylor, 1982). And the combination of ethnicity and crime found in the major cities may be polarizing public opinion on social issues—civil rights, welfare, and so on—in a perhaps explosive way (Stinchcombe et al., 1980).

All these and more are some of the costs of the fear of crime that accompanies city life in the United States. While our review in this section suggests that the reality of crime is not usually so strongly connected to urban residence as it is today in America—in fact, the United States in the 1980s is quite extreme in this respect—some greater amount of property and vice crime does typically accompany city life. And thus we can conclude that crime and its fear, albeit not the panic we see today, is part of the social context of the urban experience.

SUMMARY

There is one dimension of the urban context we have not discussed: ambience—the pace, the rhythm, the taste, and feel of a place; the quality that makes New York different from Paris, as well as a large city from a small town. This is a dimension hard to capture by scientific techniques. Balzac, for instance, warns us that

> Paris is indeed an ocean. Sound it: you will never touch
> bottom. Survey it, report on it! However scrupulous your sur-
> veys and reports, however numerous and persistent the ex-

plorers of this sea may be, there will always remain virgin places, undiscovered caverns, flowers, pearls, monsters— there will always be something extraordinary, missed by the literary diver [1835: 17].

In our survey of social composition, we found that urban populations, compared with those of smaller communities, generally tend to be younger; less often married; composed of smaller families; more heterogeneous in ethnicity, religion, and social class; and of higher social status. We also found that urbanites are more likely to engage in bureaucratic or professional work, although that difference is narrowing in contemporary America.

These differences imply three major points: 1) the social composition of the metropolitan population forms part of the environment for individuals living in the city and may shape the way they act. 2) In many cases, this composition is the consequence of urbanism, of the concentration of population (though perhaps not in the ways determinist theory would suggest). For example, urban affluence probably results to a great extent from the economic efficiencies of concentration. 3) These traits may mislead investigations into the social–psychological effects of urbanism. We must always consider that differences between how urban and rural people feel and act may result from their demographic traits—their ages, jobs, and so on—rather than from the urbanness or ruralness of their communities.

We also found that great numbers of urban residents, particularly in nations undergoing industrialization, were once rural residents. Their adjustment, more or less successful for most of those who stay any period of time, are a major part of the urban experience. The migrants tend to be a superior selection of the rural population. The newcomers' capacities to adapt and integrate themselves successfully into city life challenge the popular theory that the anomie of rural migrants explains urban disorder. Actually, migrants are less likely than natives to contribute to conflict in the city. At the same time, for migrants and city-born alike, an important feature of most urban settings is the presence of multitudes of rural migrants who affect the experience of all. And today we are witnessing a substantial reversal of this age-old migration flow. In some Western societies, the rural-bound migrants outnumber the urban-bound ones.

The stranger is a pervasive aspect of the city's social context, in that each person is often surrounded by people whom he or she does not personally know. More critical, these strangers represent particular subcultures—subcultures that may positively influence the individual or that may conflict with the individual's own subculture.

Linked to this strangeness, the social context of city life is also distinguished from country life by crime. Theft and vice are generally greater in urban than in rural communities. But today, in the United States, that contrast is especially stark and is accompanied by differences in violent crime as well. Together, the reality of crime and the company of strangers create a sense of danger in urban life.

chapter 5

Social Groups in the City: Secondary Groups

The reflective visitor to the city, having assimilated its physical features and appreciated its complex social makeup, begins to speculate about consequences. What does all this mean—the hustle and bustle, the businesses and stores, the variety of races and religions, and all the rest; but most of all, the sheer size? What does it imply for the lives of city-dwellers? To pursue this curiosity, the visitor might begin a regular schedule of city-watching from a favorite and well-placed vantage point. If lucky, that observation post could be a sidewalk cafe in Paris or Barcelona in the spring, where scrutinizing passersby could alternate with sips of espresso and a perusal of the back pages of the local newspapers. (Our visitor would not be conspicuous, because people-watching is a favorite pastime of the natives, too.) In short order, the observer notices not only distinctive people, but distinctive groups among the passersby: families on outings; businessmen on their way to a working lunch; adolescents engaged in horse-play. These observations might lead to the specific query that introduces the topic of this chapter and the next: What is the fate of social groups in the city?

For sociologists, this is a critical question. People do not deal directly with the masses who form the city; instead, people lead their lives in a much smaller frame, with the few persons who inhabit their social worlds. These worlds—ethnic enclaves and professional circles, for example—are composed of *social networks,* groups of people who tend to see one another, care for one another, and depend on one another. Peoples' experiences of the environment are mediated by the experiences and values of the persons around them, in their social networks.

To know how the urban setting affects people, we must therefore know how it affects social networks. That is why the theoretical controversy about urban life concentrates so much on the quality of social relationships. Determinist theory holds that cities weaken the cohesion and efficacy of personal networks in favor of impersonal institutions, which in turn brings anomie and deviance. [Wirth wrote: "The superficiality, the anonymity, and the transitory character of urban social relations . . . (leads to the loss of) the spontaneous self-expression, the morale, and the sense of participation that comes with living in an integrated society. This constitutes essentially the state of *anomie,* or the social void (1938: 153)."] Compositional approaches argue that personal networks are largely immune to ecological forces such as community size, and that, therefore, individuals are unaffected. [Reiss (1955: 47): "No matter what the size of a community may be, when a person acts in small situational contexts his behavior is apparently subject in large degree to direct primary controls."] Subcultural theory suggests that urbanism does shape social networks, by nurturing and changing the social worlds within which these networks are imbedded, and thereby complexly affecting individuals (see Chapter 2). But all these theories assume the critical importance of social networks.

For this discussion, social networks can be divided into several common-sense groups—kin, friends, neighbors, and the like. This chapter will consider *secondary groups*—social networks that are typically *not* most intimate to individuals, in which not all facets of their personality are involved, groups that are more often voluntary (sometimes called *Gesellschaften,* "associations"). In this list are included the residential community, formal associations, class and occupational groups, special-interest groups, and neighborhoods. Chapter 6 will consider *primary groups* (sometimes called *Gemeinschaften* or "communities")—social networks that typically do involve individuals intimately, with which they are fully identified, and that are ends in themselves—ethnic groups, friends, and kin. For both these groups, the key question is: How does the urban setting affect the structure and cohesion of social networks?[1]

THE COMMUNITY

The largest social group in a community is the entire community itself. The term *community* has several meanings, but here it refers simply to a group of people who reside in the same settlement. Our concern in this section is how the size of a community—the population of a settlement—affects relationships among members of that community. In particular, we will ask two connected questions. First, how does urbanism affect the cohesion of the community? Are large communities, for example, less harmonious and less likely to act in a unified way than small ones? Second, how does urbanism affect the individual's attachment to the community? For instance, are people in large towns less involved with their communities than people in small towns?

Simple arithmetic provides one answer to these questions. Residents of a village (say, 500 persons) can reasonably expect to know personally someone from almost all the families in the community. But residents of even a modestly sized city (say, 25,000) cannot hope to know more than a fraction of their fellow citizens.[2] In the small town, birthday parties are announced in the newspaper; in the big city, few deaths are even listed. As size increases, the chances of a community being bound together by personal ties among all its members drops rapidly. To the extent that cohesion requires such relationships, it seems doomed in great urban communities.

Other arguments do not depend on arithmetic to depict "the eclipse of community" in cities (Stein, 1960). Determinist theory suggests that both the differentiation accompanying urbanism and individual adaptations to urban stress threaten the community's solidarity.[3] Interestingly, subcultural theory makes a similar prediction, though *without* assuming that anomie is involved. As its size increases, the community is less united because distinctive subgroups emerge. These groups—occupational-interest groups, lifestyle groups, and political groups, for example—clash with one another, divide the community, and draw the allegiance of their members away from the community as a whole. (Compositional theory does not seem to speak to this issue.)

How can we test the proposition that community cohesion and peoples' community involvement are reduced by urbanism? A survey conducted in England asked each respondent if there was an area around his home which he felt he belonged to, and if so, what its area was. In communities of under 30,000, people tended to identify the entire town as "home," but in populous cities "home" was a set of nearby streets (Great Britain, Royal Commission, 1969: 151–162). We noted before that American surveys show that city residents today are less satisfied with their communities than town residents are with theirs (Louis Harris Assoc., 1979). (Perhaps, the rate of emigration also indicates residents' feelings of attachment to their communities. But there is not much difference in rates of leaving between large and small communities.[4])

Probably the best expression of community dynamics is its politics. There are some problems in using it as an index of the social relationships within the community, but politics has certain advantages.[5] It is relevant to all adult members of the community; it tends to reveal community harmony or division; it is one way individuals demonstrate their involvement in the community or their disengagement from it; and we have useful research on urbanism and community politics.

The two general questions about urbanism and community life will be translated into two specific questions about urbanism and politics: How does urbanism affect the political system of a community? And how does urbanism affect the involvement of people in its politics?

Political systems are, in fact, affected by size (see Dahl and Tufte, 1973). In essence, they follow the principle of structural differentiation—the larger the community, the more distinct are political roles and functions. As small towns grow to cities, they develop more complex and formal governmental functions and agencies, typically in response to emerging demands for services such as sewer construction, refuse collection, policing, care of the destitute, and recreation (for case studies, see Wolf, 1976; Blumin, 1976; Frisch, 1972). Villages have part-time mayors and council members who hold monthly meetings in school auditoriums; cities have professional administrators who work full time in office buildings. Small towns rely on volunteers to staff fire departments, bureaus, and the like (see Sokolow, 1981). City governments are more formal, complex, and bureaucratic. They are also more significant in people's lives and, in general, more effective than small-town governments (see Prewitt and Eulau, 1969; Aiken and Alford, 1974; Dahl and Tufte, 1973: 87).

More significantly, as community size increases, so do political disagreements and divisiveness. To be sure, small towns are often rent, sometimes violently, by arguments and feuds (Konig, 1968). But the general rule is that the larger the community, the more disagreement there is on more topics among more factions. There is more conflict, more contested elections, more lobbying by interest groups, and a higher turnover in administrations. The likelihood of group violence also increases. Thus, urbanism is indeed related to a decline in community cohesion.[6]

These conflicts arise, at least in part, from the high stakes of urban politics. In the United States, city politics concern not only the issues of land use and educational policy that flare up in small towns, but also in matters of major "public goods," such as mass transit, housing projects, utility regulation, and social-service programs. With often millions of dollars and hundreds of jobs at stake, battles can be fierce. In Europe, where governments control yet more—owning utilities and much of the housing, for example—city politics have become major battlegrounds (see Castells, 1983).

Urban politics is more conflicted than small-town politics also, perhaps, because there is less consensus in cities about what to do with those high stakes. In the view of the Chicago School, cities suffer a "breakdown" in the shared system of values, of the "moral order." The "atomization" of the society makes agreement more difficult. From the subcultural viewpoint, consensus is shattered by the "buildup" of small interest groups, each exercising increasing power in the public arena.[7]

On the second question: How involved individuals are in community affairs is influenced by two particular considerations (besides any possible anomie or emergence of subcultures). One is the importance of a town's public affairs and the interest those affairs generate. Larger communities have an advantage in this respect, since their controversies usually concern more significant aspects of residents' lives. But the second factor works to the disadvantage of large communities. Once again, it is a matter of simple arithmetic: The number of decision-making positions (mayor, council member, friend of council member, or "community elder") does not keep pace with the number of people in a town. Thus, the larger the town, the smaller the proportion of its residents who can fill one of these roles.[8] Generally, the average person has less influence on public affairs in urban than in rural communities, so he or she likely will not engage deeply in urban politics. (On these two countervailing forces, see Greer, 1962: 149–151.)

Studies around the world confirm that, in general, the larger a community, the less interested and active are its citizens in *local* politics. These urban–rural differences in political involvement are large in some countries and small in others, but they form the prevailing pattern.[9] In an American survey in 1977, for example, 23 percent of the big-city residents said they had worked with others in the community to solve a local problem, but 34 percent of small-town and country residents said they had done so. A similar contrast appeared when respondents were asked if they had ever contacted a local official (Louis Harris Assoc., 1979: 132).

But the relatively smaller interest of urbanites in local affairs does not mean that they are politically apathetic. They tend to be interested instead in national and international affairs.[10] (This preference is partly, but not entirely, a result of the urbanites' higher level of education.) Thus, urbanism tends to turn people away from local *to translocal* affairs. The reason is not clear but may be, according to subcultural theory, that emerging group affiliations—by ethnicity, or occupation, or lifestyle—stimulate members' interests in the groups' national situations.

Studies of voting habits find roughly the same pattern. As the size of the community increases, in economically developed nations, voter turnouts for local elections drop off; but turnouts for national elections increase slightly. In the less-developed nations, the larger the community, the smaller the turnouts for both types of elections.[11] The explanation for these international differences seems to lie in the nature of voting as a political act. In the American experience, political battles increase voter interest and result in large election turnouts. This does not seem to be true in the villages of many nations, where voting is more of a social ritual often supervised by village elders. One study showed that in Japanese villages even politically apathetic citizens went to the polls, but that this was not true in the cities, where village elders could not pressure citizens to vote (B. M. Richardson, 1973). In this vein, a student of French politics refers to villagers' involvement as participation without interest (Hamilton, 1967: 258–259; see also Kesselman, 1966).

The larger a community, then, the less interested its citizens tend to be in its politics. And when they are interested, they are much more divided. This is evidence of an urban "loss of community," if we mean by "community" cohesion and consensus among all the residents of a town. But is this evidence of the urban anomie predicted by determinist theory? It appears not. First, we have seen that city-dwellers are no more apathetic on the average than rural residents; instead, their attention is concentrated elsewhere than the town. Second, controversy and contention, although evidence of a divided community, are not evidence of anomie; instead, political disputes indicate that people are aggressively pursuing their separate group—if not their community-wide—interests. Organized fights are the result of social engagement, not individual estrangement. [For an illustration, see Glazer and Moynihan (1970).] Subcultural theory explains this urban divisiveness as the product of cultural variety, of small groups now large enough to challenge the rule of the dominant group. Subcultural theory can also help explain the decline of residents' interest in the local community, as noted earlier. The large subcultures of cities challenge people's allegiance to a group based primarily on geographic proximity. People's commitments become centered in social and economic subcultures, with concerns that transcend the community—for example, in racial groups or national unions.

These findings on politics, however explained, raise again a question that concerned the Chicago School sociologists: How can the "moral order" be maintained in the city? Compared to smaller places, cities are conflict ridden and draw less loyalty from their residents. Perhaps the simple answer is that the moral order is not maintained as well as in small towns—cities limp along in divisiveness. Or perhaps moral order, in the sense of stability based on shared values, is replaced by a form of negotiated order—a stability based on political arrangements among competing groups (see Suttles, 1968; Kornblum, 1974; further discussion in Chapter 8).

FORMAL ASSOCIATIONS

According to determinist theory, urbanites must compensate for their lack of strong personal relations by turning to formal associations, such as sports clubs and mutual loan societies, to maintain ties to their community and to achieve their ends. For instance, unmarried persons in small towns are "fixed up" by mutual, matchmaking friends; but in the big city, single people presumably must more often rely on clubs for meeting potential spouses.[12]

As illustration of this view, a historian explains the proliferation of organizations in Philadelphia over the course of the nineteenth century by the residents' reaction to the loss of informal intimacy. Feeling increasingly isolated in the rapidly growing city, they rushed into formal associations (Warner, 1968: 61). Similarly, the philanthropists who set up YMCAs during that century believed that they were providing young urban migrants with substitutes for the families and neighbors they had left behind (Boyer, 1978).

Subcultural theory also predicts that people join formal associations more frequently in large communities, not because these associations are substitutes for personal relationships, but because they are *certifications* of them. When the acquaintances who share a hobby become numerous enough, for example, they may form a club. The club does not replace the original relationships; it makes them official.

One often-observed process seems, at first, to support the determinist expectation. Rural migrants to cities commonly establish formal associations soon after their arrival. In some ways, these associations substitute for rural kinship groups. The leaders occasionally exercise the authority that in rural areas is reserved for family elders. But studies of these associations suggest that their formal quality is usually only a veneer, applied (often for political purposes) to essentially *informal* relationships based on ethnicity or village background. For instance, a group of urban migrants from the same village may wish to participate in the annual carnival parade. To do so, they need official recognition from the municipal authorities; so they constitute themselves as a formal club, complete with officers. This kind of group is usually not very "formal" in the sociological sense.[13]

Historical and anthropological studies that follow associations over time tend to show that formal groups emerge as immigrants get settled, usually as a product of ethnic size and success rather than as a reaction to isolation. The first German immigrants to Milwaukee, for instance, joined horticultural and musical societies set up by natives and Irish immigrants. But as their numbers grew in the 1850s, they created their own parallel German societies (Conzen, 1976: Chapter 6).[14]

Contemporary studies in Western nations cast doubt on any

causal link between city dwelling and associations. Some researchers have estimated the number of memberships in organizations held by individual residents of large cities and found that most of them belong to no associations or to only one besides their church. Comparative studies done in the United States, Canada, Mexico, Great Britain, Italy, and Germany show that rates of membership in formal associations do *not* differ by size of community. Research also indicates that association members have generally low rates of participation (such as attending meetings), and that such participation is equally low in both large and small communities.[15] These findings are most consistent with a compositional argument that there are no differences between urbanites and ruralites.

Perhaps, a determinist might say, the critical issue is the functional significance of the associations, rather than simply membership or degree of participation. In large communities, such organizations may be psychologically more important to individuals than they are in small communities. Unfortunately, we have little evidence to test this proposition. One study suggests that church memberships are especially important as sources of social ties for *small-town* residents (Fischer, 1982a). People seem by and large to use their formal affiliations as ways of cultivating informal personal ties, not as substitutes for these ties. Membership in an organization is often valued because the association provides a place to pursue and develop friendships. The scanty data suggest that the formal organizations of cities come not to replace or overshadow, but perhaps only to supplement persisting informal subcultures (Gutkind, 1965; Fischer, 1982a).[16]

SOCIAL CLASSES AND OCCUPATIONAL GROUPS

In the previous chapter, we saw that the larger a community, the more numerous and distinct its social classes. The question here concerns the extent those social classes—defined for present purposes as strata of people with roughly the same amount of affluence, power, and prestige—form the bases for meaningful social groups. Does urbanism affect the likelihood that members of the same social class will maintain personal relationships with one another, identify themselves as members of a class, and act in unison?

According to determinists like Simmel and Wirth, the answer is yes, because, much like formal associations, social classes based on economic status are part of an impersonally integrated society. Grouping around class and occupational interests is consistent with the instrumental relationships urbanites are assumed to have.[17] Subcultural theory would seem to agree that class- or occupational-based groups increase with urbanism—not as part of increasing formalism, but as a result of the critical masses that foster subcultures. There are simply more people in each of the class and occupational groups.

Social class is generally a prime basis for personal ties and community division in all places, from villages to metropolises. Many studies of small towns show class cleavages to be deep and divisive. An anthropologist found, in an American farming community in the 1940s, that the rural tradition of mutual assistance was expressed frequently, but that all the exchanges of neighborly aid were among farmers of comparable income. That is, help was class segregated (Kimball, 1965). A small mining town in another study was constantly in conflict in the 1950s because of bitter and often violent class divisions (Lantz, 1971). Newburyport, Massachusetts, a small city of 17,000 in the 1930s, was the subject of a famous sociological study, the major point of which was that personal relationships in the community were kept largely within class lines (Warner et al., 1963). A similar conclusion was drawn from a study of men in the large city of Cambridge, Massachusetts in the 1960s: They drew their friends mostly from their own social classes (Laumann, 1966).[18]

Class underlies social divisions virtually everywhere, but the question for us is: Does the *degree* to which this is true vary by community size? We have some indications—from studies of *conflict* between social classes—that class distinctiveness and cohesion do increase with community size. Analyses of voting patterns in America typically find that political differences between classes increase with urbanism. In small communities, blue- and white-collar workers tend to be similar in their party preferences; but in the larger towns, white-collar workers vote predominantly Republican, and blue-collar workers vote predominantly Democratic. Apparently as size increases the numbers in each class, the likelihood that voters' contacts are exclusively with members of their own class also increases, thereby making them more "class-conscious"

(Ennis, 1962; Campbell et al., 1964: 203–204; Hamilton, 1972: Chapter 6).

A study in France (Hamilton, 1967: Chapter 6) found a slightly different pattern: Left-wing voting within the working class was greatest in the medium-sized, not the largest, cities. The reason, the researcher suggested, was that French industrial policy had directed factory construction to those cities, and that was where workers had much in-group and relatively little out-group contact. The key again was the relative size and concentration of workers. We are reminded of Karl Marx's claim that revolution should arise in cities, not the countryside, because that was where workers could meet and support one another.

Other forms of class conflict, some of them violent, also increase with community size. For example, strikes grow disproportionately with the population size of metropolitan areas, largely because workers are more unionized in larger communities (Lincoln, 1978; Bennett and Earle, 1982). Studies conducted by Charles Tilly and his associates indicate that European cities were disproportionately the sites of collective violence, which in turn was largely the direct or indirect expression of class divisions (Tilly, 1974; Tilly et al., 1975).[19] Such conflict and disorder has been interpreted by determinists as symptoms of societal breakdown and anomie. Park (1916: 109), for example, wrote that "Strikes and minor revolutionary movements are endemic in the urban environment," because "the community is in a chronic condition of crisis," in turn because "human relations are likely to be impersonal and rational." But, evidence suggests that the urban tendency to class violence results from organization and cohesion within economic groups in the city, not from disorganization and collapse (Tilly et al., 1975). That is, cities generate class conflict by "intensifying" competing economic groups.

Moreover, political economists argue that class conflict is an inevitable part of city development. For one, cities are where the wealth of a society and its control are centralized. Sharp contrasts between the haves and the have-nots are always part of the urban scene. [The disgruntlement of many city residents with their communities may arise from this conjunction—not from absolute deprivation but from the comparisons they make to the showy affluence of the urban elite (see Rodgers, 1980)]. And the changing land-use patterns of the city involve the constant extraction of profit by owners from tenants, even as the specific forms of land use change. In one period, tenement landlords may crowd poor people into dilapidated buildings at relatively high rents with low services. In another period, with a changing urban economy, land speculators may push tenants out of those same inner-city units to renovate and settle them as condominiums to "invading" middle-class people. In all instances, class tensions can spark into open conflict.[20]

Urbanism apparently increases the solidarity of social classes, making it more likely that they will be the sources of personal relationships and the bases of collective action. One analysis, shared by the Chicago School and subcultural theory, is that urbanism enlarges the importance of *occupation* as a basis of social affiliation. Indeed, broad social classes as such may be most important in modestly sized towns, where, for example, the lawyers, bankers, and doctors might jointly form a single clique. But in cities each occupation is probably more apt to form its own group; and, in the larger cities, the process probably evolves to the point where tax lawyers, trial lawyers, and divorce lawyers each have their own separate set. The argument is that the larger cities have larger numbers of people in each occupation and that this produces small social worlds based on occupation. Each occupationally distinct set of people forms internal allegiances, develops a characteristic outlook and style—in short, becomes a potential subculture. As Park noted long ago: "In the city every vocation, even that of beggar, tends to assume the character of a profession and the discipline which success in any vocation imposes, together with the associations it enforces [1916: 102]."[21]

What evidence do we have for this contention? Small towns with one or two people working in most occupations are not likely to develop many occupational subcultures. But it does not necessarily follow that occupationally based social groups emerge in large cities. Historically, guilds arose in the cities—work organizations that had some qualities of subcultures. And several sociological studies suggest that urbanism encourages occupational subcultures today.

The longshoremen of Portland, Oregon, present an example. A longshoreman-turned-anthropologist has described how members of this occupational group not only work together but also see each other socially, largely come from the same nationality groups, marry each other's sisters, and recruit relatives into the union. (But they are not likely to be neighbors—a point that will be important later in this chapter.) Accompanying these dense relationships is a distinctive identity, style of behavior, and set of habits and beliefs (Pilcher, 1972).

Another example is offered in *Union Democracy,* one of the classics of sociology, where the author explores the social world of printers in New York City. Like the Portland longshoremen, printers are socially intertwined and quite distinctive, and they form a subculture that, in turn, is divisible into successively more distinct groups according to religion (Lipset et al., 1956). Even prostitutes, criminals, and skid-row alcoholics have social circles and subcultures of their own in cities (Oelsner, 1971; Bahr, 1973).

All the preceding occupations are to some degree special; for instance, they have irregular or unique working hours. Unfortunately, we have few studies of "average" nine-to-five workers. Nevertheless, the argument is both simple and plausible: People get to know other people whom they meet at work or deal with as professional colleagues; they also share common backgrounds and interests with others in their line of work. This is true everywhere. But what occurs with an increase in population is that the size of an occupation becomes sufficient to permit, even to encourage, the formation of subcultures by which each occupation becomes a somewhat separate and self-sufficient social world. People establish the major portion of their personal relationships within the group of their work colleagues, they become involved in the institutions of the subculture (its organizations, meeting-places, newspapers, etc.), and they tend to exhibit its particular style of behavior in such things as their dress, language, and attitudes.

On the other hand, occupational worlds may be very intensive in small communities that have only one or two industries. In towns where a large proportion of the population works in the same place—say, the local mine—or in the same business—say, the ski resort trade—occupation-based ties are probably quite strong.[22]

We do not have any direct evidence that urbanites are in fact more or less involved with work colleagues. One 1977 California survey tested this proposition (Fischer, 1982a) and found *no* substantial differences in the respondents' ties to coworkers according to the size of community. If anything, the people in the medium-sized places were a bit more likely to report work-based friend-ships.[23] Until more studies are done, the plausible link between urbanism and occupational worlds remains only plausible, not proven.

SPECIAL-INTEREST GROUPS

People often join together to pursue common interests—chess, politics, charitable works, scuba-diving, or opera-going. Sometimes such groups are formal—as in political parties, or chess clubs. More often they are informal—the group that plays basketball together on Sunday mornings, the amateur musicians who jam on Saturday night, the regular customers at a local bar. In these groups the commonality is produced by some shared, special interest. Are such groups more likely to form in larger communities than in smaller ones? If so, what implications follow?

Earlier, we examined some fragments of data about formal associations. Even less information is available about informal as-sociations. In the absence of much hard evidence, we must there-fore fall back on reasonably informed speculation. In Chapter 3 we noted that the advantage of cities in providing services and facilities arose because cities could command sufficient numbers of clients—critical masses of them—to support a variety of institutions. The analysis of special-interest groups pursues the same logic. Large populations concentrated in small areas permit people with particu-lar pastimes, causes, or life-styles to get together regularly.

Illustrations of such urban groups abound. In the thirteenth-century Chinese city of Hangchow, all sorts of societies, legitimate and not, "responded to the desires of lovers of the same art, believ-ers in the same faith, or of natives of the same district, to meet together and fraternize. Only a great city could have such a variety of them" (Gernet, 1962: 222). In seventeenth-century London, ado-lescent apprentices to various occupations formed a youth subcul-ture, complete with clothing styles, customs, and periodic brawls (S. R. Smith, 1973). That tradition lasts to the modern day in many European cities where dissident youth form a politicized social movement and even have relatively distinct "youth ghettoes."

Homosexuals provide another contemporary example of people who often wish to enjoy each other's company in their own milieu. Apparently, homosexuals commonly drift from smaller communities to the large metropolises—such as San Francisco, New York, Los Angeles, and Chicago—because the cities provide a large enough pool to provide liaisons, friends, services, and locales such as gay bars. The larger cities also appear to be more tolerant—an attitude that itself is in some part a result of the size of the homosexual community. (In San Francisco, politicians take serious account of the homosexual vote).[24]

Certainly, not all types of special-interest groups become more common as city size increases. Hunters, for example, more often find fellowship in rural areas (Lizote and Bordua, 1980). But special-interest groups should generally be more prevalent in cities. Our same California survey that failed to find a connection between urbanism and work friendships did find one between urbanism and pastime friendships. Especially for people who were particularly committed to their leisure, the more urban the community, the more associates they reported with similar interests (Fischer, 1982a).[25] But we have only that one piece of "hard" evidence.

Assuming that special-interest groups are relatively more common and more important in larger than in smaller communities, what consequences follow? The answer depends on how we interpret special-interest groups.

For the determinist school, members of special-interest groups are instrumentally engaged with each other as means to an end.[26] Illustrations include the group that plays basketball together regularly, and the coffee-house intellectuals who debate one another each night over cups of espresso. In both examples, the activity is the essence—if not the totality—of the relationships; personal interaction—that is, people treating each other as unique persons—is relatively rare. Moreover, these instrumental ties challenge and replace personal ones. For example, people would prefer to discuss their anxieties in encounter groups rather than with their friends or family. The intimate web of relationships common to rural life fades as a consequence, replaced in the city by shallow, single-purpose ties. "The growth of cities," wrote Park (1916: 110), "has been accompanied by the substitution of indirect, 'secondary,' for direct . . . 'primary' relations in the association of individuals in the community." This is the determinist interpretation.

An alternate interpretation of special-interest groups is that they *supplement* personal ties. Some data suggest that the two go

together.[27] Interest groups sometimes usurp functions otherwise performed by intimate associates—for example, when a girl prefers to
play chess with fellow chess buffs rather than with her father. But
such activities are not the central functions of the family nor of other
intimate groups. And, sometimes, special-interest groups can provide a source of primary ties, a way of making friends. In either case,
the groups do *not* undermine intimacy.

These two analyses are speculative. In the next chapter, when
we discuss friends and family, we will be better able to assess the
effects of urbanism on intimacy. Before that, we must consider the
unique type of group known as the neighborhood.

THE NEIGHBORHOOD

Neighbors—whom we initially define as a set of people who live
near ("nigh") to one another—are often considered by the general
public and scholars alike as a "natural" social group. Like the
family, the neighborhood commands early-on the intense loyalties
of its residents and their intimate involvement with one another.[28] In
this view, isolation from the neighborhood portends a person's
alienation; disintegration of the neighborhood threatens social disorganization (Nisbet, 1967; Durkheim, 1893; 300).

An anguished Los Angeleno pleaded several years ago for a
resurgence of neighborhood roots. She felt that the lack of next-door
ties must explain part of the city's crime problem, even of residents'
marital problems. "It is a sickness of soul to live such isolated lives.
Could we not make once again neighborhoods into 'real' neighborhoods where people know each other and care about each other
as our forefathers usually did?"[29] This sentiment is shared by a wide
range of Americans, from left-wing community organizers to a
conservative president who said, in 1981, that Americans are
"members of their communities and the answers to their problems
can be found on the streets where they live," in voluntary action,
rather than in the national government.[30]

Popular understandings often also include the notion that
neighborhood cohesion—that is, the degree to which neighbors
form an intimate and active social group—is seriously impaired by
urbanism. In this view, the city is exemplified by apartment-house
neighbors who never greet each other, much less know each other's

names; and the small town is seen as the heartland of neighborliness. More than one recent presidential candidate has used his small-town upbringing to certify his ability to apply a spirit of "neighborliness" to America's urban problems. Residents of large cities have even come to accept their unneighborly image—so much so that contrary incidents are viewed as exhilarating exceptions. The *New York Times,* for example, prints stories of apartment-house or block parties as heartening beacons in the generally gloomy neighborhood life of the city.

This view of the urban neighborhood is central to the determinist theory. Like other primary groups, the neighborhood is presumably weakened by urbanism. The Chicago School thought that, with the exception of ethnic ghettoes, "in the city environment the neighborhood tends to lose much of the significance which it possessed in simpler and more primitive forms of society," and that "where thousands of people live side by side for years without so much as a bowing acquaintance, these intimate relationships of the primary group are weakened and the moral order which rested upon them is gradually dissolved [Park, 1916: 98, 111]." Ties to the locality are loose or sundered; people are independent of and anonymous to their neighbors—it is all part of the general anomie and isolation of urban life.

How do the facts match up with both the popular and scholarly impressions? Compared with residents of smaller communities, do city-dwellers less often know, interact socially with, and care about their neighbors? In general, the answer is *yes.* Most relevant studies indicate that, on the average, the larger the community, the less the involvement with neighbors. For example, an American survey conducted in 1968 asked respondents, "About how many people in this neighborhood do you know by name?" In nonmetropolitan places, only 3 percent of the interviewees said fewer than 3; 70 percent said that they knew over 20 or "all" of their neighbors. In the center cities of large metropolitan areas the results were quite different. Twenty-two percent responded with fewer than 3, and only 27 percent said 20 or "all." Similar reports come from other studies in the United States and abroad.[31]

These findings do not indicate that cities lack neighboring and neighborhood vitality. Indeed, some prime examples of vibrant local groups studied by sociologists come from large cities: Boston's North and West Ends (W. F. Whyte, 1955; Gans, 1962b), London's

East End (Young and Willmott, 1957), New York's Greenwich Village (Jacobs, 1961), and Chicago's Addams Area (Suttles, 1968). Descriptions of these places show that neighborhoods can thrive in the center of the metropolis. Yet as Suzanne Keller (1968), a noted student of the neighborhood, has pointed out, these locales are in some ways out of the mainstream (a point to which we will return later). The pattern of the mainstream, where most people and places are found, is of less neighborhood cohesion in larger than in smaller communities.

Similarly, rural life is no guarantee of neighborliness. In the rural United States, homesteading meant that the most families were terribly isolated, particularly during the preautomobile days. Insanity was common on the farm and often attributed to loneliness. One observer of life among Scandinavian immigrants in the plains states wrote in 1893 that "These people came from cheery little farm villages. . . . Think for a moment about how great the change must be . . . to an isolated cabin on a Dakota prairie, and say if it is any wonder that so many Scandinavians lose their mental balance."[32] Nevertheless, as a general rule, people living in smaller places— although perhaps not on dispersed farms—tend to be more involved with neighbors than are city-dwellers.

The Neighborly Person

How might we explain this general pattern? One explanation is urban anomie. But a simpler, compositional explanation is that differences in who urban and rural residents are explain this difference in neighborhood involvement. Neighborly types of people tend to live in small communities, and people who are not prone to "neighbor" end up in cities. To explore this proposition, let us consider who the neighborly person is.

First, neighborly people are likely to be long-time residents of the neighborhood. Although people newly arrived in the area often exhibit a flowering of sociability, that bloom tends to fade. Time permits the meetings and remeetings that root people to a place. Second, the neighborly type is likely to be raising a family. Children keep their parents tied to a neighborhood in a variety of ways: Because of their children, parents search for amiable places to live, and they take on local responsibilities (such as the PTA); children meet the next-door children, leading the parents to meet; and raising children often means that someone is home during the day. Third, the neighborly type is likely to be older. Youth contributes to roaming, and age contributes to staying put. Fourth, the likely-to-neighbor is a person who tends to be at home during the day—a retiree, or, most likely, a homemaker; and, being at home means having more opportunity (and more need) to see the people nearby. Fifth, working-class people tend to rely on their neighbors more ✓ than do middle-class people. Although the affluent may actually *know* more of their neighbors, those less well-off depend more on neighbors. Finally, one important trait involves not the individual alone, but the neighborhood itself: commonality. Sharing common values and common needs creates bonds between all people, including neighbors. Such shared interests usually arise from common statuses—age, occupation, ethnicity—and similar life-styles. Thus homogeneity contributes to neighboring.[33]

This list of characteristics explains, at least in part, why urbanites tend to neighbor relatively little. On most counts, city-dwellers are less likely to have the traits associated with neighboring than do people outside the city. Instead, urbanites are more likely without children, younger than the average, working away from home, affluent, and living in heterogeneous neighborhoods.

But these personal and neighborhood characteristics do not completely account for the very sizable differences between large and small communities in neighborhood life. Apparently, something additional, related to urbanism itself, decreases social interaction in the large locality.[34] Urban anomie is the determinist's suggestion for what that "something additional" is. I propose an alternate explanation, one that requires us to examine more closely the concepts of "neighbors" and "neighborhood." This explanation has been called a "minimalist" theory of neighboring (Hunter, 1979).

Any group of people who happen to live near one another may be called "just neighbors." This meaning of neighbors must be distinguished from a weightier meaning: an intimate social group composed of people who live nearby (what many might consider to be "real neighbors"). An intimate group can arise from a set of "just neighbors" under certain specific conditions. Those conditions are less commonly found in cities.

The first condition that generates social bonds out of "just neighbors" is functional necessity. That is, people in a locality join together to meet certain local needs. There are, for one, internal functions: in rural areas—harvesting, barn-raising, road maintenance; in cities of an earlier era—street cleaning, maintaining the well; in both places—enforcing the norms of proper behavior. There are also external functions—foreign relations, so to speak. In many political systems, rewards are divided territorially, areas must compete with each other, and people are treated by others partly on the basis of where they live. These, too, are problems calling forth neighborhood cooperation.[35]

Cities of an earlier era had much more distinct neighborhoods than modern cities do, and thus can illustrate the way these conditions work to promote cohesion. Consider medieval Damascus again. Each section of that city contained about 500 persons who usually shared an ethnic or occupational identity. The city administration recognized the various quarters as autonomous entities, with sheikhs appointed from each quarter to represent it to the municipal government, to help administer the collective taxes, and to ensure the enforcement of ordinances. The quarters were so distinct and self-reliant that it was not uncommon for fierce battles to erupt between them. Little wonder, then, that they were "small, integrated communities . . . analogues of village communities inside the urban agglomeration [Lapidus, 1966: 95; see, also, Abu-Lughod, 1971: 71–79]."

Other dramatic examples of achieving neighborhood unity through conflict come from contemporary urban shantytowns in Latin America. The residents, called *favelados* in Brazil, are treated as outcasts by their national governments and are thus forced to rely on their own communal resources for providing necessary public services. That cooperation, along with the battles against the authorities, creates cohesion where none had existed (Dietz, 1979: 93; Leeds, 1973; Cornelius, 1973). In North America, neighborhood cohesion is occasionally produced by a threat from outside such as highway construction, ethnic invasions, school busing, or other needs to deal with external organizations (e.g., see Coleman, 1971: 673; Gottdeiner, 1977; Taub et al., 1977).

These internal and external functions can bind neighbors together but do not necessarily bind them with ties that are personal. Rather, they can be specifically instrumental ones. Rudolf Heberle (1960: 9) has described the traditional rural German neighborhood in this way: "Neighborhood, as a social relationship, is originally indifferent in regard to emotional–affectual attitudes of neighbors to one another. Neighbors will do certain things for each other, whether they like each other or not." A recent study of small-town Austria suggests that villagers are wary of getting too emotionally close to their neighbors (Crowe, 1979: 74). The point is that functional interdependence generally leads to instrumental relationships among neighbors. These, in turn, make it more likely that personal relationships will also emerge—but they do not guarantee that they will. A study of neighborhoods in Seattle hints that personal bonds are less likely to emerge from functional interdependence today than they did 50 years ago (B. A. Lee et al., 1982)—perhaps because of changes in the two other conditions that foster local intimacy.

The second condition is the existence among neighbors of other relationships besides living near one another. Relatives, co-workers, members of similar religious or ethnic groups will tend to have close ties. Being neighbors may help strengthen those ties, but the source of the intimacy is not the neighbor relationship itself. A rural village provides an example. Anthropologist Conrad Arensberg (1968a) discovered a great deal of cooperation among the countrymen of a remote Irish farming village during the 1930s. But when he carefully examined who actually helped whom, he found that "in every case an extended-family relationship was involved." These farmers were greatly intermarried, so that by helping their kin, they were simultaneously helping many of their neighbors. But it was the kin tie that called forth the mutual assistance. A study of a Mexico City shantytown revealed a similar pattern: Residents had very intense ties with a few of their neighbors, but the relationships arose out of separate personal histories, especially out of kinship and common hometowns, not out of neighborhood solidarity (Lomnitz, 1977).

A third condition that encourages local interaction is difficulty in sustaining extra-local interaction. When people face impediments in making contact with others not near them—as do children, housewives with young children, the ill, the aged, and the poor—they must either make friends with neighbors or be isolated. If they make the first choice, that often involves associating with people who are not ideally appropriate (Keller, 1968: 84; Fischer, 1982a).

Three examples illustrate the point. A natural "experiment" occurred in Hobart, Tasmania, when a collapsed bridge split the town for about a year and required a long alternate route. One effect seemed to be that some people saw friends on their own shore more often. Yet even more people became lonely from not seeing their opposite-shore friends. When the bridge was restored, old, cross-town ties were quickly restored (Lee, 1980). The second illustration comes from the history of rural French villages. Peasants used to spend winter evenings in *veillées,* gatherings in a barn where people chatted, did their craftwork, courted, and kept warm. With the coming of warmer homes, and especially, of the bicycle, *veillées* were reduced to a sparsely attended old folks' tradition (Weber, 1976: Chapter 24). The third story comes from contemporary Chinese cities where, researchers report, people see a great deal of their neighbors and little of their kin and friends, at least as compared to prerevolutionary days and to Hong Kong. The reasons include, in addition to governmental programs that encourage neighborhood interdependence and activity, heavy time constraints posed by work schedules and major difficulties in access to transportation and communication (M. K. Whyte and Parish, In Press). In these cases, neighboring seems a secondary substitute for more preferred social interaction.

These three conditions—functional interdependence, prior relationships, and lack of alternatives—increase the likelihood that people will have personal relationships with those who live nearby. *The larger the community* (and the more modern the society), *the less likely* will each of these conditions be found. Consequently, neighborhood interaction declines with increases in urbanism.

Urbanism and the Neighborhood

In modern cities, the responsibility for many internal functions such as safety, street cleaning, and education rests at a higher level than the neighborhood. (This can be a problem when the city fails to serve certain neighborhoods. The cry of "community control" is then often raised.) City-wide allegiances also dissipate the unity derived from dealing with external relations. There certainly remain many divisive neighborhood issues—such as where traffic will be routed—but they are often overshadowed by city-wide concerns, such as police practices. Racial, religious, class, and ideological divisions that cross-cut the entire city compete with territorial divisions for the interest and commitment of the residents. As Heberle (1960: 9) puts it:

> The reciprocal obligation between neighbors is a consequence of their proximity and interdependence. Where interdependence ceases because of the availability of services as in the city, proximity no longer constitutes the basis for a categoric social relationship. Neighbors may now choose to what extent they want to associate with each other.

Instrumental ties among neighbors and the emergence of personal ties out of them become less probable.

The second condition—the proximity of kin, coworkers, and so on—is also less likely to be present in larger settlements. The wider housing market of a city makes it possible for associates to be physically dispersed and still maintain contact with each other [as in the earlier example of the Portland longshoremen who were socially connected in many ways, although they were not especially likely to be neighbors (see, also, Frankenburg 1965)].

Third, the larger the community, the greater the choice *not* to neighbor. That is, urbanites have more options in selecting whom to interact with, and their more compatible associates may live outside the neighborhood. Park (1916) describes it this way: "The easy means of communication and of transportation [in the city], which enable individuals to distribute their attention and to live at the same time in several different worlds, tend to destroy the permanency and intimacy of the neighborhood." Suzanne Keller (1968: 48) put it crisply: "Village life makes neighboring mandatory. . . . In cities this type of neighboring . . . is mandatory no longer."

An illustration comes from a study conducted by Susan Freeman (1970) in a tiny Castilian hamlet, one of the least urban places we will encounter in this book. The several families living there were closely (though somewhat primly) bound together as neighbors, partly because they depended on one another, partly because many were kin, and partly because there was no other choice. The last condition rankled many a resident. Freeman (1970: 199) concludes her study by describing the ideal social life as the average person in the hamlet imagined it.

> It is attained in a large and dense settlement where within the one town or barrio he can find all the companionship he needs, where he can select his own associates, and where the people he works with are not the only available friends. This idea is fully realized only by emigration [to a larger community].

Urbanism reduces the likelihood that the conditions needed to bring active group life to neighborhoods will jointly occur. This general rule is dramatized by its exceptions. Many urban neighborhoods *do* harbor active and intimate social groups. But, they usually fit one or more of the following descriptions: being threatened from outside, being an ethnic or occupational enclave, or being populated by people with little physical mobility (for example, home-bound wives).[36]

An example of an occupational enclave is our familiar case of South Chicago. Residents there were heavily involved in neighborhood life: They identified emotionally with neighborhoods such as Irondale or Millgate, and they strongly resisted incursions by outsiders. The reason for their fierce localism in the midst of a huge metropolitan area was that the residents shared an important and dominant involvement in the nearby steel mills. And on top of the occupational similarity was the ethnic homogeneity of specific neighborhoods. In exceptions such as South Chicago, neighborhoods can be cohesive in the most urban of areas; but they are exceptions (Kornblum, 1974; Warren, 1977).

Urbanism, in general, makes concrete the abstract distinction presented earlier—the distinction between "just neighbors," a set of persons who live near one another, and the intimate social group that can develop from "just neighbors." Urbanism tends to reduce the role of neighbor toward its bare essence (although it hardly ever becomes stripped bare, even in the largest cities). That basic role seems to involve two essential norms or rules of behavior. The first is: Be ready to assist your neighbor at those times when physical proximity is important—either in an emergency, or when the assistance costs little and it would be silly to force the other person to go long distances for it (for example, in the United States, loaning a cup of sugar). The second norm is simple: Don't be offensive. Good neighbors don't disturb or offend the people next door (or lower the property value of their dwelling). These are the same normative expectations generally held for any people in close physical proximity, when they are standing in line, for example, or sitting on a bus.[37] Apparently, refraining from being offensive is more critical to one's neighbors than is doing anything positive with them.[38]

Even in the most urban and urbane of localities, it is, of course, true that neighbors will often be more than just neighbors. In fact, all else being equal, the nearer two people reside, the more likely it is that they will have deeper and closer ties—including, for example, getting married (Ramsøy, 1966). And in some city neighborhoods, a "good neighbor" is expected to be at least somewhat sociable. But the point is that the forces overlaying the neighborhood with primary ties are weakened in the city, thus revealing the neighborhood to be fundamentally a secondary impersonal group of "just neighbors."

What implications for the individual resident follow from the conclusion that urbanism reduces the extent and intimacy of neighborhood relationships? One exception (consistent with determinist theory) is that the absence of local ties should reduce the total of the urbanite's personal bonds. But the evidence indicates that this does *not* occur. Instead, local relationships are alternatives to extralocal ones.

Several studies support this conclusion. Eight hundred interviews were conducted in East York, an area of Toronto. Respondents were asked to name six persons to whom they "felt close" (very few could not name any). Only thirteen percent of the named "intimates" lived in the neighborhood. Most lived in Toronto, but elsewhere in the metropolitan region. Furthermore, when respondents were asked which of their intimates could be depended upon for assistance in time of need, the intimates living far away were selected as often as those closer by (Wellman et al., 1973).

Other studies report the same findings: Local ties form only a small portion of urbanites' total social bonds; nearby associates do not usually provide important social support; and people with few neighborhood friends usually have intimates elsewhere.[39] Alone, these findings cannot disprove the thesis that city-dwellers are rendered isolated by the vitiating effects of urbanism on the neighborhood. But the relative unimportance of local ties indicated by these studies suggests that the fate of social relations in general does not depend on the fate of neighborly relations. Although we need not go so far as to echo one researcher's rhetorical challenge, "Who needs neighborhoods? [Wellman, 1972]"—some persons certainly do—many individuals seem to do well without them.

There is yet another possible consequence of reduced neighborhood ties in cities: a breakdown in local social control. As one student of the Chicago School put it:

A large part of the city's population lives much as do people in a great hotel, meeting but not knowing one another. The result is dissolution of social solidarity and public opinion. . . . There

> is . . . no common body of experience and tradition, no
> unanimity of interest, sentiment, and attitude which can serve
> as a basis of collective action [Zorbaugh, 1929: 251]."

Concretely, if neighbors do not associate with one another, they can less effectively establish a *local* moral order, to control rowdy children, to compel residents to keep up their property, and so on.

Some evidence exists that neighborhoods with "unneighbor-ly" traits are the most prone to crime. For example, neighborhoods where people are not at home and those where residents move frequently tend to suffer (e.g., see Roncek, 1981). Police repeatedly encourage people to get to know their neighbors as a crime-fighting strategy. Whether this connection between crime and lack of neigh-borliness reflects an absence of cohesion or something simpler—for instance, the kinds of people who live in such places, or the absence of curious neighbors to report untoward events—is not clear. But we can argue that, while people may not need neighbors, neighborhoods need people who do.

Neighborhood Movements[40]

In the last several years, journalists have reported an upsurge of neighborhood organizations and local activism within America's large cities, crediting such movements not only with local successes, such as blocking highways, but also with unified action and power at the municipal level in cities such as Houston and San Francisco (the phenomenon may be worldwide [Castells, 1983]). Whether or not a "new" neighborhood movement exists is not evident. Many neighborhood groups have existed for a long time as homeowners' and improvement associations (Lee et al., 1982). And neighborhood action—sometimes violent action—is common in American history (e.g., Schneider, 1980). But there are reasons to believe that neighborhood activism has indeed increased. One reason is that the "War on Poverty" launched in the 1960s left in its wake organizations and trained personnel dedicated to fostering "community control" (e.g., see Katznelson, 1981). Another is that remnants of the New Left seemed to have turned from defeats at the national level to action at the local level (see Boyte, 1981). An example of that redirection is the Santa Monica, California, Campaign for Economic Democracy, which successfully organized local tenants to establish rent control. A third source of movements is the various "urban crises" of the 1970s, exemplified in the bankruptcy of Cleveland and the near-bankruptcy of New York, which have led to so much deterioration of public services that residents have mobilized in response (Castells, 1978).

What does such an apparent resurgence imply for our understanding of neighborhoods? The movements call upon a shared American ideology about the "natural" neighborhood—a call coming from both the left of the politcal spectrum and from its right, as illustrated by the earlier quotation from President Reagan (see, also, Berger and Neuhaus, 1977). Yet, the movements do not seem to involve an upwelling of communal togetherness—in fact, they seem to have little to do with personal ties among neighbors—but rather other concerns. Some are mobilizations to combat threats such as crime or shut-downs of hospitals. Others are, crudely speaking, homeowner associations moved to the city: organizations of middle-class people who have "gentrified" poor inner-city areas (e.g., Hunter, 1975; see, also, Chapter 9, this volume). And yet others actually reflect nonterritorial concerns—race, age, lifestyle, and so on—argued under the label of neighborhood issues.

To the extent that people in a neighborhood share a fate and have a common interest in city services, land-use policy, property values, and so on, the potential for organized action exists. The stronger the threat, the likelier the collective action; and threats have been great in recent urban history. Yet anything lasting, or personal, or "communal" arising from these actions is unusual.

SUMMARY

In this chapter, we concentrated on the way secondary social groups are affected by urbanism. The largest group in a community, the community itself, becomes less cohesive the more populous it is. As local political affairs demonstrate, urban communities are more strife-ridden than rural ones, and tend to lose the attention of their residents to the national and international scenes. One reason for this may be the sharpening in urban places of social class lines and perhaps the emergence of meaningful groups organized around occupations. People in large communities can also more easily join in special-interest groups, because there are more people at hand who share whatever the interest, hobby, or political orientation may be. One urban–rural difference that is expected but does not appear is membership in formal associations—urbanites are no likelier to be members than ruralites. In any case, the determinist assumption that formal associations involve impersonal relations is not necessarily true; associations may instead be places to pursue quite personal relationships. Finally, we examined the relative weakness of the urban neighborhood in some detail. Something about urbanism seems to reduce the likelihood that personal, primary relationships will emerge among a group of neighbors. The Wirthian thesis is that the feebleness of neighborhood life in cities is part of general urban anomie. But a better explanation may be that urbanism brings with it some "freedom from proximity." The ready availability of many potential associates outside the immediate vicinity allows people to construct social networks that extend beyond the neighborhood. What then develops are "localities of limited liability" (Janowitz, 1967; Greer, 1962)—neighborhoods where only a minimum is expected and demanded of neighbors, where the formation of closer bonds is a matter of personal taste, and from which residents can leave with little emotional loss.

Many of the trends described here—the lesser importance of community-wide and neighborhood ties and the greater importance of specialized, nonterritorial ties in the city—were apparent to Louis Wirth and his associates at Chicago. They interpreted these trends as evidence of urban anomie. Persuasive as such an interpretation is, it is inconsistent with other facts: that urbanites are not more involved than ruralites in formal associations, nor do they rely more on formal ties, and that they obstinately personalize what seem to outsiders to be the impersonal connections of occupation or special interest. Furthermore, we should doubt the assumption that groups based on residence—the community and neighborhood—are in essence primary and personal.

Another possible interpretation of these findings is based, in part, on subcultural theory. According to this view, a residential group is not primary in the sense that the family is. Residential groups are sets of people who live near one another. What urbanism does is to place even more people within easy reach of the individual, and thereby to provide more bases of association than the locality alone. And thus urban residents seem, in a sense, to replace associates that rural people draw from the neighborhood with friends they draw from work or special-interest contexts (Fischer, 1982a: Chapters 8–9). (Modern technology, through rapid transportation and communication, may have much the same effect as urbanism.) In this larger population, there are likely to be many people—critical masses of them—who are more personally suitable for the individual than those who happen to be in his or her local area. Thus it is easier for people in cities to build social networks and to live in social worlds distinguished by class, occupation, or interest. [Keller (1968: 61) calls it "a shift from a neighboring of *place* to a neighboring of *taste.*"] Consequently, residential groups lose some, although hardly all, of their members' commitments to translocal associations (see Webber, 1968b).

This interpretation suggests that there is greater freedom of association for urban than rural individuals, and probably a greater compatibility among urban associates (see Fischer, 1982a). It also raises one of the thematic tensions discussed in Chapter 2: community versus individualism. Some have argued (for example, Nisbet, 1967) that groups based on freely chosen association cannot satisfactorily replace "natural," inherited groups in maintaining the "moral order" of a society, that the traditional groups better socialize, bind, and integrate the individual into the social whole.[41] This argument will be easier to evaluate once we have considered the nature and strength of urban personal life and "moral order" in the chapters that follow.

CHAPTER 6

SOcial Groups iN the City: PRimaRy GROUPS

Of the many social groups the visitor to the city observes, the most significant to the residents are the smallest—those made up of the few people they know fully and intimately. These relatives and close friends are the *primary groups* that help shape our personalities, influence our values and opinions, encourage or restrain our actions, and that give us the most grace and the most grief. Our individual experiences of the world are filtered through these primary groups and largely interpreted in ways they have taught us.

Primary groups also are vital to society. They form the basic units of which it is made, much as cells are the basic elements of the body. In traditional cultures, people seem to be recognized not as autonomous beings, but instead only as interchangeable parts of families or clans. When primary groups are weakened, society is weakened. People drift off separately, and society becomes disorganized, atomistic, and vulnerable to anomie.

Determinist theory argues that city life weakens such intimate groups, and that urban societies consequently tend to be anomic. Cities produce structural differentiation and psychic overload, both of which cause personal ties to wither. Their emaciation is accelerated by impersonal urban institutions that usurp the functions of friends and relatives. The ultimate consequence is a tendency toward individual alienation and social disintegration (see the detailed discussion in Chapter 2).

Both compositional and subcultural theory maintain that intimate relationships are just as common in the city as in the countryside. Subcultural theory adds a twist: Primary groups are alive and well, but the urban experience does *change* them. Both the composition of close relationships (that is, the kinds of people who are intimates) and the character of those relationships are different in small-versus-large communities. They differ, at least in part, because the urban setting provides individuals with a variety of people with whom they can be involved and a variety of subcultures in which they can participate. For instance, because the choice of potential friends is ordinarily greater in an urban setting than a rural one, urban friends should be, on the average, somewhat more compatible than rural ones. Similarly, urbanites should rely on relatives for assistance less often than ruralites do, because there are more sources of aid in the city. But from either perspective, compositional or subcultural, the urbanite is embedded in intimate groups, and is *not* isolated in "the lonely crowd."

In this chapter, we will examine the condition of primary groups in the city, in particular ethnic groups, friends, and family. Does urbanism reduce the vitality and social significance of these primary groups? Are they changed in any other respect? What implications can we draw for a person's urban experience?

ETHNIC GROUPS

Cities differ dramatically from smaller communities in their greater variety of racial, regional, and religious groups. We can think of these as "ethnic groups": subsets of people within a community who are linked, through descent, to a common race, or religion, or place of origin, or a combination of these. (Because of the genealogical nature of ethnicity, I have placed the topic in this chapter on primary groups.) Typically, each group is also distinguished by a particular culture—tradition, values, customs, and style of action—although just how distinctive the ethnic subculture is varies. For example, Americans of Mexican origin tend to have a way of life more distinctive from other Americans than do those of, say, Danish origin.

Beyond this simple definition, the concept of ethnicity is flexible. Some cases may warrant making finer distinctions than others.

In small communities, for example, it might be enough merely to distinguish Italian–Americans from non-Italians; but in large communities, distinguishing among Sicilians, Neapolitans, and Northern Italians might be appropriate. The most critical bases of ethnic differences vary from country to country: race and nationality of origin in America, region in France, tribe in Africa, caste in India. But, essentially, we are dealing with descent-based cultural groups.[1]

The Chicago School sociologists held ambivalent opinions about ethnic groups in the city. On the one hand, Park, Wirth, and their colleagues were struck by the stubborn survival of ethnic enclaves in modern cities; those enclaves were significant pieces of the urban mosaic. But they were also convinced that these residual ethnic cultures would ultimately be destroyed by the forces of "rationalization" in the city (see Wirth, 1928; Park and Miller, 1921: 296–308) and were "communities in process of disorganization [Zorbaugh, 1929: 192]." First, ethnic groups were declining as sources of personal relationships and locations for social activity. And second, in the city, the cultures of ethnic groups were quickly becoming less traditional, less distinctive, and less controlling of individual behavior.

In contrast, compositional theories (Gans's in particular) consider ethnic groups to be the kind of small social units that are unaffected by ecological variables like urbanism. Subcultural theory provides a complex prediction. On the one hand, urbanism generates various alternate bases of association besides ethnicity: Groups founded on occupation or life-style or special interest (Chapter 5). These subcultures attract people's allegiances and, through personal contacts and diffusion of values, modify the cultures of ethnic groups. On the other hand, the concentration of many ethnic-group members and intergroup conflict should have the same vitalizing effects for ethnicity that they do for other subcultures. This urban vitalization should be especially important for small minority groups. We should expect, therefore, to observe *both* processes—weakening and strengthening—and to see them working against each other. In some instances, defections from and dilutions of the ethnic group will predominate. In others, cohesion and cultural integrity should be maintained, perhaps even deepened. Although the relative balance will vary according to specific circumstances, we should observe both subcultural vitality and intergroup diffusion as results of urbanism.[2]

What do the available studies indicate is the actual fate of ethnic groups in the city? The weight of the evidence is that they persist *and* they change.

Persistence of Ethnic Groups

Scores of anthropological studies have been conducted on urban populations around the globe—on such groups as Italian–Americans in Boston; on Andean villagers living in Lima, Peru; Serbian migrants to Zagreb, Yugoslavia; tribesmen from the bush in cities all around Africa; rickshaw drivers in Dacca, Bangladesh; and Irish families in nineteenth-century London. Repeatedly, the researchers have "rediscovered" ethnicity. They describe people who restrict their social ties largely to persons within their own ethnic group, who identify themselves as members of that group, and who maintain the distinctive customs and traditional values of their particular culture.[3]

There is, to be sure, great variation in the extent that particular ethnic groups remain distinctive and cohesive in urban settings. Persistence depends on characteristics of the group—its size, migration pattern (as individuals or families; see Chapter 4), occupational position, political leverage, cultural features, the discrimination it faces, and so on[4]—and on features of the particular city: its ethnic composition, economic structure, housing patterns, politics, and so forth (e.g., see Peil, 1981; Lazerwitz, 1977; and Nelson, 1981: 92–93). In the United States, our impression is that some groups, such as blacks and Jews, are set off more from the mainstream of society than are other groups, such as the Irish and Germans (Fischer, 1982a: Chapter 17); and that some cities, such as Boston, have more distinctive ethnic groups than have other cities, such as Houston. Nevertheless, the overall conclusion from urban ethnographies around the world is that ethnicity is remarkably persistent in major cities.

That people tend to emphasize social ties with fellow ethnics shows up in several ways: Most kin and friends are in a person's own ethnic group; marriages occur predominantly between fellow members (sometimes great efforts are made to recruit wives from home villages)[5]; and clubs and associations tend to have exclusive ethnic memberships.

When people identify themselves, they think of themselves as

Chinese in Bangkok, as Bretons in Paris, or as Armenians in New York. In South Chicago, for example, old animosities between Serbians and Croatians (regions of what is now Yugoslavia) still contribute to tensions between their American descendants (Kornblum, 1974; Kneeland, 1978). Urbanism can even *create* a new form of ethnic identity, in that self-identification may become more encompassing: For example, New Yorkers of Neapolitan origin identify themselves as "Italians." Some evidence for persistence in ethnic identity comes from studies of voting in American cities that indicate a continuing preference by electors for candidates of their own ethnicity unto the third generation of immigrants.[6]

Maintaining ethnic customs and values is a third way people demonstrate persistence. In South Chicago, some of the Slavic customs practiced by third-generation residents are so traditional that more recent immigrants from the "old country" find them bizarrely out of date (Kornblum, 1974). But in most cases that sort of cultural purity is not maintained in the city, not at least with regard to what might be termed "peripheral" cultural items.

The customs, values, and artifacts of a culture can be scaled from "central"—those characteristics reflecting the fundamental, almost preconscious, aspects of a culture (such as implicit understandings of the social world, ultimate life values and goals, and styles of interpersonal relations)—to "peripheral"—those that are relatively incidental aspects of a culture (such as dress styles, specific rituals, and political attitudes, items not integrally linked to a culture's ethos). Peripheral items are easily changeable, in the sense that, within a generation or two, minority ethnic groups in a city adopt all or parts of such cultural patterns from the predominant group. But, the central cultural items of ethnic groups seem to persist to a notable degree even in the largest cities.[7]

These conclusions about urban ethnicity are based mainly on studies conducted only in large cities; in that way, they are limited. They rarely contrast the ethnic group in the city with its counterpart in smaller settings.[8] Probably the purest form of ethnic culture— outside of the "old country"—would be in isolated, single-group hamlets. There are certainly examples of ethnic minorities thriving in such places—for example, Swedes in rural Minnesota, Mennonites in Pennsylvania, and Sikhs in California—where they can separate themselves from other populations. But in most instances such rural ethnic enclaves dissipate quickly (Hine, 1980: Chapter

8). The issue for us is whether, over a range of groups and societies, an urban location is generally more or less conducive than a small-town one to a minority's ethnicity. Comparative evidence usually shows, in fact, that ethnicity is generally as or more significant in the city than in the countryside.

Consider some studies: Anthropologists following migration to the rapidly growing cities of Africa have frequently described a process labeled "re-" or "supertribalization." Becoming an urbanite is often associated with increased awareness of, pride in, and self-conscious attachment to the individual's tribe. This attachment often manifests itself in tribal organizations and in tribal conflict.[9] Anthropologist Edward Bruner (1961, 1973a) studied a Christian tribe in Indonesia, called the Toba Batak, both in its home village and in the largely Moslem city of Medan. He found that attachment to traditional norms concerning family life was at least as strong in Medan as in the village. A sociologist polled third-generation Ukrainian–Canadians living in a small, exclusively "Ukrainian" town and others living in a larger, ethnically heterogeneous city. The respondents in the larger, more differentiated community were more resistant to assimilation and identified more with their Ukrainianism than those in the smaller town (Borhek, 1970). Three political scientists investigated the extent to which Polish–American voters in a Chicago ward and in a rural county of Illinois were inclined to select a candidate on the basis of ethnicity. The Chicago voters were markedly more likely to choose the candidate with the Polish name than were the rural voters (Lorinskas et al., 1969). And finally, in the Northern California Community Study (Fischer, 1982a: Chapter 16), we found that city-dwellers more often than residents of small towns identified themselves as "ethnics," had associates from the same group, and were organizationally involved with the ethnicity.

There are, to be sure, bits of evidence pointing the other way, but on the whole, these and similar studies (e.g., Neilli, 1970; Cornelius, 1971) suggest that the vitality and integrity of ethnic groups is not necessarily sapped by urbanism and is sometimes even strengthened by it.[10] In the long run, ethnic minorities probably do assimilate and "disappear" (e.g., see Alba, 1976; Montero, 1981; Woodrum, 1981), but they seem to persist longer in cities than in small towns.

How might this be explained? It may be that the forces in the urban setting that Wirth thought weakened ethnic groups simply do not exist or are not very powerful. It may be that the kinds of groups, or the kinds of individuals, residing in cities are especially ethnically oriented to start with. This would be a compositional suggestion— that ecological factors are of little consequence.

We have some evidence that composition explains a major part of urban–rural differences in ethnicity. In the United States, for example, some of the most culturally distinct groups—the Jews, Chinese, and blacks, for instance; the foreign-born, in general—are especially likely to concentrate in the great metropolises. But, when these and other aspects of composition, such as people's age and education, are taken into account, a tendency for the urban ethnics to be more "ethnic" than their small-town cousins remains.[11] A subcultural explanation would be that countervailing urban forces work to bolster ethnicity. We will discuss two such forces here, elaborating arguments originally presented in Chapter 2.

The first of these two forces is the by-now-familiar achievement of critical mass. Large numbers make it possible for people to find friends and spouses within their own group. For instance, the chance that a Catholic will marry within the faith increases with the size of the Catholic population, so that it is more probable in large than in small American cities (J. L. Thomas, 1951); the same is true for Jews (Rosenthal, 1967; see, also, Blau et al., 1982). The larger the group, the likelier it is that yet more members will be drawn into the city. There are many cases of "chain migration" in which residents of one region or village will move into a particular niche in a particular city, such as newspaper vendors in Tunis coming from a specific Berber village (Findlay, 1969: 61), or children's cloak-makers in turn-of-the-century New York all being from Minsk, Russia (Rischlin, 1977: 183). This may be, but often is not, accompanied by ethnic concentrations in particular neighborhoods.[12]

The larger the ethnic group, the greater also the support for institutions that reinforce ethnicity: churches, newspapers, stores, clubs, political organizations. These institutions link people to their groups, exercise authority over members, protect them from outsiders, help attract fellow ethnics, and constantly remind them of their identity. In Chapter 3 we cited a study of immigrants to Montreal that showed that national groups with such institutions were best able to maintain ethnic cohesion and boundaries. And having those institutions was partly a function of simple numbers (Breton, 1964;

Karnig, 1979; cf. Stephens, 1979). Similarly, another Canadian study found that the likelihood of French-speakers passing that language, rather than English, onto their children as a mother tongue depended on how numerous and segregated the French were in a community (Lieberson, 1970). Yet an additional example of the same process comes from a study of American Indians in San Francisco. Powwows provide important social and ritual functions in Indian communities, but until 1962, few Indians in the Bay Area could perform the necessary rites. People had to drive back to the reservations for the powwows. Now that the Indian population of the area has grown, powwows have been held in the city and have helped unite the Indian community (Hirabayashi, 1972: 82).[13]

The larger the city, the larger—in general—are its various ethnic groups. And in turn, the larger an ethnic group, the more likely it is to preserve its culture and its social boundaries. [When an ethnic group happens to be large in small towns, we will see many of the same phenomena there (Fischer, 1982a: Chapter 16).] It may even become possible to maintain in the midst of the city an isolated ethnic world, where the signs and the language spoken on the street are foreign (Lopata, 1967; Mathiasson, 1974).

The intensification resulting from concentration affects primarily or only *small* minority groups. In country towns, their few members tend to be absorbed by the wider community; in the city, although they may be the same percentage of the population, the groups' greater absolute numbers help preserve ethnic cohesion. For large and predominant ethnic groups—such as European Protestants in America—size would seem to make little difference.

In Chapter 4, we noted that ethnic variety, although not inevitable, is a common accompaniment to urbanism. In Chapter 5, we suggested that urbanism tends to generate subcultures founded on bases *other than* ethnicity. These subcultures can, and often do, have tense relations with one another which, in turn, promotes ethnic distinctiveness, ethnic boundaries, and ethnic consciousness. Cross-cultural contacts can result in violence. More commonly, they simply lead to mutual revulsion, because members of each group view the others from their own cultural perspective. Repelled and disgusted, the members are more than ever convinced of the virtue of their own group.

As a case in point, African "supertribalization" results largely from tribal members seeing for the first time, in the city, people who look, act, and believe differently than they do. This experience raises their tribal consciousness. The Toba Batak, the Indonesian group, also exhibit this process. In the following passage, Edward Bruner describes encounters between the Batak and the Sundanese majority in Bandung, Java.

> Most Sundanese have not had much experience with Batak although all are familiar with the Batak stereotype of a rough and aggressive person. The Sundanese and the Batak each approach the initial interaction guided by their own customs and emotional set, and at first they judge the other by their own standards. What the Sundanese define as being crude the Batak interpret as being honest, straight-forward, and strong. What the Sundanese regard as refined behavior the Batak regard as being evasive, insincere, and feminine. Each group feels morally superior to the other and at least initially the behavior of each tends to validate these stereotypic evaluations. Each group in doing what it thinks is right and proper behaves in ways that the other feels are morally deficient [Bruner, 1973a: 265].

There are many examples of such cultural clash in the American urban experience as well. Describing the Addams area of Chicago, Suttles (1968: 61–72) notes common misunderstandings between blacks and whites. Their styles of dress, of physical and verbal expression, and even modes of eye-contact differ (LaFrance and Mayo, 1976). What one considers honest the other perceives as rude; what one considers polite the other perceives as hostile.

Sally Merry (1981) describes similar tensions between Chinese–American residents on the one hand and their black and white neighbors on the other in an East Coast housing development: Suspicions arising from differences in expressiveness, voice level, sexual norms, display of wealth, views of how to attain success, and so on (see also Ginsberg, 1981). Students in ethnically integrated high schools commonly report intergroup tension and voluntary resegregation.[14] We like to believe that intergroup contact fosters understanding, but in the typical situations that ethnic groups meet one another—often unequal and impersonal, sometimes competitive—the contact leads to friction and to each group believing that the other is unworthy of trust and friendship (see also Nelli, 1970; Borhek, 1970; Gans, 1962b).

This ethnic friction is more likely to occur in city than in town, because that is where minorities are visible and where contacts occur. Small-town residents tend to be more ethnically *prejudiced,* but big-city residents actually *experience* more hostile ethnic encounters.[15] Thus ethnic suspicion and distrust tend to increase with urbanism (Fischer, 1982a: Chapter 18).

The ultimate outcome of intergroup tension is occasionally overt ethnic conflict. Sometimes violent, such conflict is more likely to occur in large than in small communities. Racial violence during the 1960s in the United States, for example, was especially concentrated in the larger cities (Spilerman, 1971; Morgan and Clark, 1973; Danzger, 1975). The concentration of blacks in the metropolitan areas created more friction with whites, a greater sense of black pride and unity, and a greater feeling of power (Karnig, 1979)—all of which made collective violence more likely.

This aspect of urbanism's influence on ethnic consciousness—intergroup contacts—probably affects majority or *large* groups more than it does minorities. The latter must confront the predominant group almost everywhere, town or city. But the predominant group usually does not confront minorities in sizeable numbers or activity except in cities. It is there, then, that the large groups must confront the growing power of the small.

Change in Ethnic Groups

Ethnicity both persists and *changes* under the influence of urbanism. As we have known since at least the time of Thomas and Znaniecki's *Polish Peasant* (1918), Poles in Chicago are hardly identical to their cousins in Polish villages. The changes can be grouped into the same categories of social ties, identity, and customs that we used to discuss persistence. But before examining the ways urbanism modifies each, let us consider the forces that produce the changes.

Some of these forces are incidental to urbanism and are not unique to cities: disruption and family separation resulting from migration, and changes in language and occupation that accompany a move from one society to another. A study of rural migrants in Bombay, India, for example, revealed that they had given up some religious rituals, not necessarily because of Bombay, but because their new jobs made the services more bothersome to perform than when they were farmers (Prabhu, 1956; Husain, 1956).

Besides such factors connected to migration, two familiar ones are peculiar to urbanism: the numbers of people and the heterogeneous contact among them. These are the very same forces that support ethnicity. Community size modifies ethnic groups because it supports the development of alternate subcultures based on other factors, such as occupation, life-style, and age. These subcultures tempt defections from the ethnic culture—as when young professionals turn their backs on the old ethnic neighborhood. Furthermore, a large city with a sizable, predominant ethnicity becomes a precarious environment for small minorities. Even when they are tolerated by the majority group, the small groups must modify at least their public behavior. That was the fate of the Batak in Java, and of most minorities in white, Anglo–Saxon, Protestant America.

We have noted that contact among groups often leads to repulsion and conflict. But it can also lead simultaneously to diffusion—to the adoption of selected life-styles, beliefs, or objects from other groups. Usually, subordinate groups adopt cultural items from predominant ones, but the influence can operate both ways, as in the case of urban black culture and its influence on whites.

The forces of intergroup diffusion modify the social ties of ethnic-group members. People almost inevitably make connections across ethnic lines, with close involvements sometimes growing out of what began as impersonal relations between members of different groups (e.g., see Baskauskas, 1977). Frequently, people drift away from the ethnic group, committing themselves instead to subcultures based on profession and life-style. Or sometimes they marry into another ethnic group, as is becoming increasingly common among middle-class, urban Africans (Little, 1973: 131). It is remarkable that this weakening of ethnic boundaries has not happened faster than it has in the United States, which is a difficult environment for pluralism.[16] Note that, in crossing ethnic boundaries, the "defectors" are not left drifting, isolated without any bonds; rather they have been drawn into an alternate social world. Note as well that the defection leaves behind a more purified core of committed ethnic-group members—"a saving remanent."

The same sorts of pressures alter ethnic identity. In particular, intergroup contact in cities creates an allegiance to larger ethnic categories. For example, in peasant China, people saw themselves as members of a village, sometimes as members of a region (say, Cantonese); in American cities, they are "Chinese," an identity not traditionally stressed back home. In the African bush, people see themselves essentially as members of specific family lineages; in the cities they are identified as, and identify themselves as, members of the tribe. Sometimes, in the larger cities, the process reverses. There come to be so many immigrant Chinese, for example, that distinctions by province are again important.[17]

And ethnic culture—traditions, customs, institutions— changes. For instance, organizations develop that did not exist in the rural homeland: mutual-benefit societies, credit unions, ethnic newspapers, political clubs. These are partly cultural borrowings from other groups and partly adaptations to new economic conditions and to hostility from other groups (the B'nai B'rith Anti-Defamation League is an example of the latter).

Customs and traditions are altered. Sometimes the alteration is toward more cultural distinctiveness, often as a response to threats from other groups (Horowitz, 1977). For example, one Indian caste, finding itself in competition with other migrant groups in the city of Madras, redefined its traditional rules of membership and changed its customs to encourage in-group marriage. Both moves helped consolidate the caste's political and economic strength (Barnett, 1973). Another example is the trading tribe of West Africa, the Hausa, who live in Nigerian cities dominanted by the Yoruba tribe. Earlier in this century, Hausa leaders initiated a vigorous Moslem revival, probably as a political tactic to fight off potential competitors (A. Cohen, 1969).

But the more common changes in ethnic cultures are probably those that blur the lines between groups. For example, the Toba Batak in Java learn, as they must to succeed in that society, to lower their voices, to display "refined behavior," and generally to adopt Sundanese ways. Batak children change even more, so much that they come to judge their own families by Sundanese standards (Bruner, 1973a). Or French–Canadians learn English to succeed economically, and some families end up shifting to English altogether (Lieberson, 1970).

The extent to which an ethnic group's structure and culture can be altered is dramatized in the African urban experience. In rural areas, the African tribe is the entire society, economy, polity, and culture. In urban centers, the tribe is an ethnic group: a category of people, an identity, a source of relatives and friends, an instructor in belief and behavior. In these ways, the tribe distinguishes the individual from others with whom he or she shares a common society, economy, polity, and national culture. The tribe becomes, instead of *the* social world, just one social world among many (see Epstein, 1967).

For all these changes, ethnic boundaries nevertheless remain, and cultural cores persist. What is altered most are the peripheral items, such as style of clothing or taste in food; least altered are basic understandings of the world. People identify themselves with, display the cultural traits of, and find their most intimate social ties within their ethnic groups. Cases of ethnic assimilation into the urban melting pot, of course, occur—as do cases of continued ethnic purity. Most ethnic groups are in between, their particular balance of change and constancy depending on their internal characteristics, the society around them, their distinctiveness from other groups, the distance from their homeland, their flow of migration, and other such traits. Urbanism is one force for persistence. The tide of history moves most groups toward assimilation, but that tide is resisted at least somewhat in the large cities.

In sum, the critical mass and the cross-cultural contact that accompany urbanism bolster ethnicity in various ways. And simultaneously, these same forces stimulate competing subcultures that can change ethnic groups and lure their members away. In most societies, urbanism produces in ethnic groups a combination of both constancy and change. At the same time that the multicultural people of a city dress, speak, work, and play in shared ways; they trust and relax with "their own"; interact in a style peculiar to "their own"; pursue goals particularly stressed by "their own"; and urge their children to marry "their own."

FRIENDS

Friendship is a complex social relationship. To sociologists, it is complex conceptually as well as perhaps personally. Unlike being neighbors or relatives or coworkers, being friends is not ascribed or structured from outside, but is instead a state freely chosen by the people involved (Suttles, 1970; Allan, 1979; cf. Fischer, 1982c). To be sure, most friends are simultaneously neighbors, coworkers, kin, or connected in some other way; rarely are they *just* friends (Shulman, 1972). We tend to select as friends people we know in some other context. These contexts are the "pools" from which we draw our friends. Our first question concerns what effects urbanism has on these pools and the process of selecting friends from them.[18]

From the standpoint of arithmetic alone, the larger the community, the greater the number of people who can meet and befriend one another—in theory. One apparent implication, then, is that the more urban the community, the greater the available choice in friendships, and, consequently, the more compatible are the friendships that actually result. Another implication is that urban friendships are more likely to involve *just* friendship and no other relationship.[19]

Actual differences between large and small communities are, however, not nearly as great as these calculations imply. Neither in urban nor in rural settings do people canvass their entire town for friends; instead they select them from relatively small pools or milieus—the work place, neighborhood, social club, and so on. These friendship pools are probably not much more populous in cities than in small towns. Still, urbanites most likely have modestly greater choices when selecting friends. Urban friendship pools are probably somewhat larger, are more numerous, and their populations do not overlap as much as they do in small ones (see Barker and Gump, 1964). What differences does this theoretical contrast make to the actual patterns of friendship of urban residents?

The theory of urban anomie suggests that intimate relationships are eclipsed in the city by impersonal ties, so urbanites have fewer friends than ruralites do. Although surrounded by and in ceaseless contact with people, city-dwellers rarely communicate at a personal level. Simmel (1905: 58) refers to "the brevity and scarcity of the inter-human contacts granted to the metropolitan man." Park (1916: 125) compares people in the city to people "in some great hotel, meeting but not knowing one another. The effect . . . is to substitute fortuitous and causal relationships for the more intimate and permanent associations of the smaller community." Should an urbanite claim to have friendships, they are in truth shallow and transient ones. The same authority who earlier proclaimed the death of primary groups described such "friendships" in these terms: "People who live in cities may think they have lots of friends; but the word friend has changed its meaning. Compared with friendships of the past, most of these new friendships are trivial" (Alexander, 1967: 241).[20] And all this is consistent with Americans' belief that small towns have the "friendliest" people (Louis Harris Assoc., 1979).

In contrast, compositional theory asserts that friendships, like other intimate connections, should be no less common or meaningful in cities than in the countryside—at least once we take into account city–countryside differences in age, education, and so on. Subcultural theory agrees, and goes further: Urban friendships should be somewhat more intimate than rural friendships, because they are likelier to emerge from distinctive, homogeneous, and freely chosen subcultures (the subcultures themselves partly produced by concentration).

For evidence, we turn first to the ethnographic studies that have been conducted in cities around the world. These studies repeatedly find that city-dwellers *do* have friends. There are, to be sure, specific cases that closely fit the image of the lonely urbanite: skid-row alcoholics whose "friendships" last only as long as the shared bottle (Bahr, 1973; Hertz and Hutheesing, 1975); unemployed men who hang out on ghetto street corners, whose "friends" pass out of their lives without exchanging last names (Liebow, 1967; Hannerz, 1969; cf. E. Anderson, 1978). But these are exceptions. The general rule is that city-dwellers, apparently no less than country-dwellers, have friends from whom they draw both emotional and material support.[21] By comparison, studies of some small communities suggest that their residents might actually have the weaker friendships. Reports of peasant life are replete with accounts of hostility, suspicion, and feuds that estrange many people from most neighbors who are not also their immediate relatives.[22]

Survey studies affirm the same general conclusion. Few city residents report themselves to be without friends. For example, only 1 percent of men interviewed in San Francisco in the 1950s said that they "never" saw people informally; 8 percent reported seeing friends and relatives only a few times a year; but one-half reported seeing such people more than once a week (Bell and Boat, 1957). Similarly, less than 5 percent of respondents to a survey conducted in Lansing, Michigan, said that they had no "best friends" (Smith et al., 1954).[23]

A number of reservations about these studies should be noted: For one, they are not comparative. Although the percentage of friendless people in the city may seem low, that proportion may still be higher than that in rural areas. Nor do these studies take into account factors that may mask urban–rural differences in friendships (for example, the fact that urban people tend to be younger than rural people). Finally, we find that the surveys usually cannot distinguish deep relationships from trivial ones when both are simply called "friendships."

Several comparative surveys have found that urbanites are just as involved in friendships as are ruralites. One of the most exact studies was conducted in the Nashville, Tennessee, area by Albert Reiss, Jr. (1959b). Men in the city and in the rural hinterland—both on and off farms—were asked to provide "time budgets," that is, to recount exactly how and with whom they had spent the previous working day. Urban men reported spending *more* time with friends, as against secondary associates, than the rural men did. Patricia Crowe (1979) interviewed people from various communities in the province of Tyrol, Austria. She found that the city-dwellers had more friends than did residents of towns and villages, and that the urbanites were also more open to close friendships. (Her explanation is that small-town residents felt that their communities were too closed-in and familiar, and that this inbredness would complicate personal relationships.) In the northern California study, we asked survey respondents to tell us which of their associates were their "friends." Some of the results are displayed in Figure 9.[24] The urban respondents named *more* friends, ranging from an average of 11.2 for those living in or near San Francisco to 7.5 for those living in small towns far away (see unstriped bars in Figure 9). To a great extent, this finding is explained by population composition—the city residents tended to be young and educated, the small-town residents older and uneducated. When such compositional factors are taken into account, a much smaller difference emerges: from an average of 10.0 friends for the most urban to 9.1 for the least urban (the "adjusted estimates" shown by the shaded area). These three studies, and others, reinforce the conclusion that urbanism does *not* impair friendship.[25]

But, perhaps some quality of friendship differs from city to countryside? Not much evidence supports that conjecture either. A study or two suggests that urbanites may visit with their friends a bit

Figure 9
NUMBER OF FRIENDS REPORTED, BY URBANISM OF RESIDENCE, NORTHERN
CALIFORNIA, 1977

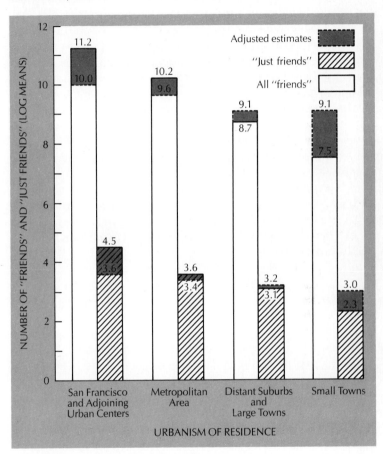

Source: Fischer (1982a: Chapter 10; 1982b).

less often than do ruralites, but that city people are at least as close
to and engaged with their friends—and probably more so—than
country-dwellers are with theirs (Fischer, 1982a; Crowe, 1978,
1979).

There are other dimensions of friendship besides quantity and
quality, and on some, city and town do seem to differ. One is the

source of the friendship: From what context or pool do people draw their friends? The northern California study suggests, consistent with indications from other research, that residents of small places more commonly turn to neighbors and fellow church members; residents of large places more commonly draw on farther-away associates whom they met in various ways (Fischer, 1982a).[26] Figure 9 shows, in the striped bars, the number of friends that respondents named who were "just friends"—that is, friends who were not simultaneously coworkers, or neighbors, and so forth. Urbanites named a greater proportion (and number) of such "just friends," suggesting that they had more social ties outside of any specific social context—sort of "free-floating" friendships. Urban friendships seem also to be a bit more *homogeneous*—in age, ethnicity, religion, and interests—than small-town ones (Fischer, 1982a).[27]

Evidence that urban friendships are more dispersed, specialized, and homogeneous is, as yet, too skimpy to yield firm conclusions. But one conclusion does appear relatively strong: Urban people have no fewer and no less intimate friendships than do small-town people.

FAMILY

Our study of social groups in the city has gradually moved from those that are most distant from the individual toward the most intimate group of all, the family. The family of origin—the family into which one is born—is the immediate shaper of one's life-chances and life-views; the family of procreation—spouse and children—is one's main investment and reward, sadness and joy. The family is also the basic unit of society, and its major instrument for teaching and social control.

In the traditional sociological view, as expressed by the Chicago School, urbanism weakens the family by producing institutions that have "deprived the family of some of its most characteristic historical functions" (Wirth, 1938: 161) and that tempt defections from its members. Community size and structural differentiation provide alternatives to the family for economic support, emergency help, leisure activities, and other services. So, too, in this view, other social groups in the city—such as work friends and club associates—draw people away from home. These losses of function and attention sap the authority of the family and render remaining family ties tenuous, narrow, superficial, and unfulfilling. Consequently, society, which is dependent on the family for sustaining and restraining people, suffers disorganization and anomie.[28]

Compositionalists contend simply that kinship persists in the city. Oscar Lewis (1965: 494) reported that, for his respondents in Mexico City, "family life remained quite stable and extended family ties increased rather than decreased." The family may be affected by economic differences between urban and rural communities (such as the number and type of available jobs), but it is not seriously affected by population size as such. Subcultural theory takes seriously the challenge to family allegiance posed by other sources of attachment that arise in the city, such as commercial services and social groups. But whether these alternatives actually weaken the family depends on yet other issues: whether one social bond precludes another to any significant degree; whether family relationships are weakened or strengthened by loss of certain functions; and so on. We will return to these considerations later.

An important distinction is sometimes made between the nuclear and the extended family, in which "nuclear" refers to the immediate family of husband, wife, and children, and "extended" refers to remaining close relatives such as aunts, grandparents, and in-laws. Most theoretical analyses and empirical data meld the two. We will largely do the same here.

We begin with the basic demographic facts. First, the larger a community, the less likely it is that its residents live in families. Single adults living alone or in unrelated groups are more common in city than in countryside. In 1980, 28 percent of metropolitan households and 23 percent of nonmetropolitan households in the United States were "nonfamily"—single people or roommates (BOC, 1982a: 43). And the contrast has been growing. Second, divorce and desertion rates tend to be greater in larger communities, although this is not universally true. In America today, urbanism is related to family dissolution. For example, in 1975 the rate of divorce in metropolitan areas was 15.7 per 1,000 married women, the figure was 13.0 in nonmetropolitan areas (Plateris, 1978).[29] Third, families have historically usually been smaller in larger communities. Fourth, when there are children, those born in urban areas more often tend to be illegitimate than those born in rural areas (see Chapter 8). And, fifth, members of extended families are less likely to share a common household in urban than in rural areas (Laslett, 1973; Goode, 1963; Hughes, 1975).

These demographic patterns indicate that the larger a community, the less common and the smaller are its families. But there are many exceptions to the rule; and the differences are often small. For instance, although households composed of extended families are the ideal in many societies, the actual statistical norm around the world in urban and also in rural places is the nuclear-family household (Gulick, 1973; Laslett, 1973). Many circumstances, housing and labor-market conditions in particular, shape household structure, overriding the urban–rural consideration. In particular, housing shortages and economic stringencies requiring pooling of resources may push urban families to live together, as is true in urban Peru, where households are actually larger than those in rural areas (Tienda, 1978).[30] We should also note that American demographic differences are largely produced by center cities. That is where singles, divorcees, and unwed mothers are concentrated; in the suburbs, nuclear family households are at least as common as they are in small towns.

In short, there is a typical, albeit not universal, relation between urbanism and nonfamilism, which calls for explanation. A determinist interpretation fits well: These differences are signs of the urban disintegration of the family. A compositional explanation would concentrate on self-selection: Certain kinds of people—the young and unmarried, the upwardly mobile, the nontraditional—disproportionately migrate to cities, and it is their presence that accounts for the differences. The research that would permit us to choose between the two explanations has yet to be done. In any case, these statistics do not speak to the essence of the question: the social–psychological quality of family ties. Single persons have relatives; divorced persons remarry; small families can be intimate. What we want to know about is family cohesion.

Sociological studies of family cohesion provide an even more complex story than do census data on family structure. They suggest that urban and rural families differ on two dimensions. Kin (mainly extended kin) are more dispersed geographically in large communities than in small. For example, in an American survey conducted in the late 1960s, families living outside metropolitan areas were about 12 percent more likely to report having relatives within walking distance than were families in metropolitan areas.[31] Similarly, the northern California study showed that urbanites were more geographically distant from their kin than were small-town people from theirs (Fischer, 1982a; 1982e). This difference in distances means that relatives in nonmetropolitan areas see one another more often than do those in metropolitan areas. A national study found that rural fathers and sons lived nearer each other and thus saw each other more frequently than did urban fathers and sons (Klatzky, 1971). Geographic separation probably makes some but considerably less difference in how often relatives telephone, or write letters, or assist one another (see Fischer, 1982e). In any event, this urban dispersal of kin occurs in various societies (see Schnaiberg, 1970; Bruner, 1973b; Koyama, 1970).

And as Wirth (1938), Ogburn (1954), and others suggested, the family probably serves fewer functions in the city than in the countryside. Chapter 3 documented the wealth of facilities and services available in cities. This wealth implies that urbanites can, more often than ruralites, satisfy their needs (for a job, advice, recreation, a meal, etc.) outside the family. For reasons discussed in the previous section, urbanites probably involve themselves socially less often with kin and more often with friends than do ruralites. They should also rely less on those relatives. Bits of research tend to support these conclusions: City-dwellers less often pursue leisure activities with their immediate family than country-dwellers do (Fischer, 1982a; Swedner, 1960; Leevy, 1950); and urbanites distinguish among their personal associates when seeking services, turning, for example, to friends for job advice and to kin for aid during illness (Roberts, 1973; Litwak and Szelenyi, 1969). But research also cautions us that these urban–rural differences are not great. Even though they have outside alternatives, city-dwellers turn first and most often to relatives for assistance (Wellman et al., 1973; Goode, 1963: 70–76). Especially during the initial period of migration, new urbanites typically rely strongly on their kin (Butterworth and Chance, 1981: 95; M. Anderson, 1971). Moreover, although urban services and urban friends *permit* people to look outside their family for satisfaction of their wants, they do not *compel* them to do so (see Fischer, 1982a: Chapter 7).

The urban context also seems to require of the family a some-what different set of material functions. Gugler and Flanagan (1978: Chapter 7) stress that the African family, for example, may in the city no longer be a single economic unit or household, but it is a sponsor of education, migration, job opportunities, and the like (Gutkind, 1974: 103–121).

Urbanism tends to disperse kin and to alter and specialize the instrumental functions of the family. Does it also weaken the per-sonal importance and the emotional intensity of the family relation-ship? The general thrust of the evidence indicates that it does *not*. Over and over again, ethnographic reports from around the world tell us that kinship persists and even thrives in the city. A classic study in this vein, one which helped shape a consensus in sociology on this issue, was conducted in Bethnal Green, a dense and gritty working-class borough of London (Young and Wilmott, 1957). The investigators reported that "We were surprised to discover that the wider [extended] family, far from having disappeared, was very much alive in the middle of London." They discovered that young couples chose to stay near their parents, and, indeed, depended on their mothers to help them find flats nearby. Husbands and wives saw their "mums" frequently, the women averaging four times a week, and family get-togethers at "mum's" were common. In all, Bethnal Green was an extended-family neighborhood in which kinship dominated the residents' lives. Discoveries such as this one of familism in the city have become so common as to make the finding virtually a truism (See Gulick, 1973: 1003ff.)[32]

Survey studies conducted in many cities find that residents report frequent contact with their kin and that urbanites both see and depend on their relatives more than on any other associates. Two California studies conducted in the 1950s serve as examples. Half the Los Angeles housewives interviewed in one survey re-ported seeing relatives at least once a week; less than 10 percent said they never saw kin (Greer, 1956). Forty percent of men inter-viewed in San Francisco reported seeing kin more than once a week; only about 15 percent reported never seeing kin (Bell and Boat, 1957). These studies, and more recent ones, show that rela-tives are seen more often, cared about more, and relied on more for assistance than are friends, coworkers, or neighbors.[33]

The ethnographic and the survey studies of kinship in urban

areas are both subject to the now-familiar reservation that they are not comparative. Because each study was conducted in a single location, it cannot tell us whether the kinship involvement in the city was greater or less than would have been if the study had looked at comparable rural populations. Some comparative studies have been done on family relations. A few have examined frequency of contact; others have looked at the number of kin living with, or accessible to, individuals. The results are quite mixed.

A few studies found no essential differences by size of community in the extent of contact with kin (Crowe, 1979; Key, 1968; Swedner, 1960; Koyama, 1970). An example is the Nashville time–budget study mentioned earlier: City men averaged about as much time with their families as did men in the countryside (Reiss, 1959b). A few studies reported that rural people saw their kin more often, or were emotionally closer to their kin than were urban people (Klatzky, 1971; Tsai and Sigelman, 1982; Schnaiberg, 1970; Winch and Greer, 1968).[34] That is the general impression from the northern California survey, too, where urbanites relied less and spent less time with kin, especially extended kin, than did small-town residents (Fischer, 1982a).[35]

Still other studies report the opposite: more closeness to kin in urban than in rural areas (Bultena, 1969; Youmans, 1977; Palmore et al., 1970).

The few comparative ethnographic studies repeat these contradictions. For example, Bruner (1962) reports that the Toba Batak residing in the city of Medan saw more relatives than did the Batak in the home village; but the urban contacts were less frequent, less "personal, intimate, and familial than in the village." Yet, other comparative ethno-graphic studies report stronger family ties in the city (Lewis, 1952, 1965; Butterworth, 1962; Shack, 1973). One thorough historical study contends that family affection was greater in urban than in rural nineteenth-century France (Weber, 1976: 167ff; Stone, 1977; Shorter, 1975).

If a conclusion can be drawn from all these conflicting studies, it is this: In general, there are no major differences by size of community in the extent to which people are bound to their *nuclear* families, but urbanites do seem less bound to their *extended* kin.

The conclusion that urbanism is unrelated to the cohesion of the immediate family is buttressed by those few studies that are comparative and that also take into account the physical distances between kin. One, mentioned earlier, examined how often male relatives got together; once distance was held constant, there were no differences between urban and rural men (Klatzky, 1971). This study suggests that nothing about urban life, other than distance, lessens contact with kin.[36] In the northern California study, we found that urban respondents were actively involved with fewer relatives than small-town respondents were and although they got together with their relatives less often. Otherwise the quality and intensity of their bonds with the kin they did see were as intense as those of the nonurbanites [excepting some estrangement from parents (Fischer, 1982a: Chapter 7, n. 22)].

The ways that spatial distance from kin, contact with kin, and family solidarity affect one another should be carefully considered. The farther people live from their relatives, the less often they will see one another face-to-face. We have seen that urbanites usually live farther from their kin than ruralites and are thus more often discouraged from visiting relatives. But the critical issue is the extent either to which distance or frequency of contact determines the social and emotional intensity of personal relationships. Certainly, the more easily people can come into contact, the more they can develop a relationship. But there is evidence that long distances and infrequency of contact do not necessarily impair basic family ties. Relatives may be far away and rarely seen, yet still be considered intimate, written to or telephoned, cared about deeply, and turned to in time of need. (And the old saying that separation makes the heart grow fonder is doubtless often true.) Relationships survive not only the large city but long distances as well.[37]

Just as distance should be taken into account when assessing urban–rural differences in family ties, so should other variables, such as age, social class, and the question of whether people still live in the place they were raised in. Only a few studies have controlled for such factors. Some have found no substantial and independent urban–rural differences in familial relationships (Reiss, 1959b; Schnaiberg, 1970; Palmore et al., 1970).[38] And the results of the northern California study suggest that, all else equal, urbanites are involved with *fewer* relatives, especially to fewer extended kin, but are *just as close* to the kin they are in touch with, as are small-town people (Fischer, 1982a: Chapter 7).

Recap

Drawing together the bits of research reviewed here, we can make a few general statements about urbanism and the family: First, the larger the community, the less "complete" the average family. City-dwellers are slightly more likely to be unmarried, or without children, or with fewer children, or divorced or separated, than are people outside the cities. Second, the larger a community, the more the extended family tends to be geographically dispersed; the less often uncles, aunts, and so on, live in the household. But the great urban–rural difference that once was thought to exist—exemplified in the mistaken idea that the typical rural household in Western societies contained three generations—does not (Laslett, 1977). The spatial dispersion means somewhat less-frequent meetings of kin. Third, the larger the community, probably the somewhat fewer and different the functions the family serves. It tends to specialize in child-rearing, companionship, and emotional succorance; other institutions, groups and people in the city can meet further needs of the individual. And fourth, urban life tends—although the evidence here is murky—to encourage people to disregard their extended kin.

These effects of urbanism seem not to impair the intimacy and depth of nuclear family ties. (Divorce will be discussed in a moment). Such qualities of kinship do not decline as a consequence of increases in urbanism. Although the frequency of contact among kin may be affected, family ties seem as close and as psychologically important in the city as in the countryside. It is worth speculating briefly about why family intimacy would *not* be weakened, in view of the apparent reduction in the material services city families provide their members. Perhaps—contrary to the assumption of theories that expect the breakdown of urban families—economic, recreational, service, and other such ancillary functions are not the stuff of which family strength is made. That "stuff" is more personal, emotional, and psychological. Indeed, certain functions may actually interfere with intimacy (sharing a business, for example, may cause a falling-out between brothers). Furthermore, the urban setting does not *require* that such functions be performed outside the family; it merely *permits* them to be. For instance, parents may still prefer to ask relatives to sit for their children, even though commercial baby-sitting services are available in the city. The presence of alternatives often allows urban families to *choose* which functions will be performed within or outside the household. Similarly, the reduction of family control over members is basically the reduction of coercive control, such as the threat by fathers not to will the farm to their sons (see M. Anderson, 1971). Emotional control is likely to remain in the urban family.

But what of divorce? It tends to be more common in cities than in countryside, and certainly seems to evidence family break-up, if not "breakdown." True enough. But divorce is a curious issue, even for experts in the family. Divorce and remarriage (over three-fourths of divorced people remarry, usually quite quickly) may well lead to closer family ties than does remaining in unhappy marriages (see Chernin, 1981; Bane, 1976).

One specific exception to this rosy picture must be noted because of its important role in contemporary urban America: inner-city black families. There is some evidence that these families may suffer from the encounter with urban life in ways families of other ethnic groups have not. One study concludes that

> the black extended family in the city is most likely to deterio-
> rate. Crime, delinquency, truancy, abortion, the formal adop-
> tion of children, the institutionalization of the aged indicate
> that the extended family is failing to fulfill its traditional func-
> tions. Further, little communal support and mutual aid is avail-
> able in urban black neighborhoods to take the place of the
> deteriorating extended family. Human relationships among
> urban blacks are atomized for the most part . . . With increas-
> ing loss of kinship ties among urban blacks, there is also an
> increasing loss of sense of community [Martin and Martin,
> 1978: 91].

The reasons why the black family should have fared so differently from that of other rural-based groups [such as Italians (Yans-McLaughlin, 1971)] who moved to American cities is not clear. One possibility is that generations of discrimination in the North pre-vented black relatives from helping one another find jobs and housing (Bodnar, et al., 1979; Lieberson, 1970; Furstenberg et al.; 1975), thus weakening family allegiance (cf. Stack, 1974). Escalat-ing proportions of unmarried mothers since 1960 and similar indications suggest that family strains for urban blacks have gotten rapidly worse in this generation (Chernin, 1981: Chapter 4) for reasons scholars do not agree about. Whatever the explanation for the exceptional fate of black families, it is of serious concern to all Americans, especially as many center cities have become predominantly black.[39]

The general findings on the family and the city described here have clear implications for the theoretical controversy this book is presenting. Determinist theory predicts the breakdown of the urban family; that prediction is in most cases not confirmed. Compositional theory predicts no effects of urbanism *per se* on the family; this prediction is closer to the facts. The urban–rural differences we discovered could be explained in terms of the composition of the urban population: Urbanites tend to be young, and young people tend to have few children, to move away from home, and to turn away from the family for companionship. Urbanites tend to hold higher social positions than ruralites, and people of higher status depend less on relatives for aid and can afford to live farther away from their kin. These and similar facts may suffice to explain the modest urban–rural differences in family structure without recourse to subcultural theory. The latter makes much the same prediction as compositional theory, but it also stresses the presence of institutions and groups in the city that supplement family functions and thereby render the family a somewhat more specialized primary group. And indeed, we did observe some alterations in geographic distribution, the role of extended kin, and so forth. In either case, an accurate theory of urbanism must incorporate the fact that, while the family may be changed by the city, it remains alive and well.

SUMMARY

The quality of people's lives depends greatly on whether they belong to intimate social groups—groups of people on whom they can rely, who provide both moral support and moral restraint. These personal networks are the indispensable ingredients for integrating the individual into society and for maintaining social cohesion.

Urban people belong to such groups at least to the same extent as do rural people. Whether by answering survey questions or by their other behavior, city-dwellers demonstrate that they have people whom they can call on for friendship, advice, and assistance. Urbanites probably draw on different associates for different kinds of involvements more often than ruralites do. Friends might supply sociability, coworkers advice, relatives long-term assistance, and neighbors emergency aid. Compared with the small-town resident, the city-dweller probably turns more often to different individuals for specialized relationships. This one knows a good lawyer; that one is fun at parties; the other is supportive when one is upset.

Specialization does not seem to reduce the meaningfulness and intrinsic value of social ties. But neither can we say that it increases them. In any case, the difference between city and countryside ought not to be exaggerated; for all sizes of community, kin rank nearest and dearest, and associates are largely drawn from within the ethnic group. City and countryside differ in the extent to which people turn to those physically nearby. Urbanites usually can and do go beyond their immediate vicinity to gather the personal elements they need to construct a viable social world. (In Chapter 5 we mentioned the constraint felt by the residents of a Castilian hamlet because they could not do the same.)

What happens to primary groups under the influence of urbanism? They persist and they change. They persist in that urbanites are as involved in intimate relationships as are ruralites (or more so). And they persist in that each of them—the ethnic group, friends, the family—exists as a distinguishable and vital group in the city. As theorists of primary-group breakdown point out, the city provides a multitude of competitors, of alternate bases of association. These other social worlds often challenge and alter ethnic groups and the family. But two important points about that challenge should be remembered: First, to leave one social world for another does not mean the loss of primary ties, but only their transference. People who neglect their extended kin in favor of friends met in a professional context are not without intimate ties, it is just that they have formed different intimate ties. Second, and more important, the availability of other acquaintances, friends, and intimates in the urban setting does not rule out close ties with kin (or, indeed, neighbors). Urban relationships do not replace those found in rural areas; they add to the choices of relationships. This is also Bruner's conclusion about the social relationships of the Toba Batak in Medan.

> It is a process of addition, not substitution, and the quantity of social relations is not fixed. Those Batak who relate more to non-kin may be said to be more urbanized and modernized, but this does not mean that they become less Batak, or that they renounce their ethnic affiliation, or that they cut ties with their fellow villagers and clansmen. They are urban and Batak at the same time [Bruner, 1973b: 391].

Primary groups in the city also change. They change in that friendships based on job or interest are slightly more preferred to those based on neighborhood or to kin, as compared to relationships in the country (see Fischer, 1982a: 118–122). They change in that they are more dispersed over space, and that they are somewhat more specialized in function. But these changes are neither so great in extent nor so significant in effect as to weaken the social–psychological role of primary groups.

If a single lesson can be distilled from all this, it is that people in both city and countryside lead their lives not on the huge scale of complex metropolises or of vast prairies but in small, intimate, private social worlds. There may be differences in the style and composition of those private worlds, but little in their quality.

cHAPTER 7

THE INdividUAL iN THE City: STATES of MiNd

Our visitor to the city has now had time to observe the urban scene. He or she might leave the café, enter the passing throng, and, by interviewing people in the crowd, seek to understand them. What are city-dwellers like psychologically? How do they think, and what kinds of personalities do they have?

The theoretical controversy reaches its climax in questions of this sort. According to determinist theory, city life poses a harsh dilemma for the individual. On the one hand, urbanism creates psychological stress at the time that it weakens the social support that could help ease the strain. The probable outcome is psychological disorder—anxiety and irritability at best, severe malfunction at worst. On the other hand, people can adopt various ways of coping with that stress that, in effect, alter their personalities and styles of life. "The process of building defenses against the city inevitably molds the identity of the man doing the building [Sennett, 1969: 9]." These coping defenses include becoming aloof, cynical, superficial, and mercenary. Both compositional theory and subcultural theory, however, deny that urban life poses this dilemma; they assert that neither effect—mental disorder nor personality alteration—occurs. In their view, the stresses probably do not exist; even if they did, social support is available in the city and would buffer any pressures.

In Chapter 8, we will consider the second horn of the determinist dilemma—that the urban experience forces people to alter
their personalities and life-styles. In this chapter, we address the first
horn—that living in cities produces psychological stress. In our
examination of urban states of mind, we first review a school of
thought and research called "crowding studies." Some observers
argue that urban densities violate intrinsic human needs for space,
causing serious harm. Then we focus directly on the relationship of
urbanism to psychological stress and disorder. Next we examine
"urban alienation." And, finally, we consider whether living in
cities makes people unhappy.

As always, we must remember that the urban experience is
plural, varying according to the city-dwellers' personal traits, specific communities, and specific locations within the city. The importance of specific location has been underlined by studies of the
mental pictures ("cognitive maps") people have of their cities.
When asked to draw maps of their cities or to indicate familiar
locales, people tend to exaggerate the size or detail of their own
neighborhoods in relation to the rest of the urban area. On these
maps everything except the immediate neighborhood tends to resemble the vague *terra incognita* of medieval maps. The extent to
which this distortion occurs is partly a function of how far individuals regularly travel in the metropolis—for example, employed
women know more of their communities than do homemakers—
and partly a function of how often traversed the various locales are.
Locations in Manhattan are usually recognized by New Yorkers
from all the boroughs, but Queens is generally a mystery, even to
residents of Queens (Milgram et al., 1972).[1]

URBAN CROWDING

Recent years have witnessed a popular metaphor of city life: teem-
ing cages of rats climbing over, fighting with, and devouring each
other, with a few animals sunk in listlessness or engaged in rodent
parallels to juvenile delinquency and homosexuality. This is the
picture of population density among rats conveyed by the experiments of John B. Calhoun (1962). It is a great and often irresistible
temptation to draw conclusions about human crowding from such

studies. In a relatively typical statement, one psychoanalyst asserts that

> many people find life in cities irritating and exhausting [because] they are compelled to control aggressive impulses which arise solely as a result of overcrowding. It is also probable that it is because of wider spacing between individuals, which is usual in the countryside, that rural folk are less tense, more neighborly, and often better mannered than their urban counterparts [Storr, 1968: 37].[2]

Similarly, a U.S. senator warns that population density causes "the erosion of trust between people [Sundquist, 1975: 21]." What are the theories and what are the *facts* about human crowding, its consequences, and its relevance to city life?

Starting in the early 1970s, psychologists and sociologists loosed an avalanche of speculations and of studies—experiments, surveys, and ecological analyses—on human crowding.[3] Organizing all this outpouring would require another book, but a summary can be made. The following one will suggest that the rat-cage image of urban life *probably is wrong and probably is irrelevant.* There may be negative effects of living in overcrowded apartments, but there are no established negative effects of living in dense neighborhoods. This is not even a useful way to think about city life.

Crowding Theories

The general argument is this: Living in a large community means that people will find themselves in specific settings with relatively high ratios of people to space. The denser those settings, the more crowded people feel. This density and the sense of crowding create psychic strains and tensions requiring relief. Relief must be found—for example, by aggression or withdrawal—or the stress will produce mental or physical illness. Urban crowding thus leads to antisocial adaptations or psychopathology. A psychiatrist warns that overstimulation, an aspect of urban life, "is a social and public-health problem no less grave than overpopulation, pollution, and the growing scarcity of natural resources [Lipowski, 1975:

219]." A variety of theories or models follow this general line of analysis, and we will examine five of the more important ones [for others, see Fischer et al. (1975); Baldassare (1979)].

1. *High density creates problems of interference and problems in distributing resources.* This theory is the simplest and places the least emphasis on mental strain: The more persons in a limited area, the more likely they are to trip over each other's feet, and the more subdivided the available goods—whether food, tools, or fresh air—must be. The ensuing competition and confusion can cause problems (see R. E. Mitchell, 1974; Stokols, 1974; Wicker, 1973). In particular, child-rearing is likely to be difficult in cramped quarters: Children have no place to study, their noise upsets parents, and so on (Michelson and Roberts, 1979).

There may well be psychological spinoffs from this experience of clutter. As in other situations where people are beset by deprivations of various kinds (e.g., job insecurity), the repeated inability to control one's environment, here in the form of interruptions and lack of privacy, may lead to passivity and fatalism (Rodin, 1979). But at base the problem is a practical one: the organization and control of activities. (Indeed, ecological models of urban development explain that cities and neighborhoods change in ways that lead to better organization for handling competition over land and resources.) This model has the obvious and reassuring implication that as long as interaction is well organized and there are sufficient goods for all, no ill effects need result from density. The other theories, however, are more dramatic and controversial, because their arguments are that problems arise from density for reasons *other than* simple interference.

2. *High density generates stress because, as part of their evolutionary heritage, human beings have a territorial instinct.* This territorial theory holds that the more people in a place, the more likely it is that any individual's (or group's) area will be invaded; "natural" reactions to such an invasion—aggression, physiological changes, and self-destructive impulses—will then be mobilized. A standard example is the youth gang defending its "turf." This theory has been popularized as "the territorial imperative," and, in effect, portrays urbanites as caged "killer apes."[4] ("We have caged ourselves in zoos of our own creation; and like caged animals, we have developed pathological forms of behavior [van den Berghe, 1974:

787]."") The basic implication of this theory is that the only non-destructive relief for crowding is to uncrowd.

For various reasons, it is doubtful that humans actually have such a territorial instinct. One is that instincts develop and persist because they provide an evolutionary advantage to a species. For some, such as grazing animals, a territorial instinct would help distribute the members evenly across the available resources; for others, the instinct may help protect nests. But it is not advantageous for humans, who instead survive best by living and working together, not by spreading thinly across the landscape. A second reason is that instinctive behavior is rigid. For example, the display of territorial defense among animals is usually reserved for specific times and places, such as mating season and near nests. Such stereotypy is *not* characteristic of human behavior with regard to territory. Third, many animals—especially the apes, who are most closely related to humans—show few or no signs of a territorial instinct. Finally, the emphasis on instinctive behavior ignores humans' unique character as a culture-bearing species. It is precisely the triumph of brain over biology that distinguishes *homo sapiens*.[5]

3. *The presence of other people in "unnaturally" high numbers and in close quarters produces physiological or psychological overstimulation.* This model, related to the second, is also drawn from animal studies, but it is not as insistent on human aggressiveness. Some versions hold that density leads to "overstimulation," causing adrenal glands to enlarge, average physical size to diminish, disease resistance to wane, pregnancies to abort, and other behavioral abnormalities and stress-linked physiological changes to occur. Crowding produces these effects perhaps because of the strain of constant interaction ("social pressure"), perhaps because of increased competition for resources, or perhaps because of an instinct to reduce population size; opinions differ about the reason. The reduction of population size upon reaching high densities is often observed among animals; it rebalances numbers and resources. (The rebalancing is not a result of starvation, but is instead a biological and social reaction to the density itself.)[6]

The specifically psychological version of this theory is the "psychic overload" model we discussed earlier (Milgram, 1970; S. Cohen, 1978; see Chapter 2, this volume). In a crowded environment, many things are going on that demand a person's attention.

Eventually, he or she becomes fatigued from trying to handle all the stimulation or develops some destructive or antisocial way of coping with the onslaught.

Specific cases of overstimulation exist—and of understimulation, too—but this argument is open to several critiques: The overstimulated image of city life probably is false (Fischer, 1978b); people often can and do adapt without harm to a level of stimulation (Geller, 1980); and strategies to cope with stimulation need not have any harmful side-effects—for example, people can "selectively withdraw" from encounters with strangers, but preserve their relations with kin and friends (Baldassare, 1979). In any event, these overstimulation arguments imply, like the territorial ones, that separation and small numbers are biological necessities.

4. *High density generates stress because it leads to frequent violations of the "personal space" surrounding each human being.* This is a less biological and more social version of territorial theory. Personal space has been defined as "an area with invisible boundaries surrounding a person's body into which intruders may not come [Somer, 1969: 26]." Consider how we calculate our distance from strangers in public settings, or retreat from a conversational partner who has become overly excited, advanced too closely, and is spraying his or her *bons mots* into our face. Common experiences such as these suggest that we each are surrounded by personal "bubbles" that cannot be invaded without producing distress.[7] Again, the only relief would appear to be separation, or uncrowding.

We will consider this theory later in more detail, but one observation is in order now. Although the reactions described by the notion of an invasion of personal space are no doubt real, the proper interpretation may not be one involving "bubbles," but one based on the fact that people vary their interpersonal distances as a way of communicating nonverbally. Our physical postures and distances convey messages to those around us. In this view, keeping inappropriate distances from others is poor etiquette. A stranger who stands too close conveys a message not unlike an indecent verbal proposal. Such an interpretation of how personal space operates is more optimistic about avoiding the ill effects of crowding, for we take room density into account when we interpret people's nonverbal communications (see Watson, 1972). This observation leads us to the final theory of crowding effects: a cultural rather than biological model.

5. *High density generates stress when the socially defined standards for what are appropriate distances between persons are violated.* These standards depend on the situation, the specific people involved, the place, and the society. (For example, American standards for housing assign ten times as much space to each individual as Japanese housing standards assign [R. E. Mitchell, 1975]). Expectations about spaces are subject to a tacit etiquette, and tension occurs when anyone violates the rules of that etiquette. According to this view, typically dense situations should not cause psychological stress because, being typical, crowding is expected (see Stokols, 1972a; Baldassare and Feller, 1976). What New Yorker seriously expects much elbow room on the subway at rush hour?[8]

These five specifications of a general crowding theory are not incompatible, but each has its own implications: The more biological theories imply that density (almost) invariably means trouble; the more social ones imply that people can handle a reasonable amount of density when their culture leads them to expect it.

Crowding Research

Studies on crowding can be ordered into four groups: studies of animals, studies of people placed in dense situations, studies comparing neighborhoods and communities of varying densities, and surveys of people living in conditions of varying densities.[9]

Scientists have analyzed the population patterns of a great variety of animals in the wild, and they have conducted experiments in which animals were permitted to multiply unchecked in laboratory pens, as in Calhoun's rat studies, or in which animals were placed in cages and groups of different sizes. Despite some contradictory results, a few general conclusions about animal density appear justified. Clearly, there are natural mechanisms for population control in some species [deer, for example (Christian et al., 1960)] that operate to keep the numbers in the group down (even in cases where there is abundant food). These mechanisms involve biological changes: As population increases, so do rates of sterility, age of maturation, incidences of mortality. In certain species these mechanisms also involve changes in social behavior; rats, for instance, exhibited violence, withdrawal, and subgroup formation in Calhoun's studies.

But we cannot draw any straightforward conclusions about the behavior of people in crowds from these animals studies. While physiological and behavioral changes do occur in some species as a result of crowding, it is also true that similar alterations sometimes occur during periods of isolation! The significant changes usually occur only in the most extremely dense conditions (as was the case in Calhoun's rat pens), and smaller variations in density show only slight changes. In any case, these animals studies seem to have little relevance for humans; the human species probably lacks both the need for and the availability of instinctual devices for population control. Instead, the collective social character of human subsistence patterns makes dense aggregation—with the exception of extreme cases such as over-filled refugee camps—generally beneficial, and nurtures man's special nature: culture.

Among the studies of humans are a long series on personal space, which have found that people avoid others and protect themselves when approached closely. In a classic study, the "target" was a student sitting alone at a college library table. The experimenter's confederate selected, based on a random schedule, a seat at varying distances from the target person. When the confederate ignored other available chairs and sat in one next to the target, the student tended to get disturbed, and either left or placed books in between them (see Somer, 1969). In addition to experiments, researchers have observed the systematic methods that people use to distance themselves from one another. For instance, investigators have noted that when one member of a conversing pair starts to inch forward, the other will generally match these moves backward, and apparently do so unwittingly. Such findings support the notion that people have personal "bubbles" of space.

Personal-space studies have also documented the fact that the size of the "bubble" varies tremendously—by person, situation, and culture (Tedesco and Fromme, 1974; Heshka and Nelson, 1972). It comes as no surprise that the response of many men to the intimate proximity of an attractive female is not at all like their response to the intimate proximity of a beefy football player. So, too, different situations evoke different responses to interpersonal distances. Proximity that we find intolerable on some occasions—say, moments of private contemplation, or in our private quarters—we accept, even welcome, on other occasions—at parties, rallies, discotheques. Finally, there are major cultural variations on the spatial theme: For example, Latin Americans stand closer to one another than do North Americans, Arabs closer than Scandinavians (Hall, 1966; Baldassare and Feller, 1976).

Such variability in spatial behavior suggests that a bubble metaphor is less appropriate than a body-language metaphor. Just as cultures use different symbols for verbal communication, so they use different symbols in nonverbal communication. Space is a mode of nonverbal communication, and varying distances are signals in that mode. One study, for example, found that people interpreted another's proximity as an expression of need (Baron and Bell, 1976). In other circumstances, it could be interpreted as a threat or an advance. That is why a person, when unavoidably pressed against another person in an elevator or subway, often uses other nonverbal cues, such as looking away, to say in effect: "Don't misunderstand; this is *not* an intimate message." The implication of all this is plain: If spatial relations provide a language or are governed by an etiquette, they can be readily modified for crowded situations—presumably with no pathological consequences. That is, when people are "too close" to us in situations understood as necessarily crowded, we also understand that they are not broadcasting messages that should disturb or anger us.

Another and rapidly expanding body of experimental research attacks the issue by placing people in dense situations and observing the consequences. In a common type of study, groups of volunteers—usually those overworked guinea pigs, undergraduates—are brought into one of two rooms: one considered an appropriate size for a group of that number, or one quite cramped for such a group. For an hour or two, the groups discuss assigned topics, play games, perform tasks, and, of course, fill out questionnaires.

The results of these American experiments have not been very consistent, but a few general findings seem to emerge. One is that people in a dense room do not automatically feel crowded. Various aspects of the situation can affect the sensation of crowding, such as the architecture (Schiffenbauer et al., 1977), past experiences of density (Stokols et al., 1979), and the activity in the room (Rodin et al., 1978). People, especially men, in denser conditions do tend to report being more uncomfortable and irritable than those in more spacious conditions. And, many studies indicate—although a goodly number dispute it—that crowding impairs people's ability to perform tasks either while in the dense setting or just afterward.[10] Whether such disruptive consequences appear or not seems also to depend on other circumstances, such as just how crowded people expected the room to be (Klein and Harris, 1979) and whether they had any control of the experience once in it (Rodin et al., 1978). In all, we can show experimentally that, under certain circumstances, people placed in dense settings do react negatively."[11] Just how relevant such experiments are to understanding urban life is, however, an open question.[12]

The third category of crowding research consists of studies that correlate the densities of physical areas with their rates of social pathologies. These include housing studies—the areas are rooms or dwelling units—and neighborhood or census-tract comparisons within cities. (Some have even foolishly extended such comparisons to states or nations.) The general result is familiar. Those housing units or census tracts with higher densities tend also to be the ones with higher rates of crime, disease, social breakdown, aggression, and so on.

But, as usual we must consider what other factors common to both density and pathology might be creating a spurious correlation—the appearance of causality where there really is none. Some are evident: Because space in and around the home is almost universally desired, the people who lack it are, in general, those usually unable to obtain the good things in life—the poor; the minorities; and the socially, physically, and psychologically handicapped. When statistical controls for these disadvantages are introduced, it appears that the density level of neighborhoods has virtually *no* discernible effect on indicators of pathology. Overcrowded households may produce some problems, especially for children, but the results are still tenuous (Choldin, 1978).[13] It is more nearly accurate that suffering people come to live densely than that density causes suffering.

Finally, researchers have examined a variety of surveys to see whether living in high-density conditions affects people's answers to questions about their feelings and social behaviors. The results have been mixed. Studies looking at the consequences of *neighborhood density* seem to indicate that people prefer more spacious surroundings and object to the noise and bother of too many neighbors. But they have failed to show any deep psychological or social harm.[14] One thorough study (Baldassare, 1979) suggests that living in dense neighborhoods may lead people to shun neighbors and strangers but *not* to lessen their general social ties—a form of "selective withdrawal."[15] [This finding echoes the one that urbanites are less involved with neighbors (see Chapter 5) and more wary of strangers than are ruralites (see Chapter 8).]

Surveys on *building density,* particularly those comparing people in high-rises to those in low-rises, also are mixed, some showing clear negative effects (McCarthy and Saegart, 1979) and others not (Michelson and Roberts, 1979; Michelson, 1977; Edwards et al., 1982). Several studies conducted on students in college dormitories suggest that high-rise and long-corridor layouts are disliked and can disrupt school and social activities.[16] One suggestion is that in high-rises residents often do not know one another, which may in turn create anxiety about strangers, and fear of crime.

Also contradictory are survey studies of *household crowding,* the number of people per room (Booth and Edwards, 1976; Booth and Cowell, 1976; cf. Gove et al., 1979).[17] At most, only a modest case can be made that intense crowding in the home is sometimes disruptive and stressful, especially for children and others with little power to command space.[18]

An intriguing side note is that the findings that density has ill effects come largely from American studies. Foreign studies tend to find little in the way of psychological or social effects, even at quite high levels of density (Mitchell, 1971; Anderson, 1972; Ginsberg and Churchman, 1981).

In sum, the mounds of research conducted on density and crowding have *failed* to establish general social or psychological consequences caused simply by living amidst many other people. Living in a very crowded apartment appears to be unpleasant and to create some stresses, although these problems usually occur only at extreme levels. Living in a dense building or neighborhood poses problems of dealing with strangers. But overall, we must conclude that *no proof* yet exists that density—at least in the normal range

Americans encounter, excluding places such as prisons and submarines—has the dire effects claimed by the crowding theories.

Crowding Theory Reconsidered

Having looked at a variety of research studies, we can now reconsider the state of crowding theory. Its most general proposition is that the more dense a situation, the more likely people are to feel crowded, thus stressful, and often to be forced into inadequate adaptations. The upshot of this argument is a conclusion like that of anthropologist Edward Hall (1966: 165): "The implosion of the world population into cities is everywhere creating a series of behavioral sinks [the pathological condition of Calhoun's rats] more lethal than the hydrogen bomb." The evidence gathered to date does *not* support this claim, since density has generally *not* been found to have such effects.

When high density does have effects, the most appropriate specific models seem to be those of resource distribution and of cultural standards. That is, when density is so high or poorly managed as to prevent children from sleeping, problems can occur. One reviewer concludes: "It is not high density *per se* that brings negative aftereffects but the aversive events that *sometimes* accompany high density [Sundstrom, 1978: 61]." Or when density violates a cultural standard of proper distance—what is fine at a party is too close in an airport lounge—people come to *feel* crowded, to view the circumstances as inappropriate and, consequently, to be upset—though not necessarily deranged. (Indeed, to the extent that owning space is itself valued, as it is in North America, simply not having the space may create feelings of deprivation.) These non-biological interpretations of crowding have less pessimistic implications than do instinct theories about our ability to deal with the particularly dense occasions of urban life—and they are likely more correct.

Something like "overload" certainly often occurs. If one hears a television blaring from next door, a stereo blasting from above, and clattering from the kitchen, concentrating will be hard. (This may be less a result of density and more a result of poor soundproofing.) And something that looks like "social overload" does occur in dense settings, in that residents cannot all know one another and may be on guard against strangers. But no evidence of *psychic* overload exists in this pattern—simply, evidence that the more people one sees, the smaller the proportion one can know personally.

Beyond these considerations about urban crowding is a much more general one: *How relevant is the entire topic of crowding to an understanding of the urban experience?* Many researchers and commentators assume, seemingly without serious reflection, that by understanding crowding they understand city life. Those who write about territoriality and interpersonal spacing suggest that they have explained why cities have high crime rates (e.g., van der Berghe, 1974; Lorenz, 1966). A reviewer of the crowding literature includes in his book a chapter entitled "In praise of cities," again implying a close link between the two subjects (Freedman, 1975). Researchers often casually move from reporting the results of a crowding experiment or small-scale study to making speculations about urban life (e.g., Freedman and Ehrlich, 1971; Sherrod and Downs, 1974; Griffit and Veitch, 1971). This connection is *not at all certain* (Baldassare and Fischer, 1976), and often reveals the authors' unfamiliarity even with elementary urban sociology, such as the fact that densities of American cities have been declining for decades.

It would be foolish to say that a city is "like" the crowded rooms used in experiments. It is somewhat more plausible to say that city life involves more frequent experiences of crowding. But how many urban occasions *are* actually dense? How much of urban life *is* crowded? In Chapter 3, we saw that contemporary American urbanites are no more crowded *in their homes* than ruralites are in theirs. Concentrating on stereotypic crowd scenes, during rush hours for example, may lead to gross overestimates of the average daily experience of the people in these crowds. Even assuming that interpersonal crowding in small spaces is at all relevant to understanding the urban experience, the resource and the cultural models imply that high densities need not lead to pathologies. No matter how small the amount of physical space per person, when resources are well distributed (as in small but well-built apartments) and people's expectations are in line, social life can proceed quite well. For instance, an efficient mass-transit system could move large numbers of people in dense vehicles comfortably, perhaps pleasantly.

Studying the consequences of density in micro-environments *is* important for understanding various aspects of living in cities—for instance, as an aid in designing housing units or planning neighborhoods. These lessons have sometimes been learned painfully. For example, housing programs in Rio De Janeiro moved people from shantytown shacks into high-rise apartments. Although the residents now received more inside space, the high-rise design caused even worse problems than had simple crowding. These are important implications of crowding research.

But crowding theory seems to have little utility for understanding urban ways of life or the consequences of living in cities. Of even less utility are analogies to rat cages.

If rat cages and laboratory rooms do not contain the answers to our questions about urbanism and mental states, perhaps direct studies of urban psychology do.

PSYCHOLOGICAL STRESS AND DISORDER

The idea that urban life creates a pathology is central to determinist theory. Wirth (1938: 156) wrote: "The necessary frequent movement of great numbers of individuals in a congested habitat causes friction and irritation. Nervous tensions which derive from such personal frustrations are increased by the rapid tempo . . . under which life in dense areas must be lived." But psychological alterations supposedly occur to urbanites for other reasons besides nerve-rattling congestion: the breakdown of primary groups and of the moral order. The functional integration that arises in their stead "does not . . . insure the consistency and integrity of personalities. . . . Personal disorganization, mental breakdown, suicide, delinquency, crime, corruption, and disorder might be expected under these circumstances to be more prevalent in the urban than in the rural community [Wirth, 1938: 162]." But determinist theory also describes a way people can avoid psychological distress—adoption of a particularly urban type of personality, cool and calculating. Unlike that viewpoint, neither compositional nor subcultural theory expects that such a choice—mental disorder versus interpersonal estrangement—need be faced, because intimate social groups encapsulate human psyches in the city as well as they do elsewhere.

The question here is: Does living in cities produce psychological stress or disorder? (Or, as the jacket cover of one book asks rhetorically, "Can the city drive you crazy?") Americans certainly seem to believe it does (Carpenter, 1977a; Srole, 1978a).

"Stress"—nervous tension, anxiety—is invisible as such, but there is scientific consensus on its symptoms: irritability, physical weakness, fear, hypertension (high blood pressure), insomnia, and the like. Do we find that urban people have these symptoms more often or to a greater degree than nonurban people?

The ethnographic studies cited in earlier chapters yield a mixed-to-negative answer. From most reports, for instance, those on residents of London's East End or Boston's North End, little evidence indicates that urbanites suffer especially from stress. Other studies, particularly of rural migrants recently arrived in the city, do describe serious tensions. The newcomers occasionally feel lost, anxious, and overwhelmed—at first (see discussion on migrants in Chapter 4). This distress would appear to be a result more of the problems of adjusting to a new home than to the fact that it is an urban home. Furthermore, as we saw earlier, most studies of migrants indicate that satisfactory adjustments apparently come pretty quickly.

Survey studies of stress symptoms are either mixed or contradict the hypothesis that urbanism causes tension. The U.S. National Health Survey cited in Chapter 3 shows that stress-related health problems are *not* regularly associated with community size. For example, the differences between urban and rural people in rates of hypertension and hypertensive heart disease were generally small. The only major contrast was among black males, who suffered much more hypertension in *rural* areas—perhaps as a result of diet (NCHS, 1973).[19] A New Zealand study found that how often tranquilizers were prescribed—presumably a sign of anxiety levels—did not vary between large and small towns.[20] As part of a major study conducted on modernization, researchers administered a "psychosomatic symptoms test" to carefully selected and matched samples of men in six developing nations. The test asked questions such as whether the respondent suffered from insomnia or "nerves." The investigators concluded that no substantial relationship existed between such symptoms and the amount of their urban experience (Inkeles, 1969). In sum, the data available to date does not support the urbanism–stress-symptoms hypothesis.[21]

Social scientists have used various indicators to measure community differences in psychological disorder ("mental illness"). Admissions to mental hospitals, for example, generally tend to be higher in cities than in rural areas (Clinard, 1964; Mann, 1964; but cf. Szabo, 1960). But several problems with this indicator keep us from concluding that urbanism leads to mental disorder. We know from Chapter 3 that facilities for detecting and treating psychological problems are more readily available in urban areas, and this could account for their higher rates of hospitalizaton. Other research shows that urbanites are more likely than ruralites to define problems as psychological and to seek professional help (Veroff et al., 1981b), probably because the city-dwellers are generally more liberal and avant-garde. Rural people are more likely to consult a minister. From Chapter 4 we also know that migrants to cities occasionally move there with rural-grown psychiatric problems. (It is widely believed in California that mental patients "deinstitutionalized" from hospitals in the 1970s drifted into the large cities.) Disturbed people may cause more trouble in cities than in rural places and thus be more often hospitalized. Finally, we should note that what conventional citizens consider "crazy" is often simply the unconventional behavior of members of "deviant" subcultures, not the symptoms of deranged minds (Srole, 1972).

Suicide and alcoholism are perhaps less ambiguous signs of psychological disorder than are hospital admissions. In the nineteenth century, suicide rates were almost always higher in cities than in the countryside (Gibbs, 1971; Dublin, 1963; Durkheim, 1897); today there is no consistent difference (Gibbs, 1971; Srole, 1978b).[22] The pattern prevailing in the last century might have been the result of the unique difficulties in the rapidly changing early industrial city. The absence of differences in this century might reflect a "leveling" of urban–rural distinctions.[23] Or the data might be faulty: Urban–rural differences in the earlier century may have simply reflected the greater efficiency of record-keeping in cities. (For example, in Catholic countries, fewer deaths may have been categorized as suicides in rural than in urban areas because of the Church's relative strength in the countryside and its condemnation of suicide.) In any case, suicide statistics *today* do not suggest that urbanites are more mentally strained than ruralites.

In the United States, recorded alcoholism and death from

cirrhosis of the liver are more common in urban than in rural places (Trice, 1966; Sauer, 1980). In France, the opposite is apparently true (Szabo, 1960). The by-now-familiar difficulties in the data confound a comparison on alcoholism just as they do on suicide: The behavior may be more visible and better recorded in cities; and rural people with problems move to the city—to drink or to die. Using a different method, an American poll found little difference among communities in whether residents reported having a problem with drinking in their own families (GOI, 1981, #186).

Rather than try to interpret muddled institutional statistics, some investigators have gone into the field to measure psychological disorders directly. Most have used paper-and-pencil tests to assess levels of "adjustment." These tests have usually been administered to children, and the rural–urban comparisons have varied greatly: farm versus village, village versus town, or a single city versus its hinterland. Of 17 such studies, 3 found that personality problems were more common in the larger places, 5 found them more common in the smaller communities, and 9 found no differences. But in most of the studies the differences were quite small, and the investigators did not take into account income and other differences among the groups of children.[24]

A few investigators have used brief diagnostic instruments to survey general populations. The most comprehensive effort was, once again, the National Health Survey. From 1960 through 1962 the NCHS examined almost 7,000 adults. They were asked to report whether they suffered from any of 11 symptoms of "psychological distress," including having had, or sensing the onset of, a nervous breakdown. Sociologist Leo Srole (1972) obtained a compilation of the results broken down by community size (see Figure 10). Besides the fact that women reported more symptoms of distress than did men, the data show that residents of larger communities reported *fewer*, not more, symptoms than residents of smaller communities. A similar survey done in the early 1970s apparently showed *no* urban–rural differences in symptoms of distress (Srole, 1980: 18).

Other American surveys of psychological well-being are consistent with these results. A recent survey of "the inner American" found that city-dwellers reported worrying more than did otherwise similar residents of small communties, but city-dwellers also reported fewer symptoms of anxiety and fewer self-doubts—in all, at

Figure 10

U.S. PSYCHOLOGICAL DISTRESS SYMPTOM SCORES, BY COMMUNITY SIZE,
FOR 6,672 WHITE ADULTS, 1960–1962

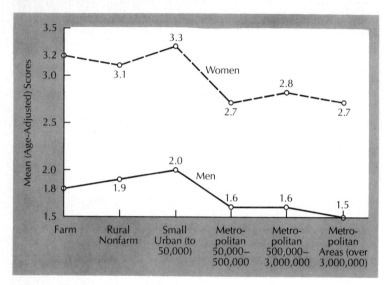

Source: Srole (1978: 481).

least as good mental health (Veroff et al., 1981a: 425–431). The
northern California study found no appreciable psychological consequences of city or small-town residence (Fischer, 1982a: Chapter
4). A 1972 poll found no difference by community in whether
respondents reported having a family member who needed clinical
help (Louis Harris Assoc., 1976). *In sum, the evidence fails to
support the claim that urban life is psychologically damaging*
(Freeman and Giovannini, 1969; Schwab et al., 1972).[25]

From this review, several problems make it hard to draw firm
conclusions about urban–rural differences in psychological disorders. Such differences can be spurious—the result of statistical
procedures, the "drift" to cities of the disturbed, the greater availability in cities of efficient detection, and, in some cases, the labeling
as disorder of what is merely unconventionality. But on the basis of
the available evidence, we *cannot* say that the urban experience
induces mental strain or derangement. (Nor can it be said that urban
life is especially beneficial for psyches.)

If these conclusions are true, why do people have such a strong impression that cities are mentally harmful? Perhaps the impression arises because many ill people drift to cities, or because disturbed behavior is so much more visible in cities than in the countryside, or because we tend to label as disordered behavior that is really only foreign, or because we cannot imagine that anyone can live downtown without becoming frazzled. Whatever the reason, despite our widespread notions that city life inflicts psychological damage, we have no evidence that it is so. It probably is not so.

ALIENATION

The concept of *alienation* is heavily weighted with philosophical and political connotations. It seems to imply all sorts of social–psychological anguish. As used here, alienation is a person's sense of separation from the society around him or her (see Fischer, 1976). Alienation assumes various forms, depending on the part or parts of the society an individual feels detached from.[26] We will consider how such forms of alienation may be affected by urban life, and we will evaluate statements such as the following one found in a research report to the U.S. government: "All contemporary trends associated with the emergence of alienation are directly or indirectly tied to the growth of very large urban environments [Elgin et al., 1974: 64; see Seeman (1971) and White and White (1962) for reviews of "urban alienations"]." We will consider the forms called "powerlessness," "normlessness," and "social isolation."

Powerlessness

The most intensively studied variety of alienation is powerlessness, the sense that people cannot determine the outcomes of their own behavior. Fatalists—who believe that no matter what they do, the gods or Lady Luck will decide their lives—feel powerless. People who do not think they can succeed do not make much effort to do so, and when they do make an effort, they frequently fail. The personal traits that determine powerlessness are varied but largely involve actually lacking power, such as being black or poor (Seeman, 1972; Rotter, 1966).

Urban life has been seen as bound to create feelings of power-lessness. Wirth, for example, refers to "masses of men in the city being subject to manipulation [1938: 163]." Lewis Mumford (1961: 547) writes of the modern metropolis as

> a world where the great masses of people, unable to achieve a more full-bodied and satisfying existence, take life vicariously, [live] remote from the nature that is outside them, and no less the nature that is within [and] are progressively reduced to a bundle of reflexes, without self-starting impulses or autonomous goals.

The mass of people, the complex structure of society, the disintegration of personal social groups—all these kinds of elements emphasized by determinist theory should leave people convinced of their powerlessness.

Careful survey research has *failed* to support such expectations. In the United States, at least, there is no connection between people living in a large community and whether they express powerlessness, even when correcting for traits such as education (Fischer, 1973a; Schooler, 1972; Photiadis, 1967). Ethnographies of peasants in some other nations tend to portray these *rural* residents as quite fatalistic (e.g., Foster, 1960–1961; Banfield, 1958). Similarly, studies do *not* show urban migrants to be generally defeated or discouraged by the city environment (see Chapter 4). More often, we read of cases such as the peasant migrants to Mexico City who experienced a "loss of fear" when they moved—the fading of general anxieties they had in the village that strong and malevolent forces plagued their lives (Butterworth, 1962).

In sum, the extent to which people believe that they can act successfully to achieve their goals is not reduced by urbanism; in some nations, it may even be greater in urban than in rural settings.[27]

Normlessness

Normlessness refers to people's sense of detachment from social norms or rules, rules they feel no reason or obligation to obey. The person who thinks that "anything goes," or that "the ends justify the means" is normless (see Durkheim, 1893; Merton, 1938a; Clinard, 1964). If the urban condition is particularly anomic, city-dwellers should exhibit a tendency to dismiss the enfeebled norms

("Everyone cheats; why shouldn't I?"). But if urbanism vitalizes subcultures, we should expect as much if not more attachment to group norms in cities as in the countryside.

This comment about subcultures points to a crucial distinction: Whose norms? If the concern is for the rules of the majority, then there is strong evidence of urban normlessness. Official rules are broken far more often in cities than in rural places, and city-dwellers are especially likely to challenge prevailing values (see Chapters 4 and 8). But our interest here is psychological: the question of people's attachment to any norms at all. Thus the proper concern is whether urbanism weakens or strengthens people's beliefs in the rules of their own particular groups. Do urbanites tend to operate nihilistically, outside of *any* moral system?

A classic portrait of city life is of the peasant lad who leaves home, turning his back on the "old country" ways to "make it" in the big urban world. We should not be misled into considering this to be normlessness. The Italian boy from Boston's North End who cuts his ties to Little Italy as he enters college is, except perhaps during the transition period, not normless. He has been attracted by an alternate subculture and its norms. As people abandon one group, they usually enter another, rather than hang suspended in a moral void. The review in Chapters 5 and 6 of social groups in the city indicated that, not only do the traditional normative systems of ethnic groups persist in the city, but that urbanism stimulates the emergence of new sources of normative regulation, such as occupational and special-interest groups.

The implication is that urbanites are not more apt than rural-ites to be normless, not at least in terms of their own subcultures. We can go further: To the extent that urban groups are more specifically tailored to their members' interests than are rural ones, city-dwellers will be *more* attached to their groups' norms than will country people. This urban norm*ful*ness would support a subcultural rather than a determinist model. In any case, there is little evidence of distinctly urban norm*less*ness.[28]

Social Isolation

Social isolation refers to a sense of loneliness or of rejection by others. Here we meet one of the most prevalent ideas about city life—that the urbanite feels alone in the midst of the crowd (Riesman, 1952). One urban planner writes: "The people who live in cities are often contactless and alienated. A few of them are physi-cally lonely: almost all of them live in a state of endless inner loneliness" (Alexander, 1967: 239). In the last chapter, we reviewed evidence indicating that the urbanite was not in fact alone. But the possibility remains that the experience of cities—its masses of strangers, for example—might create a *feeling* of loneliness or alienation anyway. The issue, we will see, seems to be: alienation from *which* others?

Ethnographies of urban life usually describe feelings of social involvement, not of isolation. At the same time, some ethnographies of *rural* communities, at least peasant ones, describe intense suspicion and hostility. The description of a French village by anthropologist Laurence Wylie is representative of these rural portraits. He reports having been constantly warned about *ils*—"the others"—the ones who could not be trusted:

> Most people believe that it is wise to keep important things to oneself, to avoid involvement with "the others" insofar as it is possible. At the same time, contact with other people is important for them. [So] when they are with other people they are cordial, friendly, hospitable, even jovial, but this behavior is superficial [Wylie, 1964: 204–205].[29]

Comparative surveys of how much people feel isolated are rare. Among the more common indicators instead are questions measuring general *distrust*—for example, "Do you think that most people would take advantage of you if they got a chance, or would they try to be fair?" American surveys during the 1970s tended to show that city-dwellers were a bit likelier to answer "would take advantage" and to give distrustful replies to similar questions (although it is possible that these differences developed only in recent years).[30] In one study, questions were combined into "distrust" scales for four 1960s surveys (three American, one British). The results of the analysis were similar in all four surveys: When one takes into account the fact that urbanites tend to be younger, more affluent, and so on, the connection between community size and distrust increases. It appears that urbanism independently, albeit slightly, *does* increase feelings of suspicion about other people (Fischer, 1973a).

Given the evidence that urbanites are not in fact isolated, why do they seem to feel more estranged, or at least distrustful? Let us ask first: Of *whom* are urbanites distrustful? The answer seems to be that urbanites do not feel estranged from fellow members of their *own* groups, but they do feel that "out there," beyond their own groups, are other, very different people, the "strangers," those who would "take advantage" (Fischer, 1981a; 1982a: Chapter 18). And, given the higher rates of crime in cities, some distrust is to be expected and probably sensible, and perhaps only the product of the last decade or two (House and Wolf, 1978). Thus, there seem to be two kinds of social isolation: from the general world of strangers, a form that *is* more common to urbanites; and from personal associates, a form of isolation that is *not* more common in city than in countryside.

Summary

Taking powerlessness, normlessness, and social isolation as three important varieties of alienation, we conclude that urban people are *not* especially alienated.[31] This conclusion was foreshadowed by the evidence examined in Chapters 5 and 6. Individual personality is created and maintained by the intimate groups of society—particularly, family and friends. The finding that these groups persist in the urban setting should lead us to expect the findings in this section, an equal level of overall alienation. But we note one important qualification: Urbanites, more than ruralites, distinguish what it is that they are alienated *from*. City-dwellers adhere to their own groups' norms, but they are more likely to challenge the wider society's norms; and although they are socially integrated with people in their personal worlds, they are somewhat estranged from the wider community.

HAPPINESS: THE URBAN DISCONTENT

Our question in this section is: Do urban and rural residents vary in their reports of happiness and satisfaction with their lives? The answer seems to be that they did not before, but now they do.

In Chapter 2, we reviewed the evidence that people, especially North Americans, tend to express dissatisfaction with large communities. Urbanites say that they generally prefer to live in more rural places, and more often than ruralites, report that their community has an unsatisfactory "quality of life." This assessment partly reflects the pastoral ideal, but it also reflects grievances about specific features of American cities. Residents of large communities tend to report less satisfaction than residents of small communities with various important attributes of their towns, such as schools, housing, taxes, and safety (and they report more satisfaction on far fewer items; Fischer, 1973b; Hawley and Zimmer, 1971). These concrete sources of discontent explain a great deal of the negative attitudes residents have to their cities (Marans and Rodgers, 1975; Rodgers, 1980).

People's feelings about their communities are important in trying to understand the relationship between urbanism and happiness. But more to the point are people's feelings about their own lives, their personal contentment or despair. Does urbanism generate some deep, chronic malaise? The answer is complex.

Apparently, in the developing countries of the world, the answer is clearly no. In an early-1960s survey, city-dwellers reported as much as or more happiness than did people in the countryside (Cantril, 1965; Fischer, 1973b). The differences cannot be accounted for simply by the fact that the urbanites tend to be better off materially. These results also are consistent with other studies, discussed earlier, which found that migrants to Third World cities were overwhelmingly satisfied (Nelson, 1981).

But in advanced societies, especially the United States, we find a tendency for reported contentment to *drop* slightly as one goes from rural areas to the big cities—a tendency that would be even more accentuated if urbanites were not economically better-off than are residents of smaller places. Moreover, we find that this satisfaction gap has *widened* in this generation. For example, the Gallup Poll periodically asks, "In general, how happy would you say you are—very happy, fairly happy, or not very happy?" In analyses of such polls conducted in 1952, 1957, and 1963, I found no appreciable differences by size of community (although a small degree of urban discontent showed up when I adjusted for personal traits). By the late 1960s and 1970s, there were noticeable differences by community in the Gallup Polls. In 1977, for example, 45 percent of small-town and rural respondents answered "very happy"; of respondents living in cities of 50,000 to 500,000 population, the figure was 40 percent and 36 percent for those in still larger cities (GOI, 1978: #156). In 1981, about 50 percent of respondents in towns of under 50,000 answered "very happy"; in larger towns, the figure was 40 percent (GOI, 1981: #189). Other national surveys of the 1970s, using somewhat different probes and procedures, also found that urban residents reported slightly less contentment than did people in smaller places.[32]

We now confront yet another puzzle: Urban life does not seem to impair mental well-being, but seems, at least in America today, to reduce expressions of happiness. How can this be explained and what does it mean? And why should this gap have developed recently?

There are several possible answers, including these: One, the patterns may reflect a new cultural change: an increase in Americans' degree of introspection, their willingness to own up to difficulties rather than to simply give conventional answers, a new frankness that began in the urban centers [for similar suggestions, see Veroff et al., (1981a, 1981b); Rodgers (1982)]. Two, the poll results may reflect growing pessimism in America. From the mid-1950s into the 1960s, Americans' reported happiness dropped notably and then levelled off in the 1970s (T. W. Smith, 1979; Rodgers, 1982). City-dwellers led the change in attitude. For example, between 1963 and 1973, the percentage of metropolitan residents optimistic about the future dropped 13 points (from 64 to 51 percent), but the optimism of rural residents dropped only 4 points (from 60 to 56 percent; see GOI., 1973, #103).[33] If so, then perhaps an eventual rebound in American morale will also be led by urbanites.

A third possibility is that the lower level of reported happiness reflects the "cost" of urban life, the sacrifice people make to enjoy the fruits of the city (Hoch, 1972). This cost could have increased greatly in the last 20 years of the "urban crisis," a product of increasing crime, decay, loss of services, and so on. For example, the difference between how satisfied big-city Americans were and small-town Americans were with their children's education more than doubled between 1963 and 1973—quite likely reflecting a growing perception of problems in big-city school systems. [In line with this argument, there is evidence that urban "distrust" developed only in the late 1960s, tied to the rise of crime (House and Wolf, 1978).] Combine this historical change with the fact that the American ideal has always been the house in the small-town suburb—an ideal that became increasingly out of reach in the 1970s—and one can understand some degree of bitterness on the part of city-dwellers left behind (see Fischer, 1973b). Whether this discontent might change in the next 20 years depends on policies and events we cannot foresee. In the meantime, we have the paradox of mentally healthy but slightly disgruntled urbanites.

SUMMARY

This chapter has taken an initial look at the urban psyche. Do city-dwellers, unable to adapt completely to the social and individual experiences of urban life, suffer psychologically? Or do urban social groups nurture psyches as healthy as rural ones? We reviewed a popular theory that interpersonal crowding violates human nature and generates serious pathology, and found this thesis more myth than matter (and perhaps just plain immaterial). On a more general level, we found that urbanites are apparently *not* more stressed, disordered, or personally alienated than ruralites. Certain subtle effects of urbanism were noted: Cities probably attract more people labeled "sick" than rural places do; parochialism within urban subcultures (as well as urban crime) probably creates some suspicion of and anxiety about "others"—a form of alienation from the wider public community, though not from people's private communities; and contemporary large cities may be creating a measure of discontent for their residents, perhaps because of today's "urban crises." Yet, in general, the urban psyche seems none the worse for its urban experience.

    In terms of the theoretical controversy we have been pursuing, these conclusions seriously challenge the determinist position. The psychological disorganization determinists predicted to accompany the social disorganization of urban life has not been confirmed (neither, for that matter, has the social disorganization). Thus, compositional and subcultural theory are more supported by the available evidence. But we have considered in this chapter only one horn of the determinist dilemma—that the urban environment causes psychological distress. In Chapter 8, we will consider the other horn—that urbanites maintain their psychological balance only through specific alterations of personality, alterations that produce a distinctively urban type of individual.

CHAPTER 8

THE INDIVIDUAL IN THE CITY: PERSONALITY AND BEHAVIOR

Urban people are on the whole just as mentally healthy as their rural counterparts. Determinist theory argues that to avoid psychic stress and sustain this health, city-dwellers must adapt themselves to the psychological and social demands of city life. These adaptations—for instance, indifference to strangers' pleas or nonchalance amidst bizarre events—produce a uniquely urban type of personality. In the first part of this chapter, we will examine several styles of behavior thought to be especially characteristic of urbanites. Do city-dwellers in fact develop special patterns of social interaction? If so, is that done to insulate themselves from excessive demands?; and does that simultaneously estrange them from other people?

In the second part of this chapter, we will expand our investigation to include general social attitudes and behaviors. We will ask, in particular, whether urbanism induces people to be unconventional and deviant. That topic will lead us to look closely at one form of deviance, crime. How can we explain the especially high rates of urban crime? Then we will review how the key findings of the last few chapters might resolve the theoretical debate launched by Louis Wirth. The chapter closes with a consideration of whether and how well the "moral order" is sustained in the metropolis.

BEHAVIORAL STYLES

Folk wisdom has it that the country boy who journeys to the big city must be on his guard in dealing with the natives there. Should he seek a casual, friendly conversation, he will find to his dismay that the city-dwellers are too busy rushing from one transaction to another to be casual and too suspicious and insincere to be friendly. Worse still, the "city slickers" may attempt to exploit the rural innocent.

As we have often found to be the case, determinist theory and popular image are in this instance quite similar. The folk tale highlights three key aspects of what is ostensibly the "urban" personality: Urbanites juggle different social roles with separate people, so that they are always "managing" several distinct identities; they are impersonal, exploitative, and even aggressive toward others; and they are indifferent to others' needs because they do not want to "get involved." The determinists contend that people develop these habits to adapt to the contingencies of urban *public* life, but the behavior becomes so habitual that they permeate urbanites' entire social styles, not only with strangers, but in their *private* lives as well. As one author writes: "Withdrawal soon becomes a habit. People reach a point where they are permanently withdrawn, they lose the habit of showing themselves to others as they really are, and become unable and unwilling to let other people into their own world [Alexander, 1967: 253]."

The contrary point of view, held by compositional and subcultural theory, is that the dilemma posed here—suffer psychic stress or change personality—does not exist, because social groups that protect psychological stability persist in the city. Compositionalists would expect to find no urban–rural differences in personality or behavioral style other than those resulting from the differences in the populations' ages, ethnicities, social class, and so forth. Subcultural theory is more complex, expecting some differences in public behavior to arise from the meeting in the city of diverse subcultures—for example, some degree of suspicion and hostility.

Multiple Identities

One argument holds that city-dwellers live in several and separate social worlds and that they adopt a different personality in each. "By virtue of his different interests arising out of different aspects of social life, the individual acquires membership in widely divergent groups, each of which functions only with reference to a certain segment of his personality [Wirth, 1938: 156]." And this "makes it possible for individuals to pass quickly and easily from one moral milieu to another, and encourages the fascinating but dangerous experiment of living at the same time in several different . . . widely separated worlds [Park, 1916: 136; see, also, Frankenburg, 1965; Craven and Wellman, 1973]."

According to one line of thought, this multiple-group membership creates an extreme individuality not seen in traditional societies (Simmel, 1922). According to another line, this causes people to have many identities. As an employer at work, the city-dweller may be a tyrant; as a husband at home, a mouse; to his poker pals, a hail-fellow-well-met; and so on. In each role, with each group, the person is a different "self." The psychologist William James wrote, "A man has as many different selves as there are distinct groups of persons about whose opinion he cares" (quoted by Gergen, 1972: 31; see, also, Mead, 1934: 142). In this view, urbanites, compared with ruralites, are adept personality manipulators, changing their identities with the ease of changing hats. In either case, life in many worlds is thought to alter personality.

There are two variations on the argument that urbanism promotes multiple personalities. The first states that there are simply many more social roles and social worlds available in typical cities than in typical rural communities, so that urbanites regularly move through a greater number of them than ruralites do (Meier, 1962: 8). The structural differentiation of cities—their varied jobs, services, and special-interest groups—indicate that urban communities on average offer a relatively great number of social roles.

But the extent to which this difference between communities applies to individuals is not clear. For any given resident, there may not be significantly more roles in large places than in small. His or her job, for example, though perhaps more specialized in the city, is still only one job. The village may have a single school teacher for all grades, but the city has dozens of teachers and administrators, yet each person still holds a single job. Indeed, to pursue the analysis, we may come to the opposite conclusion—that *rural* people do more role changing. Small social systems commonly lack enough people to fill all their positions, so that many people are pressed into double or triple service. The proprietor of the country store may also run the post office and be drafted to act as mayor.

Larger communities have a full-time professional in each role (see Barker and Gump, 1964; Wicker, 1973; Morgan and Alwin, 1980).[1]

More important yet is the distinction between possibility and actuality. Perhaps a peripatetic person can hold 3 jobs, be a member of 10 clubs, have 20 close friends, and play 4 sports on the side, and have a better chance to do all this in city than in countryside. But few of us can make use of *all* of our opportunities. What evidence we have from time budgets on daily activities does not indicate that urbanites engage in hyperactive role changing (Brail and Chapin, 1973; Reiss, 1959b; and what evidence we have on residential mobility shows no greater place changing.[2]) Urban–rural difference may reside not in the *number* of roles people have, but in the *choice* of roles that they have. The urban-dwellers' advantage may be the wider range of options they can take or leave, as their taste dictates. Usually they leave them.

If we consider, not social *roles*, but social *worlds*, one study does indicate that urbanites tend to belong to more subcultures than do small-town residents—mostly because the latter tend not to belong to any distinctive subcultures at all (Fischer, 1982a: 231–232). But does this difference makes a psychological difference? The literature on "marginal man" (especially the acculturating immigrant) describes the person who is simultaneously in two worlds—as potentially torn by conflicting expectations and as vulnerable to "personal disorganization" [e.g., Zorbaugh (1929: 176); he may also attain greater ego strength (Simmel 1922)]. But the evidence on acculturation does not support such claims (e.g., Baskauskas, 1977).

Linked to arguments that urbanites frequently change roles is the popular perception that city life is lived at a faster "pace" than is rural life and that this, too, has psychic complications.[3] City-dwellers seem to be away from home more than rural people (Weber and Burt, 1972), perhaps because they more often indulge in public leisure activities (see "Activities," pp. 98–100). But otherwise, little evidence exists that the average urbanite's life is any more hectic than the comparable ruralite's—*except* for the public's certainty that it is!

There is a second and more common argument that urbanism promotes multiple identities. It is based not on the number of roles but on the separation of roles. "People in rural society tend to play different roles to the same person [while] people in urban society tend to play different roles to different people" (Frankenburg, 1965: 287). In smaller communities, the argument goes, people are more likely to "play" neighbor, coworker, fellow club member to the same audience; in larger communities they play these same roles to different audiences (see Craven and Wellman, 1973; Southall, 1973b). Once again, the implication is that ruralites are compelled to maintain a generally consistent identity, for they are constantly with the same people; urbanites need not be consistent—perhaps cannot be consistent—and are more likely to have two (or three, or four) identities.

The discussion of social groups in Chapters 5 and 6 lends some plausibility to the argument. Such groups are more functionally specialized in urban than in rural places; various primary and secondary relationships probably overlap somewhat less often in large than in small communities. For example, a survey of poor families in Guatemala City showed that in most cases the respondents' associates were either kin or neighbors or coworkers or friends, but were usually no more than one of those. This segregation of social relationships increased with length of residence in the city (Roberts, 1973; Pons, 1969: 259). Conversely, descriptions of life in small villages suggest that the residents deal with one another in many ways (e.g., Boissevain, 1973; Freeman, 1970; Wylie, 1964); for example, they are coworkers *and* neighbors. It is from cities that we usually get dramatic stories about "double lives," such as the respected family man who has another family elsewhere in town.

Evidence that urban relations are particularly specialized would be necessary but not sufficient to demonstrate that urbanites actually maintain multiple identities, that they change personalities as they go from relationship to relationship. City-dwellers can distinguish the rules and expectations specifically appropriate to each of their role relationships (Roberts, 1973; Plotnicov, 1967), but apparently so can country-dwellers (Foster, 1961). For instance, rural people discriminate between the expectations appropriate to neighbors *as neighbors* and to the same people *as relatives* (Arensberg, 1968a; Freeman, 1970). Apparently, we have *no direct evidence* that urbanites display different personalities to their various associates; nor have we indirect evidence in the form of psychic stress resulting from urbanites' efforts to manage their multiple selves (see Chapter 7). Indeed, multiple and segregated relationships need not result in psychic or social difficulties (Fischer et al.,

1977; Fischer, 1982a: 139–144). People who have chosen and maintained such multiple roles probably do so because both the material and psychological rewards from those relationships usually outweigh the logistical problems of managing them (Sieber, 1974; Gergen, 1972; Thoits, 1983).

Unfortunately, the topic of multiple identities is another in which the speculation outweighs the evidence. The best current guess is that urbanites *could* maintain separate personalities more easily than could ruralites. The city's variety and insularity of sub-cultures and city-dwellers' simple proximity to many milieus permit it. But we simply do not know if in fact they do.

Impersonality

In Chapter 2 we noted the determinist view that one important way urbanites adjust to city life is to adopt an impersonal orientation to other people—to perceive and deal with them only with respect to the functions they perform and not as unique persons. Simmel (1905: 49) referred to the urbanite as "calculating"; "the metropolitan man reckons . . . often even with those persons with whom he is obliged to have social intercourse." Park (1916: 109) wrote that urban "human relations are likely to be impersonal and rational, defined in terms of interest and in terms of cash." Bus drivers are just drivers of the bus; their family life, political attitudes, and personal troubles are irrelevant. Each person is interchangeable with any other so far as it comes to having the function performed.

As a description of public interaction with *strangers,* impersonality is neither surprising nor terribly interesting; we can hardly be intimate with everyone we encounter on a busy street. The significance of the topic lies in impersonality as an *orientation,* when people are impersonal even when they need not be, and even with people they know relatively well. Does this cool orientation enter their private lives? Do urbanites have more pervasively impersonal styles than ruralites?

We have no easy way to measure impersonality, and therefore no easy answer. Observers have the general impression that urban *institutions*—schools, organizations, courts, and so forth—are more impersonal than rural ones, following general principles in all cases regardless of the persons' unique characteristics or backgrounds. No doubt, this tends to be so, if for no other reason than the fact that the people involved are likely to be strangers to one another. [But it is an impersonality that can be perhaps more fair to those involved, treating all alike (e.g., see Hagan, 1977).]

Still, the issue of central concern is whether urbanites' psychic make-ups are altered by these institutional as well as other experiences to being characterologically impersonal. The available bits of evidence suggest that the answer is no. Sensitive ethnographers have provided many descriptions of urban people who are highly personal and particularistic in their attitudes and behaviors, at least toward members of their *own* social worlds. Groups we have already encountered—steelworkers in South Chicago, Italian–Americans in Boston, the working class in the East End of London—and many others like them belie the image of great urban impersonality. At the same time, ethnographers have found clear instances of impersonality in small communities. One investigator described people in a small Appalachian mining town as impersonal, isolated, cynical, and suspicious (Lantz, 1971: 246), and reported that "the general impersonality found in Coal Town permeated relationships in the family" (p. 149). The ethnographic literature has too little evidence to allow us to answer the question in the affirmative and some to suggest a negative conclusion (e.g., Gulick, 1980).

And we have practically no relevant survey evidence. One study attempted to measure the degree to which workers in six developing nations held "modern" attitudes, attitudes that reflected some degree of impersonality, such as feeling that nepotism is wrong. The investigators found no independent effects of urbanism (Aksoy, 1969).[4]

No doubt, the *public* experience of city life is more impersonal than that of small towns. We are simply less likely to know, as individuals, the persons we run into in public when we are in the city (Fischer, 1982a: 60). But there is no evidence that this impersonal style comes to pervade urbanites' *private* relations.

Exploitation and Hostility

Beyond impersonality, there is exploitation (using people) and hostility (abusing them). In the determinist city, where the moral order is weak and "anything goes," rapaciousness is expectable, perhaps even sensible. Wirth (1938: 156) argued: "The close living together and working together of individuals who have no sentimental and emotional ties foster a spirit of competition, aggrandizement, and mutual exploitation." Simmel (1905: 53) describes "latent antipathy and antagonism" always ready to burst out into aggression. We should therefore find that residents of large communities are more exploitative of and hostile toward one another than residents of small ones. Subcultural theory *also* anticipates more exploitation and hostility in urban than in rural communities. But, there is significant difference in the two sets of expectations. For subcultural theory, the urban tension results not because city-dwellers are hostile, but because more contact occurs between members of very different subcultures. Taking advantage of or fighting people in one's own group is considered morally reprehensible, but doing the same to one of "them" is often considered legitimate.

Descriptions of such selective exploitation come from a variety of places. In Indonesia, both the urban and rural Toba Batak think it acceptable to fleece the outsider in a business transaction. But transactions with non-Batak are much more common in the city than in the countryside and, thus, so are incidents of cheating (Bruner, 1973b: 380). In a slum area of Chicago, some blacks justify "ripping off" white storeowners who are themselves viewed as exploiting the neighborhood (Suttles, 1968; Molotch, 1969). And, in Ghana, members of other tribes and Europeans are often considered fair game for petty theft (Clinard and Abbott, 1973: 87). In short, some exploitation across group lines is to be expected as a consequence of intergroup contact in the city.

Similarly, outbreaks of public hostility may well be more common in city than countryside. In a 1976 French survey, urban respondents more often reported having disputes with others such as police, neighbors, merchants, and people waiting in line than did residents of small communities (Lech and Labrousse, 1977). Such a difference would in part reflect the fact that urban encounters in public are usually between strangers (if we know the fellow who dents our fender, we are less likely to scream at one another) and in part reflect the fact that urban encounters in public are more often between people who are strange to one another (see Chapter 4) and in that way offend one another. The issue for us is, again, whether this public experience is connected to a type of urban personality—exploitative and aggressive—that also exhibits itself in personal life.

The little evidence available provides only mixed support. A series of experiments done with Third World children suggests that the urban ones may be more competitive than the village children.[5] In the French survey just cited, the city-dwellers more often said they felt aggressive. But they did not actually report more incidents of aggression in their private lives.[6] Other surveys tapping some dimension of exploitativeness or hostility fail to find effects of urbanism.[7] (Later in this chapter, we will consider another indicator of aggression—rates of violent crime.)

It is reasonable to expect, whether from subcultural theory or simply from the fact that city life is life among strangers, that there will be more hostile public encounters in cities than in small towns. And that seems to be so. We might also expect, whether Wirth was right or not, that these irritating experiences could carry over to private life. For example, the child who gets into fights at school may become aggressive toward her siblings. But, so far, we have *no evidence* of such an effect. Instead, it seems that there is a segregation of public and private experience, so that the typical urban person is no more exploitative of or hostile toward *his or her "own"* than the typical rural person.

Indifference: "Don't Get Involved"

The stabbing murder in 1964 of Kitty Genovese in Kew Gardens, New York City, sent a wave of despair across the country. Over 30 neighbors had heard Ms. Genovese's screams, but none tried to help her or even to phone the police. Popular oracles and mass-media savants saw in this sad event the nadir of humanity in the city. The murder became the archsymbol of callousness, a theme developed in the many newspaper stories that quickly followed.[8]

Determinist theory expects that being indifferent is a basic adaptation to the stressful demands of the urban setting. Simmel (1905: 50–53) used words such as "reserve," "aversion," and "blasé." Milgram (1970: 1462) wrote explicitly: "The ultimate adaptation to an over-loaded social environment [the city] is to totally disregard the needs, interests, and demands of those whom one does not define as relevant to the satisfaction of personal needs." Are urbanites more likely than ruralites to avoid getting involved? If so, is adaptation to overload the explanation?

Social psychologists responded to the Genovese case and the subsequent public furor by conducting studies grouped under the label of "bystander intervention." Researchers investigated the conditions that facilitate or impede intervention in a crisis. Experiments were conducted simulating emergencies under controlled conditions, both in laboratories and in "real world" settings (e.g., see Berkowitz and McCauly, 1972). For example, a study was conducted on New York's Lexington Avenue subway to see, among other things, whether people would be more likely to help a stricken individual if he appeared to be a heart-attack victim than if he appeared to be drunk. [The answer in this case was yes (Piliavin et al., 1969); these researchers also found that New Yorkers were almost universally quick to help!]

What determines whether or not people help? There are many reasons of course, but of special interest to us is group size. Early studies found that people were less likely to help someone in a simulated emergency if the observers were in a group than if they were watching the crisis alone (Latané and Darley, 1969). Later research suggested that this group inhibition on helping is not a result of the bystanders' indifference, but instead is an outcome of difficulties in collective decision making: of trying, first, to determine whether the situation is actually an emergency, so that one does not foolishly interfere in others' personal affairs (for example, do yells in the apartment next door indicate that a crime is in progress or simply a family quarrel?); and then of deciding who should act (see, also, Christman and Ofshe, In Press). When a crisis is obvious, people in groups seem as willing to act as individuals alone (e.g., see Darley et al., 1973). The thrust of this and other research on bystander intervention is that the failure to act is probably *not* in most instances a product of callousness, but a product of circumstance.

The amount of tumult—traffic, noise, activity—surrounding a crisis may also inhibit helping (F. Weiner, 1976; Kamman et al., 1979). This finding could substantiate the defensive indifference Milgram describes: people protecting themselves from overload. Or instead, it could reflect the problems of noticing and dealing with a crisis when in a confusing situation (see Korte, 1978).

Various studies have now been conducted to see whether there is a connection between urbanism and people's willingness to help strangers. Most involve staging "emergencies" in large cities and small towns—for example, stopping people on downtown streets and asking for small change, or calling phones at random and asking for assistance.[9] The findings of these studies are mixed, but generally indicate that help is indeed *less* forthcoming in larger than in smaller towns (Korte, 1978, 1980).

Why? Is it because urbanites are indifferent? Or is it because of urban circumstances? Crime and the fear of crime are certainly critical urban circumstances. Good samaritans have been victimized. For example: "'I was trying to be a good neighbor and now my wife is dead,' said Earl Harshman, the victim of a brutal beating at his home by two men he permitted to use his telephone."[10] Police warn people to "always be on guard if a stranger approaches you for any reason—to ask for a light, directions, the time, or the like."[11] How risky it seems to help someone does affect people's willingness to help (Holahan, 1977). Because the risk of being victimized is greater in cities, especially American cities (see Chapter 4), it is reasonable that urbanites would be more wary of helping strangers than small-town people would.[12] One study looked at a particular kind of helping: letting a survey interviewer into one's home. The findings showed, first, that city-dwellers were more reluctant than those in small communities to do the interviews; but second, that this contrast between urban and rural rates of refusal had largely developed during the 1960s; and third, that most—not all—of the urban–rural difference could be accounted for by variations in community crime rates (House and Wolf, 1978).

Other aspects of urban situations besides the greater risk of crime may also explain differences in helping. One is that incidents requiring help are more often likely to occur with other people around, so that the paradox discussed earlier, bystanders in groups being less impelled to help than bystanders alone, would occur more often in cities. Each person's studied composure in the face of a crisis misleads the others into believing no crisis exists. Another aspect of cities is the greater availability of official help there, particularly, of course, police. This, too, is likely to discourage bystanders from acting directly. In the French survey described earlier, respondents were asked what they would do if, at night, they heard cries for help. There was no difference, by urbanism, in whether people said they would help, but the more rural respondents said they would intervene directly, and the more urban ones said they would call the police (Lech and Labrousse, 1977: 269). Finally, we should also note again the circumstance of strangeness. Bystanders in cities are less likely to be like the person in need—of the same ethnicity or subculture—and for that reason, too, are less likely to help (Korte, 1978).

These are all *situational* aspects of city life that seem to inhibit helping strangers. But does this experience, and does presumed urban overload, make city residents less helpful types of *personalities?* Here we have even less evidence, but it suggests *not.* Faced with the identical circumstances, people from urban backgrounds appear to be at least as willing to help as people from small-town backgrounds (Holahan, 1977; Weiner, 1976). Very different evidence on "altruism," such as charitable contributions (Alford, 1972: 349) and support for government programs to aid the needy, also indicate that urbanites are at least as good-hearted as others.

Thus, people in cities are apparently less likely to offer aid to strangers in need than are people in smaller communities. This seems to be explainable by several concrete circumstances that accompany city life (especially anxiety about crime). But according to available evidence, people in cities do *not* seem to be any more indifferent or callous than people elsewhere.

In this chapter and the last, we considered the determinist proposition that the urban experience offers people a harsh choice: Either succumb to the psychological strains of living in cities, or adopt a personality that estranges them from other people (or both). In the previous chapter, we concluded that there was little support for the notion that city-dwellers suffer particularly from psychological stress. In this chapter, we have reviewed a few suggestions concerning the alterations in personality that city-dwellers are said to make to avoid this stress. The results here have been more complex and more perplexing. The evidence suggests that urbanites *are* more likely to behave in public impersonally, exploitatively, hostiley, and indifferently. That pattern seems to be explainable by the social circumstances of city life; in particular, the company of strangers, the clash of subcultures, and the fear of crime—not necessarily by "overload" or "social disintegration." In any case, the evidence also suggests that these forms of *public* action do *not* permeate *private* life, do not become psychological predispositions. As individual personalities, city people seem to be as personal, warm, and caring as country people.

Urbanites in Public

Yet, a nagging question remains: If this conclusion is true, why is the impression so strong that urbanites are cold, indifferent, and perversely individualistic? One possible answer is the general antiurban prejudice that exists in Western culture (see Chapter 2). Another answer is that the impression results from encounters with special sorts of people who are disproportionately found in cities—merchants and bureaucrats, for example. More interesting than either of these is the possibility that city living systematically promotes the impression that urban residents are personally cool, blasé, and hostile even though they are not. Consider two ways this might happen.

Social behavior is a function of both situation and individual personality, and urbanites often find themselves in public situations that *call* for impersonal behavior—behavior that, when we observe it performed by others, we attribute to personality.[13] Buying milk at the supermarket, waiting at a corner for the "walk" sign to flash, standing in the ticket line at a movie—in many such situations urbanites are in the presence of strangers. (Small-town residents in similar settings often at least recognize the people around them). The proper etiquette with strangers in these circumstances is to be politely impersonal, not to intrude, not to annoy. Each individual may actually *feel* very personal—eager to talk, sexually attracted, hostile, curious, and so on—but usually will not act on those feelings. Consequently, while individuals sense themselves to be involved and sensuous persons, they see around them what seem to be cold and aloof people. [Sometimes, some special circumstances—getting stuck in an elevator, for instance—breaks down the etiquette, and people are surprised to discover how warm others can be; see Goffman (1971)]. Similarly, if people witness someone in danger, they may feel surges of concern and sympathy, but still refrain from intervening for reasons we discussed earlier. Each of them might then conclude that he or she is the only concerned person in a crowd of apathetics. In this manner, urbanites might form the impression that all their fellows are callous and distant, even if none of them are.

Lyn Lofland (1973: 178) makes a similar observation: The city-dweller "did not lose the capacity for knowing others personally. But he gained the capacity for knowing others only categorically. [He] did not lose the capacity for the deep, long-lasting, multi-faceted relationship. But he gained the capacity for the surface, fleeting, restricted relationship." That is, a feature of the urban experience may be that it teaches people how and when to act impersonally. A study conducted in Malaysia illustrates the point. The social life of two neighborhoods in the city of Kuala Lampur was compared with that of a village 19 miles away. Malay culture has two styles of interaction (in terms of address, for example)—one formal, the other informal and used with intimate associates. The formal style was much more evident in the city than in the village. This difference was not a result of the city-dwellers having become impersonal types of people, but instead a result of their more frequent encounters with strangers. It was found that in and near their homes urbanites, as well as villagers, were informal; there was no difference in their ability to have familiar, personal relationships (Provencher, 1972).

A second reason for the impression that urban residents are impersonal may be their frequent encounters with people from different subcultures. We are usually more open and familiar with, and less exploitative of, those like ourselves than those who are distinctively different. In small communities, public encounters will occur relatively more often among people who are are, if not acquaintances, at least from the same social world, and in large communities such contacts are more often across cultural lines. Consequently, people in cities may well experience coldness or abuse more frequently and from people who are hardly cold or abusive in their own social circles. Probably even more common than actual abuse is simple miscommunication between people of different backgrounds, which leaves each one feeling abused by the other. Harvey Zorbaugh (1929: 243) described this in Chicago's North Side in the 1920s.

> According to their backgrounds, these persons and groups react very differently in identical situations. And they fail to understand each other's reactions. They look upon each other as "common" or "snobbish" or "queer" or "foreign" or "out-landish" or "red." . . . The city becomes a mosaic of worlds which are totally incomprehensible to one another.

Confrontations between blacks and Jews in many large American cities illustrate the tension and distrust that can arise from intergroup encounters. Blacks often succeed Jews in neighborhoods and jobs, replacing those who have moved on to better homes and positions. During the turnover, members of the two groups frequently meet in inauspicious circumstances, as, for example, landlord and tenant, shopkeeper and customer, supervisor and worker. Blacks often feel—sometimes rightly—that they are being discriminated against and exploited; frustration and hostility follow. Jews often feel—sometimes rightly—that middle-class blacks will be followed by "bad elements" who will depress land values, increase the crime rate, and drive the remaining Jews out; fear and suspicion follow. One Jewish woman living in a transitional neighborhood put it this way: "I'm not prejudiced; I'm just scared" (Ginsberg, 1975: 144; 1979; Gans, 1969; Cuomo, 1974).

These two analyses can help explain how cities may have especially many impersonal encounters, when, in fact, city-dwellers are not actually especially impersonal people.[14] There are many circumstances in urban life when people must interact with strangers. Friendly intimacy is not to be expected in such meetings. Yet simply because they find themselves in such circumstances more often than do ruralites, urbanites need not be any less warm and engaging. The impersonality lies in the *situation,* not in the *people.*

In much of the preceding discussion, we made a distinction between public and private life. A separate public world seems, as the classical sociologists observed, to emerge with the growth of the community. In the archetypal village, people appear to know "everyone" they meet, at home, at work, and in between. Encounters with strangers occur rarely, though when they do they are often described, in fact, as tense moments. In the city, there is a distinctly public life, amidst strangers, that is part of almost everyone's routine; it has an atmosphere and an etiquette that separates it from residents' private worlds. The private life is not, as some imply, just family life. It includes coworkers, fellow organization members, and scattered friends. Also, the line is not sharply drawn. For example, as one gets to know people on a new job, the "private world" expands. But the complexity of living both privately and publically is, as Simmel and others observed, a feature of urbanism.

Where these earlier formulations failed is in assuming that residents' private lives and their personalities were molded in the form of public life, that if public encounters were impersonal or hostile, then people themselves became that way. We have found, instead, that urbanites seem to maintain the integrity of their private selves even while coping with an impersonal outside world.

Thus far in this book we have undermined a large number of popular images about urban people. We come to one more: the city-dweller as unconventional, offbeat, and deviant. But this image is not undermined by the evidence; it is supported.

THE UNCONVENTIONAL URBANITE

The conviction that cities breed deviant ways of life is central to any urban theme, whether it is paean to urban progress or a denouncement of urban decadence. For sociological theory the unconventionality of urban behavior is also a central concern. The basic point of Wirth's theory was to explain the phenomena observed by the Chicago School—crime, vice, delinquency, family breakdown, and bohemianism and other new life-styles—which they labeled "pathologies" and "social disorganization." Is this keystone proposition of determinist theory—that urban-dwellers are disproportionately "deviant"—valid? Yes.

But let us be clear about what *deviant* means here. At one end of the continuum of values and beliefs are those we term "traditional" or "conventional," those usually held by a majority of the society. They tend to be the older values, the ones celebrated on ritual occasions—God, Country, and Motherhood, for example. At the other end of the continuum are the "unconventional" or "different" values and beliefs that lead to practices the general society considers criminal, immoral, crazy, innovative, or just odd. Sometimes applauded but more often castigated, these actions are called deviant.

As a general rule, the larger the size of their community, the more likely it is that people will hold unconventional values and beliefs, and display unconventional, deviant behavior. This appears to be almost universally true—across different cultures, different periods of history, and different realms of life. Of course, what is unconventional in one era often becomes traditional in the next. (So that sometimes only a minority hold the "traditional" position.) But in two respects this historical process of the odd becoming the usual also demonstrates the connection of urbanism to unorthodoxy. First, as they become orthodox, new ways spread through the cities and then to the countryside. Thus rural people are generally the last to surrender the old ways. Second, even as the urban-bred deviance of yesterday becomes the nationwide tradition of today, further deviations from *that* norm emerge in the cities, so that the process does not cease. For example, as the consumption of alcohol became an unremarkable habit almost everywhere in the United States, the use of marijuana arose in and began to disseminate from the larger cities (e.g., see Johnston, 1973). We have something like ripple effects in still water: Waves move outward from the point of disturbance, each followed by yet another (Fischer, 1978c, 1980).

We are familiar with this idea as applied to fads and fashions, whether it be the spread of urban dress styles to the French countryside in the last century (Weber, 1976: 229) or the craze for jogging in America in this century (GOI, 1978: #151). The point here is that a similar process of *cultural diffusion* from city to countryside operates with respect to even more fundamental values and actions.

Let us be specific about urban unconventionality: Some types of behavior in the cities are so seriously unconventional that they are considered to be crimes. We saw in Chapter 4 that cities have a perverse "advantage" in rates of crime. At least for property and vice crimes, the association between urbanism and criminality is found in most nations in most times. Later in this chapter, we will examine explanations for the connection between urbanism and criminal deviance.

More distressing yet from the perspective of the "powers that be" is the tendency for cities to harbor the politically radical and to be the arenas of rebellion. Karl Marx once lamented that peasants could not lead the revolution because they were too dispersed to organize, a problem that did not hinder the urban proletariat.[15] Though not completely prescient, Marx was describing an empirical uniformity: French political turmoil in the nineteenth century was particularly urban (Tilly, 1974; Lodhi and Tilly, 1973). So were American racial uprisings in the twentieth (Spilerman, 1971; Danzger, 1970, 1975; Morgan and Clark, 1973), spreading then to smaller places (Midlarsky, 1977). A survey of American males conducted in 1969 revealed that the larger a man's community, the less likely he was to support the use of violence to protect the status quo (for example, police action) and the more likely he was to endorse violence for social change [Blumenthal et al. (1972); similar French attitudes appear in Lech and Labrousse (1977)]. In belief and in behavior, urban-dwellers tend to be more politically radical than rural-dwellers (Ward, 1979; Lipset, 1963: 264–267).

An interesting exception to this has been suggested: imperial China. There, rebellions traditionally arose in the countryside and moved against the cities (e.g., see Murphey, 1954, 1972; Balazs, 1964). It appears that governmental control was so great that dissent could only flourish away from central authority.[16] Urban insurrectionists would flee to the countryside (Balazs, 1964)—as did Mao Tse Tung in the twentieth century. But in other respects imperial Chinese cities were more "deviant" than the countryside (see review in Fischer, 1978a). And today, Chinese dissent does emerge in urban centers [as in the case of the "Cultural Revolution" of the 1960s (Baum, 1971)].

Less threatening to the "system" but only slightly less threatening to many people is what might be termed moral deviance—behaving and believing in ways that, if not illegal, are at least considered wrong or distasteful by the central groups in the society. Deviance of this kind includes sexual irregularity, divorce; bizarre physical appearance, drug use, nontraditional family roles, indifference or hostility to religion, and the like. Although it is not always the case, urbanites are usually more unconventional or "immoral" than ruralites in most nations, most times, and on most issues. Figure 11 presents a sample of such differences in the United States during the 1970s and 1980s. The percentages show a generally regular, though not dramatic, increment in the willingness of respondents to endorse or allow nontraditional behaviors as the size of a community increases (Glenn and Alston, 1967; Glenn and Hill, 1977; Larson, 1978; Stephan and McMullen, 1982).[17] We referred to one interesting pattern earlier: As ruralites became the last holdouts against the consumption of alcohol, urbanites turned to (turned *on* to?) something newer still, marijuana.

Much of the difference between the cities and small towns is a result of composition: Urbanites tend to be younger, more educated, more commonly unmarried, and so forth. But several studies suggest that these factors do not fully explain the lesser traditionality of urbanites; something about urban residence *itself* seems to encourage such attitudes.[18] Moreover, a few studies have found that where people were raised—city, town, or farm—can be as strong an influence on such attitudes as the size of their current communities, suggesting that places of residence contribute to the general cultural orientation people carry through life.[19]

The topics sampled in Figure 11, ranging from religion to sex, represent a broad domain of "social morality." We can examine three specific areas in this domain more closely.

Attachment to traditional religious institutions and beliefs decreases as community size increases. This is evident in how strictly religious people are, although sometimes it is less clear in how often people attend religious services [which partly serves as sociability

Figure 11
PERCENTAGE OF RESPONDENTS ENGAGING IN NONTRADITIONAL BEHAVIOR,
BY COMMUNITY SIZE

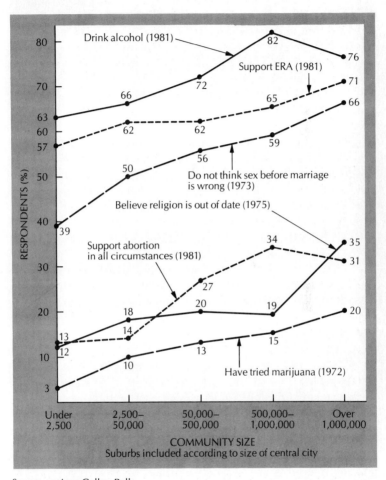

Source: various Gallup Polls.

(Fischer, 1975c)]. Cities both harbor and tolerate deviant religious
sects and atheists. Even the minimal religion which urbanites hold
tends toward the less fundamentalist and more dissenting. These
urban–rural differences appear across most (though not all) contemporary societies.[20]

But historically, this urban–rural difference has not always meant less religiosity in the city. In fact, the orthodox religious traditions now defended in the countryside spread from the cities and replaced yet more ancient beliefs in rural places. Modern Catholicism, for example, spread from Paris to the French hinterland before the nineteenth century (Weber, 1976: 344ff.). In premodern England, religious changes occurred in urban-spawned waves: First, Catholicism was preached from the towns to the rural "heathens," and then, after the Reformation, many towns became the centers for preaching Puritanism to the rural "papists" (Clark and Slack, 1976: 145–152). The basic phenomena seems to be, then, religious *innovation,* rather than simply religious skepticism.

Sexual attitudes and behavior, to the extent that we can tell, follow the same pattern. In surveys of Americans' views concerning premarital sex, birth control, abortion, nudity, pornography, and the like, the larger the community, the more common are endorsements of the nontraditional opinion [see Figure 11, and Reiss (1967)]. The proportion of couples living together out of wedlock—as well as the willingness to admit it—increases with city size (Reinhold, 1979). Similarly, homosexuality seems more common, more open, and more tolerated in larger communities (Hoffman, 1968: 38; Harry, 1974; Fischer, 1982a: 55ff; Stephan and McMullen, 1982). This is another realm of mores in which urbanites are relatively deviant. (Excluded from consideration here are those "primitive" societies in which sexual behavior considered liberal in the West is traditional).

There are particularly good records available on rates of illegitimate births, which in part reflect rates of premarital sexual behavior (and in part just reflect nonuse of birth control). The general rule is that illegitimacy rates are greater in cities than in rural areas (NCHS, 1968; Shorter, 1971: 251; Clinard, 1964). This was not always so. In nineteenth-century Germany, for example, when these rates went sharply up and down, there were regions in which rural rates exceeded urban ones (Knodel, 1977; Knodel and Hochstadt, 1981). This may be explained by variations in birth-control knowledge or perhaps by fluctuations in how shocking out-of-wedlock births are. In any case, "innovative" sexual activity is generally spawned in cities.

A third and related area of social morality is family structure and family life. In Chapter 6, we pointed out the ways they differ in rural and urban places. In cities, families are less often formed, as people remain single longer; they are more often broken by divorce; and they tend to be smaller. These differences can be attributed to various factors, including urban–rural differences in age and economic opportunities. But one of these factors is values; urban-dwellers are more willing to accept alternate family structures than are rural-dwellers. Residents of cities typically want slightly fewer children than do people in the countryside (GOI, 1974, #107: 28; Coombs and Sun, 1981), exercise less patriarchal authority over their children (Douvan and Adelson, 1966: 310–315), are more egalitarian in decision making (Fischer, 1975c), and so on.

The birth records allow us to look especially closely at changes in family size over a long period. As noted in Chapter 4, urban fertility rates have usually been lower than rural ones. During the latter part of the nineteenth century, birth rates dropped sharply in Western societies—and typically dropped first and fastest in the cities, falling later in the countryside (Sharlin, 1980; Knodel, 1977). This lag is probably a result of urban-to-rural diffusion of the technology *and* the will to control births. Such a spread from the cities of new, Western ideas about the family is occurring in developing nations today (Coombs and Sun, 1981; Gugler and Flanagan, 1978: Chapter 8; Gutkind, 1977: 103–121). In China, a similar process had started before the Communist revolution and was then pushed by the new regime in its effort to erase contrasts between town and country. Yet, even there, the peasantry resists such newfangled ideas as birth control and women's rights (Yang, 1959; Terrill, 1975). Thus, in this realm of social morality, as in religion and sexual practice, the city leads the countryside away from tradition.

Another facet of "unconventional" behavior is innovation, including the invention of gadgets, the production of new fads, the adoption of alternate life-styles, and artistic creation. In all these endeavors, too, cities are usually first and foremost, and have almost always been so. Images of rural tinkers notwithstanding, science and engineering are particularly urban. Art, music, literature—their relation to the city is a commonplace. And it is also a commonplace that most innovations diffuse from cities to rural areas, spreading down the urban hierarchy from larger cities to smaller ones, and outward from the cities to the surrounding areas (e.g., see Hagerstrand, 1967; Pedersen, 1970). Cities produce the material and cultural advances of their societies, in addition to producing a high proportion of their societies' crime and immorality.[21]

It is often argued that these urban–rural differences are rapidly disappearing. As the world enters the age of instantaneous communication, thousand-mile jaunts by jet, and cross-national allegiances, urban and rural increasingly become one. In the United States, city- and small-town persons alike read *Time*, watch Monday Night Football, see Hollywood movies, hum the same top-40 tunes, work for national corporations, belong to the Lions Club, and buy at J. C. Penney's. In this synchronized society, how can tastes, values, or life-styles differ greatly from urban to rural?[22]

These developments in communications and transportation, together with the convergence between urban and rural places in many social and economic characteristics (see Chapter 4), have indeed probably lessened cultural differences between city and countryside. Passing fads and lasting faiths no doubt diffuse far faster today in modern societies than they did in the nineteenth century, with the automobile, television, and telephone now having turned many rural areas into metropolitan suburbs. And yet, the homogenized society has *not* arrived. The material we reviewed here—on insurrection, social values, innovation and the like—shows that urban–rural differences persist even in the United States, even in the last half of the twentieth century. We have no evidence that the cultural gaps have substantially narrowed, and some evidence indicates a few gaps have not narrowed at all (Willitis et al., 1973; Glenn and Alston, 1967; Fischer, 1978c) or have even widened (Williams et al., 1976; Fischer, 1980). As one rural sociologist put it,

> Implicit in their reasoning [those expecting homogenization] was the assumption that the rate of rural social change would have to exceed that of urban social change, since it was obvious that rural society would have to catch up if the rural–urban gap was to be closed. So far the catching up has not taken place, and there are sound sociological as well as ecological reasons for believing it may never take place [Ford, 1979: 14].

With respect to basic social values, as well as fads and fashions, change lags in the countryside. Rural people alter their attitudes later and more slowly than do urbanites. And as we suggested earlier, although the ruralites are adopting the new attitudes, still newer deviations are arising among the city-dwellers (Friedl, 1964). As a religious orthodoxy spreads from the cities to the small towns, challenges to it arise in the cities. Perhaps, divorcees come to be tolerated in rural hamlets, then there arises the issue of accepting unwed mothers. Specific issues may pass, but there will always be issues, one following the other outward (see Fischer, 1978c, 1980).[23] And, in general, urbanites will be disproportionately found on the unconventional side of those issues.[24]

We come now to a critical juncture in this book. Many popular descriptions of urbanites have turned out to be inaccurate, but this one—that urbanites are unconventional—is indeed accurate. The larger their community, the more likely people are to believe in unconventional values and act in unconventional ways. Why?

THE THEORETICAL CONFRONTATION

A satisfactory theory of urban life must explain the greater unconventionality of city-dwellers, and it must do so in a way consistent with the other facts of urban life.

The determinist theory of the Chicago School was, in great measure, an attempt to explain the new social forms—so evident in Chicago—as a result of urban anomie, the shredding of the moral order and the fraying of individuals' bonds with that order. This social disintegration releases people's inhibitions to deviance and innovation.

The Wirthian analysis can certainly find support in specific and dramatic cases: hobos on skid row, immigrants suffering from cultural shock, community conflict, and so on. Yet the conclusion to be drawn from the last few chapters must be that this analysis does not work. In the majority of tests, predictions about city life derived from the theory of urban anomie—that primary ties are replaced by secondary ones, intimate relationships decline, rules of morality weaken, individual personalities are disordered or transformed—do not hold. These varieties of disintegration are supposed to explain how urbanism creates deviance. If the predictions of alienation and anomie do not stand the test, neither does the theory.

Compositional theory has a simpler explanation: Urban–rural differences in belief and behavior are produced by differences in social composition. More often than ruralites, city-dwellers are young, without family responsibilities, highly educated, and members of minority groups. These are characteristics usually associated with unconventional life-styles, and they thereby explain the urban–rural contrasts in deviance. Furthermore, the rural migrants who swell the city population are distinguished in part precisely by their willingness to change their way of life. These facts are sufficient to explain urban unconventionality; size and density are unnecessary.

Compositional analysis goes far toward providing an explanation. But although age differences help account for urban mores, occupational differences for political views, ethnic differences for religious beliefs, and so on, such differences in background do not suffice. The great historical and cross-cultural consistency in the connection of urbanism with unconventionality, the wide variety of ways this unconventionality is manifested, and frequently large gaps between urban and rural cultures—all these challenge the adequacy of an explanation that points only to the somewhat less consistent and often smaller urban–rural differences in social composition. Furthermore, it raises yet another problem: Why do unconventional individuals choose to move to cities? Finally, as discussed above, several studies of unconventionality have statistically controlled the variation in social composition between large and small communities. They tend to find that a modest, but consistent, effect of urbanism remains, and that it cannot be explained away by the characteristics of the residents. In sum, the relation of urbanism to unconventionality is too substantial to be completely explained by compositional theory.

Nor can these findings be fully explained by other nonecological theories—notably, Marxist political economy. The cultural gaps are not simply the product of a particular economic regime, but appear in very different societies and historical eras (see Fischer, 1978a).

And so we come to subcultural theory, which argues that population composition and economics do partly explain urban unconventionality, but size and density also have consequences. They facilitate the congregation of people with common interests in numbers sufficient to form viable social worlds. Urban concentration affects the minority, the unconventional, and the deviant most. The average citizen can find comradeship almost anywhere; but the more unusual people are, the larger the population they require to find their like. It is the availability of these deviant congregations in cities that explains urban unconventionality.

Creative people are found everywhere, but cities permit them to find collaborators and audiences. Thus, cities are centers of art and science. Discontented citizens are found everywhere, but cities permit the militant ones to meet, to organize, to mobilize. Thus, cities produce insurrectionary movements. People with eccentric tastes and habits are found everywhere, but cities concentrate enough of them to allow each variety to sustain a way of life and to systematize its philosophy. Thus, cities produce distinctive lifestyles. [Robert Park once wrote: "The small community often tolerates eccentricity. The city, on the contrary, rewards it. Neither the criminal, the defective, nor the genius has the same opportunity to develop his innate disposition in a small town that he invariably finds in a great city" (1916: 126)].

The city's special conduciveness to unconventionality results not only from the growth of sizable social worlds, but from their interaction as well. These culturally dissimilar worlds of the urban mosaic occasionally touch, rub, and scrape. In the process, new ideas and new ways are adopted by members of more conventional groups. Construction workers and junior executives in the 1970s grew the beards and long hair that in the 1960s they associated with "dirty hippies"; middle-class matrons defend civil liberties for homosexuals; working-class people are slowly convinced of liberal, sociological explanations of the causes of crime; white teenagers slap palms and yell the latest catchwords from the black ghetto. Everywhere, in city and in countryside, the national culture exercises social influence as heavy and as constant as atmospheric pressure. But in the cities, subcultures that are ethnic, exotic, avant-garde, or deviant exert some counterinfluence, one consequence of which is the further intensification of urban unconventionality.

The theoretical debate comes down to this: Urbanites are relatively unconventional. Determinists explain this with a theory of urban alienation and anomie for which there is little evidence. Compositionalists explain it in terms of population traits, but this is only a partial explanation. Subcultural theory argues that urbanism itself generates deviance, but does so without generating anomie. It does so by nurturing varied social worlds—vibrant and cohesive and frequently unconventional.

Explaining Urban Crime

Of all the forms of urban unconventionality, the one of greatest concern today is crime. How well do the alternate interpretations of the urban experience explain the link between cities and criminal deviance?

In Chapter 4 we reviewed the current state of knowledge: In most societies and most historical eras, larger communities suffer more property and vice crime than do smaller communities. Violent crime, though, is *not* usually associated with city life, and in Western history has actually tended to be more typically rural. (But today in the United States—and perhaps increasingly elsewhere—violent crime *is* also greater in the cities than in the small towns, and so is an exception to the general pattern.) Let us consider how these findings might be explained, concentrating first on property and vice crime. Keep in mind that we are not trying to establish the causes of crime in general—that has more to do with age, economic inequality, and the like than with urbanism—but to explain why, within the same society, urban and rural rates of crime tend to differ in these ways.

Many explanations have been offered; more than one are probably valid. Some theories try only to explain the phenomenon of urban crime; others, drawn from global theories of urban life, try to explain urban deviance in general. In the first category are explanations such as the following: There is more crime in cities because there is more to steal in cities.[25] There is more crime in cities because the less privileged members of the community are more likely to see fruits of affluence—in store windows, worn by people they pass on the street, in cars that drive by—and to therefore feel deprived, angry, and willing to take what they want (Blau and Blau, 1982; Shelley, 1981). There is more crime in cities because of their physical layout and because people do not know one another, both of which make it easier to get away with a crime. (FBI statistics do show that fewer serious crimes are "cleared by arrest" in cities than in small towns, although that is not so for burglary and theft.[26])

Whether any of such speculations are correct, what is more interesting to us are those explanations of urban crime that are also general theories of urban life. Compositional explanations contend that urban crime results from the concentration in cities of those types of people likely to be criminals. In general, crimes are committed by all sorts of people—perhaps at equal rates if tax evasion, price-fixing, influence-peddling, filching office supplies, and other crimes of the affluent are fully included. But, the crimes that worry people most (such as burglary, robbery, and assault) are disproportionately committed by males (who were 81 percent of the people arrested in 1980 for serious crimes in the United States), young people (81 percent of arrestees were under 30; 49 percent were under 20), and members of deprived minorities [43 percent of arrestees were nonwhite or Hispanic (Webster, 1981: 199–207)]. In contemporary America, blacks are particularly prone to commit serious crimes.[27] In other times, it has been other subordinate groups. For example, in 1859, 55 percent of the people arrested for crimes in New York City were Irish-born (Glaab and Brown, 1967: 96). Although not commonly recorded in official statistics, it is also clear that "street crime" is disproportionately committed by low-income people of whatever race (Hindelang et al., 1979). The concentration in large cities of such groups, especially of young minority men, appears to explain much of the connection between urbanism and serious crime (Worden, In Press). One exception even "proves" the rule: In the Soviet Union, the highest crime rates are not in the largest cities, but in the smaller, frontier cities, apparently because rural migrants—largely, young men—are not allowed to move to cities such as Moscow and Kiev, and those cities are off-limits to people with criminal records (Shelley, 1980).

Population composition explains a great deal of the link between cities and crime—but not enough. Analyses of American and some foreign data suggest that the community differences, especially in property and vice crimes, are too great to be accounted for solely by social composition.[28] What is it about urban life itself that contributes to crime?

Some versions of determinist theory answer that question (e.g., Wolfgang, 1970; Clinard, 1978; Shelley, 1981). Fundamentally, the argument is that urbanism "breaks down" the social groups that normally control individual behavior. That collapse of social control "releases" individuals' impulses to violate the rules—to steal, to rob, to kill. Bits of evidence suggest that people outside the control of traditional social groups (such as the unmarried or the fatherless) are most likely to commit crimes, but there is *not* much support for the rest of the argument.[29] In particular, we have seen throughout the previous chapters that urban life does not seem to break down social groups. And this explanation has another problem: If urbanism releases criminal impulses, why is not violent crime also a consistent product of city life? Why has that historically been more rural?

We turn, instead, to a subcultural explanation of urban crime: Most property crime is socially produced—committed by groups or by people taught and supported by groups.[30] Most criminals, especially full-time professionals, depend on fences for selling "hot property," syndicates to protect them, and associates to train, aid, and befriend them (Cloward and Ohlin, 1961). This, of course, contradicts the disorganizational assumption: crime is a product of social cohesion instead of social breakdown.

Large population size provides a "critical mass" of criminals and customers for crime in the same way it provides a critical mass of customers for other services. The aggregation of population promotes "markets" of clients—people interested in purchasing drugs or the services of prostitutes, for example; and it provides a sufficient concentration of potential victims—for example, affluent persons and their property. Size also provides a critical mass of criminals sufficient to generate organization, services, and full-time specialization in crime. An English police officer in the 1830s wrote: "The thieves in a village are not the same as the thieves in town. They [the village thieves] all work occasionally [Tobias, 1972: 68]." It is in ways such as these that cities are found to promote criminal subcultures.

This subcultural analysis of crime as a way of life, as a profession, is more consistent with the evidence than is a determinist explanation. Crime for profit generally expands with urbanism, as do other activities for profit. (Recall that robbery, although officially called a violent crime, is a crime for profit.) Crime for passion (violent crime), on the other hand, does not generally expand with urbanism. Crime for profit is definitely a subcultural phenomenon, and thus changed by urbanism; passionate, violent crime is largely psychological and is not affected by urbanism.

But can this analysis also explain that in the United States today violent crime *does* increase with urbanism? To do so, I would suggest combining subcultural and compositional theory: High homicide rates in American cities are partly an accompaniment of the general criminal subculture and, in part, of the concentration there of violence-prone populations, but it is not the result of "breakdown."[31]

First, nonviolent crime for profit often brings violence in its wake. Much bloodshed occurs among people dealing in illegal substances such as cocaine (Zahn, 1980) and in other vice operations. The 1980 homicide rate of 66 per 100,000 in Miami, Florida—2.5 times that of New York City—was clearly a result of drug wars. Criminals often have violent falling outs. In New York City in the 1970s, more than 70 percent of murder suspects had prior criminal records, as did over half the murder *victims* (Buder, 1977, 1978). As crime for profit increases, which it has in the last 25 years, so will this sort of violence—and it will show up most in cities.

Violence is also used against innocent civilians in the course of crime for profit—muggings, shooting witnesses to burglary, and the like. A large portion of cities' homicides are of this kind, and it may well have increased in recent decades with the great increase in handguns.

Then there is a third, and most common, kind of violence: crimes of passion among friends and relatives. In 1980, at least 51 percent of homicides were committed by kin (16 percent or more), friends (7 percent), neighbors (1 percent), or acquaintances (27 percent), and at least 45 percent involved a personal argument (Webster, 1981: 12–13; D. Black, 1983). In the recent past, such personal homicide was an even greater proportion of all homicides (Wolfgang, 1970). This personal kind of homicide does *not* seem to increase with urbanism in the United States, but homicide committed by strangers *does* seem to increase with urbanism (Parker and Smith, 1979). That is, homicidal outbursts against the people we know—which one would expect to accompany urban life if cities created strain and released passions—does *not* typify urban violence. Instead, it appears that urban violence tends to occur in the course of crime for gain and as part of a criminal subculture.

This first explanation for contemporary American urban violence is that it is an accompaniment of property crime, not a sign of impulsive "release" in the general public. The second, and related, explanation is that contemporary American cities have an unusual concentration, to levels of "critical mass," of violent subcultures. These are ethnic or regional groups, usually less than three generations removed from *rural* regions that have traditions of great bloodshed (such as the American South), where violence is a particularly common method of settling disputes. These groups have been termed "subcultures of violence."

In the United States today, a fraction of the urban black population seems caught in such a culture. The rate of death by homicide was about 37 per 100,000 for blacks in 1980 (versus under 7 for whites), and all but a few of the known killers of blacks were also black.[32] Because much of street crime is also concentrated in the ghetto, we have a particularly volatile combination of property crime and violence. Some sociologists strongly challenge the idea that some cultures promote violence, but the idea nevertheless helps explain certain facts: that violence is very much a family affair, that great variations occur among societies in rates of violence, and that subgroups differ so much (e.g., the death-by-homicide rate for Asian–Americans is about 5 per 100,000). The second argument, then, is that American cities suffer subcultures of violence on top of subcultures of crime.[33]

In sum, the best evidence suggests that urbanism is typically linked to property and vice crime, not because cities break down social groups, but because cities build up the opportunities and social supports for such crime. Why there is in addition a link today between American cities and violent crime is more difficult to account for, but a subcultural model still seems preferable to a theory of urban alienation. And thus we come back to the same basic analysis we used in understanding less-traumatic forms of urban unconventionality: Composition of the population explains much of urban unconventionality, but not all of it. The rest is best explained, not as the outcome of social disintegration, but instead as the outcome of subcultural intensification.

MAINTAINING PUBLIC ORDER

One reason popular views and older theories of urban unconventionality are apparently wrong is that they confuse the public and private realms of urban life. We have seen that the way individuals act in public is typically assumed to reflect their personalities, when really it usually reflects the public situation. Similarly, the seeming "disorderliness" of city life—the clashes of culture, public tension, group conflict—is interpreted as the result of social breakdown.

This is an incorrect interpretation in that it assumes a breakdown of urbanites' private social worlds (for instance, that intergroup conflict occurs because individuals' impulses have been "released" by the absence of family or friendship bonds). As far as we can tell, urbanism does not impair the solidarity of people's intimate circles. But that breakdown interpretation *is* correct in another sense: The large community is less able than the small one to maintain a collective, community-wide consensus—a "moral order"—than is the small one.

In the village, peace and decorum are maintained by a shared cultural consensus and are defended against dissenters by gossip and ostracism (R. Smith, 1961; Weber, 1976: 399). Unusual and contentious behavior is suppressed, particularly because personal conflict in a small community can be extremely disruptive (Colson, 1974). So neighbors carefully watch one another and try to mobilize the community against someone who gets out of line.

City people are also scrutinized and disciplined through gossip and ostracism. But this social control is not performed by the community at large, nor typically by neighbors. It is performed by urbanites' associates in the "little worlds" of the city mosaic, by members of the small subcultures in which they participate. (For example, it is likely that people's coworkers or friends, rather than their neighbors, will tease them if the clothes they wear are out of fashion.) What happens, then, to the public order of the community when the interests and values of those little milieus clash, even when neighbors can have very different moral understandings from one another because they participate in very different social worlds? We can fairly say that there is a "breakdown" in the "moral order" of the community (see Arkes, 1981). Public order is not maintained by shared values and collective action; instead various groups act on their own, often at cross-purposes.[34]

This fractured moral order is, I suggest, chronic to cities in general. Add on to it the problem of crime, especially American violent crime, and the question arises: How is any public order at all maintained? Why does not big-city life simply collapse?

To some extent, order is *not* maintained. Chapter 5 described how conflict is more pervasive in cities than small towns, and we have just reviewed the higher rates of crime in cities. And yet, excepting a few desperate cases such as Belfast, Northern Ireland and Beirut, Lebanon in the 1970s, large cities do not descend into chaos. Even cities as heterogeneous, jammed, and troubled as Tokyo, London, and New York, function day to day. People go to work, services are provided, life goes on fairly regularly and predictably. What ways have evolved to preserve this precarious public order in cities?

One is that the authorities and other groups with power often prevent subcultural heterogeneity from arising in the first place. In many ancient cities, specific ethnic or occupational groups were kept outside the city walls. And today the more homogeneous cities do appear to be the more peaceful ones. Another solution is for one ethnic group to completely dominate the city. Peace can be preserved by exercising full authoritarian control. A very common, albeit partial, solution is segregation. Medieval cities were typically divided into semiautonomous cells by nationality and guild. And American metropolises have become quite segregated into separate municipalities by social class and ethnicity. This reduces disputes over taxing, schooling, policing, and so on, at least for the people who can buy their way into suburban enclaves. Then there is public order by negotiation among those groups sufficiently mobilized to exercise some political leverage. The politics of New York City has always been a fascinating example of ethnic- and interest-group horse trading (Glazer and Moynihan, 1970). But negotiation is a precarious "solution," because behind much of the bargaining is the possibility, even the implicit threat, of open conflict in the form of demonstrations, strikes, and violence. Often the possibility becomes reality.

On a personal, day-to-day level, the incipient chaos of city life is held at bay by a public etiquette (Lofland, 1973). This etiquette, the reserved and impersonal style we often mistake for a constricted personality, allows strangers with clashing values to deal with one another even in the absence of a strong moral consensus. It permits such amazing public phenomena as the jamming together of thousands of strangers in New York subways at rush hour or of a half-million people on a southern California beach with relatively little trouble (Edgerton, 1979).

Order is maintained, even in the megacities. But it is often maintained under conditions of great moral dissensus. And it is a precarious order, broken briefly on occasion and frequently in danger of complete collapse.

SUMMARY

In Chapter 7, we considered one horn of the dilemma posed to urbanites by traditional determinist theory—that their price for residing in the city is psychological stress and alienation. We found little evidence of such costs. In this chapter, we considered the other horn—that urbanites avoid the stresses of the city by altering their personalities and social interactions in ways that ultimately estrange them from other people. Little evidence could be marshaled to substantiate this prediction either. Instances of seeming impersonality, exploitation, and callousness probably do occur more often in urban than in rural communities, even though urban *people* are no more impersonal, exploitative, or callous than rural people. These experiences occur when strangers are together (for instance, in bus stations), or when there is contact between members of different subcultures (for instance, in changing neighborhoods). Cities are more often the locales of these estranged *situations* than are small towns, but city people are not necessarily more commonly estranged than are small-town people.

Perhaps the psychic or social pains of city life are too subtle, too camouflaged, or too spiritual to be measured by the crude instruments of social science. Plausible arguments along this line can be constructed. But *plausibility* is promiscuous and will couple readily with most theories that come by, no matter how incompatible the theories are with one another. Plausible arguments could also be constructed about hidden psychic costs of rural life, the dangers of monotony, overly intertwined social ties, or absence of recreational outlets. A debate between these arguments cannot be resolved except by recourse to whatever instruments social scientists can command, no matter how crude. To date, we have little reason on the basis of scientific measurement to believe that city life in general creates such hidden psychic harm.

But there *are* reasons to believe that urban residents are particularly wont to unconventional views and to behave in unconventional ways, in realms of life ranging from politics to sex and religion. The best explanation seems to be subcultural theory. The congregation of large numbers of people permits the minorities and "deviants" to establish active and supportive subcultures, and to influence the majorities around them.

This production of subcultures also helps explain why cities have more property and vice crime than do smaller communities. Criminal and quasi-criminal social worlds can flourish more easily in cities, just as can other small social worlds. The unusually violent nature of crime in modern American cities needs further investigation. But even that can be better understood as a subcultural phonomenon than as the outcome of "breakdown" and "release."

The profusion of vital and varied social worlds characteristic of cities has implications, as well, for mental states and behavioral styles. We might indeed expect some traces of worry or some untoward incidents to occur because of interaction across cultural lines. So, for example, urbanites tend to distrust the vague category of "most people" slightly more often than ruralites do. In the urban setting, these "most people" frequently include those who are clearly foreign and perhaps deviant—those who may be threatening or upsetting.

Worry and hostility might be expected to arise in such unconventional surroundings. Such anxieties, which determinist theory interprets as psychological deterioration brought on by the failure of primary groups to sustain individual psyches, is, subcultural theory contends, the product of public confrontation among differing cultural groups. The public order of cities lacks the moral uniformity more common in villages, so that encounters among strangers are problematic, relations among groups are prone to conflict. In this fragile moral order, it is not surprising that tension and battle often arise. What is perhaps more surprising is the fact that urbanites are at least as mentally sound as ruralites—which is testimony to the health of people's intimate personal networks and the solidarity of social worlds within the complex urban mosaic.

CONCLUSION

The portrait of urbanites that has emerged in the last few chapters is this: The urban community is one of plural social worlds; urbanites' relationships are specialized in function and spatially dispersed, but even so their circles of acquaintance and attachment mark out only a small portion of the city's people; most of their personally important experiences occur within a single subculture or two, which are distinguished by occupation, ethnicity, life-style, or some combination thereof. This small circle, occasionally supplemented by outside ties, provides urbanites with the social affiliation and the psychic support they need to help them meet their life goals. These small social milieus fulfill the same functions in the city or the countryside, but the more unconventional ones can fulfill those functions and can flourish better in the city.

The plurality of subcultures in the city splits asunder any community-wide moral order into many parochial varieties. The person who lives in a more unusual subculture generated or enhanced by urbanism will exhibit values and behaviors that deviate from the common norms. But almost all urbanites, conventional or not, seem able to participate in the wider urban arena, while still maintaining a base in a cohesive home milieu, and are thus able to conduct their lives in no more stressful, alienated, isolated, or dehumanized fashion than rural persons do. Healthy personalities, of whatever social persuasion, are bred in intimate, personal groups. Those groups flourish in small and large communities alike.

CHAPTER 9

WiThiN ThE METRopoLis
City and Suburban Experiences

In developed nations, urban settlements have grown to encompass hundreds of square miles and most of the population. Urban places are no longer compact cities with a few outlying villages, as in our grandparents' childhoods; they are now vast urban regions containing many centers of activity (Muller, 1981). In the United States, most urbanites live, and increasingly also work, outside the core city, in the suburbs. So, we now turn our attention from contrasting the urban and nonurban experiences to examining the variety of experiences *within* the metropolis.

Although there are many variations we could examine, urban sociologists have stressed the contrast between city and suburb. In the previous chapters we tried to answer: What are the effects of urbanism on a person's social life and psychological traits? In this chapter our question is: What are the effects of *suburbanism* on an urban person's social life and psychological traits? We will follow the same procedure in answering the second question as we did in answering the first: comparing and contrasting the milieus, social groups, and personalities of suburbanites to those of city-dwellers. (*Note carefully:* in this chapter, the term "city" refers specifically to the *center city* and not, as it did in the previous chapters, loosely to the entire metropolis.)

Suburbs are not new, although they have grown tremendously

in the last few generations. Ancient and medieval cities had suburbs of sorts—clusters of dwellings just outside the city walls, where low-caste groups or long-distance traders often lived. Elites frequently owned country estates at distances from the city that we would now label suburban. The great expansion of suburbs started in the late nineteenth century in conjunction with new transportation technologies: the commuter train, the omnibus, and most especially, the automobile. These inventions and advancing industrialization made possible a new type of urban system in which the work place was separated from the home; thus the commuter and the "bedroom" suburb were created. Before the automobile a commuter could go, at best, 6 miles in 60 minutes, so that urban development was effectively restricted to 100 square miles. The car and later the freeway increased the 60-minute radius to 35 miles and thereby opened up 2,000 square miles for urban settlement. In 70 years, the potential size of urban areas has multiplied 40-fold (Hawley, 1981; Zimmer, 1975; Warner, 1962).[1]

Suburbs have expanded rapidly in the United States, especially since World War II, and by now more Americans live in suburbs than in center cities or nonmetropolitan areas. Figure 12 shows the rapid growth over the years in the number of people living in urban areas, but outside the centers. In 1960, it was about one-third of all Americans; in 1980, about 40 percent. In fact, the figure is an underestimate. If one adds in the communities that had grown large enough by 1980 to be officially classified as metropolitan, the suburban percentage is 45.[2]

One example of such growth is the "I-270 corridor" outside Washington, D.C. in Montgomery County. In the early 1960s, the interstate highway was completed and linked inner suburbs such as Bethesda to the small towns in northwest Maryland's rural countryside, such as Gaithersburg and Germantown. Almost immediately, high technology industries and governmental agencies planted themselves along the 33-mile highway, housing construction boomed, and retail outlets opened branches. Between 1960 and the mid-1970s, the population along the corridor jumped from 10,000 to 62,000 people (Barringer, 1977).

The nation's factories, businesses, and services are moving outward, too, so that each year fewer suburbanites need visit the city to work, shop, or play (Kasarda, 1976; Muller, 1981). For example, 80 percent of New York City's suburban workers have

Figure 12

U.S. SUBURBAN POPULATION GROWTH, 1900–1980: NUMBER OF PEOPLE IN
CENTER CITIES, OUTSIDE CENTER CITIES, AND IN NONMETROPOLITAN PLACES

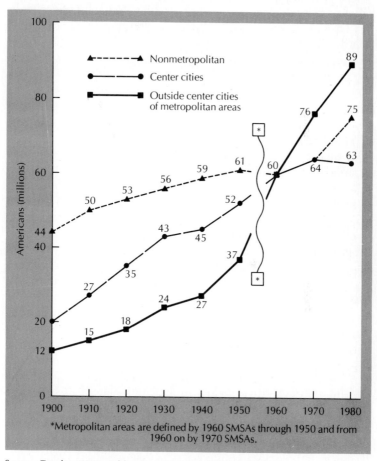

*Metropolitan areas are defined by 1960 SMSAs through 1950 and from
1960 on by 1970 SMSAs.

Source: Taeuber (1972: Table 19) and Long and DeAre (1982a).

jobs in the suburbs (Feron, 1978; Hoover and Vernon, 1959;
Hacker, 1973); over one-third of Detroit's suburbanites *never* visit
downtown for reasons other than work (Lansing and Hendricks,
1967; Zikmund, 1971; Schwartz, 1976b); and most of the New York
suburbanites do not identify themselves with the city (Feron, 1978).

This sprawling suburbanization pattern familiar to North

Americans is not typical of other societies. Outer metropolitan areas vary greatly from nation to nation. In northern Europe, for example, where there has been central planning, suburban communities are more commonly high-density clusters of apartment buildings, businesses, and industries surrounded by open space (Popenoe, 1977, 1980; Hall, 1977). In Israel the outlying areas of Tel Aviv, Haifa, and Jerusalem are composed of old cooperative farms, immigrant housing projects, Arab villages, as well as new middle-class housing (Gonen, 1976). Yet the North American suburb is of more than parochial interest: Suburban sprawl is becoming increasingly common in metropolises around the world (Hoyt, 1969; Hawley, 1981; London and Flanagan, 1976).

Before we can consider the consequences of North American or other suburbanization, we must pause to define "suburb." In spite of all the contemporary interest, we have no commonly accepted interpretation of the word. Indeed, people *living* in suburbs do not clearly know what a "suburb" is and whether they live in one (Hummon, 1980; Silverman, 1982). The U.S. Census defines a suburb, roughly, as the part of a metropolitan county or set of counties that lies outside the political boundaries of the center city. For example, the Hollywood district is a part of Los Angeles, so it is considered center city; but Beverly Hills is another municipality, so it is classified as a suburb. This political definition is the one used in the statistics presented in Figure 12.

A political definition of suburb has some uses in the U.S. case. For example, city lines are quite important in metropolitan politics and school systems. But sociologically it is a limited definition (Treadway, 1983); there is little reason to believe that social life changes abruptly from one side of the city line to the other. When we defined "urban," we argued that the simplest definition—population size—was the best. Here as well, the simplest is the best—distance: *A suburb is a locality within a metropolis relatively distant from the center of population.* Just as "urban" was defined as a matter of degree (degree of size) so "suburban" is defined as a matter of degree (degree of distance). In the previous chapters, "urban" and "city" were used as shorthand terms for relatively large communities; in this chapter, "suburb" is used as a shorthand term for relatively distant localities, and "city" for relatively central localities. As before, when specific data and research are considered, we will have to accept the definitions used by the researchers; fortunately, these criteria will usually be strongly related to distance.[3]

THE IDEA OF SUBURBIA

Scholarly opinion on the suburban experience has fluctuated sharply in this century (Schwartz, 1980). Suburban residence was praised mightily early on for combining the cultural and economic benefits of city life with the physical and spiritual wholesomeness of rural life (see Chapter 2). Ebenezer Howard, father of the "new town" concept, proclaimed: "Town and country *must be married,* and out of the joyous union will spring a new hope, a new life, a new civilization" (cited by Donaldson, 1969: 23; Tarr, 1973). By the middle of the century, social critics saw the suburbs differently, as the home of mass society's "organization men"—conformers, status seekers, anti-intellectuals, and neurotics (e.g., Riesman, 1958; Whyte, 1956). This critique of suburbia has eased in recent years, but other critiques have replaced it. In particular, many view suburban housing restrictions as locking low-income and minority families into decaying center cities (Downs, 1973) and suburban sprawl as a waste of natural resources (Whyte, 1968; Canter, 1974).[4]

Whatever the vagaries of intellectual opinion, popular opinion on suburbia is strongly favorable. As we discussed in Chapter 2, most Americans would prefer to live in a small town near a large city—in other words, a suburb. A few surveys have asked respondents whether they preferred to live closer to or farther from the metropolitan center than they currently do. Usually, most persons (60–70%) prefer their present distance, whatever it is; but the remainder select "farther" much more often than "closer," by 3 or 4 to one [see Lansing and Ladd (1964); Lansing and Hendricks (1967); Butler et al. (1968); for Londoner's opinions, see Young and Willmott (1973: 47)].

Conversely, opinions about the center city are, and have been increasingly in the last few decades, negative. Many Americans have felt as Henry Ford did: "We shall solve the city problem by leaving the city."[5] Today, as generations of urbanites grow up who have lived only in the suburbs, the city becomes more and more fearsome and foreign place. A journalist recently reported that suburban Boston teen-agers tend to see that city as a dark and dangerous combat zone. One 17-year-old said, "The city is dirty and crowded and full of crime and I'm glad I'm isolated from it. My parents never wasted their time going in and neither will I. I don't want to be any part of it [Henry, 1978]." To be sure, some speak the way Ed Koch, mayor of New York, does: "Have you ever lived in the suburbs? . . . It's sterile, it's wasting your life. And people do not wish to waste their lives after they've seen New York."[6] But most Americans by far would strenuously disagree with His Honor.

Actual migration patterns are consistent with these more typical preferences. Many more people move out to the suburbs than in toward the cities. Suburban ideology may influence this movement by encouraging people to seek "a country home in the city." But rustic ideals are probably not as significant today as they were early in the century, at the time of the largely upper-middle-class migration to the suburbs (see Tarr, 1973; Warner, 1962). Most people move from one home to another for concrete reasons—most importantly, space for growing families; and good schools, safety, the physical condition of the neighborhood, and convenience.[7] Americans do indulge a cultural taste for the single-family house (see Chapter 3), often justified as beneficial for raising children. They are willing to commute quite far to live in a nicer home (Louis Harris Assoc., 1979: 77–79). The great suburban expansion of the last generation should probably be attributed less to suburban ideals and more to suburban practicalities. When middle class families seek spaciousness, indoors and out, at prices they can afford, they largely find it in the suburbs.[8]

No sociological theories of suburbanism have yet been developed that are as comprehensive as the Chicago School's determinist theory of urbanism. The most thorough statement specifically about the suburban way of life is the compositional one, coming in response to the 1950s critique of suburbia. To the contention that living in the suburbs created conformism, conservatism, frantic consumerism, lonely and bored housewives, harassed and status-hungry husbands, spoiled and neurotic children, and so on, these scholars answered that there are no effects of suburbanism other than purposeful ones—for example, the opportunity to garden or make other use of open space. If city and suburban people act differently, they do so because different kinds of people moved to each place (Gans, 1962a, 1967; B. Berger, 1960; Bell, 1959, 1968).

But we can apply determinist *and* subcultural theories to the suburban question: To the extent that more suburban places in the metropolis are less dense and farther from population concentration, they should bear roughly the same relation to more central places as rural communities bear to urban ones. On what, specifically, the resulting contrasts in ways of life are, determinist and subcultural theory, of course, disagree.

THE CONTEXTS OF SUBURBAN LIFE

Just as cities vary greatly from one another, so do their suburbs. One important distinction among suburbs is their developmental histories. Some American suburbs have grown gradually as a result of population "spill-over" from the city (Warner, 1962). Others are "instant communities" that developers built virtually overnight in what was yesterday open land [Levittown, New Jersey, for example; Gans, (1967)]. In a third category are "engulfed towns"— communities that were once autonomous villages or small cities but have since been surrounded by the metropolis (Dobriner, 1963: 127–141). Somewhat different social patterns are likely to arise in each type. Because of marketing decisions made by its developer, the "instant" suburb, for example, is likely to be more homogeneous in the ages and incomes of its residents than most neighborhoods [at least at first; Popenoe (1977)]. And the engulfed suburb often becomes the scene of a great deal of "oldtimer"—"newcomer" conflict.

Suburbs are heterogeneous in other ways as well, ways similar to those that differentiate city neighborhoods, such as class, age, race, and religion. One geographer has suggested that there are four basic types of American suburbs: the exclusive upper-class suburb (e.g., Grosse Pointe, Michigan); the middle-class, family-centered suburb most common in the stereotype (e.g., Los Angeles' San Fernando Valley); the working-class suburb (e.g., Union City, New Jersey); and the "cosmopolitan" enclave [e.g., Cambridge, Massachusetts; see discussion in Muller, (1981)]. In addition there are black suburbs, old industrial suburbs, new high-technology suburbs, and suburbs that are largely shopping malls. All this diversity is significant, for the life-styles of blue-collar suburbanites resemble those of blue-collar city-dwellers more than they do those of white-collar suburbanites. In general, differences among suburbs are greater than the overall differences between a city and its suburbs. This great variability should be constantly kept in mind, even as we endeavor to draw general conclusions about cities and suburbs.

The Physical Context

The physical environment of suburbia is, as we noted earlier, a significant public attraction. In general, the farther from the center of a metropolis, the fewer the irritants produced by congestion: crowds, noise, dirt, and pollution.[9] This is clearly perceived by the public. City residents note irritants as major drawbacks to their neighborhoods, and suburban residents note their absence as positive features. This contrast appears to explain in part why suburbanites are more satisfied with their communities than city dwellers are with theirs (Hawley and Zimmer, 1971; Marans and Rodgers, 1975; Louis Harris Assoc., 1979: 94–95).

Probably more significant in producing this satisfaction is housing. Each mile farther from the metropolitan center adds exponentially to the land available for building. In general, the more distant from the center a plot of land is, the less valuable it is commercially, and again in turn the less costly it is for home building. Thus, the construction of single-family houses is cheaper in the suburbs than in the center city. And, as a general rule, the more distant a neighborhood is from the center city, the higher its proportion of single-family houses (Evans, 1973; Treadway, 1969). Nearly 70 percent of U.S. suburbanites have their own houses, but less than one-half the city residents do (BOC, 1979: 1). A glance back at Figure 3 (p. 61) reminds us that suburban housing is on the average more spacious, valuable, and generally desirable than center-city or nonmetropolitan dwellings.

Several consequences flow from the relative concentration of single-family houses in American suburbs. Homeowners are likely to stay longer in a neighborhood. The house encourages suburbanites to spend more leisure time at home (tending the lawn, making repairs, etc.), to entertain family and friends, and to be interested in the neighborhood and involved with their neighbors (Michelson, 1973a, 1977; Gans, 1967; Berger, 1960). The lower density means that stores and services are beyond walking distance, and thus the purchase of a second or even a third car for wives and teen-age children is more likely (Foley, 1975).[10] And, given the general preference for such housing, lower density means that suburbanites are usually more satisfied with their locations than city residents are with theirs (Louis Harris Assoc., 1979; Stueve et al., 1975).

The price suburbanites pay for a pleasant environment (in addition to the cost of a house) is difficulty and time in reaching services and facilities. This is being quickly alleviated, at least in North American suburbs, as jobs, stores, and entertainment places spring up there (Muller, 1981; Kasarda, 1976). Though residents on the city's rim are disadvantaged by their dispersed residential patterns in attracting services, these suburbanites have the counterbalancing advantage of relatively large disposable incomes. A preeminent symbol of suburban facilities is the grand shopping mall, which in some areas has taken on the aspect of a suburban downtown, complete with loitering adolescents and crime (King, 1971; Muller, 1974). Nevertheless, suburbanites must generally travel farther for services and live more often without them. This is particularly so for more specialized services and for persons with more specialized needs or whose mobility is restricted, such as the elderly.[11]

This trade-off—the physical setting and house versus ease of access—is consciously perceived by most people when they decide where to move. The majority choose, when they are in the position to choose, a nice house in a less accessible location (Lansing, 1966; Butler et al., 1968).

Suburbanites tend also to be disadvantaged in public, as well as commercial, services, particularly in public transportation and in medical care. But there is one quite notable exception, at least in the United States: schools. Suburban residents are considerably more pleased with their public schools than are center-city residents, especially compared to residents of the larger cities (Louis Harris Assoc., 1979: 110). School quality is one family-centered concern that motivates many moves to the suburbs. It also reflects one of the relatively unusual features of *American* metropolises, that schools are locally financed and run, so that it matters for urbanites' children (and for their tax rate) whether their home is on one side or the other of a district line.

THE SOCIAL CONTEXT

The various metropolitan communities are marked not only by particular physical contexts, but also by particular social contexts.

Population Composition

One dramatic difference between city and suburb in the United States is racial composition. In1980, 23 percent of the center-city population was black (up three points since 1970) in contrast to about 6 percent of the suburban population (up one point; Long and DeAre, 1981). Furthermore, blacks who are officially suburban have been largely confined to ghetto areas that have trickled over city lines and to small ghettos in satellite cities, at least until quite recently. In fact, the entire growth of suburbs in the United States has been linked to the issue of race—in part of a result of "white flight" and in part a cause of increasing racial segregation.[12]

In general, non-natives have, in the modern era, congregated in center cities rather than suburbs. Although in the 1970s Asian and Hispanic immigrants to the United States often moved to suburban areas—perhaps because of black concentration in the cities—the pattern still held in 1980: 10 percent of city residents recorded by the census were foreign-born; in the suburbs the figure was 6 percent (Hebers, 1983b).

City-dwellers and suburbanites also differ consistently in life cycle. Young adults in the prefamily stage and elderly people whose children have grown up tend to live in cities. Married adults between the ages of 25 and 44 and their children under 18 tend to live in the suburbs.[13] In 1980, 34 percent of suburban households included a married couple and children; among city households the figure was 23 percent. The figures were just about reversed for the percentage of single-person or unrelated-people households (Hebers, 1983a). In general, the farther from downtown a neighborhood is, the higher the proportion of child-rearing families (Anderson and

Egeland, 1961; Guest, 1971). Current mobility patterns in metropolitan areas are reinforcing these differences: Young adults are moving inward; slightly older, married, and child-rearing adults are moving outward (Long and Glick, 1976).[14]

City and suburb also differ in social rank. Although suburbanites tend to be slightly more educated and to hold more prestigious jobs than city people do, the two groups differ most in income. In 1979, the median income of suburban *households* in the United States was 35 percent greater than that of city households—$20,158 versus $14,967 (Hebers, 1983a). The gap for *families* was smaller but still substantial—about 30 percent—as was the gap in income *per person,* about 18 percent. (Remember, suburban families are larger than city ones.) Moreover, the difference seems to have widened during the 1970s. Median suburban family income exceeded median city income in all but 2 of the 20 largest metropolises.[15] Residential moves are still augmenting these differences, as high-income families move outward and low-income families are stuck in the center (Hawley and Zimmer, 1971; Farley, 1976; Olsen and Guest, 1977). Although it is foolish to imagine that suburbanites are uniformly wealthy—a good many are working-class—they are on the average wealthier than city-dwellers.[16]

Although this description of suburban affluence is probably familiar to any casual observer of America, it is actually a historically unusual pattern. We learned in Chapter 3 that preindustrial cities largely had an opposite pattern. The rich people of Moscow in 1897, for example, lived near the center, and the poor lived on the outskirts (Abbott, 1974). The same was true for U.S. urban areas (Ward, 1971); Conzen, 1975) until the middle classes started moving out in the late nineteenth century—moving out, some historians argue, precisely to avoid the lower-class immigrants flooding into the cities (Walker, 1978; Schneider, 1980). Meanwhile, rich–inside and poor–outside continues for metropolises in the industrializing nations, for cities that matured before their nations had industrialized (Schnore, 1965; Hoyt, 1969), and even for a few remaining metropolises in the southern United States (Schnore, 1972; Schlitz and Moffitt, 1971). Nevertheless, the "North American" form, with affluent residents living on the outskirts, deserves close attention, because most major metropolises not yet there are evolving toward it. The growing middle classes around the globe are moving out of the cities to the peripheries (Hoyt, 1969; Hawley, 1981; Schnore, 1965; London and Flanagan, 1976).[17]

The differences in racial and class composition between cities and suburbs in the United States are one of the few contributors to the American "urban crisis" that is truly *urban* in nature. That is, the demographic structure of the metropolis is a major part of the problem. The ability of the affluent to segregate themselves and their tax moneys behind suburban political walls has left the center cities with immense social and physical services to support [including those such as museums, road maintenance, and police and fire protection for suburbanites commuting to work or "on the town" (Kasarda, 1972a)], but without the financial or human resources to succeed. It is ironic that the person who can manage the price (and color) of admission to many suburbs—that is, purchasing an expensive house—can also enjoy "rebates" in the form of better services for lower taxes.

Suburbanites and city-dwellers also differ in migration histories. Generally, residents of center cities move more frequently than do residents of suburban rings (Long and Boertlein, 1978a), although the American differences are small. In 1977, 35 percent of city households had been in their current homes less than 18 months, but for suburban households the figure was 31 percent (BOC, 1977a: 6). But perhaps more important, city movers typically stay in the same neighborhood or district, and the suburbanites tend to change communities. Movers from city to suburb outnumber those going in the opposite direction by about 3 to 1. And suburbs absorb most of the migration into metropolitan areas from smaller communities (Farley, 1976). Consequently, suburbanites are more often unfamiliar with their neighborhoods, not yet firmly rooted, in the process of planting those roots. Suburban communities tend to be newer, and, as a result, to have fragile social and political structures (Gans, 1951, 1967).

The last aspect of social composition we shall consider is homogeneity. As many have suspected, suburban neighborhoods tend to be slightly more homogeneous in class, race, religion, and life-style than are city neighborhoods.[18] The consequences of greater homogeneity could be (though need not necessarily be) slightly more cohesion, conviviality, and consensus in suburban than in city neighborhoods.

A Middle-Class Return?   During the 1970s, journalists filed reports from many center cities around the United States of an "urban revival." The signs of what seemed to be a phoenix-like resurgence were dramatic: waterfront complexes in Boston, newly scrubbed brownstones in Brooklyn, luxury high-rises in northside Chicago, brightly painted victorian flats in San Francisco. What appears to be happening is a "return to the city" by the suburban middle class. What *is* happening?

Many center-city neighborhoods are being fixed up, some by their long-time residents and probably more by newcomers who are wealthier than the people they replace. Part of that replacement simply reflects familiar processes of residential turnover, probably accelerated by the inflation in housing costs during the 1970s (Goodman, 1979). (What might have been affordable on a craftsman's salary in 1960 required a professional's salary in 1980.) But a significant portion of what is so visible in many cities is *gentrification*—the concentrated settlement and renovation of specific working-class or poor neighborhoods by affluent newcomers (NUC, 1978; Clay, 1980; Laska and Spain, 1980).

In the initial stages of gentrification, what might be called "bohemian" types of people—usually unmarried—"pioneer" a low-income neighborhood, typically one with some historical and architectural charm. Couples follow, as do businesses; professional renovators and speculators buy in; the locale becomes "chic"; and affluent families eventually make it an established neighborhood (Gale, 1980). The "gentry" tend to be young, white, highly educated, often although not always childless, and professionals by occupation—*not* middle-class white- or blue-collar workers. Commonly, they are *not* returning to the city. Rather, they tend to have been raised in small towns or suburban areas, moved to the city earlier as renters, and were now buying their first homes.[19]

Why gentrification is happening now is not clear. It may be caused by a combination of factors: the coming to adulthood of the baby-boom generation during a period of stagnant housing supply, an inflation in suburban housing costs that make city buildings comparative bargains, the overextension of suburban commuting distances, or perhaps a new love for city life on the part of many people (London, 1980; Clay, 1980; Gellen, 1982). Whatever the forces at work in the United States, we should keep in mind that gentrification has been happening in Europe—the word comes from Britain—for quite a while.

Also unclear is how widespread the upgrading process actually is. In Europe, enough affluent people have replaced working-class residents in the center cities to significantly alter the social geography of places like London and Amsterdam (Hammett and Williams, 1980; Kandell, 1978). But this has *not* happened in the United States, at least not yet (Spain, 1980; Long, 1980). We have seen that the overall gap in income between city-dwellers and suburbanites actually widened in the 1970s, even in actively gentrifying places like Washington and San Francisco. If the urban revival remains limited and selective, then we may see a continuation of the current American social geography: small pockets of elite neighborhoods within a depressed center city, surrounded by broadly working-class and middle-class suburbs. But if middle-class people follow the professionals into the inner city, we may see in the next generation a new, more European, pattern: a middle-class downtown, circled by a ring of working-class neighborhoods and suburbs, surrounded in turn by more distant middle-class suburbs and "ex-urbs" (see Gellen, 1982).

As of now, gentrification is displacing a small, although notable, number of lower-income people [(Grier and Grier, 1980); more are displaced by simple inflation]. And we do not know just where the displaced are going (NUC, 1978). But the process, as limited and isolated as it may be, is a growing source of conflict as potentially displaced residents resist—politically and otherwise—what they see as invaders. This tension is no doubt a major contributor to campaigns around the country for rent control and limits on condominium conversions. The 1980s will see just how sizeable gentrification—and its accompanying conflict—will be.

Activities   The social contexts of city and suburb are also defined by the typical activities of the people who live there. American suburbs have usually been thought of as the sites of home activities, such as child-rearing, and cities were the work and commercial recreation sites. Never completely true, this becomes less true every year.

There always were factories and businesses in the suburbs, and their number has increased rapidly in recent years. By now, most of the jobs and most of the retail sales in large American metropolises are in their suburbs (Muller, 1981: Chapter 4; Kasarda, 1978). The critical issues are not just the amount of work done in city and suburb, but also the type of work done. On the first count, it remains as a general, though weakened, rule that commercial and industrial land use declines with distance from the center, and residential land use increases. Cities still house more work activities per acre and per resident than do suburbs. On the second count, center cities tend to have proportionally more professional, administrative, and white-collar work; but blue-collar manufacturing jobs have shifted to the suburbs, where lower land costs permit cheaper factory construction. Suburbs are increasingly attracting the white-collar jobs, too—in office parks, for example (Muller, 1981)—but those still remain relatively centralized. These employment and residential patterns often create a daily criss-cross commute in American metropolises: Some white-collar workers travel from suburban low-rise homes to city high-rise offices; some blue-collar workers travel from high-rise city apartments to low-rise suburban factories (Guest, 1975).

City-dwellers and suburbanites also differ in their leisure activities. Residents closer to downtown tend to use public facilities such as theaters more, but suburbanites tend to be more involved in home activities, such as gardening and entertaining friends (Gruenberg, 1974; von Rosenbladt, 1972). This difference in part reflects the residential choices of people with different tastes (Zelan, 1968; Bell, 1968), but studies of people who moved from city to suburb indicate that they actually changed their leisure pursuits, often without having intended to (Michelson, 1973a; Gans, 1967; Clark, 1966). House ownership and child-rearing, both more common among suburbanites, "root" leisure activities. But suburbanism itself has an effect (Gruenberg, 1974; Wallden, 1975). That effect probably involves simple distance: Theaters, restaurants, and the like tend to be inconveniently far away for suburbanites (von Rosenbladt, 1972) so suburbanites stress home activities instead (Zikmund, 1971; Lansing and Hendricks, 1967).

Increasingly, it seems, one thing suburbanites do not do with their leisure time is go to the city. One-half of the New York suburbanites polled in 1978 said that they went to the city less than five times a year for nonbusiness reasons; one-quarter said "never."

And the more recreational facilities near their homes, the less often suburbanites visited the city (Madden, 1978). City residents, however, are even less likely to visit the suburbs in their free time (Louis Harris Assoc., 1979: 242, 246), so the cities are still, comparatively speaking, the leisure centers.

Crime   Criminal activities show sharp city–suburban differences, largely as a function of differences in social composition. In preindustrial urban developments, deprived groups reside on the outskirts, and so do the criminals; crime therefore *in*creases with distance from the center (Herbert, 1972: 217–221; Abbott, 1974). In modern cities, such as American ones, crime is found in the center where the low-income groups are, and it *de*creases with distance (Herbert, 1972: 199ff.). This difference, like many others, is in flux: Suburban crime rates in the United States are rising more rapidly than are city rates (McCausland, 1972; Malcolm, 1974). Nevertheless, people in the suburbs are safer from crime than are people in the city. Federal Bureau of Investigation statistics for 1980 indicate, for example, that suburbanites ran about one-third the risk of being murdered, one-fifth the chance of being robbed, and one-half the chance of being burglarized as did city-dwellers (Webster, 1981: Table 14). Victimization surveys show similar results.

Suburbanites also feel safer: In one survey, more than 50 percent of the city residents interviewed said that they thought it was unsafe for them to walk outside at night; but "only" 20 percent of suburbanites felt it was unsafe to do so (Marans and Rodgers, 1975: Table 18). City-dwellers more often complain about crime, and fear of crime is a contributor to Americans' preferences for suburban over city living.[20] [Indeed, crime has become synonymous with the word "city" for many American urbanites (Silverman, 1982).]

Most of the differences in social context between American cities and suburbs are not very great. (And they are differences in *averages,* which mask great internal variations.) And these differences are often reversed in other nations. But they form a consistent pattern, and one increasingly typical elsewhere. This brief overview of American suburbs' physical and social structures suggests that, on the average, these places are in some ways like affluent small towns within the metropolis. Except for their wealth, the distant communities of American metropolises tend to be to the central communities as rural places are to urban ones: less dense, greener, more socially homogeneous, more typically composed of families, and safer. If suburbs are indeed small towns in the metropolis, then they are meeting the aspirations of most of their residents.

SECONDARY GROUPS

Any attempt to contrast the lives and behavior of suburbanites to those of city-dwellers runs into major obstacles. One, both sets of people are urbanites. Socially and economically, they are part of the greater metropolitan population, working, shopping, and playing at many of the same places and with the same people. Thus, suburbanites are not likely to act in markedly distinct ways (except insofar as their personal traits, such as education or age, incline them to do so). Second, though there has been much popular interest in suburban life-styles (Donaldson, 1969), the amount of careful, comparative research is quite limited. Consequently, we shall have to tread lightly and speculatively over a number of questions in this field. Of the secondary social groups in suburbia, we shall consider three: the community, the neighborhood, and the special-interest group.[21]

The Community

Attention to the community as a social group highlights once more the features of metropolitan life peculiar to the United States. This nation's home-rule tradition disperses power to local units. Suburbs are autonomous political organizations that exercise a good deal of power over taxes, schools, police, zoning, and other important concerns. This is unlike other nations, where most or many of these functions are performed by the national or metropolitan governments. To move across the line from an American center city to its suburb, or from one suburb to another, is often to find a drastic change in types of schools, tax rates, the quality of public services, and the like. Consequently, interest in the suburban community is more than good citizenship; it often means, more significantly than in the city, the protection of low taxes, high-quality (typically segregated) schools, and property values (Schneider and Logan, 1981). The role of these political lines becomes dramatized when the autonomy of the suburb is threatened, as in the case of attempts to bus children from the center city to local schools or in efforts to create metropolitan-wide governments. Suburbanites fight these moves strenuously.[22] In addition, the small size of suburban polities should make each resident's opinion count more than it would in the city; he or she should feel more politically efficacious.

These characteristics of U.S. suburbs should promote political involvement, thus making more cohesive "groups" of them. But, a number of suburban characteristics lessen involvement. Many residents are relatively new to the community (Alford and Scoble, 1968); many, if not most, workers hold jobs outside the community (Martin, 1959; Verba and Nie, 1972: Table 13-2); and suburban politics are likely to be overshadowed by those of the center city (Fischer, 1975d). So, for example, suburbanites, though more educated than city residents, are less likely to know their local political leaders (Hawley and Zimmer, 1971: 67ff.; Verba and Nie, 1972: Chapter 13) and no more likely to vote in local elections (Greer, 1962: 40; Hawley and Zimmer, 1971).

Perhaps the best description of suburban politics is that it is an apathetic but arousable consensus. Most constituencies are socially and ideologically homogeneous. Consequently, there is usually widespread, if implicit, agreement on political philosophy, and few issues generate excitement. Semiprofessional officeholders are commonly allowed to act as trustees of the general accord so long as they care to do so. [Contrast this to the deep divisiveness and chronic conflict of large cities, as discussed earlier (Chapter 5, passim; Chapter 8, pp. 217–218).] In the normal course of events, suburbanites do not get very involved in community affairs (Prewitt and Eulau, 1969). And they tend to be relatively satisfied with their local government (Louis Harris Assoc., 1979: 126). But this appearance is misleading. When the consensus is threatened by a challenge from without or a schism from within, suburbanites become very active (Black, 1974) and are more likely than city-dwellers to act in concert (Louis Harris Assoc., 1979: 132). Metropolitanization, school busing, zoning changes—these are the kinds of issues that arouse the latent community "group." We can conclude that, in the suburbs, all else equal, the political community *is* a more significant social group than in the city.[23]

The Neighborhood

Another territorial unit, the neighborhood, is also more cohesive in the suburbs than it is in the city. Research in the United States and abroad is virtually unanimous on this point. Whether measured by visits with neighbors, concern for the local area, local activities, or almost any equivalent indicator, suburbanites are more involved in the neighborhood than are city-dwellers (but still less involved than rural residents). In a 1977 survey, for example, 72 percent of American city residents said that people in their neighborhood kept "pretty much to themselves"; but 55 percent of suburbanites did [and 44 percent of town residents (Louis Harris Assoc., 1979: 120)]. Suburbanization is not always associated with increased neighboring; some people—those with special tastes or members of minority groups—are actually more isolated in suburbia. We shall return to these people later. And the intensity of suburban neighboring may be dropping as more and more wives take jobs (Silverman, 1983). Yet for the bulk of the population, suburban life is associated with more neighborliness.[24]

Though there is some consensus on city–suburban differences in neighboring, there is none on the explanation for it (Fischer and Jackson, 1977). Researchers point to the personal characteristics of suburbanites, such as their young children and high income (Michelson, 1977). Although these provide a partial explanation, they do not account for all of the differences. A few studies have found that suburbanites are more neighborly than city-dwellers even when taking into account such differences (e.g., Tomeh, 1964; Fava, 1959; Tallman and Morgner, 1970). Other studies followed the same people from city to suburb and found that they tended to increase their neighboring after the move (Michelson, 1973a, 1977; Clark, 1966; Berger, 1960). These latter investigations cast doubt as well on the theory that neighborly personalities are drawn to suburban life, and that self-selection explains the city–suburban difference (Bell, 1959, 1968; Fava, 1959). Some self-selection no doubt occurs—people who love to neighbor might find the neighboring in suburbia an extra incentive to move there—but this is not a significant reason for moving. And there seems to be little self-selection according to sociability [Baldassare and Fischer (1975); Michelson (1973a); Michelson et al. (1973); there is some self-selection according to preferred leisure activities—gardening versus attending the theater, for example, (Zelan, 1968)]. Other explanations of suburbanites' proclivities for neighboring include the argument that the detached house is conducive to local social life (Gans, 1967; Dobriner, 1963), that neighboring is a result of pioneer eagerness in brand-new communities (Marshall, 1973), and that local involvement is a result of suburban homogeneity (Donaldson, 1969; Gans, 1967).

One more explanation should be considered: distance. Suburban neighborhoods are often inconveniently distant from the bulk of the population and from metropolitan attractions. Consequently, friends and activities outside the neighborhood are relatively costly to see, and so suburbanites tend to "settle" for local relationships (Fischer, 1982a, 1982b). The problem is particularly acute for suburbanites with travel constraints, such as teen-agers or carless housewives. This explanation is consistent with longitudinal studies of people who moved to the suburbs, which indicate that new suburbanites must make major efforts to maintain contact with their associates in the city. Quite commonly, those associates are dropped in favor of closer, local ones (Clark, 1966; Michelson, 1973a). This analysis explains the cohesion of the suburban neighborhood by the basic nature of suburbia: its peripheral location in the metropolis (Fischer and Jackson, 1977).

Whichever explanation(s) future research confirms, the difference is clear: Suburbanites tend to be more involved in their neighborhoods than are city-dwellers. Fitting this fact together with others—the significance of the community, leisure time spent at home, house ownership, and child-rearing—suggests a general style of life we might call "localism." People's activity and attention are directed toward the immediate locality and its residents. To be sure, some forces pull suburbanites *away* from their localities, including associates in the city, jobs outside the area, the necessity to travel far for services, and the easy mobility of middle-class families with two or more cars. Nevertheless, the countervailing tugs of the suburban neighborhood—the home, children, congenial neighbors, suburbanism itself perhaps (that is, distance)—appear to be stronger, with the net result being a somewhat more localized way of life.[25] Additional evidence of suburban localism comes from the relative weakness in suburbia of nonlocal special-interest groups.

Special-Interest Groups

Suburban communities certainly have their share, or more, of fraternal associations, PTAs, garden clubs, and the like. These are broad-based and usually local interest groups. Less common are the groups that cater to the atypical resident. Members of ethnic minorities, single people, people with unusual tastes—compatible groups are scarcer for them, even though their "Middle American" neighbors are surrounded by congenial groups. The small size of each unique population leads to a poverty of specialized services and facilities for them, and thus further deprivation.

Consider two examples. Widely dispersed across the town, frequently carless, and lacking places to go and things to do, adolescents are commonly disgruntled in suburbia (Popenoe, 1977). This problem was illustrated recently by confrontations between police and teenagers in Foster City, California, a suburb of the San Franciscan peninsula. Police explained that the troubles were the result of "boredom" among the youth. (On their part, the teenagers said that the troubles were the result of "boredom" among the police.) A second example is provided by Herbert Gans, in *The Levittowners*. The population of suburban newcomers he studied included a number of Jewish women who were interested in cultural activities. They found, to their frustration, that they were too few, and too far from places and people in Philadelphia, the nearest city, to satisfy their desires. People like these, outside the mainstream, are impaired in their efforts to form special-interest groups. Gans concludes: "The smallness and homogeneity of the population made it difficult for the culturally and socially deviant to find companions. Levittown benefitted the majority but punished the minority with exclusion . . . [with] 'the misery of the deviate' [1967: 239]."

The feebleness of translocal special-interest groups thus helps reinforce the suburban pattern of social life centered on the community and the neighborhood.

PRIMARY GROUPS

The effects of suburbanism on *primary* groups are quite modest but are still consistent with the tendency toward localism.

The 1950s vision of suburbia saw *ethnic* differences dissolving in its melting pot. Not many studies have been done on suburban ethnicity, but a few notable ones have looked at Jews. These found that Jewish suburbanites continue to identify themselves as Jews and, more importantly, that their intimate social relationships are almost exclusively with other Jews, even when they live in over-whelmingly gentile communities. The people in the studies reported simply feeling more "comfortable" and "at home" with their coreligionists. But the research also revealed notable declines in adherence to Jewish religious ritual and belief among these sub-urbanites when compared to the practices of their parents. (This change was mostly a result of generational differences, or of upward social mobility, and minimally of suburbanism itself.) Nevertheless, Jews remain a distinct and meaningful ethnic group in suburbia (Sklare and Greenblum, 1967; Goldstein and Goldscheider, 1968; Gans, 1951, 1957, 1967). If this case can be generalized to unstud-ied groups, it implies that nothing is inherently inimical to ethnicity in suburban life (Lieberson, 1962; Alba and Chamlin, 1983).

But one major qualification should be noted: So long as ethnic group members remain few or widely dispersed, they face the harsh choice of isolation or assimilation. In these studies, the Jewish families who were early settlers in their communities anxiously awaited the arrival of others so that they could establish both formal and informal associations. Where they remained scattered, religious identity was weakened (Goldstein and Goldscheider, 1968). And some ethnic groups fare less well. Gans notes in *The Levittowners* that "groups without a strong subcommunity were isolated, notably a handful of Japanese, Chinese, and Greek families [1967: 162]." The persistence of ethnicity partly depends on the concentration of sufficient numbers in the group. Thus, concentrated and segregated ethnic groups in suburbs should persist. But those conditions are less often met there than in the city. Two survey studies suggest that suburbanites less often had friends of the same ethnicity than city-dwellers (Jackson, 1977: 71; Fischer, 1982a: Chapter 16). All told, suburban residence probably reduces ethnic cohesion slightly.

Another proposition in what has been termed the "suburban

myth" (Donaldson, 1969; Berger, 1960) concerns *friends*. It holds that suburban residence promotes a peculiar sort of "hypersociability": People are involved with many friends, but those friendships are superficial. From the evidence at hand, it appears that suburbanism is associated neither with a greater number of friendships nor with shallower ones than city residence.[26] But these are two modest differences, already alluded to, between city and suburban friendships.

First, suburbanites' friendships tend to be slightly more localized than those of city residents. Suburbanites are a bit likelier to draw their friends from among their neighbors. For many new settlers on the urban fringe, there is a gradual fraying of bonds with friends who were left in the city, and the braiding of substitutes with neighbors.[27] In Chapter 6 we suggested that one difference between rural and metropolitan friendships was that the former were more geographically concentrated. Within the metropolis, suburban neighborhoods lead toward a more rural pattern of local ties.

Second, suburban neighbors often cannot replace other friends for those who are too young or too old, who are members of ethnic, racial, or class minorities in their neighborhoods, or who are adherents to atypical life-styles. These people have problems finding friends in the locality (and they find it difficult to form special-interest groups). Consequently, those who can travel long distances to see friends do so, but those who cannot or will not travel that far are often isolated in their suburban houses (Gans, 1967; Tomeh, 1964).

The elderly provide one case in point. Because of physical and financial problems, they tend to be relatively immobile, and therefore suffer more acutely from problems of access than do younger people. A study of the elderly conducted in San Antonio, Texas, found that the farther from the center they lived, and the fewer friends they reported, the less active socially, and the lonelier they were (Carp, 1975; Bourg, 1975; Cantor, 1975).

Another case is low-income residents of cities in the underdeveloped world, where private cars are rare and public transit very slow and undependable. Studies suggest that those living on the outskirts tend to be more socially isolated than poor people who manage to find accommodations in the center city (Roberts, 1973; Perlman, 1975; Kemper, 1975).

Other than the localization of friendships and the relative

isolation of atypical people, there appear to be no differences between the friendship patterns of North American city and suburban residents—or, at least, no differences not attributable to suburbanites' affluence, child-rearing, and other traits that differ from those of city-dwellers.

Much of journalistic speculation about suburban life has concentrated on the damage suburban residence might do to the *family* (Donaldson, 1969). Scholars, too, have been concerned, worrying, for example, that the long commuting times spent by fathers would lead to mother-centered families (Burgess and Locke, 1953: Chapter 4). This concern is ironic, in light of the public's opinion that suburbs are ideal for family life. In 1977 Americans polled on what was the best place to raise children ranked suburbs above cities (but below the country); 82 percent said that large cities were the worst place (Louis Harris Assoc., 1979: 157–159). The indoor space of a suburban house provides individual privacy; a yard and a quiet street allow children to play in safety; the grounds and the structure promote leisure activities at home; the house itself serves as an investment and symbol of achievement; the schools are probably better; and the social environment is less threatening.

Most movers from cities to suburbs desire and expect to alter their lives in a more familistic direction, and they usually do (Gans, 1967; Michelson, 1977; Bell, 1959, 1968). Suburbanites more often say they are satisfied with their communities as places to rear children than city residents do (Louis Harris Assoc., 1979: 103). This does not mean that suburban families are more cohesive or "healthy" than comparable ones in the city; there is little solid evidence on this issue, on marital relations, or on the quality of child-rearing.[28] People are generally convinced that suburbs are good places for families; we have little empirical reason to dispute or confirm that belief.

But, when we view the status of the *extended* family as well as that of the nuclear family, one blemish in this portrait of suburban familism appears. A few studies suggest that movers to the suburbs tend to underestimate how inconvenient it will be for them to see their kin—parents, in-laws, siblings—after their move. At first they try to stay in touch, but over time the frequency of interaction often declines, with local friends eventually replacing the relatives in many suburbanites' social lives.[29] This does not appear to bother husbands very much but seriously disturbs many wives.

A well-known case of family separation occurred when young families moved from Bethnal Green, the working-class district of London described in Chapter 6, to Greenleigh, a recently built housing estate on the outskirts of London. Contact between the suburbanites and their parents was difficult, and the resulting feeling of separation was strong, especially among the women. Though they tried to stay in touch—"When I first came I felt I had done a crime," said one woman, "It was so bare. I felt terrible and I used to pop back to see Mum two or three times a week [Young and Willmott, 1957: 133]"—almost inevitably they were isolated. When the researchers returned to Greenleigh a few years later, after it had become more populated, they found that neighborhood social life had grown and significantly eased the women's isolation (Willmott, 1963).

In sum, the effects on primary groups of living in the urban center or the urban periphery apparently are modest. Movers to the suburbs are much like movers within the city; those who have a choice choose homes and neighborhoods to match their life-styles and to promote their private lives (Michelson, 1977). Insofar as people correctly anticipate the changes that result from their moves, they presumably protect their primary ties or alter them in desired ways. Hence, we should expect suburbanism by itself to produce few differences in social relations. But anticipated or not, one modest effect does seem to occur: a modest constriction of social networks, on two dimensions. A slight spatial constriction occurs that results in more localized activities and relationships than occur in the city, particularly for the less mobile. And there is a modest constriction in variety, with people who are relatively atypical in the suburban population finding themselves more isolated from their fellows than would be the case in the city. (Even these differences are, we must repeat, small.)

Unfortunately, these conclusions are based largely on studies of *moves* to suburbia, rather than on suburban residence alone. Most researchers have concentrated, often by necessity, on recent arrivals to the suburbs; and studies of long-time suburbanites are relatively rare (Hawley and Zimmer, 1971; Zelan, 1968). Increasingly, suburbanites are people who were also raised in suburbia—in 1978, only one-third of New York suburbanites had ever lived in New York City (Madden, 1978)—and yet we know little about those people (Fava, 1975). Thus, we face the uncertainty of whether city–suburban differences *or* lack of differences are a result of the *residence* or the *move*. Until further studies are completed, any conclusions we draw must be qualified this way.

THE INDIVIDUAL IN SUBURBIA

There is little reason to expect the mental state or the personality of the suburbanite to differ from that of an otherwise comparable city-dweller. Coresidents of a common metropolis, suburbanites and city-dwellers alike have presumably chosen, within the constraints of their family budgets, neighborhoods that maximize their preferred balance of amenities and accessibility. We should find differences between suburban and city people of similar backgrounds if one or both of two conditions hold: If certain personalities are selectively drawn to suburbia, or if suburban residence has *unanticipated* consequences.

Some early speculations suggested that either or both of these conditions would produce a difference in the types of personalities, levels of stress, rates of mental illness, and overall morale of city and suburban residents—to the disadvantage of the latter. One sociologist asserts, for example: "We can clearly see the most grievous human loss that life in the suburb entails. Dedication to a status-dominated life-style forces individuals into a rigid mold from within which they can see only limited aspects of human reality. . . . Emotional growth stops at [a] 'juvenile' phase [Stein, 1960: 286; see review in Donaldson (1969)]."

Available data do not support such speculations. There are differences in *tastes* between those who prefer suburbs and those who prefer cities; the gardeners move outward, the gourmets move inward (Zelan, 1968; Fugitt and Zuiches, 1973; Michelson, 1973a). But there is as yet little evidence that suburbanism attracts or produces people who are stressed, disordered, or alienated.[30] Indeed, the most likely psychological change when the average American moves from city to suburb is an increase in happiness. Perhaps because of the specific amenities of the suburban home and perhaps because of the achievement it represents in American society, suburbanites are usually happy with their moves (Gans, 1967; Berger, 1960) and slightly happier with their communities and their entire lives—other factors held equal—than city-dwellers (Marans and Rodgers, 1975; Fischer, 1973b).

But this conclusion does not hold for specific sets of sub-urbanites for whom suburbia can be anguishing. These people, whom we singled out before, are those whose age, social class, ethnicity, or life-style make them "cultural deviates" in their sub-urban neighborhoods, where they usually live because of error or lack of choice. In the suburbs, these people tend to be isolated from congenial associates and activities. In the city, they are more likely to reside in appropriate neighborhoods; but even if they do not, it matters less, for they have easier access to people and places outside the neighborhood. For those in the American "mainstream"—middle-class, middle-browed, raising children, and so forth—the difference between city and suburb on this score is largely moot. They can find their like almost anywhere (and in a suburb most of all). When members of the cultural minorities can, they hold on to social ties outside the suburbs through the active use of the car and telephone. When they cannot, or when traveling wearies, they risk loneliness, boredom, and unhappiness.

Many studies have been conducted on one vulnerable group—women in general, homemakers in particular. Researchers have found that women are more critical of suburbs, more dis-pleased with moving there, and more likely to suffer psychologi-cally from the move than their husbands. Employed men daily travel away from home to a milieu usually more interesting than the one they left; they return to a house and a neighborhood that provide quiet relaxation and pride of achievement. Women, whose first loyalty has traditionally been the home, must often forego having a job because there are none conveniently near. For many home-makers, moreover, the house and neighborhood represent hours of housekeeping drudgery, boredom if they step outdoors, and no other involvements. Gans (1967: 226) reports the complaint of a working-class woman in Levittown: "It's too quiet here, nothing to do. In the city you can go downtown shopping, see all the people, or go visit mother." (These problems seem to be less common in the high density suburbs of Europe, and perhaps the suburbanization of employment and leisure in American metropolises will help here.) To be sure, most women adjust, finding friends and diversions nearby, and supplementing those with trips and phone calls. Nevertheless, many in this group suffer psychologically in suburbia.[31]

Efforts have been made to pinpoint the source of this home-makers' malaise. Suggestions include the hard labor of "keeping" a house, or the move itself with its tearing up of roots (men maintain job associates and do not seem to care much about losing touch with relatives), or the particular mix of persons in suburban neighborhoods. These hypotheses may all be valid. If so, they do not indict suburbia, because none of them is unique to the suburbs or to moving there. But we have some evidence that peripheral location itself also contributes to women's unhappiness: William Michelson (1973a) conducted an exact study in the Toronto area in which families were interviewed before and repeatedly after moves to residences of varying types. Few major unanticipated changes upset these families, but one was the isolation and boredom of some suburban housewives, ills that were relieved only partly by neighboring. Many women continued to complain of problems resulting from the distance to the city, for example, or from the absence of things to do other than housework. (Ironically, those who spend the most time in the suburbs, housewives, are least happy with it; but those most happy with it, husbands, are least often there.)

The available evidence on city–suburban differences in *social behaviors and attitudes* is quite limited.[32] Bits of research suggest that most differences can be explained by associated characteristics of suburbanites—their education, stage in the life-cycle, home ownership, and the like. "Unconventional" or deviant behavior—crime, for example—occurs relatively less often in the suburbs than in the city. This is largely because unconventional persons shun the suburbs, or are shunned by them, rather than because suburbanism suppresses deviance. It was once thought that people who moved to suburbia subsequently changed their political allegiance from Democratic to Republican, but that notion has been largely discredited (Wirt et al., 1972; Wattell, 1959; Gans, 1967). Suburbanites are relatively more involved in their local churches than are city-dwellers, but that activity appears to be part of their greater localism, rather than an indicator of reawakened faith.[33]

Other notions about suburban life-style find even less support. The thesis that suburbanism promotes conformity (Whyte, 1956;

Dobriner, 1963: Chapter 1) remains a speculation (Gans, 1967). The argument that suburbs attract or produce consumption-driven people (Bell, 1959; 1968) still lacks substantiation. And the suggestion that suburbia debases cultural tastes (Riesman, 1959) probably mistakes correlation for causality. People who prefer "high culture" tend to prefer the city (Zelan, 1968; Michelson, 1973a) and tend to feel isolated in the suburbs, but suburbanism itself probably does not suppress intellects. Speculations such as these are often, in essence, city-dwelling intellectuals' critiques of middle-class American life-styles, critiques that blame places for the ways of life people bring to them (see Donaldson, 1969; Gans, 1967).

And yet, as we have suggested, distant location may have some modest effects of its own, such as encouraging a more neighborhood-, home-, and family-centered lifestyle, discouraging the development of distinct subcultures and creating problems, of isolation and boredom for some immobile types of people. Otherwise, suburbanites seem little different from more centrally located metropolitans of similar social background.

REFLECTIONS ON THEORIES

Earlier in the chapter, we suggested that we could try to apply the three original theories of urbanism to this topic.

Determinist theory implies that, since suburbs are less dense and heterogeneous than center cities, they should produce stronger primary groups, less psychic stress, more intimate behavioral styles, and less deviance than cities do.[34] Little evidence currently available supports any of these predictions—except the last.

There are a number of small-town features often found in the suburbs that most people deeply appreciate—the quiet, the spaciousness, the greenery, and the homogeneity. But so far as we can tell, these environmental characteristics do not alter fundamental psychological states or processes, although they increase residents' satisfaction with the community.

The compositional stance is that any social–psychological variations between city and suburb result from the characteristics of the people who can and want to live in those communities, and not to ecological factors like density or distance. Herbert Gans' conclusion, drawn from his classic study of Levittown, New Jersey, is worth quoting at length:

> When one looks at similar populations in city and suburb, their ways of life are remarkably alike. . . . The crucial difference between cities and suburbs, then, is that they are often home for different kinds of people. If one is to understand their behavior, these differences are much more important than whether they reside inside or outside the city limits. Inner-city residential areas are home to the rich, the poor, and the non-white, as well as the unmarried and the childless middle class. Their ways of life differ from those of suburbanites and people in the outer city, but because they are *not* young working or lower and upper middle class families. If populations and residential areas were described by age and class charac-teristics, and by racial, ethnic, and religious ones, our under-standing of human settlements would be much improved. Using such concepts as "urban" and "suburban" as causal variables adds little, on the other hand, except for ecological and demographic analyses of communities as a whole and for studies of political behavior [Gans, 1967: 288–289; see, also, Gans, 1962a; Berger, 1960].

This view appears to be generally accurate. We have seen the extent of selectivity involved in suburban residence: Singles move away, families move in; whites are welcomed, blacks are not. These and other selectivity factors certainly explain far more than distance from downtown does. But there remain some effects of sub-urbanism, some modest differences between city and suburb, that are regular and patterned and not fully explained by self-selection. In particular, there is the localization of social life and the relative absence of unconventionality in suburbia. These differences bring us to our third theory.

Subcultural theory can be extrapolated to deal with intramet-ropolitan differences: The vigor of a subculture depends on how many people of a certain type there are in a community and on the access (in travel time and cost) that those people have to one another and their institutions. Here, then, is a variable applicable to the issue at hand: *distance*. The farther apart people reside, the more costly it is for them to come together, and the less likely it is that they will do so.

Distance from the center of the metropolitan population reduces the access of suburbanites to people and places in the center or other side of the area. And because of their peripheral location, most American suburbs are less densely populated than cities, and this in turn hampers the ability of suburbanites to attain a critical mass. City-dwellers, conversely, are in the midst of the center's density and roughly equidistant to the various suburbs. Other things being equal, suburban residents would consequently have less opportunity to form or participate in vigorous subcultures than would city-dwellers. [This effect is not as pronounced in European suburbs which, although peripherally located, tend to be dense and planned to encourage gatherings (Popenoe, 1977, 1980).]

But at least two factors mitigate the depression of subcultural life in American suburbs. One is the automobile. Cars and freeways permit suburbanites to travel great distances very rapidly, and thus to participate in groups throughout the metropolis. The second is self-selection. Those persons who most need population concentration—members of cultural minorities, for example—tend not to move to the suburbs; and those who do move are the ones who are best able to travel far and who are best able to accept "Middle American" culture. Thus, the distance of suburbia for the most part has only modest effects.

Nevertheless, it has effects: an emphasis on local, rather than metropolitan, activities and relationships; the isolation of people, such as many housewives, who underestimated suburban distances and are unable to overcome them easily (see Michelson, 1973a; Clark, 1966); and, for those persons out of the "mainstream" culture, the paucity of satisfactory social networks and supportive subcultures.

City–suburban differences in ways of life result largely from self-selection, but also, I suggest, from the relative difficulty suburbanites have in getting together with people other than their immediate neighbors. In this way at last, suburban neighborhoods have, in contrast to city localities, a "rural" flavor. According to subcultural theory, they should—and, indeed, they seem to—recapitulate features of nonurban areas: less subcultural vitality, variety, and intensity; less deviance; more localism, but no fundamental psychological differences. Scott Greer (1972: 63) observed that "the culture of the suburb is remarkably similar to that of the country towns in an earlier America." And that is just what most American suburbanites probably want!

SUMMARY

Suburbs are metropolitan neighborhoods lying some distance from the center. Residents sort themselves out within the metropolis on the basis of their personal characteristics—largely their needs for space, their travel times from work, and their abilities to pay. Distance is fundamental to these calculations and the consequent sorting out, so that the suburbs become home to somewhat distinctive residents. In the United States (and, increasingly, elsewhere) suburban residents, more so than city-dwellers, are middle-class, raise children, and are members of the predominant ethnic stock. They have come to the suburbs mainly for a house, outdoor space, and physical amenities—available at prices they can afford; although social factors, such as crime and school quality, also encourage Americans to locate in the suburbs. Inner-city renovation, "gentrification," may be noticeable, but it has not yet altered these patterns.

Understanding suburban life and social psychology must begin with these two related observations: The kinds of people found in suburbia differ in their backgrounds from those found in cities, and suburbanites are in the suburbs for particular reasons. Suburbanites may act differently from others, but the difference is probably a result of traits they brought with them (for example, being hardy consumers because they are affluent), or of personal tastes they have been able to satisfy by moving to the suburbs (puttering around the house instead of attending ballet), and not so much an effect of suburbanism itself.

Yet there is a pattern of differences between people in the suburbs and people in the cities that might reasonably be attributed to suburbanism (peripheral location) itself. Extrapolating from the evidence to some extent, the pattern is that social life is localized, occurring in and focused on the locality; and minority or unconventional subcultures are relatively rare, a fact that is largely a result, but also partly a cause of, the relative scarcity of unconventional people.

There is apparently no substantial *net* effect of suburban residence on mental states. But this net balance is composed of two divergent trends. Most people who have moved to the suburbs enjoy their homes, pleasant environment, and congenial (i.e., homogeneous) neighborhoods. But other people (such as adolescents, elderly people, housewives, ethnic minorities) often find suburban life too localized, and themselves too isolated from compatible associates and activities. These people, who are often in the suburbs because of lack of choice or foresight, are vulnerable to boredom, loneliness, and discontent.

The latter group is outnumbered by those who find that suburbia suits them quite well. And, in general, the unintended consequences of suburbanism are few and modest—just as the effects of urbanism are mainly few and modest. These two factors share another commonality. We have argued in this book that urbanism fosters the growth of distinctive subcultures. Suburbanism, we have argued in this chapter, seems to produce at least a small decline in cultural differentiation; in some sense, it is, as David Riesman (1959) has implied, a form of "deurbanization."

chApter 10

The Urban Future
Conclusions, Projections, and Policies

> The central problem of the sociologist of the city is to discover
> the forms of social action and organization that typically
> emerge in relatively permanent, compact settlements of large
> numbers of heterogeneous individuals. Only by means of [a
> workable theory of urbanism] will the sociologist escape the
> futile practice of voicing in the name of sociological science a
> variety of unsupportable judgments concerning such problems
> as poverty, housing, city-planning, sanitation, policing, market-
> ing, transportation and other technical issues. While the soci-
> ologist cannot solve any of these practical problems—at least
> not by himself—he may, if he discovers his proper function,
> have an important contribution to make to their comprehen-
> sion and solution. The prospects for doing this are brightest
> through a general, theoretical, rather than through an ad hoc
> approach.
>
> —Louis Wirth

The noted sociologist George Caspar Homans once began the end
of a book by asserting: "According to my lights, a last chapter
should resemble a primitive orgy after a harvest," in which the toiler
"is no longer bound by logic and evidence but free to speculate
about what he has done" (Homans, 1974: 356). Lacking that full
measure of Homansian bravura, I will not engage in any orgy of
speculation, but only carouse a bit. I will attempt to draw some

general conclusions about the urban experience, consider what the urban experience promises to be like in the coming decades, and employ what we know about city life to enter current debates over urban policies and policies affecting urban people (a distinction that will become clear later).

CONCLUSIONS

Considering the research reviewed in the last seven chapters, what can we conclude about the competing theories of urban social psychology and about the themes found in Western culture concerning urban ways of life?

Determinist theory holds that urbanism weakens intimate social groups and isolates people, eventually producing social disorganization. Some research supports this theory: Urban social structure is differentiated and specialized; social groups defined by territory show signs of being eroded in cities; and other groups, such as the family, are altered in various ways. Most importantly, urbanism is associated with high rates of deviant behavior, as dramatized by the rate of violent crime in modern American cities. The precarious state of the urban "moral order" is also evident in bitter dissension with the community over rules and mores.

But most of the critical sociological research does *not* support the theory of urban anomie. Instead, it suggests that intimate social groups persist in the urban environment; that urbanites are connected firmly to others, to networks of social support, and to moral systems; and that urbanites do not suffer disproportionately from psychological stress and malfunction.

The compositional position maintains that there are *no* significant social–psychological consequences of urbanism. To be sure, ways of life often differ from community to community, but they do because the personal characteristics of residents—their age, job, income, ethnicity—differ from place to place or because the specific economies and histories of the communities differ. They do *not* result from urbanism, or population concentration, itself. The small social milieus—home, workplace, friendships—that determine individual social behavior are not seriously affected by such gross ecological factors as population size.

Compositionalists can point to evidence that: intimate social circles survive in large cities; individuals are integrated into meaningful networks; social, behavioral, and psychological phenomena tend not to be related to community size, and when they are, the associations are usually a consequence of personal variables, such as age and income, not ecological variables, such as city size. Yet the compositional description of urban life is not entirely correct; many features emphasized by Wirth and his associates are indeed especially common in urban locations, such as structural differentiation, the weakness of locality-based networks, intergroup conflict, deviance, and "social disorder." In sum, the compositional thesis is better but not wholly adequate.

The subcultural theory of urbanism in some ways synthesizes the two theories. The concentration of population has social psychological consequences, but not of the sort Wirth described. It nurtures distinctive subcultures, encouraging new ones to emerge and old ones to be strengthened. The subcultures in turn generate the "Wirthian" phenomena that compositionalists have the greatest difficulty explaining: deviance, social turmoil, intergroup conflict, and the splintering of the moral order. These result not from alienation, anomie, and normlessness, but from the growth of many diverse and divergent subcultures, each with its own moral order. At the same time, subcultural theory, along with compositional theory, predicts that intimate social relationships and psychic balance will persist in the urban setting. In short, subcultural theory subsumes the empirically correct predictions of the determinist and compositional theories but avoids their errors.

It does more. It accounts for other distinctive features of the urban experience. Locality-based groups—the community and neighborhood—are usually less cohesive and active in cities than in the countryside, because population concentration stimulates allegiances to subcultures based on more significant social traits. Intergroup suspicion and conflict arise in cities, even though city-dwellers are not especially hostile and expoitative personalities, because tensions result from the mingling of different moral systems in the city. And the subcultural model helps us understand what is unique about the *sub*urban experience.

To conclude that subcultural theory most fully explains urban social psychology is not to conclude that it has been demonstrated as true. Hardly. Many research issues remain gapingly open, and still others are raised by the theory itself. Many of the empirical generalizations presented in this book are based on limited research. Among the topics needing deeper study are the relationship of urbanism to personality types and problems; the specific features of primary relationships altered by urbanism; the sorts of unconventional behaviors that typify large communities and the kinds of people who engage in them; and the relative importance of social-versus-impersonal support for individuals across communities. Few of the key propositions considered in this book have been fully investigated.

The subcultural approach stimulates questions like these: Along what lines do subcultures vary? What size critical mass is necessary for which features of subcultures? What kinds of individuals are tied to more than one subculture, and how do they manage their lives in separate social worlds? How much do communication and transportation technologies mitigate the need for population concentration? And, quite important, what means emerge in metropolitan communities to maintain a minimum, common moral order among their divergent subcultures—for example, what etiquettes reduce conflict among people, and what negotiation procedures are used to resolve disagreements among groups (Fischer, 1982d)? These queries only illustrate the common observation that, in the sciences, every answer raises yet more questions.[1]

Sociology is only one mode of apprehending the world. Another is collective folk experience, often expressed in cultural stereotypes. In Chapter 2, we considered four themes in Western culture dealing with urban life. On the evidence reviewed here, It would seem that those beliefs tend to be valid *descriptions* of experience, but misleading *explanations* of experience.

The first theme is the polarity of rural nature versus urban artifact. Cities do disrupt many natural processes, as in the pollution they produce; and they also generate the social and economic support necessary for the artifacts of civilization. But the social–psychological elements of the polarity are more problematic. Urbanites may be more "rational" than ruralites, but, if so, the difference probably results from their greater educational experience rather than greater urban experience. Urbanites may appear guileful, but that impression probably results from contacts between subcultures, rather than from personality.

The second popular theme is rural familiarity versus urban strangeness. The evidence supports this description in broad terms but amends it significantly. The important feature of urban encounters with strangers is that they involve meetings of different subcultures, with all that implies for uncomfortable or antagonistic interactions. And the strangeness of urban life—unknown persons, opportunities, thrills—does not supplant familiar experiences but *supplements* them. Some city people go beyond their small social circles to join in the wider, stranger urban scene; others, for instance, those Gans has called "urban villagers," rarely encounter those "foreign" worlds directly. But virtually all urbanites have their intimate milieus, so that their urban experience involves public strangeness as well as private familiarity.

Given the focus of this study, the most significant theme is that of rural community and cohesion versus urban individualism and alienation. At first glance, certain features of urban life seem to confirm this image: for example, the urban locality is less cohesive, and social ties are more geographically dispersed than in the countryside. But closer study reveals that this stereotype is in error; urbanites are involved in meaningful social worlds, in fact, in a great variety of them. This theme would be more accurate if phrased as the unity of rural commun*ity* versus the multiplicity of urban commun*ities*. The individualism of urban life, such as it is, is not one of solitary freedom and despairing alienation, but rather one involving the personal choice of communities and the singular expressions of those social worlds.[2]

The fourth and final theme is rural traditionality versus urban innovation. This is, in great measure, an accurate picture. To be sure, tradition frequently persists in the heart of urban areas, as in ethnic enclaves, and change does occur in rural areas, as in agrarian uprisings; thus it is an exaggerated picture. Nevertheless, deviance, nontraditionalism, and change are disproportionately spawned in urban environments. Our investigation qualifies the stereotype by suggesting that beneficial innovation and destructive deviance may be two sides of the same urban coin; they are produced by the same forces. Despite our best efforts, there may remain an irreducible amount of "bad" changes that accompany the "good" ones generated in cities, and vice versa.

Thus, it appears that the cultural themes about urban life are at least superficially true. The rural youth journeying to the great metropolis would, in general, experience a more artificial environment, "a world of strangers" and strangeness, a milieu of *seemingly* estranged and normless individuals, and frequent encounters with novel and perhaps threatening behavior. These urban experiences are predicted by folk sociology, which thus serves its purpose well. That is, cultural beliefs are constantly being tested against common experience; in most cases, they should be, as general rules of thumb, correct. But they are also frequently mistaken in particular and systematic ways indicated by a scientific sociology.[3]

These systematic errors perpetuate biases about urban life that research indicates are not true, particularly the belief that cities produce social isolation, amorality, and psychological disorder. Two sources of bias involve perceptual distortion. One is the habit of believing in the concrete and visible and disbelieving in the existence of the abstract and unapparent. So, for example, urbanites appear to be friendless partly because their friends tend to be geographically dispersed and so, not visible. Ethnocentricism is another source of perceptual bias. We tend to interpret the behavior of strangers in terms of our own cultural standards, so that we often decide that strangers who do something we find immoral or offensive must be immoral or offensive people, when they may be acting quite properly according to the standards of their own culture.

Other biases arise from the way folk explanations develop. They tend simply to be deterministic: If city people act a certain way, it is because cities make them be that way. Such explanations are often blind to the subtler processes at work—the fact that urbanites may live at a faster pace than ruralites because they more often hold high-pressure jobs, for example, or that urbanites tend to live alone because unmarried people choose to live in cities. (This is the problem of "spurious correlation.") Another bias in popular explanations is attributing the actions of other people to their personalities but attributing our own behavior to external circumstances. For example, we might interpret formality by a stranger in a public place as a product of his or her unsociability, but we see our own formality as simply appropriate to a public setting.

In these ways, the cultural themes about the urban experience turn out to be a complex and fascinating mélange of roughly correct observations and systematically erroneous interpretations. In sociological research, the actual state of affairs is usually found to be much more complex than our preconceptions lead us to believe; this clearly holds for the urban experience.

In the United States, one of those "roughly correct observations" has had serious effects on individual behavior and political decisions. American cities are seen—and rightly so—as places of great criminal violence. This observation has greatly influenced the American perspective on cities and the national dialogue on urban politics.[4] The violence has been attributed to the nature of urban life itself. This explanation is in error; great metropolises in economically advanced nations around the world are quite safe places in which to live (although their nonviolent crime rates may be relatively high). American urban violence is an aberration of the society much more than of its cities. Yet it is hard for people to think about urbanism in this country without having such a thought chased out of their minds by just plain fear. The observation makes explanation difficult.

PROSPECTS OF THE URBAN FUTURE

Where do we go from here? The thumbnail history of cities presented in Chapter 1 pointed out that cities are relatively new and that large metropolises are unprecedented in the development of the human species. We are now speeding toward an urban future that has outlines we can only vaguely discern and human consequences we can barely guess at. Nevertheless, let us conjecture. Drawing on our knowledge of the contemporary urban experience, what might future urbanism be like, and what sorts of urban experience might result?

Sober statistical projections have yielded startling predictions. These projections essentially extrapolate the history of the last few decades into the next few. Using such procedures, Kingsley Davis estimated in 1972 that by the year 2000 about 25 percent of the people in the world would live in cities of over one million (at that time, only 12 percent lived in such cities), and that there would be three metropolises of more than 64,000,000 people each and one of more than 100,000,000 (in 1980, the wider New York area contained only about 16,000,000). Projections made for the United States by Jerome Pickard (1972) indicated that its metropolitan population would grow from 71 percent to 85 percent of the nation by the year 2000. The wider Los Angeles region would expand from 10,000,000 to about 22,000,000, and the New York region to about 25,000,000. Many zeroes.

Valuable as they are, these projections are inevitably limited in at least two ways. They cannot incorporate into the calculations the political, technological, or cultural events that push the future out of the trajectory set for it by the past. Unanticipated changes in trajectory have already cast doubt on the projections. World population growth has slown down a bit (Nossiter, 1980). In the developed nations, including the United States, metropolitan populations have actually shrunk relative to nonmetropolitan ones—opposite to these predictions (see Chapter 4). The New York region, for example, lost 5 percent of its residents in the 1970s (BOC, 1982a: 20). Even if the trend toward metropolitanization were to resume in the late 1980s, which is unlikely (Long and DeAre, 1982a; 1982b), this fluctuation testifies to the precarious fortunes of fortune-telling.

These projections are also limited in their ability to anticipate the shape and structure of the cities of the future. A set of predictions about the future of Western cities [drawn in part from Wurster (1963) and Chinoy (1973)] is presented schematically in Figure 13, together with representations of the urban past and present. In these drawings the height of the curve indicates population concentration, and the total area under the curve represents total population. The preindustrial, walled city was small and the populace within it highly concentrated. The modern metropolis is larger in area and population but is not as concentrated. The remaining figures illustrate possible future shapes of the metropolis, ranging from the most to the least concentrated.

It is the supercity that most captivates novelists, film producers, and authors of "pop" sociology: All the world is Manhattan magnified; families share tiny apartments within colossal buildings; and congestion's ill effects are multiplied. There are circumstances that might conceivably produce such a situation, but they are unlikely.[5] Trends in this century have been in the opposite direction—toward deconcentration—for at least 80 years.

Some have predicted a more modest reversal of the deconcentration process based on recent social changes, especially the increase in working wives, the drop in the birth rate, and the rise in

Figure 13

SCHEMATIC ILLUSTRATIONS OF URBAN PASTS AND POSSIBLE FUTURES

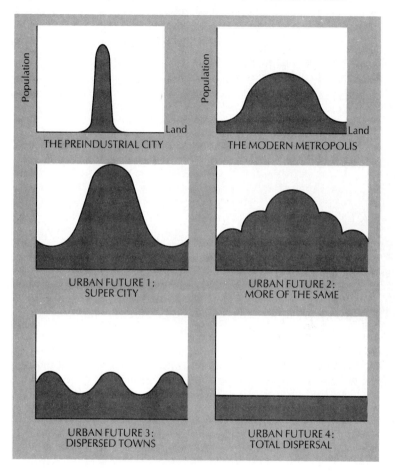

energy costs (Alonso, 1980). These kinds of changes should encourage centralized apartment living. But to date, decentralization continues, and the new apartment living is happening in the suburbs and beyond.

At the other end of the spectrum is a future (Figure 13: Urban Future 4), Total Dispersal, called the "Post-City Age" by Melvin

Webber (1968b, 1963). Advances in communications and transportation technology will eliminate the presumed purpose of cities, which is the facilitation of social interaction and exchange (Abler, 1975; Meier, 1962). Physical proximity will be unnecessary to achieve these ends because proximity through computer links and 500-mile-per-hour personal vehicles will suffice. Webber (1973: 301) forecasts:

> For the first time in history, it might be possible to locate on a mountain top and to maintain intimate, real-time, and realistic contact with business or other associates. All persons tapped into the global communication net would have ties approximating those used today in a given metropolitan region.
>
> I am guessing that early in the next century, settlement patterns will be spread broadly over the continental surface, localized at those places where the climate and landscape are pleasant.[6]

This urban future, an electronic web of households and small settlements laid lightly over the land, would be a radical departure from the urban past, for, in essence, it would be a *non*urban future, indeed a "post-city age." Without any major differentiations in population density across the inhabited landscape, there would be no cities. The urban experience would simply be a metaphor for certain ways of life thought to have been prevalent in those extinct communities. (This would not be the first time in human history that cities had declined; but earlier instances, such as after the fall of the Roman Empire, have followed a civilization's collapse, rather than an advance in technology.)

The city will probably not come to an end in the foreseeable future. For one, it is doubtful that the necessary technology will develop or be available to any but the affluent. There is more fundamental doubt: Can electronic communication supplemented by occasional visits adequately substitute for casual, in-person interaction? And can the friction of space involved in transporting objects really be brought to zero? Experiments are being conducted to determine whether television, conference calls, "videophones," and computer link-ups can substitute for business transactions, audience participation, and social interaction. We know from our own experience with the telephone that such techniques do shrink distances. But to the extent that there remain circumstances in which in-person contacts are more efficient or more satisfying than electronic ones, and to the extent that nearer still remains easier than farther, population concentration will continue. If, someday, these conditions are removed, humankind may indeed see a nonurban world. The deconcentration of the American population points in that direction, but we have a long way yet to go (if we get there at all).

Two more probable futures are cautious extrapolations of current trends. In More of the Same (Figure 13: Urban Future 2), modern metropolises continue to expand, especially in area. At the fringes, sprawling suburbs of different cities meld into one another; inner suburban areas build up with apartment houses; center cities continue to decline. Small subconcentrations of industry, business, and apartments develop in the outer areas (Muller, 1981). Dispersed Towns (Figure 13: Urban Future 3) is an intriguing variation on the dispersal pattern. Here the spreading metropolis breaks up into modest-sized towns or small cities, perhaps separated by open space and parkland, and connected by high-speed rail and highway. The old center city might continue as the nucleus of the region but would no longer dominate the area, for the towns would be largely self-sufficient. People would live at densities between those of contemporary suburbs and those of contemporary cities. Most important, they would live in communities of relatively modest size. [Two specific variations on this future are that the towns are either, one, economically and demographically similar and autonomous; or two, specialized and functionally integrated (Wurster, 1963).] We may be seeing early signs of "dispersed towns" in the form of suburban shopping malls and commercial and industrial parks.

These speculations are restricted to the economically advanced nations of the world. Any forecast at all for the developing and impoverished nations of the world—other than, perhaps, catastrophe—would be even more daring. Current urbanization in the developing nations is in some respects like that which took place in the West between 1880 and 1920. But some experts have stressed ways in which it is critically different. For one, urbanization in the Third World is outrunning the development of an economic base for it; instead of rural workers being attracted to the city by available jobs, they are coming to cities that have high rates of unemployment. Second, urban growth in developing nations is happening at a much more rapid pace than it did in the West. Third, and quite important, most of the urban growth in these nations is a result not of migration, but of the general population explosion. That is, cities and rural populations are both growing rapidly through natural increase; both are threatened by economic collapse and famine (Davis, 1966, 1972; Hawley, 1981: Chapter 12; Breese, 1969). The hope is that these nations will recapitulate Western history in two respects: a drop in the birth rate and an increase in agricultural productivity. Should these occur—there are glimmers of hope—and the present crisis be survived, then a "normal" modernization and urbanization, in which the population shifts from rural to urban areas, could occur (Davis, 1972). In that case, the urban future of the developing nations may look like a delayed version of that facing the developed nations today.

Let us return to speculate on the social consequences of the most likely future for modern cities, a future of continued modest dispersal. To consider the consequences of changes in urbanism alone, we will adopt the unrealistic but useful assumption that no other social changes are going on.

The greatest effects of further population dispersal will be in the ecological structure and size of metropolitan areas. Housing patterns will probably tend toward clustered, low-rise housing. Noise and dirt pollution will probably decrease at the points of higher concentration; whether pollution of all kinds declines or increases depends on whether dispersal leads to concentration in towns or to a more sprawling pattern that requires a great deal of automotive transportation. These changes, in general, should satisfy popular tastes. But one cost will be a modest reduction in the number and, especially, the variety of available services.

Based on what we have learned about the consequences of population concentration, the social changes accompanying further dispersal will be much more modest. Differences within communities in ages, incomes, and other traits of their residents will diminish; differences among communities might increase; economic activity and leisure pursuits will probably become more alike in various places; and the crime level will probably drop by a noticeable (though not great) degree. The cohesion and importance of locally based social groups—the community and the neighborhood—will likely increase at the expense of those founded on other bases of similarity, particularly occupation and life-style. (This prediction is contingent on communications technology not making the wonderous advances predicted for it; if it does, the trend will perhaps be reversed.)

In the personal realm, the changes are likely to be slighter. People will probably be neither more nor less integrated into primary social groups. There may be some minor changes in personal relationships; for example, family activities may expand. At most, there should be only marginal changes in personality, states of mind, or behavioral styles. For the mainstream citizen, these would include greater satisfaction with the new communities, a greater sense of belonging to the community, and less unease about strangers—the latter a consequence of fewer unconventional subcultures and greater spatial segregation. These small improvements in the peace of mind of "average" people may be accompanied by a deterioration of this feeling for many "unconventional" persons, those whose subcultures will have been diminished.

Further dispersal is likely to reduce the variety and intensity of urban subcultures, but not of all subcultures equally. Those with access to media, communications, and transport (such as affluent professionals) will be hampered only slightly; those at the other end (such as working-class ethnics and youths) will be more deprived of supportive social worlds. The consequences of this decline in subcultural variety for the society as a whole would be modest diminution in innovation and change—both "good" and "bad" change.

These prediction are based on a number of "ifs"—if the urban future is one of further dispersal, if the analyses in this book are accurate, and if nothing else changes. Of course, other things will change. Although we cannot foretell what other developments will occur—in economics (like a depression), in technology (for instance, a cheaper automotive fuel), in politics (a war, perhaps), or in other realms—we can assume that their effects on social life and personality will usually outweigh the consequences of changes in ecological patterns. For example, greater affluence, leisure time, and access to sophisticated technology by the general public will probably stimulate subcultural diversity and intensity, in spite of physical dispersal. Our speculations have served largely as a device for isolating the social–psychological consequences that urban developments, by themselves, would bring. We turn next to policies designed to shape their urban future.

POLICIES

In this section, we consider two related but distinct issues: urban policies and policies affecting urban people. The first refers to programs that would seek to alter urbanization—the size of cities, the distribution of the population within the metropolis, housing patterns, and so on. The second refers to social policies that would directly affect urbanites and dwellers in other areas as well— programs designed to reduce crime rates or increase housing, for example. A confusion between the two often results because of muddled use of the term "urban problems." The misconception exists that various social ills are found exclusively or primarily in cities, or that they are generated by city life. For some of these problems, as we have seen, even the simpler of these assumptions is mistaken: for example, poverty is more widespread in rural than in urban areas. The problems that are disproportionately found in cities are rarely caused by urbanism, and when urbanism is a contributing factor—as in crime or group conflict—it is not a major cause. In any case, virtually all so-called urban problems are also found in nonurban areas. This confusion between urban policies and policies affecting urban people intrudes itself into the formulation of specific programs, as we shall see immediately.

One of the topics recurring among planners has been the quest for the "optimal city size": the size at which the optimal mix of urban benefits and urban costs is to be found—the highest possible level of productivity, culture, and services at the lowest commensurate level of congestion, pollution, and crime (Sale, 1978; Dahl, 1967; Spengler, 1967). Once researchers have identified this best of all possible urban worlds, policy makers could design strategies to encourage the growth of cities that are now too small and the shrinkage of those that are now too large.

But most scholars seem convinced, to quote a British economist, that "the search for an optimal city size is almost as idle as the quest for the philosophers' stone" (H. L. Richardson, 1973: 131). The entire speculation is misconceived on several grounds. First, no substantial empirical findings point to a city size at which any "good"—income or innovation or governmental efficiency—is consistently maximized; or any "bad"—crime or pollution—is consistently minimized. (That is, a size that is "best" in different times and societies.[7]) In fact, some data suggest that for economic purposes an optimal city size would be larger than any we now have. We have certainly not identified an optimal size for any social–psychological variable in this book. Even if such ideals could be found, they would probably not be the same for various social goods. The size that maximizes residents' personal incomes would differ from that which maximizes their artistic creativity, or that which minimizes pollution, and so on. And how much culture is worth how many muggings, how much pollution for how much income? It would be surely be a vain task to try to sum up all these various "goods" and "bads" into a single measure.[8]

A related difficulty is deciding what it is about a social product we wish to optimize: its best, worst, or average. Do we want a nation in which each community's citizens have access to a mid-dling-good art museum, or a nation in which a few, large communities have great art museums? Do we want a nation in which everyone runs an average risk of being assaulted or one in which many run low risks and a few run great risks? Another critique is similar, but more fundamental and, ultimately, political: What is optimal for one group is unlikely to be optimal for another, and what is optimal for the "average" group is likely to be optimal for no real group at all. The optimal number of library books, ethnic taverns, discothèques, or level of traffic may suit the "average" person, but will it suit the scholar, the blue-collar worker, the adolescent, or the elderly person with a heart condition?

Finally, urbanists have been quick to point out that the economic structure of a nation depends on having a hierarchy of cities of various sizes. Small cities serve particular purposes—for example, functioning as commercial centers for agricultural regions; and large metropolises serve others—for example, national financial operations. It is quite improbable that a nation could standardize the size of its cities without suffering acute economic disruption. Similarly, a range of sizes makes it possible to satisfy a range of tastes (Price, 1978). For all these reasons, the notion of an optimal city size is a myth.

Many concede that an optimal size is a pipe dream, but they are convinced that contemporary metropolises are too large and that national policy should divert population from the most-populated to the least-populated areas. This has long been the policy in several European countries; it is favored by many American leaders, and it is endorsed by a majority of American citizens.[9] The underlying belief is that great size produces social ills; reducing urban size would alleviate those ills.[10]

Several European nations, including Britain, France, and Sweden, have pursued major "regional growth" policies. Through a variety of techniques ranging from tax credits to legal injunctions, they have tried to direct industrial development—and, thus, the jobs that attract people—away from heavily populated areas, such as the London, Paris, and Stockholm regions to places that have been losing people. Though it is difficult to judge, these policies may have helped stop urban growth and encouraged outward migration; how much is unclear (see Chapter 4 and Lichtenberger, 1976: 97–98). It is even more difficult to judge whether a net social benefit in lowered urban congestion or increased rural employment has actually been achieved. These policies are, nevertheless, very popular and politically secure (Sundquist, 1975).

In addition, the British have pursued a policy of constructing "New Towns" to help stem the growth of the large "conurbations," especially London. (On the continent, the so-called New Towns are largely suburban housing developments on the outskirts of major cities.) To reach this end, the British communities were planned to be self-contained small cities independent of the metropolis, to be sited at a distance from the centers the planners hoped (in vain) would be too far from commuting. Governmental pressure was exerted on industries to locate in the New Towns. And applicants for public housing were given preference if they were willing to move to New Towns and could fill jobs in New-Town industries.

Despite these strenuous and costly efforts, the New Town policy seems to have had mixed success. Many Britons have received needed quality housing; much as been learned about urban design and planning; and residents' experiences in the New Towns appear to be—after a difficult transition period labeled the "New-Town Blues"—a relatively pleasant one, not unlike life in an American working-class suburb. But the goal of self-containment has not really been met. The New Towns are only slightly more economically independent than are comparable unplanned communities, and the most successful ones seem to be those conveniently linked to London. Furthermore, New Towns have apparently not seriously slowed the pace of metropolitan expansion or the size of the large cities or the social problems that presumably result from "overurbanization." The British program is, in sum, mostly a successful way of controlling suburban sprawl and concentrating ex-urban growth.[11] (Two American experiments in New Towns were aborted, one by World War II and another by unexpected costs in the 1970s.[12])

There seemed, in the 1970s, a few good reasons for supporting a policy of deurbanization in the United States: It would assist those rural places that for so long lost so many of their young and productive residents, places that could no longer support vital services. Deurbanization might ease congestion in the center cities, both physical congestion and strain on social services; and it would satisfy the popular preference for redistribution, a preference that has been expressed in party platforms and governmental declarations (Sundquist, 1975; Elgin et al., 1974; Mazie and Rawlings, 1972). An inadequate but oft-cited reason for population dispersal is that it would improve social relations and ease psychic tensions among the American people. In view of the evidence we have reviewed here, that is quite unlikely. Redistribution might decrease crime rates (Clinard, 1978) and group conflict, but it would take a massive amount of migration to produce even a modest improvement in this regard (Alonso, 1970, 1975; Whyte, 1968).

There were also a few good reasons to oppose such a policy. For one, population dispersal had already started. Within American metropolitan areas, people have been dispersing outward from the center city for decades; among metropolitan areas, the largest ones have been losing ground to the smaller ones since at least 1940; and now, since about 1970, population has been shifting slightly toward nonmetropolitan areas (see Chapter 4). Second, there are serious doubts about the practicality of such a policy. The cost—in tax credits, subsidies, construction, economic dislocations, and inefficiencies—would be great and the effects are likely to be small. Third, given such expenditures, there are more efficient ways to ameliorate social problems. In fact, population redistribution is probably the most indirect and inefficient method possible to cure social ills. Instead, direct and cheaper efforts could be made to treat the problems. For pollution, taxes or fines could be imposed; for housing, rehabilitation of dwellings is reasonable; and so on.[13] Finally, for Americans' preferences for smaller communities, we should not overestimate their coherence and meaning. Opinion polls commonly express a popular ideal that few would actually do much about (Carpenter, 1977b). The distaste people express for city life is often just a way of objecting to contemporary social problems, especially to crime (Silverman, 1982). And people's rejection of cities is to a great degree a product of those problems—problems that advocates of dispersal say we should not waste money on because Americans want to leave the cities; that is, the public-opinion argument tends to be circular.

In the 1980s, in any case, the question Americans face is quite the opposite: Should the United States try to *stop* urban deconcentration? Businesses and people left the major center cities in droves during the 1970s—especially manufacturing businesses and middle-class people from northeastern cities—leaving behind fiscally and socially distressed urban cores. The debate over what, if anything, should be done depends greatly on how that deconcentration is explained. One point of view was expressed by President Carter's Commission for a National Agenda for the Eighties (1980: 100): Deconcentration has been a long-term, natural process based on "the near immutability of technological, economic, social, and demographic trends." Improvements in transport, communications, construction, and manufacturing make it reasonable for businesses to invest in the urban periphery and for people to find spacious homes there. In the coming "postindustrial" society, core cities will play a smaller role than they do now, as specialized centers for administration, culture, tourism, and the like. The government should not resist this inevitable change by trying to revitalize the big cities, but should instead help make the transition smoother and more equitable, most notably by aiding low-income city-dwellers to also move out to places where the jobs have moved.[14]

The opposite view is that deconcentration has hardly been natural, but was instead produced by decades of governmental policies. These policies include subsidization of highways (but not mass transit), agricultural assistance, regulation of the transportation and communication industries (which holds down costs in smaller communities), public works projects (that, like dams, disproportionately aid outlying areas), a free hand to local developers, financial aid to build new utility services (but not to repair old ones), and most especially, tax breaks. The Federal Tax Code has provided business with major incentives to build new plants on new land rather than to modernize old urban ones. And through the mortgage deduction on income taxes, American governments have made it much easier for middle-class people to own homes rather than to rent—indeed, has made it irrational for people in a high tax bracket not to own. Because new homes to satisfy the demand are likely to be built on the city outskirts, this, too, has encouraged suburbanization. True, the critics admit, in recent years the federal government targeted some aid to the center cities; but it was far too little and too late, they say, to make up for past policies. [In 1980, for example, the federal tax loss for the homeowners' mortgage deduction alone, $15.6 billion, was 50 percent greater than the combined federal spending for urban mass transit, community development, urban renewal, and housing assistance (BOC, 1982a: 254, 282).] In sum, if governmental policy ravaged the inner city by encouraging deconcentration, a substantial reversal of governmental policy could revive the city and the fortunes of its residents. The resulting residential and mixed-use city would, in fact, be more "natural."[15]

The experience of Western European cities suggests that there is weight on both sides of the argument. Urban areas there have also deconcentrated, and that must fundamentally have resulted from technological and economic forces. Still, deconcentration in the United States seems to be different—faster, larger, more cataclysmic, more sprawling, and more selective (e.g., decentralization here tends to remove the affluent from the core more than it does in Europe). These American traits might well be caused by policy and politics rather than "nature." If so, then a change in policy might restore some city–suburban balance, slow down the rate of deconcentration so that communities could adapt to it, and channel the outward growth in more efficient and equitable ways.

The deconcentration argument also touches on other contemporary debates. One is over gentrification (see pp. 249–252). Should the government sponsor private rehabilitation of the inner city as a way of helping bring back middle-class consumers, taxpayers, citizens, and students? Or should the government resist gentrification to prevent displacement of poor residents from their inexpensive, even if run-down, homes? Or neither? Another policy argument is over growth limits along the urban periphery. Such limits, at least in theory, should lead to more efficient, denser use of land, yet preserve open space for all. Yet in practice, critics claim, growth limits block new housing except for the rich and lead to less efficient building practices (Frieden, 1979).

Issues of growth, dispersal, and spatial policies have a quite different meaning in the developing Third-World nations. There the concern is whether the cities are "overurbanized" or "underindustrialized"—have too many people for the economic base (Kentor, 1981). Most policy makers seem to think so (even if academics are not so sure) and have instituted programs of varying severity to restrict rural-to-urban migration. In general, these policies have not stopped or significantly slowed urbanization, even in the most controlled societies such as China.[16] How much effort, if any, should be made to discourage Third-World urbanization?

Many of the preceding comments have been skeptical of policies directed to effecting social change by altering settlement patterns and population distribution (such as pressing for an optimal size). But we should not leave the impression that there can be no useful urban programs. On the contrary, much can be done to promote the efficient use of urban land, plan the growth of metropolitan areas, provide attractive and convenient low-income housing, assist rural people to obtain needed services, and generally manage the social consequences resulting from the interaction of population and space.

One issue in particular, originally raised in Chapter 9, should be noted: the political organization of metropolitan areas, in the United States. The American system of small, independent, and powerful municipalities has certainly contributed to the special problems of the inner city. In late 1975, New York City was about to go broke. Although its politicians may have done much to bring on the crisis, its fundamental problem is one almost all the major center cities face: the people and institutions that cost money are largely within the city lines; the people and institutions that can pay taxes are largely outside the city lines in the hundreds of municipalities surrounding it (Wood, 1961; Hall, 1977: 200–203). The writer Jimmy Breslin put the problem forcefully:

> The official policy of New York was to deny food or housing to
> no one. . . . From this our troubles came. New York lost jobs
> and gained people who needed jobs. Crime rose and the

schools fell and more whites fled. And now suddenly every-
body screams in horror: The city cannot pay its bills. Of course
the city cannot pay its bills. Is not a house of the poor always
poor? [*New York Times,* 20 August 1975]

Suburban municipalities can attract affluent residents through
zoning and land-development regulation, but exclude low-income
people. Through independent taxing and spending powers, they
can provide their citizens with quality middle-class services,
schools, and recreational facilities at relatively low tax rates. Their
wealthy tax base and open land also allow suburban townships to
attract modern industries that provide well-paying jobs.[17] Meanwhile, the escalating costs of maintaining an urban center increasingly in need of major capital improvements (e.g., repaving streets),
of housing low-income families who need special services, and of
sustaining cultural institutions, such as museums (which are also
used by suburbanites), are shunted to the downtown municipality.
And that municipality is rapidly losing the resources necessary to
fulfill those functions, which in turn further erodes its economic
base (Cummings, 1981). This is indeed an *urban* problem: a
fenced-in and decaying core, surrounded by exclusive, "beggar-
thy-neighbor" suburbs. (This injures not only the old center cities,
but suburban towns that fall behind in the competition for exclusivity as well.)

Urban policies directed at altering this political structure, such
as metropolitan government, would probably have notable effects
on a variety of problems. Of course, there are good arguments
against metropolitan government, as well. Pursuing the democratic
goal of individual participation in the community and "community
control" would lead us to an opposite policy: decentralization of
power and the dispersal of meaningful rights and responsibilities to
local territorial groups. The problems mentioned previously would
probably then be exacerbated. Each policy has its own benefits and
its own costs.

The localism of American government works together with
American laissez-faire attitudes about land to produce the familiar
metropolitan sprawl. To reiterate a point made by David Popenoe
(see this volume, p. 50), in the U.S., unlike most of the modern
world, peoples' use of land is largely beyond the control of the
community, beyond any effort to use it for the common good. Thus,

Americans as individuals do as they wish, largely leaving government—that is, Americans as a group—to pick up the pieces: provide schools, sewage, and police for new subdevelopments; pay social costs for the unemployed left behind by departing businesses; manage traffic congestion caused by new office buildings or shopping malls; and so on (Popenoe, 1979; Mollenkopf, 1981; Gottdeiner, 1977). Elsewhere, there are at least some planning controls that help coordinate land uses and reduce the damage to the public of private decisions (Berry, 1976a; Popenoe, 1980; Hall, 1977). The costs of government "over-regulation" are obvious and onerous; the costs of nonregulation are typically less obvious but even more onerous.

In the late twentieth century, the American city is in a unique crisis. Urban life was certainly worse in earlier times, but it usually was still better than life in the countryside. Today, urban life's relative advantages, typically economic ones, are shrinking, and its relative disadvantages, such as crime, are growing. Perhaps this is, as some argue, "natural" and we are seeing the expected end of the great urban center. But perhaps it is not and need not be so. The urban policies we adopt will determine the kind of city that emerges from the current dark era.

In the final analysis, no urban policy—that is, no policy that seeks to manipulate physical environment and spatial distribution—will have as sizable an effect on our critical social problems as would policies directed specifically at those problems. Or, as the President's Commission (1980) put it, "people-oriented" policies are likely to be more effective than "place-oriented" ones. Arguments that stress "urban" solutions to such problems as pollution, poverty, and crime are usually misinformed, visionary, and, ultimately, temporizing.

Straightforward solutions to those problems often exist, and we do not need to be sociologists to recognize them. Whether the need is to reduce pollution, poverty, crime, political disaffection, or whatever, relief is most likely to come from redistributing income, power, and social responsibility. Yet these solutions have their own costs. The difficulty in social problems is less often a technological one of finding solutions than a political one of deciding among alternate costs and who shall pay them. (This usually seems to be the case when sociologists are called upon for answers; what people really want is a magic solution that will cost no one.) The "urban crisis" is thus less a crisis in need of answers than a crisis in need of choices. While we await these choices, we must often listen to a lot of distracting and temporizing speculations about urbanism and the "decline of community."

Having said my piece about social policy and the urban experience, I will end with a few comments about the policies of people in their personal lives. The truths sociology uncovers are truths about people in general, and, as such, they are not all true for any specific person. So it is with the findings and conclusions of this book. Even when we considered specific categories of people—such as the young, or housewives, or blacks—none of the generalizations we made are valid for each member of these social categories. The individual is just that: individual in history, interests, and preferences. So, ultimately, each person must make choices founded on unique needs and desires. Some will seek and enjoy less of the urban experience; others will prefer and thrive on more of the urban experience. I hope that this book will help make these choices better informed, and that we will share a society in which each individual has the freedom to make such a choice.

NOTES

Chapter 1
Introduction: An Overview

1. General histories of urbanization include Hawley (1981), Sjoberg (1960), Mumford (1961), and Childe (1951).

2. Popular examples include Ardrey (1966) and Morris (1969). Even as serious a scholar as Kingsley Davis (1973) has worried that man's genetic heritage may be unable to adjust to cities.

3. This interpretation of "urban" is neither self-evident nor universally accepted, and a portion of the next chapter will be devoted to arguing the question. I note here only that we have other ways of defining the term, with different implications for the proper study of the issue. For instance, some scholars (e.g., Castells, 1968) believe that urbanism is so fundamentally intertwined with modernization or industrialization that the only truly "rural" communities are those completely isolated from modern influences. Since according to this view "urban" refers to general economic and cultural attributes, a modern nation such as the United States is, for all essential purposes, urban throughout. (That is, virtually all Americans watch television, buy mass-produced goods, and so on.) The resulting implication is that comparing urban and rural places and people is a vacuous exercise for no rural is left (e.g., Firey, Loomis, and Beegle, 1957). In another related view (e.g., Riessman, 1964; Greer, 1962), urbanism is not a property that communities have in greater or lesser degrees; communities are inevitably and fundamentally linked to each other. Instead, urbanism is a property of *societies*; they vary in their degree of urbanization (the scale of their institutions), and that has consequences for their communities. Had I adopted either of these positions, or other variations, the investigation in this book would have proceeded far differently. But I firmly believe that communities do form distinct entities, and, as set forth in Chapter 2, that urbanism is best defined by population size. [Further discussion appears in Fischer (1975a). See, also, Reiss (1959a); Arensberg (1965)].

4. This question, whether differences between urban and rural people are a result of urbanism—population concentration—itself, becomes a refrain throughout the book for several reasons: First, popular beliefs about urban life are basically concerned with this issue. Even casual comments on urban ways usually imply that the phenomena are inherent and inescapable concomitants of just living in the city (e.g., see Hummon, 1980). Second, social scientists' interest in urbanism derives mainly from the city's intrinsic quality of scale, a quality that means that studies of urbanism might yield lessons applicable to modern society as a whole. Third, many features common to cities of our time (such as bureaucracies and subordination to a national state) are not common to cities in other cultures and historical periods. Any effort to make generalizations about city life from these heterogeneous cases must examine the concomitants of the elementary constant in all these specific instances: population concentration. Fourth, to construct urban policy, we must determine which specific causes produce which specific effects. Is crime, for example, inevitably associated with population concentration, or does it appear disproportionately in modern American cities because of other special conditions in those cities?

5. A few authorities in the field have argued that any effort to generalize about urban life that is valid cross-culturally and historically is misguided. In particular they contend that the ways of life in preindustrial and industrial cities are qualitatively

distinct (Sjoberg, 1960; Reissman, 1964). I will nevertheless move ahead with my analyses and, by the end of the book, I will have proposed a few universal generalizations.

6. See Lapidus (1966, 1969), Abu-Lughod (1971), and Blake and Lawless (1980).

7. For a sample of general historical and cross-cultural discussions of urbanism, see Sjoberg (1960), Mumford (1961), Southall (1973a), Davis (1973), Callow (1973), Hull (1976), and Handlin and Buchard (1963). Several authors have presented historical typologies of cities, among them Sjoberg (1960, 1965a), Arensberg (1968b), and Redfield and Singer (1954).

Chapter 2
Images of City Life: Popular Views and Sociological Theories

1. A general source of ancient, classical, and renaissance views of urban–rural differences is Sorokin, Zimmerman, and Galpin (1930).

2. Regular reading of the *New York Times* yields a steady supply of introspective reflections, such as Burgess', on the city. We might also consider the New York movie. In an earlier cinematographic era, it portrayed dancing in the streets (*Singin' in the Rain*), frolicking in the grass (*Barefoot in the Park*), and the metropolis as one huge, joyful playground (*A Thousand Clowns*). Recent films have employed a sad, violent, and brutalizing New York as a vehicle for exhibiting the ills of modern life (*Midnight Cowboy, Little Murders, Death Wish, Escape from New York*, etc.). On the changing trend, see the *Times*'s film critic, Vincent Canby (1974).

3. Others have suggested alternate schemes, and similar discussions appear in White and White (1962), Schorske (1963), and Strauss (1961). For an analysis of these themes as reflected in the views of the general public, see Hummon (1980).

4. On the use of the urban–rural theme to comprehend society and modernity, see, for example, Williams (1973), Bender (1978), Weber (1976), and Gusfield (1975).

5. This finding has been and continues to be duplicated repeatedly, most often in surveys by Harris (Louis Harris Assoc., 1979) and Gallup organizations [see the *Gallup Opinion Index* (GOI)], as well as by more academic studies (e.g., Zuiches, 1981; Fuguitt and Zuiches, 1973; DeJong and Sell, 1977; and Carpenter, 1977a). But its meaning is a bit vague because people are often unclear about what a "city," or "suburb," etc., is (see n.9, this chapter).

6. *San Francisco Examiner*, 27 November 1978.

7. See, also, Fuguitt and Zuiches (1973), Mazie and Rawlings (1972), and Fischer (1973b).

8. Gallup Poll, "Urban Residents Who Want Out," cited in *San Francisco Chronicle*, 10 April 1981. A 1977 poll indicated that the larger the community, the less likely it was that residents expected to still be there five years hence ("A Populace On the Move," *San Francisco Chronicle*, 28 February 1977).

9. In analyses of the northern California survey data, Carol Silverman (1982) found that people living in the same places differed about whether that community was a "large city" or not depending in part on how much crime they perceived there.

10. For surveys on what people believe about cities and towns, see Louis Harris Assoc. (1979), Blackwood and Carpenter (1978: Table 6), and Baldassare (1982b). For a deeper analysis, see Hummon (1980).

11. Various studies highlight the characteristics of those less hostile to cities: GOI (1973, 94: 31), Zuiches and Fuguitt (1972), Louis Harris Assoc. (1979: 73), Mazie and Rawlings (1972), Cantor (1975), Zelan (1968), Bell (1959), and Dionne (1977).

12. In this regard, a survey of New Yorkers revealed that well-to-do residents of

the city were much more likely to be living there out of "free choice" than were the less economically fortunate. Forty-five percent of blue-collar workers said they had no alternative but to live in the city (Lynn, 1974: 18). See, also, Mazie and Rawlings (1972), Louis Harris Assoc. (1979: 93), and Carpenter (1977a).

13. A prior issue is the epistemological utility of the concept of urban, however it is defined. The challenge is presented, for example, by Castells (1968, 1969). See the discussion in Fischer (1975a).

14. A technical concept that comes close to capturing this definition is "population potential" (Carrothers, 1956). The relativistic definition of "city" is actually not unusual. Webster's Collegiate Dictionary defines a city as "an inhabited place of greater size, population, or importance than a town or village." A town is defined as intermediate between city and village; a village intermediate between town and hamlet; and a hamlet as smaller than village.

15. Demographic definitions also have disadvantages, one of which is determining the boundary of the city or urban area: Where does suburb become countryside? Another is the opening it provides for unusual cases. Is a downtown where no one resides not part of a city? Finally, such a reductionist definition seems to lose some of the flavor associated with the term *city*. In contrast, the other types of definitions seem to capture some of the meanings of city life as they have been expressed in Western culture. But the cost of making this connection is the sacrifice of scientific utility. For one, these definitions leave anomalous cases in limbo; for example, one author excludes from urban consideration the large settlements of the Incas, because they did not have writing (Sjoberg, 1960). Others exclude the large communities of precolonial West Africa because their economies were predominantly agricultural. More important, such definitions close off from investigation the relation among community traits. To define a city as a large settlement where certain activities occur is to preclude an inquiry into whether population size is related to those activities by asserting arbitrarily that it is. A preferable scientific procedure is to make a minimum number of restrictive assumptions and to permit a maximum number of empirical inquiries.

16. I am aware that this synopsis, based largely on Durkheim, does not do full justice to the classical sociological tradition. But it does highlight the basic features of modernization theories, particularly as they have influenced sociology.

17. The parallels are explicit. Simmel (1905: 47) wrote that "An inquiry into the inner meaning of specifically modern life . . . must seek to solve the equation which structures *like the metropolis* set up between the individual and super-individual contexts of life" (italics added). And Durkheim (1893: 299) held that "Insofar as the moral density of society is increased, it becomes similar to a great city which contains an entire people within its walls." Park's work is also explicit on this point.

18. Some have claimed that Park disagreed with Wirth's argument that urbanism leads to isolation and disorganization (e.g., Kasarda and Janowitz, 1974: 328). Park said many things, but few statements more succinctly state the thesis that Wirth championed than a passage in Park's 1916 paper: "It is probably the breaking down of local attachments and the weakening of the restraints and inhibitions of the primary group, under the influence of the urban environment, which are largely responsible for the increase of vice and crime in great cities [Park, 1916: 112]."

19. The following exposition summarizes a longer exegesis in Fischer (1972); another extended treatment is in R. Morris (1968).

20. Among the systematic adaptations Milgram lists as ways urbanites use to protect themselves from overload are attending less to any particular stimulus—for example, cutting short discussions with sales clerks when purchasing an item; ignoring low-priority demands (brushing aside beggars); blocking off intrusive stimulations (avoiding eye contact when walking through a crowd); filtering the intensity

of stimulations (using small talk to dilute any serious involvement with another person), and establishing mechanisms to divert unwanted inputs (employing a telephone answering machine). These various techniques separate people from others around them. People who adopt them become increasingly isolated and uninvolved, not only with respect to strangers, but ultimately from people they know.

21. They are said to "arise" only in the sense that communities that fail to employ them disintegrate.

22. Merton (1938a: 222–225) suggested an alternate branch in the argument that urban differentiation leads to anomie. According to his analysis, the visibility in the city of affluent life-styles raises aspirations among the general population—aspirations that will not be met in most cases. People suffering from this condition form a pool of potentially withdrawn, deviant, or rebellious urbanites.

23. Consequently, I have called this position "nonecological" (Fischer, 1975a, 1975b), a term modified from "non-materialist," used by Sjoberg (1965b). I should add that a number of ecological theories and approaches exist in urban sociology that compositionalists do not dispute—for example, those dealing with neighborhood succession. The ecological debate here speaks only to the issue of the social-psychological consequences of urbanism.

24. This is, of course, but a crude summary (see Castells, 1968, 1969, 1977; Harvey, 1973; Pickvance, 1974; Mellor, 1975; Molotch, 1979; and the collections of Pickvance, 1974 and Goering, 1978). For a defense of Wirth, see Fischer (1978a).

25. Wilkinson writes that

Save among isolated ethnic and religious enclaves, a few intentional communitarians, and some of the Native American groups, the European tradition of gemeinschaft has never fitted American communities. The time since settlement has been too short and the structural conditions were there too briefly to support the kind of interpenetration of lives and generations and the development of sacred bases of solidarity apparently necessary for gemeinschaft [1978: 118].

But compare Wilkinson's observation with that of Wolf (1976: 155ff), Bender (1978), and Nugent (1981).

26. The concept of subculture is sufficiently controversial (Clarke, 1974; Valentine, 1968: 103–114) to warrant further comment. Subcultures, as I see them, are composed of two parts: a "subsystem"—a set of interconnected social networks (in a sense, overlapping and superimposed social circles)—and the associated subculture proper—the norms and habits common to the subsystem. The term "subculture" will be used for both the network set and its culture; it is loosely synonymous with "social world." It must be understood that the defining traits of a subculture are not absolute criteria but variable dimensions—the degree of relational separateness (boundary) and internal coherence of those cultural elements. This does not invalidate the concept, but instead reveals that the specificity with which subcultures are defined is a matter of analytical purpose and empirical convenience. (The limiting case is arrived at when all interacting pairs of individuals are called subcultures.) Furthermore, a person can be a member of more than one subculture (depending partly on the minuteness of the analytical distinctions), but the number of substantial subcultures to which an individual can belong is probably severely limited by time, energy, and conflicting demands. Over 40 years ago, A. B. Holingshed (1939: 22) described a similar concept he called a "behavior system."

Persons in more or less continuous association evolve behavior traits and cultural mechanisms which are unique to the group and differ in some ways from those of other groups and from the larger socio-cultural complex. That is, every continuing social group develops a variant culture and a body of social relations peculiar and common to its members. This complex on the overt side may be characterized by discernable behavior of the group members in relation to each other, and to those who do not belong; and on the covert side, by an ethos or ideology which includes mores, codes, and other rules, which take the form of sanctions binding upon the membership in their relations to each other and to the external social world. Knowledge, techniques, attitudes, and behavior traits are all integrated into a more or less congruous system within which the participant members orient their lives and acquire status in the community and society. These constitute the criteria by which a specialized group is differentiated from other technical groups, and from the larger, incoherent "Great Society." Such a complex constitutes a behavior system.

27. What is unconventional in one period can become quite conventional in the next. When that occurs, a new deviance develops in reaction to that norm—as we saw in this chapter.

Chapter 3
Urban Life: The Physical Setting

1. The topics of urban ecology and social geography that are touched upon in this section are introduced more fully in Hawley (1981), Berry and Kasarda (1977), Johnston (1971), Herbert (1972), Yeates and Garner (1971), Schwirian (1974), and Bourne (1971).

2. Some specific cases are Teotihuacan (Millon, 1967), Cairo (Abu-Lughod, 1971), Damascus (Lapidus, 1966), Moscow (Abbott, 1974), and Osaka (Yazaki, 1973). General descriptions appear in Sjoberg (1960), Hawley (1971), Pirenne (1925), and Greenshields (1969).

3. This interpretation of the changes in urban ecology leans heavily on a transportation–technology model (Hawley, 1981), supported by several historical studies that seem to demonstrate the relationship (e.g., Warner, 1962; Conzen, 1975; Jackson, 1975). But many other forces no doubt also contributed to the modern pattern of residential segregation, some occurring before these technological changes [e.g., seventeenth-century London (Carr, 1975) and nineteenth-century Philadelphia (Hershberg et al., 1981b)].

There is some evidence that segregation, especially racial, is still increasing. See, for example, Van Valey et al. (1977), Kantrowitz (1979), and Stahura (1979) versus Hershberg et al. (1981a) who find, in contrast to Knatrowitz, a decline in white ethnic segregation.

4. These comments are based on the literature in factorial ecology. For summaries, see Rees (1972), Herbert (1972: Chapter 6), Janson (1980), and Murdie (1976). Farley (1977) cautions on the extent of class segregation. See, also, Schwirian (1974) and Yeates and Garner (1971: Chapter 11).

5. The 1977 Annual Housing Survey shows that 4.9 percent of nonmetropolitan homes were overcrowded; for metropolitan homes, the figure was 4.1 percent (4.9 percent in the center cities, 3.4 percent outside them. BOC, 1977a: Table A-1).

6. In Japan, for example (Carpenter, 1960).

7. For example, cities were particularly vulnerable to the Black Plague in the mid 1300s, sometimes losing one-half or two-thirds of their populations (Langer, 1964). In the 1600s, London lost over one-fifth of its people to periodic plagues (Clark and Slack, 1976: 89).

8. But, the difference between cities in developed and developing nations remains critical. Calcutta, for example, painfully resembles the stark description of a preindustrial environment at its worst.

9. The cost estimate was made by the Midwest Research Institute (*New York Times*, 4 September 1977). The National Academy of Science report attributed cancer deaths to smog (see also Ford, 1976). Challenges in recent years claim that the correlation can be explained by occupational differences and smoking, or air pollution for smokers only [e.g., see "Scientists Reject a Pollution Link to Higher Urban Rates of Cancer," (*New York Times*, 2 March 1979)]. A California study found lead poisoning among children living near freeways (*San Francisco Examiner*, 23 October 1977).

10. I have not separated city from suburban—as Ford tries to do—because the categories in the mortality data are not comparable to those typically used in this book. (The former data categories isolated only the most rural one-third of the suburban population.) An analysis of mortality rates for middle-aged Americans in 1970 appears in Sauer (1980).

11. These two arguments were raised, for instance, against the National Academy report that urbanites suffered lung cancer death rates twice those of rural persons (*San Francisco Examiner*, 14 September 1972).

12. Most descriptions of housing in industrializing cities are much like this one. See, for instance, Handlin (1969).

13. For example, a survey conducted in the Detroit area revealed that more than 90 percent of persons with children preferred single-family homes. The only groups who did not by a majority prefer single dwellings were unmarried and childless individuals currently living in multiple-unit dwellings (Lansing and Hendricks, 1967). See also Michelson (1970, 1977), Wright (1970), Trembly et al. (1980), and Silverman (1983). On Europe, see Lichtenberger (1976). Harvey Molotch suggests that the housing choice is more critical for city-dwellers because neighborhoods can differ so severely in cities (personal communication, 1983).

14. Another study indicated that high housing density reduced people's feelings of satisfaction with their neighborhoods. But this effect was mediated entirely by their perception of density. That is, only as it affected the extent to which people thought that their neighborhood was dense did the actual density of the neighborhood reduce their satisfaction (Marans and Rodgers, 1975).

15. R. Mitchell (1974, 1971); Edwards et al. (1982); Michelson (1977); Ginsberg and Churchman (1981); versus McCarthy and Saegert (1979). This conclusion violates many preconceptions about high-rise living. In some cases, researchers prefer their preconceptions. At a conference on housing, the chairman of the panel on space and privacy reluctantly summed up:

> We came to some conclusions that we really didn't want to, but to get on with it, I will read what we wrote down last night.
>
> We said that according to present evidence, space and privacy have only dubious and perhaps undiscovered causal relationships to health or illness. Some concern was expressed that our measuring techniques may be too crude to find the relationship between space, privacy and health which many of us believe exists. But I think what we were saying to ourselves is that we know what we are finding is not true but we don't know how to prove that it isn't [*APHA*, 1970: 10].

16. Michelson (1977), Wellman et al. (1973), Baldassare (1975), Lopata (1972: 269ff.), and Fischer et al. (1976).

17. On declining mobility, see Long (1976) and "America's New Immobile Society," *Business Week*, 27 July 1981.

18. Other sources on size and the availability of general services include Yeates and Garner (1971: Chapter 7), Swedner (1960: 107–121), Keyes (1958), and W. R. Thompson (1965). Sources dealing with specialized services include Ogburn and Duncan (1964), Abrahamson (1974), Abrahamson and DuBick (1977), Marden (1966), and Reskin and Campbell (1974). The size–services correlation holds within

the range of small communities (Johansen and Fuguitt, 1973; Allen, 1968; Harden, 1961; cf. Lincoln and Friedland, 1978) and among subparts of metropolitan areas (Yancey and Ericksen, 1979: Table 1).

19. See, for example, "Many Rural Spots Cut Off by U.S. Bus Deregulation," *New York Times*, 21 February 1983; "End of the Line for Small-Town Greyhound Stops," *San Francisco Examiner*, 23 January 1983.

20. Geographers have studied the phenomenon intensively, generally under the rubric of "central-place theory." For introductions, see Berry (1967) and Yeates and Garner (1971).

21. "Habitual Listeners," *New York Times*, 20 June 1976.

22. On complaints, see, for instance, Hawley and Zimmer (1971) and Louis Harris Assoc. (1979). Most people usually place access to services relatively low on their list of considerations when choosing a place to live (e.g., Butler et al., 1968), sometimes to their later chagrin (Michelson, 1977). See also Fischer (1973b).

Chapter 4
Urban Life: The Social Setting

1. In general, attributes of individuals, such as age or income, are "held constant" in the determinist and subcultural models. That is, the theories assume that urbanism affects individual behavior irrespective of these traits. But individual attributes are in fact correlated with urbanism *and* many dependent variables, such as unconventional behavior, thus raising the possibility that the associations of urbanism to these dependent variables are spurious. Indeed, the proposition that those associations are spurious is central to compositional theory (see Fischer, 1972).

2. General discussions of this difference can be found in Jones (1966), W. Petersen (1961); of England, in Mann (1964); of the United States in Taeuber (1972) and Fuguitt and Field (1972).

3. See, for example, Sharlin (1980), Mosk (1980), Hughes (1975), Guest (1982), and Robinson (1963). Knodel's (1977) study of nineteenth-century Germany suggests that lower urban fertility rates were caused by lower marriage rates, not lower marital fertility. Trovato and Grindstaff (1980) claim an *independent* effect of urbanism in contemporary Canada, but Slesinger (1974) finds none in the contemporary United States. Attitude studies show that urban residence is associated with a preference for fewer children [e.g., United States (GOI, #107, 1974); Taiwan (Coombs and Sun, 1981)].

4. "How Doubling Up Cuts U.S. Households," *San Francisco Examiner,* 4 April 1982.

5. Patterns of urban homogeneity have been described in various studies of preindustrial cities; of native Yoruba towns, for instance, (Krapf-Askari, 1969). But even in these types of towns, the general case was of even greater homogeneity in the countryside (Hull, 1976: 73–84; Sjoberg, 1960).

6. This point was suggested by Ann Swidler.

7. This explanation recognizes that there is not, by any means, a *national* labor market that would equalize wages—the critical assumption of the "bribe" analysis. It is also more consistent with the fact that industrial wages in places like San Francisco and Seattle are higher than those in, say, Youngstown, Ohio, or Birmingham, Alabama: Are workers in San Francisco being compensated for having to live there rather than Youngstown?

8. A study of a Guatemalan village, small town, and small city showed that villagers distinguish people only by race and wealth, but the townsmen had 7

categories of rank and the city people 10 (Roberts, 1973: 54). Similar findings appeared in a study of American college students (Lasswell, 1959). Outside observers also note greater class differentiation in larger communities (Fuguitt and Field, 1972; Ogburn and Duncan, 1964). Data on the economic diversification associated with city size is available in many sources, including Crowley (1973), Clemente and Sturgis (1972), and Betz (1972). But Lincoln and Friedland (1978) find a "shadow effect" among nonmetropolitan places—the larger, the less differentiated.

9. There is a large and burgeoning literature on urban migration, especially in less developed nations. See, for example: J. Nelson (1981), Butterworth and Chance (1981), Du Toit and Safa (1975), Gugler and Flanagan (1978), Connell et al. (1976), Ritchey (1976), and Abu-Lughod and Hay (1980). On the United States, see, for example, Ward (1971).

10. This pattern of migration does *not* imply that urbanites change residences more frequently than do rural people. Modern data indicate that rural populations are, on the average, as restless as urban ones, especially considering age differences. Evidence on mobility is available, for twentieth century America, in BOC (1968), GOI (1974, #110: 15), and for the nineteenth century, in Thernstrom (1973); for modern France, Bastide and Girard (1974a); and for pre-Western Japan, R. J. Smith (1973). Long and Boertlein (1978a, 1978b) provide international comparisons.

11. On the United States, see Tilly (1970a); France: Bastide and Girard (1974b); Africa: Hanna and Hanna (1971) and Little (1973); Latin America: Bradfield (1973), Perlman (1975), and Butterworth and Chance (1981).

12. A few recent studies showing such selectivity are Butterworth (1977), Moots (1976), and Anderson (1977). See also, Tilly (1970b), Bagley (1968), and sources cited in n. 10.

13. Recent studies showing the generally successful integration into urban life of migrants include Kemper (1975) and Lomnitz (1977) for Mexico, Whiteford (1976) for Colombia, and Laquian and Simmons (1979) for several cities. J. Nelson (1981) reviews the research on this question from around the world; Cornelius (1971) reviews Latin America, Hanna and Hanna (1971: Chapter 4) and Gugler and Flanagan (1978: 59–63), Africa; Tilly (1969; Tilly et al., 1975), Europe. On racial disorders in the United States, see Kerner Commission (1968) and on similar studies of migrants' radicalism, see Logan (1978) and Dietz (1979).

14. A sample of studies: the United States, Tilly (1965), Borchert (1981), Snyder (1971), McDonald and McDonald (1964); Latin America, Lewis (1952), Roberts (1973), Perlman (1975); France, Girard et al. (1966); for Africa, see Hanna and Hanna (1971: Chapter 3), Gugler and Flanagan (1978: Chapter 4), and Weisner (1976).

15. General sources on recent urban-to-rural migration include: Berry and Dahman (1977), Hawley and Mazie (1981), Brown and Wardwell (1980), and T. Ford (1978).

16. Calculated from Bureau of Census (1982a: 15). Among only those who had changed residences between 1975 and 1980, the probabilities were 0.22 and 0.12.

17. Another difficult-to-estimate aspect of this change is foreign immigration. In Europe, legal alien workers have partly filled-in the large metropolises (Vining and Kontuly, 1978). In the United States an unknown number of illegal immigrants may be doing the same (Alonso, 1978).

18. Although there are exceptions, for most advanced nations migration to the countryside tends to go up when the economy goes down (Vining and Kontuly, 1978).

19. Several recent studies have probed for the motives of urban-to-rural movers. Such migrants tend to emphasize noneconomic reasons—family and "quality-of-life" issues—more than people who move the other way. Whether such concerns are critical to their decisions or just "sweeteners" is not clear. No study has yet pinned

down whether a *change* in opinions or motives explains the change in the propensities to move (e.g., see Zuiches, 1981; Williams and McMillen, 1980; Long and DeAre, 1980; DeJong and Sell, 1977; Carpenter, 1977a; Blackwood and Carpenter, 1978; and Louis Harris Assoc., 1979).

20. The newspapers serving the growth areas are full of stories such as "Growth: It Drove Some People Here and It's Driving Some People Away" (Santa Rosa Calif. *Press-Democrat,* 5 February 1978); "Growth or No Growth: Georgetown Residents Face the Modern Dilemma" (Sacramento Calif. *Bee,* 23 June 1978); and "Growing pains . . . Shasta Struggles to Stay Rural" (*Bee,* 26 August 1977).

21. Official crime reports and victimization surveys show that New York City is surpassed by several others in crimes per capita.

22. See, for example, Clemente and Kleiner (1977), Stinchcombe et al. (1980: 53–54), Liska et al. (1982), and Fischer (1982a: Chapter 18), as well as Louis Harris Assoc. (1979) and BOC (1977b).

23. Gallup Poll, cited in *San Francisco Chronicle,* 22 February 1983.

24. In this connection, pollster Louis Harris told a congressional committee in 1978 that "It took close to 15 years for the cities to build a reputation for being havens of crime. [*San Francisco Chronicle,* 18 May 1978]."

25. See Gurr (1977, 1980), Wilson (1983), Ferdinand (1967, 1978), and Lane (1969, 1979). But in the latter study of homicide in Philadelphia, Lane found that the *black* homicide rate rose rapidly during the last century.

26. Among the explanations for the late twentieth-century "crime wave" are the baby boom (Silberman, 1978), class-based political turmoil (Gurr, 1977), cultural swings (Ferdinand, 1978; Fischer, 1980; Wilson, 1983), the drug trade's side effects (Zahn, 1980), increases in gun availability (Farley, 1980; Rushforth et al., 1977), and fewer people at home during the day (Cohen and Felson, 1979).

27. BOC (1982a: 178).

28. The two nations' statistics are not always comparable, of course; nor are the Canadian definitions always consistent from police force to police force (Statistics Canada, 1980: Preface). Note, also, that this figure uses 750 to 2,500 population as the base. Rural places were not clearly distinguished.

29. A 1983 Gallup poll found that 33 percent of city-dwellers, 26 percent of suburbanites, and 21 percent of rural residents had been victimized in some way during 1982 (*San Francisco Chronicle,* 22 February 1983). A census survey for 1980 reported 34 percent, 32 percent, and 25 percent, respectively (*San Francisco Examiner,* 7 April 1981). See also, Ennis (1967) and Cohen et al. (1981).

30. We can argue that biases in official crime-recording inflate the urban–rural contrast (e.g., Stinchcombe, 1963). But distortions in the opposite direction are probably greater still (e.g., lower police-to-number-of-crimes ratios and greater distrust of the police in cities). Reynolds and Blythe (1974) present evidence that suggests as much.

31. "Crime in Tokyo a Minor Problem" (*New York Times,* 3 January 1971); Michelson (1970: 154–155); "Nonviolent Cities" (*Newsweek* 5 January 1970: 33); "Buenos Aires Streets for Nighthawks" (*Los Angeles Times,* 23 July 1976); and Clinard (1978).

32. The assertions made in the next few paragraphs are based on a wide-ranging, but certainly not exhaustive, survey of the literature. For general reviews of urbanism and crime, see Shelley (1981), Wolfgang (1970), and Mulvihille and Tumin (1969); on developing countries, Clinard and Abbott (1973: 81–91). Topical studies on homicide include Wolfgang and Ferracuti (1967: 276ff) and Archer et al. (1978). On nineteenth-century America, specific historical and regional studies include Cook (1893) and Monkkonen (1975); on thirteenth-century England, Given (1977), early modern England, Tobias (1972), and modern England, Mann (1964: Chapter 2) and

H. L. Richardson (1973: 97); on nineteenth-century France, Cohen and Johnson (1982), Zehr (1975), and Lodhi and Tilly (1973); on modern France and Belgium, Szabo (1960); on nineteenth-century Germany, McHale and Johnson (1976, 1977) and Zehr (1975); on modern Scandinavia, Westergaard (1966); on the contemporary Soviet Union, Shelley (1980); on modern Africa, Hanna and Hanna (1971); on Asia, Hauser (1957: 221–233); on modern Japan, *Japan* (1967–1975); on China—old and new—see Fischer (1978a); and on contemporary New Zealand, Sheerin and Barnett (1978).

33. Archer et al. (1978) show that during the 1960s, there were six societies where the homicide rate for the largest city was *lower* than that for the nation as a whole and 18 where it was higher. The latter 18 are largely European and overseas European societies (such as New Zealand), so that for "culture areas" the division is roughly even. [Unfortunately, the use of primate cities for the comparison clouds that generally excellent analysis. In 19th-century Massachusetts, for example, Boston *and* rural areas had very high rates (Cook, 1893).] Shelley's (1981) review, as well as specific studies cited earlier, shows that, historically, rural homicide rates exceeded urban ones.

34. The rise of professional police forces in America was less closely tied to incidences of simple crime than it was to intergroup violence or class-based crime (e.g., see Schneider, 1980).

35. See also Liska et al. (1982), Taub and Taylor (1982); Hunter and Baumer (1982); and Lech and Labrousse (1977).

36. A Gallup poll of 1980 indicated that crime was a reason for moving for 30 percent of central city residents (reported in *San Francisco Chronicle,* 20 April 1981). And one study suggests that being a crime victim spurred white homeowners to "flee" the city (O'Reilly, 1981). Migration data suggest that crime may contribute to movement to the countryside (Swanson, 1983). See, also, Chapter 9.

Chapter 5
Social Groups in the City: Secondary Groups

1. A discussion of the Chicago School's conception of "social world" appears in Short (1971). On "social networks," see Boissevain (1973), J. C. Mitchell (1969), and Fischer et al. (1977).

2. Boissevain (1973) actually provides a quantitative comparison between a resident of a village and a resident of a city.

3. Wirth (1938: 152), for example, wrote that

> The bonds of kinship, of neighborliness, and the sentiments arising out of living together for generations under a common folk tradition are likely to be absent, or, at best, relatively weak in an aggregate the members of which have such diverse origins and backgrounds. Under such circumstances, competition and formal control mechanisms furnish the substitutes for the bonds of solidarity that are relied upon to hold a folk society together.

And Park:

> The form of government which had its origins in the town meeting and was·well suited to the needs of a small community based on primary relations is not suitable to the government of the changing and heterogeneous population of cities of three or four million. . . . Besides all the rest, [the voter] is too busy elsewhere to inform himself about the conditions and needs of the city as a whole [1916: 120].

4. For example, one student of nineteenth-century America concluded that:
   The probability that only between 40 and 60 percent of the adult males to be found in an American community at one point in time could still be located there a decade later held not only for most cities throughout the nineteenth and twentieth centuries; it applied in farming communities untouched by urbanization as well. . . . Approximately half of their residents at any date were destined to disappear before ten years had elapsed. . . . This was not a frontier phenomenon, or a big-city phenomenon, but a national phenomenon [Thernstrom, 1973: 225, 227; see, also, Long and Boertlein, 1978b; Darnoch, 1981].

Another possible index of community concern might be contributions to local charities. One study indicates that large-city residents were slightly *more* likely to make an effort to contribute to the community chest than were small-city residents (Alford, 1972).

5. For example, the boundaries of the political community are not always identical to those of the social community, as is true of small suburbs. This boundary problem is a particularly American phenomenon.

6. Most studies suggest that electoral competition and nonelectoral political conflict are typically greater the larger the community: Dahl and Tufte (1973), Prewitt and Eulau (1969), Black (1974), Kesselman (1966), Hamilton (1972: Chapter 6), Coleman (1957), Tilly (1973, 1974), Spilerman (1971), and Fischer (1978a). The findings are not all consistent. On urbanism and electoral competition, see, for example, Bonjean and Lineberry (1970). See, also, our later discussion on class and ethnic conflict in Chapter 6.

7. This distinction borrows from Tilly et al (1975).

8. This analysis of community participation is modelled in part on studies of differences in school sizes and the consequences for student participation in school activities (Barker and Gump, 1964; cf. Morgan and Alwin, 1980; J. Nelson, 1973). See also studies on overmanning (Wicker, 1968, 1969); for city councils, see Prewitt and Eulau (1969).

9. See discussions in Dahl and Tufte (1973) and Tilly (1973). Studies include, on international data: Verba et al. (1978), Nie et al. (1969), Burstein (1972), Dahl and Tufte (1973), Tilly (1973); U.S. data: Verba and Nie (1972: Chapter 13), Alford and Lee (1968), Fischer (1975d), van Es and Brown (1974); England: Great Britain, Royal Commission (1969); France: Tarrow (1971), Hamilton (1967), Kesselman (1966); and Japan: B. M. Richardson (1973).

10. Studies cited in n. 9 tend to support this generalization.

11. See studies cited in n. 9.

12. The substitution of instrumental and single-purpose associations for primary and diffuse groups during the process of urbanization is the essential dynamic of *Gemeinschaft* (community)–*Gesellschaft* (association) theory. Tönnies:
   All praise of rural life has pointed out that Gemeinschaft among people is stronger there and more alive; it is the lasting and genuine form of living together. In contrast to Gemeinschaft, Gesellschaft is transitory and superficial . . . a mechanical aggregate and artifact [1887: 35].

Wirth:
   Reduced to the stage of virtual impotence as an individual, the urbanite is bound to exert himself by joining others of similar interests into groups organized to obtain his ends. This results in the enormous multiplication of voluntary organizations directed toward as great a variety of objectives as there are human interests and needs. . . .
   It is largely through the activities of voluntary groups, be their objectives economic, political, educational, religious, recreational, or cultural,

that the urbanite expresses and develops his personality, acquires status, and is able to carry out the round of activities that constitute his life career [1938: 162].

13. On associations among American immigrants, see Handlin (1969), Barton (1975), Borchert (1981); on Africa: Barnes and Peil (1977), Hanna and Hanna (1971), Epstein (1967), and Little (1965); and on Latin America, Mangin (1970).

14. See, also, Blumin (1976), Barnes and Peil (1977), and Borchert (1981).

15. Single cities studied include Detroit (Axelrod, 1956), San Francisco (Bell and Boat, 1957), New York City (Komarovsky, 1946), and New Haven (Dotson, 1951). Comparative studies include Curtis (1971), Babchuck and Booth (1969), van Es and Brown (1974), and Fischer (1982a, 1973a). The last study, for example, showed that among middle-income whites, 65 percent of those living in nonmetropolitan areas and 60 percent of those in metropolitan areas never attended club meetings.

16. For other studies, see Bell and Boat (1957), Axelrod (1956), Kasarda and Janowitz (1974), Litwak and Szelenyi (1969), and Wellman et al. (1973).

17. Park, for example, said that

The outcome of [urban specialization] is to break down or modify the older social and economic organization of society, which was based on family ties, local associations, on culture, caste and status, and to substitute for it an organization based on occupation and vocational interests. . . . The different trades and professions seem disposed to group themselves in classes, that is to say, the artisan, business, and professional classes [1916: 102].

Durkheim (1893), Simmel (1905), and Wirth (1938) also refer to the rise of economic structuring. Zorbaugh (1929: 242) wrote that "primary contacts in the city tend to depend increasingly upon occupational interests rather than the contiguity of residence."

18. On small-town class conflict, see Dollard (1957) and G. M. Foster (1960–1961). On class-segregated friendships, see Laumann (1973) and R. Jackson (1977), among many other network studies.

19. For Spain, see Logan (1978); for Africa, Jenkins (1968).

20. See, among many others, Castells (1977, 1978) and collections edited by Tabb and Sawers (1978) and Dear and Scott (1981).

21. This argument can be taken to a reductio ad absurdum. I have been asked, for example, whether pipe fitters form a separate subculture. The answer is yes, if the number of pipe fitters in a superlarge city were great enough. Obviously, this does not occur in most, if any, contemporary cities. Additional factors also help determine at what threshold of size occupations will develop distinctive cultures, factors including degree of separation from other walks of life (because of schedule or physical location), exclusivity of recruitment, degree of specialized training, and degree of task-related communication, among others. [See Wilensky (1964) on the cultural differentiation of occupations.]

22. Avery Guest reminded me of this basic point.

23. In that study, I try to reconcile argument and data in two ways, raising methodological doubts about our measurement of occupational worlds and suggesting that urbanism may have two countervailing effects. The first effect is the one described here: to open up the opportunities for an occupational world. The second effect, especially strong in larger cities, is to provide more "voluntary" alternatives for social ties outside the "constrained" workplace in a manner similar to urbanism's effects on neighborhood relations (see p. 135, this volume).

24. See Mileski and Black (1972), Hoffman (1968), Harry (1974), Levine (1979), and Fischer (1982a: Chapter 18).

25. The differences held up after controlling for social background.

26. The informal associations discussed here are unofficial and smaller versions of the formal associations discussed earlier. "A special-interest group is a phenomenon of Gesellschaft," wrote Tönnies (1887: 213). It is basic to the concept of Gesellschaft that its social relations are essentially impersonal and instrumental. "A special-interest group is a fictitious being which serves its authors, expressing their common rational will in certain relationships [Tönnies, 1887: 214]." "Rational will" in this context is impersonal: "In rational relations man is reckoned with like a number, like an element which is in itself indifferent [Simmel, 1905: 49]." Consequently, "in Gesellschaft every person strives for that which is to his own advantage and he affirms the actions of others only in so far and as long as they can further his own interest [Tönnies, 1887: 77]." "Our acquaintances tend to stand in a relationship of utility to us in the sense that the role which each one plays in our life is overwhelmingly regarded as a means for the achievement of our own ends [Wirth, 1938: 153]."

27. We found that people involved in organized groups—formal and informal—tended to have more personal ties than did those not involved (Fischer, 1982a: Chapter 10).

28. an exponent of the popular view is Packard (1972), and of the scholarly positions, Tönnies (1887), Durkheim (1893), Park (1916), Nisbet (1967), and Alexander (1967). Tönnies (1887: 42) called the neighborhood the "Gemeinschaft of locality . . . a community of physical life." Park (1916: 111) described the characteristics of such natural or "primordial" relationships as including interactions that are "immediate and unreflecting . . . carried on largely within the region of instinct and feeling . . . in direct response to personal influences and public sentiment . . . and [not the result] of a rational and abstract principle."

29. *Los Angeles Times,* Letter to the Editor, 13 November 1976.

30. R. Reagan, *San Francisco Chronicle,* 3 December 1981.

31. The cited statistics are from an unpublished table prepared for Fischer (1973a). On the United States, see Louis Harris Assoc. (1979: 120), Campbell (1981: 244), Fischer (1982a), Tsai and Sigelman (1982), Bradburn et al. (1970), and Key (1968). On Sweden, see Swedner (1960); on Japan: B. M. Richardson (1973); and on China: M. K. Whyte and Parish (1983: Chapter 9). Migrants to cities often report that their home villages were more neighborly than their current places of residence (e.g., K. K. Petersen, 1971). A major exception to this pattern of findings are those of Kasarda and Janowitz (1974), who discovered only negligible associations between community size and local involvement in their secondary analysis of an English survey. Silverman (1983) reports that there is also a difference in style of neighboring: urbanites invite people over, but small-town people drop in.

32. E. V. Smalley, quoted by Boorstin (1973: 119). Contemporary observers thought that the telephone and the automobile did much to relieve the common farm-life insanity. See, for example, M. Berger (1979).

33. General discussions of neighboring appear in Keller (1968), Mann (1964), and Michelson (1970). Specific studies include Michelson (1977), Fischer (1982a), Fischer et al. (1977), Gates et al. (1973), McGahan (1972), Kasarda and Janowitz (1974), Fava (1959), and Fellin and Litwak (1963). Frolic (1971) reports comparable studies in the Soviet Union.

34. For example, in one study (Fischer, 1973a), statistically controlling for individual traits still left a large association between community size and knowing one's neighbors. Results from the northern California survey were more ambiguous but pointed to the same conclusion (Fischer, 1982a). In another study (Bradburn et al., 1970), a variable measuring "urbanization" was more highly associated with the extent to which individuals neighbored than was any other factor. Tsai and Seligman's (1982) results are similar.

35. This analysis draws heavily from Heberle (1960) and Suttles (1972). See Keller (1968).

36. This generalization assumes that social class is held constant. Neighboring tends to increase with a person's social class as part of a general increase in social activity of all kinds. Thus, well-to-do people are more neighborly (in casual interaction) than less-affluent people; but among their total social relationships, people in higher classes emphasize the neighborhood ties less than do people of lower rank (see Keller, 1968; Fischer, 1982a; Fischer et al., 1977: Chapter 7).

37. Keller (1968: 44) suggests that neighbors exchange four kinds of services— help of a casual nature, help in an emergency, joining in the celebration of special events (e.g., a birth), and assisting at cyclical events (e.g., harvests). But the latter two services are not inherent in the role. See Useem et al. (1960).

38. Ginsberg (1980) found, in an Israeli study, that residents' satisfaction with their neighborhood was not related to social involvement with neighbors but was related, negatively, to having difficulties with neighbors.

39. J. Smith et al. (1954), Bell and Boat (1957), Riemer and McNamara (1957), Tomeh (1967), K. K. Petersen (1971), Key (1968), Koyama (1970), Gordon (1977), Fischer et al. (1977), Fischer (1982a), Ward et al. (1982), Hawley and Zimmer (1971: 54), and above all, Keller (1968).

40. For general introductions to neighborhood movements, see Castells (1983), Boyte (1981), O'Brien (1975), and Morris and Hess (1975).

41. "For social control to be rigorous and for the common conscience to be maintained, society must be divided into rather small compartments completely enclosing the individual [Durkheim 1893: 300]."

Chapter 6
Social Groups in the City: Primary Groups

1. Several "conflict theorists" (such as A. Cohen, 1969; Schildkrout, 1974; Hechter, 1974; and Horowitz, 1975) have advanced the thesis that ethnicity, at least in the urban setting, is more of an economic than a cultural institution. In this view, ethnic groups are primarily economic conflict groups that employ ethnicity as a political tool. This argument over the "real" content of ethnicity is partly a matter of judgment—how distinctive must a culture be to be distinctive?—and partly one of research. Without pressing the argument, I would suggest that the identifiability of ethnic boundaries, even for political purposes, is strongly associated with cultural differences, so that without these differences political cohesion becomes unlikely.

2. At first glance, it may not be clear how both cultural intensification and diffusion can occur simultaneously. Yet such cases are common. They involve selective acceptance of cultural items from other groups. These "peripheral" items are borrowed either because they are convenient (say, clothing styles) or useful (for example, political organization). But this borrowing occurs together with an emphasis on "central" identity and core values. Examples will be given in the text. The same pattern holds true for personal contacts across ethnic lines. An anthropologist of ethnicity writes that

> It is clear that [ethnic] boundaries persist despite a flow of personnel across them. In other words, categorical ethnic distinctions do not depend on the absence of mobility, contact and information, but do entail social processes of exclusion and incorporation whereby discrete categories are maintained despite changing participation and membership. . . . Ethnic

distinctions do not depend on the absence of social interaction and acceptance but are quite to the contrary often the very foundations on which embracing social systems are built [Barth, 1969: 9–10].

3. Following is an illustrative bibliography, including texts with overviews and sample studies. North America: Gans (1962b), Glazer and Moynihan (1970), Handlin (1969, 1951), Snyder (1971); Latin America: Butterworth (1962), Butterworth and Chance (1981), Doughty (1970), Thompson (1974); Europe: Halpern (1965), Willems (1970); Africa: Shack (1973), Hanna and Hanna (1971), Gugler and Flanagan (1978); Asia: Rowe (1973), Husain (1956); generally: Southall (1973a).

4. Butterworth and Chance (1981: 98–107). For illustrative studies, see Barton (1975), Hershberg et al. (1981), Skeldon (1976), and Woodrum (1981).

5. But one study found only a weak association between having fellow-ethnic friends and marrying within the group (Cohen, 1977).

6. Wolfinger (1965), Gordon (1970), Glazer and Moynihan (1970). One complex, national survey analysis suggests that if religion and the party identification of respondents' parents are controlled, ethnicity alone does not predict political party (Cohen and Kapsis, 1977). Yet, case studies suggest ethnic lines are often city-specific and religion and parents' party may simply mediate the effect.

7. Irving Howe (1976: 618) has made a similar point in discussing Jewish assimilation:

Cultures are slow to die; when they do, they bequeath large deposits of custom and value to their successors; and sometimes they survive long after their more self-conscious members suppose them to have vanished. A great many suburban Jews no longer spoke Yiddish, a growing number did not understand it—but their deepest inclinations of conduct, bias, manner, style, intonation, all bore heavy signs of immigrant shaping. What Jewish suburbanites took to be 'a good life,' the kinds of vocations to which they hoped to lead their children, their sense of appropriate conduct within a family, the ideas capable of winning their respect, the moral appeals to which they remained open, their modes of argument, their fondness for pacific conduct, their views of respectability and delinquency—all showed the strains of immigrant Yiddish culture, usually blurred, sometimes buried, but still at work.

Gans (1962b: 208) makes such an observation on Italians in Boston: "American cities, however, could not penetrate the family circle. Thus, whereas the children who became adults of the second generation retained little of the Italian culture [meaning peripheral items], they did retain most of its social structure [a central item]."

How in practice, a researcher distinguishes, a priori, central from peripheral items is more difficult. I would suggest that the closer a trait is to basic family structure and to characteristic "ethnic personality," the more central it is, while the closer it is to being merely a material artifact, the more peripheral. Sengstock (1969), Lopez (1978), and Yans-McLaughlin (1971) present studies that illustrate this distinction.

8. There are other, similar problems common to such ethnographic studies. Researchers who have assigned themselves the task of studying ethnicity (or kinship, for that matter) tend to "see" it even where others might not. And there is a tendency to select distinctive groups for case study, often groups more ethnically defined than the average.

9. Epstein (1967); Mitchell (1970); see, also, Hanna and Hanna (1971). On tribal associations, see Little (1965); Bascom (1963).

10. For example, Guest (1982) found that, circa 1900, immigrant groups "Americanized"—i.e., lowered—their fertility rates faster in urban than in rural states.

11. In Fischer (1982a: Chapter 16), we found that, after controlling for specific ethnicity and personal traits among those who had any ethnic identification at all, urbanism tended to increase the number of ethnic associates, but not to affect ethnic consciousness or organizational membership. The argument suggested there is that being one of a few ethnics in a town full of other types fosters self-consciousness, but inhibits actual social integration into the ethnicity (Rose, 1977).

12. Ethnic group members certainly tend to cluster near one another, but the extent to which that is so varies a good deal, depending on housing and job conditions (see Nelson, 1981: 96–97; Greenberg, 1981). An earlier image of ethnic districts in American cities was exaggerated. There was a good deal more mixing of ethnic groups and rarely did any group—other, perhaps, than blacks—hold a majority (Chudacoff, 1975; Lieberson, 1970; A. Burstein, 1981).

13. Another example, this one highlighting the difficulty of maintaining ethnicity in a small community, was provided by a conference held on Jewish life in American small towns:

> "With less than 29 youngsters, 3-year-olds to high school age," said a participant from a midwestern town with 35 Jewish families, "how can we manage an effective Hebrew school to educate them?"
>
> Community centers, nurseries, homes for the aged, all-day Jewish schools, adult study programs, and other communal and social service programs are a rarity in small towns [Spiegel, 1973].

Other illustrations are provided by Suttles (1968: 150), and Doughty (1972).

14. In a survey conducted in five San Francisco area high schools, 80 percent reported occasional or frequent racial insults, and 72 percent reported occasional or frequent racial graffiti. More students picked "lifestyle differences" as the explanation for racial prejudice than any other (Hardy, 1983).

15. In a Gallup Poll (GOI, 1979: #169), the only respondents who reported an unpleasant experience with Jews were those living in the largest cities, presumably because the concentration in cities of Jews made all encounters—pleasant and not—with them more likely (see also, on black antisemitism, Marx, 1964; on segregation and school violence, Lieske, 1978).

16. Unlike most nations, the United States imposes a uniform and pervasive language and culture on its minorities. In most cases, these minorities are separated by great distance and cost from their homelands, thereby reducing the continuing support and immigration available to minorities in the cities of most other nations (Lieberson et al., 1975).

17. See Handlin (1969); Hanna and Hanna (1971); on pan-Indianism in the United States, see Price (1975); for examples from American Jewish communities, see Wirth (1928) and Rischlin (1977).

18. Popenoe (1977: 211) points out four ways that community structure can influence social ties such as friendship: by affecting the need for friends, by providing a pool of possible friends, by shaping access to those friends, and by affecting the rate of turnover in the community.

19. Yet another implication of the arithmetic is that the possible *combinations* of friends will increase geometrically with an increase in city size.

20. A reader or two have suggested that city planner Alexander is a "straw man" in this argument. Consider, then, a contemporary sociologist's comment: "Modern urban existence does give rise to impersonality, expediential relationships, social distance, opportunism, and personal isolation" (F. Davis, quoted by Berreman, 1978: 73).

21. A sample of such studies: W. F. Whyte (1955), Young and Wilmott (1957), Gutkind (1969), Pons (1969), and Roberts (1973). Other studies, many of which will be cited in the discussion of kinship, present the same conclusion.

22. See Wylie (1964), Smith (1968), Foster (1967), and Banfield (1958). Crowe's (1979) description of modern Austrian villagers points to similar distrust.

23. Other such studies include, in Detroit: Axelrod (1956); in Los Angeles: Greer (1956); in Toronto: Wellman et al. (1973); in Rio de Janeiro: Perlman (1975).

24. Figure 9 includes data not reported in Fischer (1982a). On the ambiguity of the term "friend," as illustrated in these data, see Fischer (1982c).

25. For similar findings, see Sutcliffe and Crabbe (1963), Key (1968), Kasarda and Janowitz (1974), Tsai and Sigelman (1982), and Swedner (1960). Kleiner and Parker (1976) report no differences by rural-versus-urban *origin*. Two surveys of leisure-time habits show no essential size-of-community differences in the proportions of residents who prefer to visit or entertain friends (deGrazia, 1962: 461: GOI, 1974, #105: 12). One study claims to find such differences, but the research suffers from serious difficulties (an odd sample, no third-factor controls, marginal differences), and, at best, demonstrates only that New Yorkers differ from residents of other cities (Guterman, 1969).

26. See, also, Crowe (1978) and Koyama (1970). There are a few comparative studies on the specialization of networks. Verbrugge (1973) presents data on personal networks for Detroit and for a small city in Germany. Specialization seemed to be greater in Detroit, but the comparison is crude. See, also, Frankenburg (1965) and Boissevain (1974: 71ff.). Most network surveys have been solely urban; for example, Litwak and Szelenyi (1969), Laumann (1973), Wellman et al. (1973), Wellman (1979), and Shulman (1976).

27. Peil (1981: 3) reports West African surveys on friendship that indicate more complex patterns. Unfortunately, it is difficult to apply her results, as reported, to the issues addressed here. Her conclusion about subcultural theory is worth noting:

> Factors such as the proportion of migrants in the town, especially of recent migrants, ethnic heterogeneity and cultural and political expectations, appear to be more important than size in affecting the formal and informal social life of urban residents and the subculture which they develop.

28. Wirth's statement (1938: 160–161), in more detail:

> The city is not conducive to the traditional type of family life, including the rearing of children and the maintenance of the home as the locus of a whole round of activities. The transfer of industrial, educational, and recreational activities to specialized institutions outside the home has deprived the family of some of its most characteristic historical functions. . . The family as a unit of social life is emancipated from the larger kinship group characteristic of the country, and the individual members pursue their own diverging interests in their vocational, educational, religious, recreational, and political life.

Zorbaugh (1929: 188) argued that "in practically every immigrant group, as in Little Sicily, the family is going to pieces in the conflict with an alien culture." See, also, Burgess and Locke (1953: Chapter 4), Obgurn (1954), Tönnies (1887: 229), and Park (1916).

29. See also Goode (1963), Carpenter (1960), Mann (1965: 59), and Clinard (1964).

30. On urban and rural conditions affecting household structure and family ties, see, for example, M. Anderson (1971, 1973), Greven (1970), and Kertzer (1978).

31. Results from unpublished table prepared for Fischer (1973a); see, also, Youmans (1977).

32. Other studies include, in North America: Gans (1962b), Suttles (1968), Lewis (1952), Garigue (1956); in Europe: Halpern (1965), Willems (1970); in Africa: Aldous (1962), Schwab (1968); in Asia: Vatuk (1972), Nayacakalov and Southall (1973). See, also, citations in n. 21 (this chapter) on studies of friendship.

33. For reviews of the survey literature on urbanism and kinship, see Greer (1962),

R. N. Morris (1968), and Goode (1963: 70–76). Studies include Axelrod (1956), Wellman et al. (1973), Simic (1973), Cantor (1975), and Lees (1969).

34. A related finding, but one somewhat difficult to interpret, was reported by Hadley Cantril (1965: Appendix E). Data from surveys conducted in several developing nations (Brazil, pre-Castro Cuba, Egypt, Nigeria, and Panama) indicated that people in urban places tended to have more personal fears (and hopes) about their families than did people in rural places. In more economically advanced nations (Israel, West Germany, the United States, and Yugoslavia), there were no substantive urban–rural differences in family worries.

35. A 1978 Gallup Poll found that big-city parents were less likely to report getting along well with their teen-age children than were parents in smaller places (GOI, 1978: #156). But a 1976 national survey found no such differences in reported difficulties with raising children (Veroff et al., 1981a).

36. Various studies of the elderly suggest that urban visiting with children is at least as great as rural visiting (Bultena, 1969; Youmans, 1977; Palmore et al., 1970; Winch and Greer, 1968).

37. See Litwak (1960), Adams (1966), Wellman et al. (1973), Koyama (1970), Vatuk (1972), Fischer et al. (1977), Fischer (1982e).

38. Winch and Greer (1968: 42) found no size-of-community differences in "extended familism" for nonmigrants, but found such differences among migrants, the rural ones being more familistic. This difference is probably a result of migrants having moved to small communities precisely *because* of their kin; but people tend to move to large cities for different reasons (see Bastide and Girard, 1974b; Fischer, 1982a: Chapter 2).

39. I do not intend to enter the enormous thicket of debate on this topic (nor to cite the shelves of books dealing with it)—but only to point it out.

Chapter 7
The Individual in the City: States of Mind

1. The book that sparked studies of urban cognitive maps was Lynch (1960). Other studies include Horton and Reynolds (1971) and de Jonge (1962).

2. Other extrapolators in this vein include Calhoun (1962), Hall (1966), and van den Berghe (1974).

3. Some grasp of the literature can be gained by reading recent reviews such as Altman (1978), Baldassare (1978), Choldin (1978), Stokols (1978), and Sundstrom (1978); collections such as Aiello and Baum (1979), Baum and Epstein (1978), Baum et al. (1978), and Stokols (1977); and journals such as *Environment and Behavior* and *Human Ecology*.

4. Among the popularizers of this thesis are Ardrey (1961) and D. Morris (1968). Scholars who make this argument include Lorenz (1966), Leyhausen (1965), Carstairs (1969), and van den Berghe (1974).

5. Critiques of the ethnology–territoriality model include Montagu (1973), Alland (1972), Martin (1972), S. Nelson (1974), Freedman (1975), and Fischer (1975e). See, also, discussions by Wynne-Edwards (1964) and Dubos (1970).

6. See Calhoun (1962), Hall (1966), Meier (1962), Milgram (1970), Desor (1971), Aiello et al. (1975), and Freedman (1975: 93–95).

7. See Somer (1969), Hall (1966), and Goffman (1971). Reviews and theoretical critiques appear in Watson (1972), Evans and Howard (1973), Baldassare and Feller (1976), Pedersen and Shears (1973), and Hayduk (1978).

8. This cultural model meshes with the nonverbal-communications version of the

"personal space" model. If one person moves closer to another, that person is saying, "This situation is not one of strangers, but of friends" (see Baron and Bell, 1976). The illustration of the New York subway suggests that riders come to expect and accept crowding. This deduction finds empirical support in a survey of New Yorkers (Morton, 1972), which showed that riding the subways was not related to disliking the city (though other things, especially neighborhood quality, were).

9. We cannot hope to review in detail the massive amount of research in the crowded field of crowding. See the several recent reviews of the literature cited in n. 3, as well as Fischer et al. (1975), Stokols (1977), Lawrence (1974), and Freedman (1973, 1975).

10. See reviews cited in n. 3 and n. 9.

11. One curious finding has emerged from a few studies in this line: Groups of males seem to be more upset and aggressive in small (dense) rooms than in large ones, but with groups of females, it is the reverse. In groups including both sexes, no difference was observed between the rooms. For a small sample of studies of this type of research, see Freedman et al. (1971, 1972), Stokols et al. (1973), Ross et al. (1973), and Nogami (1976). See reviews cited earlier.

12. These crowding experiments can be criticized for being of too short duration, but it is not obvious what longer sessions would show. Perhaps the negative consequences of density build up over time, or perhaps negative effects occur only when people are first placed in this rather extreme position—often forced to sit face-to-face in a small cubicle, knees practically knocking—and, over time, adjustments would be made that would reduce any ill effects. A more fundamental critique is that these experimental labs are not analogous in any straightforward way to crowded homes, much less to cities (Baldassare and Fischer, 1976; Fischer, 1978b).

13. One oft-cited study (Galle et al., 1972) presents evidence suggesting that crowding within households is related to pathologies. But there are serious questions about the results of this study (S. Ward, 1974; Loftin and Ward, 1983; Fischer et al., 1975; McPherson, 1975). In reanalysis, Galle and Gove (1979) argue that they seem to have isolated a quite small but real effect of density—probably of household overcrowding—on some pathologies, but concede that the extremely tight connection between crowding and low social status makes it difficult to draw causal conclusions. Yet another study by the same authors points to *living alone*, not crowding, as possibly pathogenic (Gove and Hughes, 1980).

14. See, for example, Baldassare (1977, 1979, 1982a) and Verbrugge and Taylor (1980).

15. A similar result is reported in Fischer (1982a: 103).

16. See, for example, studies by Andrew Baum in sources such as Baum et al. (1978) and Aiello and Baum (1979).

17. For a ferocious debate among these authors, see the *American Sociological Review* 45: 864–886.

18. See Baldassare (1979, 1981), Verbrugge and Taylor (1980), Cassel (1972), and reviews cited earlier.

19. Unfortunately, the NCHS analyses control only for age, race, gender, and, occasionally, region, but not for other factors such as diet or education.

20. The original study (Webb and Collette, 1977) reported higher prescription rates in smaller towns, but a reanalysis essentially found no differences (Webb and Collette, 1979).

21. There is an unfortunate scarcity of such studies that are comprehensive, relevant to general populations, and analytically sophisticated (e.g., systematically controlling for confounding variables). Most studies, though helpful, are limited. For instance, one study compared a small sample of Algiers residents with their kin and friends in a rural oasis, and found more tension among the former (Miner and DeVos,

1960). But a comparison of stress symptoms among residents of a slum in Lima, Peru with those of residents in a peasant village showed little difference (Rotondo, 1962).

22. No substantial contemporary urban–rural difference in suicide rate has been reported for the United States (NCHS, 1967b; Sauer, 1980), Japan (Carpenter, 1960; Isa and Tatai, 1975), or France (Szabo, 1960). A higher urban than rural rate has been reported for England (Mann, 1964: 48) and Scandinavia (Westergaard, 1966), and a lower urban than rural rate for Taiwan (Wolf, 1975). See, also, Farberow (1975: passim).

23. Roger Lane (1979) suggests that suicide has become more "democratized" in the intervening years. In the nineteenth century, for example, suicide correlated with high social status; it no longer does.

24. The 17 were totaled from those summarized by Swedner (1960: 30–45) and by Nelson and Storey (1969), plus others, e.g. Schooler (1972), Sewell and Amend (1943), and Haller and Wolff (1962). The last found signs that 17-year-old boys in two towns were more nervous than those in nearby villages, but had no greater tendency to suffer from pathological symptoms.

25. Dohrenwend and Dohrenwend (1972) reviewed a mixed bag of nine epidemiological studies that compared populations in larger and smaller communities. They conclude that mild neuroses are more common in urban areas, but serious psychoses are more common in rural ones. The studies, however, are quite limited with regard to samples, procedures, and controls for spurious relationships and for "drift." Furthermore, the differences are essentially small (see critiques by Srole, 1972, 1978b; Schwab et al., 1972).

26. These uses of alienation are derived from the work of Melvin Seeman (1959, 1972, 1975). A good history of the concept appears in Schacht (1971).

27. An interesting exception to this generalization comes from Uganda, where a small survey found that residents in the city felt more powerless than residents in a village. The researcher attributed the finding in part to the political terror of the Idi Amin regime, which was more powerful in urban areas (R. W. Thompson, 1974).

28. Various scales have been constructed to measure "normlessness," the most well-known of which is the Srole Anomia Scale. But it is not clear that these scales do measure normlessness (Seeman, 1972; Fischer, 1976); in any case, studies using them fail to show any major relationship with urbanism (Fischer, 1973a: n. 2).

29. This pattern of mistrust prevailed when the village was revisited in 1973 (Wylie, 1973). See, also, Foster (1967) and Lantz (1971).

30. This summary is largely based on several NORC annual General Social Survey tabulations, kindly provided by James Davis, which show that, year to year in the 1970s, urbanism was either positively or not correlated with distrust. Given the pattern of covariates such as education, this implies a positive net effect. House and Wolf (1978) found no effect for surveys done in 1952, 1960, 1964, and 1972, and a positive effect only for 1968. Fischer (1973a) found effects in the 1968 and in a 1971 U.S. survey and an earlier British survey.

31. We have not discussed three other varieties of alienation listed by Seeman (1972). *Self-estrangement,* which refers to alienated labor, is not directly germane. *Meaninglessness* refers to the feeling that events in the world around a person are incomprehensible. This has been researched very little, but indications (from survey items such as: "The way things are going, it is not fair to bring children into the world—agree or disagree?") are that it is not associated with urbanism. *Value isolation* refers to a lack of esteem for those goals generally considered important in an person's society. In the next chapter, we shall see that this form of alienation probably *is* related to urbanism. Finally, *political alienation* was discussed in Chapter 5, where evidence was reviewed indicating that, although alienation from political activities as such is not associated with urbanism, detachment from local politics is.

32. Controlling for self-selection factors generally sustains or expands the original difference. See, for example, Campbell (1981: 148–153), Campbell et al. (1976: 49–57); also analyzed by Rodgers (1980), Veroff et al. (1981a), and Larson (1979: 103–106). The survey we conducted within Northern California did *not* find such a difference (Fischer, 1982a: 50–51). A canvass of European polls reports no regular association of satisfaction with community size in 1973, no association in 1975, but a negative association in 1976 (Ward, 1979).

33. Some evidence for both interpretations comes from Rodgers' (1982) finding that happiness declined fastest among the young and well-educated and actually rose among the elderly and poorly educated.

Chapter 8
The Individual in the City: Personality and Behavior

1. The cited studies are of schools. They show that the larger the school, the fewer the number of positions—athlete, student leader, band member, and so forth—an average student holds. The Morgan and Alwin (1980) study is especially interesting because it shows that with respect to one activity, hobby clubs, the opposite was true: larger schools, more positions. It suggests that size reduces the number of "obligatory" roles students could hold but increases the number of discretionary ones.

2. That is, urbanites tend not to move about any more than do ruralites, and maybe even less once the immigration to the cities from the countryside is taken into account (Long and Boertlein, 1978a; Hochstadt, 1981).

3. Hoch (1976) argues that city-dwellers' time is economically more valuable, and so they rationally must live at a more hectic pace. Bornstein and Bornstein (1976) claim that people's walking speeds increase as community size increases [but for a critique, see Fischer (1978b: 136–137)].

4. Unfortunately, studies of "modernity" such as Aksoy's combine modernity as a cognitive state—a way of viewing the world, such as impersonality—with modernity as a set of values; the latter usage we will employ later in this chapter. One particular form of impersonality is ethnic tolerance or absence of prejudice. Research in North America generally finds that urban people are substantially less prejudiced—thus, more impersonal—than are rural people. But controls for social class, religion, and other covariates tend to render the differences marginal (Selznick and Steinberg, 1969; Curtis and Hawkins, 1975; Fischer, 1971; Whitt and Nelsen, 1975). Moreover, such residual differences may reflect not cognitive styles, but liberal ideologies that are currently more prevalent in cities than in small towns.

5. The results may, however, be explainable in terms of class or westernization (Madsen, 1967; Madsen and Yi, 1975).

6. Although the answers dealing with public life showed clear urban–rural differences (on the order of 10 percent between categories of urbanism), those dealing with private life were small or inconsistent. And, this study did not control for age, class, or other factors possibly related to aggressiveness.

7. Christie and Geis (1970: 318–320) found the same proportion of "Machiavellian" personalities in small and large communities. Blumenthal et al. (1972) found that rural men scored higher on a "kindness" scale but also scored higher on a "materialism" scale. Psychological surveys discussed in Chapter 7, such as Fischer (1982a: Chapter 4), do not find differences in levels of hostility.

8. Accounts in the press of this and other cases illustrates the hazards of resting sociological conclusions on news reports. The wave of "aloof witnesses" stories was

followed a few years later by a wave of "vigilante witnesses" stories, in which bystanders pursued and often attacked would-be assailants—for example, "Queens Crowd Captures a Man Fleeing Shooting"—as well as stories of ghetto residents freeing arrestees from police custody. Obviously, little is settled by counting press clippings.

9. Milgram (1970) reports a few pilot studies along these lines. Other examples include Forbes and Gromoll (1971), Korte and Kerr (1975), Korte et al. (1975), and Kamman et al. (1979). This technique is generally plagued with problems of validity—in setting up the appropriate comparisons, in creating believable situations, in holding constant spurious conditions, and so on.

10. *San Francisco Chronicle,* 19 December 1974.

11. *San Francisco Chronicle,* 5 December 1979.

12. One point in support of this analysis is that the urban effects on helping seem to have appeared only in American studies (Korte, 1978; 1980).

13. Jones and Nisbett (1972) discuss the perceptual bias people tend to show when they attribute their own actions to *situational* constraints ("I had to do it") but attribute the same behavior by another to that individual's *personality* ("He wanted to do it"). See, also, Stephan (1975).

14. Another contributor to the impression of impersonality is simple numbers. Given the larger size of the urban population, the chances are greater that someone will misbehave and annoy others there than in small towns. An illustration is provided by a widely publicized "experiment" conducted by psychologist Philip Zimbardo (1969). He abandoned a car on a Bronx, New York, expressway, and within hours it was completely vandalized. A car similarly abandoned on a Palo Alto, California, street went undamaged for days. But it was not legitimate to conclude, as he did, anything about people in large cities versus those in smaller ones. One crucial fact is that far more people passed the Bronx car than passed the Palo Alto car, exposing the former to much greater risk. The New York people were not necessarily any different from the Californians. (Moreover, the cars were left in neighborhoods of very different social class; the Bronx expressway is a notorious dumping ground for ailing automobiles; and the places chosen were hardly representative of each type of community.)

15. Peasant revolts are, of course, common and were actually the rule in Communist successes. But, peasant uprisings are usually, at least at first, restorative and not radical (Hobsbawm, 1959; Tilly et al., 1975). The advantages of peasants over urban workers in modern times have probably less to do with motivation than with the tactical advantages of remote bases (see Gurr, 1971).

16. Actually, peasant revolts have often also occurred in Western history (Hobsbawm, 1959; Tilly et al., 1975). One of their interesting features—shared as well by the Chinese case—is that they tend to be *conservative* revolts. (See n. 15.)

17. Tolerating unconventionality is correlated with engaging in it (Fischer, 1982a: Chapter 6).

18. Fischer (1975c, 1982a: Chapter 6), Hoch (1972), Glenn and Alston (1967), Glenn and Hill (1977), Lowe and Peek (1974), Nelson et al. (1971), Williams et al. (1976), Willitis et al. (1974) versus Grasmick (1974) and White (1973: 27–28); Swedner (1960: 30–45).

19. Glenn and Hill (1977), Fischer (1975c; 1982a: 74), Stephan and McMullen (1982), and Grasmick and Grasmick (1978). But we should note that this is urbanism as *recollected* by respondents.

20. For some studies, see Fischer (1975c, 1982a), Nelson et al. (1971), Nelson and Potkin (1977), Perlman (1975: 143), Schnaiberg (1971), Seligson (1972), and the review by Argyle (1968). Roof (1976) suggests that the effect of urbanism is mediated by a dimension of localism versus cosmopolitanism. There are occasional negative

findings, such as van Es and Brown (1974) and Gulick (1980). Cross-cultural analysis of this issue is confounded by the fact that cities are also the sites of religions' "great traditions"—as we noted in the text.

21. On urban innovation and diffusion in general, see Turner (1940) and Rogers (1962). On inventions, see Ogburn and Duncan (1964), Feller (1973), Merton (1938b: 211–224), Higgs (1975), and H. L. Richardson (1973: 40–43).

22. A long list of scholars make this sort of claim, including Stein (1960), Greer (1962), Friedman and Miller (1965), and Palen (1979). See analysis in Sjoberg (1964, 1965a).

23. Lest this process seem like an irreversible juggernaut, there are cases in which the diffusion can be stymied or reversed—when, for example, historical events change the context [e.g., the rise in crime has reversed trends of opinion against the death penalty; Fischer (1978c: 157)], or when there is a strong traditionalist reaction (e.g., against the Equal Rights Amendment).

24. The argument I have made is neutral about the *content* of the unconventionality, implying that conservative as well as radical dissent will arise and diffuse from cities. Gerald Suttles and Mark Baldassare have suggested to me that there may be an inherent tendency for urban unconventionality to be liberal (in the classic sense of the word—emphasizing individual liberty against community control), because the constant process of innovation demands and produces tolerance for deviation.

25. Cohen et al. (1980) and Cohen and Felson (1979) suggest a sophisticated version of this argument, that property crime is a function of the amount of property and the absence of "guardians" staying home. Both are greater in cities.

26. Webster (1981: Table 20). The geography of communities as a factor is also implicated by the finding that robberies are more likely to occur on streets, the larger the community (Cohen et al., 1980).

27. This is *not* a false impression based on discriminatory police practices. Surveys of victims also show that blacks disproportionately commit serious crimes (Hindelang, 1978).

28. See, for example, Worden (In Press), Hoch (1974), Cohen and Johnson (1982), Zehr (1975), and Applebaum and Follett (1978). Shelley (1981) fairly well documents the wide and universal gap between urban and rural rates of property crime.

29. We have seen that unattached young men are most likely to be criminal. Indicators of social isolation seem to predict ecological rates of crime (Blau and Blau, 1982; Roncek, 1981). Crime rates are highest in areas and in historical periods of greatest rural-to-urban migration (Shelley, 1981; McHale and Johnson, 1976, 1977; Zehr, 1975)—presumably as a cause and an indicator of "breakdown," although that is debatable.

30. On the group nature of delinquency, see Erickson (1971), Einstadter (1969), and Cloward and Ohlin (1961), among others. See general discussion in Wilks (1967: 140–142).

31. Actually, once violent crime reaches very high levels, it may itself generate a social breakdown conducive of further crime.

32. Rates estimated from Webster (1981: 8) and *Statistical Abstract* (BOC, 1982a). Offender data are presented in Webster (1981: 9–10) and indicate that about 94 percent of blacks were killed by blacks. On racial differences, see Lane (1979) and Farley (1980).

33. This analysis of urban violence is pursued at greater length in Scherer et al. (1975: Chapter 8) and Fischer (1980). The major source on the topic of violent subcultures is Wolfgang and Ferracuti (1967). The kind of evidence offered *for* the proposition that certain subcultures teach their members to use violence readily includes, first, statistics showing huge variations between particular groups (the poor, the black, etc.) and others in rates of criminal violence; and second, ethnographic

descriptions of group differences [e.g., Hanna (1982); Merry (1981); Horowitz and Schwartz (1974); but see, also, Rossi et al. (1974)]. The kind of evidence presented *against* the proposition is the absence of major differences between such groups and the rest of the population in their answers to survey questions concerning violence and personal experiences with noncriminal violence (Erlanger, 1974; Ball-Rokeach, 1973). Although the documentation in support of the negative position is substantial, I am not fully convinced that the probes used in these surveys capture the essence of the "subculture of violence" thesis: that certain groups have, and perpetuate through socialization, a higher tendency to resort to violence and, consequently, greater proportions of their members who commit serious violence. An alternate interpretation of the data might be that of a "breakdown" model: Black culture does not value violence, but its ability to control its youth has broken down in American cities.

34. This is roughly what Zorbaugh meant when he said that Chicago's Lower North Side was not a "community":

> There are a few customs that are common at once to the "Gold Coast" and to "Little Sicily," and there is certainly no common view which holds the cosmopolitan population of this whole region together in any common purpose. Furthermore, the laws which prevail are not a communal product, and there is no organized public opinion which supports and contributes to their enforcement. In fact, it is doubtful whether, in any proper sense of the word, the "Lower North Side" can be called a community at all [*1929: xvii*].

Chapter 9
Within the Metropolis: City and Suburban Experiences

1. To what extent transport innovations caused, followed, or facilitated suburban expansion is still a matter of historical inquiry. Hershberg et al. (1981a), for example, claim that housing demand and prices mobilized suburbanization before there was effective and cheap transportation [and for yet another view, see R. Walker (1978)].

2. The statistics in Figure 12 further underestimate suburban growth because they include annexed areas within center cities (Kasarda and Redfearn, 1975).

3. Defining "suburb" requires more comment. Any satisfactory definition should neither severely violate nor bow to the common usage of the term. Therefore, any definition that categorizes a locality near the central business district as a suburb, or an area on the urban fringe as city, is unsatisfactory. A number of suggested criteria fail this test. These criteria include residential land use (what does one do with center-city residential areas?); density (outlying apartment areas exist; inlying low-density areas, though uncommon, do exist); housing type (most metropolitan areas have single-family housing throughout); commuting (virtually everyone who works commutes); recency of development (what do we do with engulfed villages or redeveloped downtowns?). To define suburbs in terms of "familism" begs the sociological question about the relationship between suburbanism and ways of life. The political definition has its virtues, but also its anomalies. (Los Angeles is a classic example. The "suburb" of Compton is a "stone's throw" from city hall, but it takes about an hour from downtown on the freeway to reach the city limits at the north end of the San Fernando Valley.) Virtually all of these definitions have something to recommend them; and virtually all are strongly related to distance. But none do quite as well as distance.

Five arguments support a definition based on distance: (1) distance appears in many common usages of suburb—for example, that a suburb is an outlying *and* residential area, or an outlying *and* low-density area; (2) distance is related to the historical meaning of the term—a residential area outside city walls; (3) distance is cross-culturally useful; in foreign nations, many of the other variables are inappropriate (e.g., political lines) or inconsistent there (e.g., residentiality), but distance is a simple universal; (4) distance determines the other definitions—for example, the farther out, the easier it is to maintain low density; and (5) distance is parsimonious and a simple ecological variable.

4. The basic sources on popular and scholarly views of suburbia are *The Suburban Myth* by Scott Donaldson (1969) and a chapter with a similar title in Bennett Berger's *Working-Class Suburb* (1960). Schwartz (1976, 1980) provides recent overviews.

5. Quoted by Flink (1976: 39).

6. Quoted from *Playboy* in the *San Francisco Chronicle,* 25 February 1982.

7. See Rossi (1955), Butler et al. (1968), Michelson et al. (1973), Michelson (1977: 138–142), Marshall (1979), and Fischer (1982a: Chapter 2).

8. Three research items support this conclusion. Guest (1972a) found that the concentration of child-rearing families in outer areas can be explained statistically by the spaciousness and newness of the dwellings. A recent study of movers in metropolitan areas found that those moving from the cities to the suburbs were *not* much more likely to endorse prosuburban views than were those moving within the city (Butler et al., 1968). And another national survey found that suburbanward movers moved overwhelmingly for personal reasons, such as a recent marriage. But they were more likely to have moved for neighborhood reasons than were the cityward movers (Goodman, 1979). For a thorough discussion of the effects of housing economics on suburban expansion, see Evans (1973).

9. Most studies cited in the Chapter 3 discussion of pollution point out that irritant levels are lower in suburban than in central districts.

10. In 1977, about one-half of the suburban households in the United States had two or more cars; only about one-third of city households did (BOC, 1977c).

11. Von Rosenbladt (1972) provides a tally of services by distance from the city center in a German community and Yancey and Ericksen (1979: Table 1) do the same for Philadelphia. On complaints by suburbanites about lack of services, see Warner (1962: 158), Hawley and Zimmer (1971), Michelson (1973a), and Louis Harris Assoc. (1979: 110–114). Gans (1967) and Popenoe (1977) point out that groups with specialized needs, for example, adolescents, suffered most from this problem. On the elderly, see Bourg (1975). Suburbanites tend to travel farther to schools, churches, stores, and jobs than do city residents. But they seem not, on the average, to spend more *time* on these trips, because a higher proportion of suburbanites than city-dwellers drive cars. See Hawley and Zimmer (1971), von Rosenbladt (1972), Oi and Shuldiner (1962), Stegman (1969), and Michelson (1977).

12. See Farley (1976), Muller (1974), Berry et al. (1976), Marshall (1979), and Frey (1979), versus Guterbock (1976).

13. In 1977, 44 percent of suburban households had children under 18; for city households the figure was 35 percent (BOC, 1977a: 5). Another factor at work may be the tendency for city apartment managers to bar children.

14. Modell (1979) presents complex arguments and data contending that the familistic American suburb is a relatively new, post-World War II, phenomenon.

15. The figures are drawn from Heber's (1983a, 1983b) early report of 1980 census data or calculated from various tables in the 1981 *Statistical Abstract* based on current population surveys (BOC, 1982a: 432–441). See, also, Long and Dahman (1980) and Roof and Spain (1977).

16. Some have failed to find social–class differences between cities and suburbs. Anderson and Egeland (1961) and Guest (1971) report that occupational prestige did

not increase much with distance from city center in their ecological studies. The problem seems to have been the use of prestige instead of income. The census reports that, within occupational types, suburbanites earn more than city-dwellers (Burt and Weber, 1972: Table 116). Preparing Fischer and Jackson (1976), we found, in a sample of white males in Detroit, that distance from the city center was correlated about 0.3 with respondents' family income, though only about 0.2 with their education and occupational prestige. Another problem that has bedeviled the literature on this issue is the technical difficulties that arise as a result of arbitrary city boundaries (Schnore, 1972).

17. The historical reversal in the association between suburbanism and social class is briefly explained in Chapter 3. See Evans (1973: Chapter 10) for a more sophisticated economic model. In the United States, young and small metropolitan areas less often exhibit the pattern of suburban affluence than large metropolises do. This appears to be a result partly of statistical artifacts produced by political boundaries, partly of often having developed in the automobile age rather than the trolley era, partly of less-developed transit systems in smaller communities (which reduce the attraction of suburban residence), and partly of less congestion and deterioration in their centers (making city residence less offensive). See Schnore and Winsborough (1972) and Guest (1972b).

18. In unreported analyses prepared for Fischer (1982a), we found a strong correlation between a neighborhood being suburban and local informants considering its residents to be homogenous in life-style. On the other hand, Farley (1976) reports no association of distance with demographic homogeneity. Methodological difficulties confound analyses of homogeneity. One problem is the measurement of variability: Inevitably, it seems, the measure is affected by the direction of skewness in the distribution of the given attribute, thus producing a correlation between measures of central tendency and measures of dispersion. Another problem is the unit of analysis. At the largest level, city municipalities versus suburban townships, the latter are more homogeneous than the former. At the smallest level reported in the literature (census tracts), the results are ambiguous (Fine et al., 1971). This probably results from the different areal sizes of city and suburban tracts. At intermediate levels—zones and neighborhoods—it appears that suburban localities are slightly more homogeneous than city localities (Kish, 1954; Bradburn et al., 1970). For a discussion of the methodological problems, see Roof and Van Valey (1972).

19. Studies of gentrifiers include Laska and Spain (1979), Gale (1980), Goldfield (1980), Bradley (1977), N. Smith (1979), and Hammett and Williams (1980). See Laska and Spain (1980) for a general collection discussing "Back to the City."

20. On complaints about crime and its relation to residential moves, see, for example, Louis Harris Assoc. (1979) and BOC (1977b: 14–15). Aggregate analyses suggesting that crime contributes to outmigration from cities include Marshall (1979) and Frey (1979) versus Guterbock (1976).

21. For the purposes of completeness, brief comments about the two omitted secondary groups are in order. 1) *Formal associations.* Two contrary speculations have been offered in this regard: one that suburbanism produces a veritable mania of joining and organizational activity (Whyte, 1956); the other that the drain of commuting reduces organizational participation, at least for males (Martin, 1959). There seem to be no major differences in membership not explainable by personal characteristics (see, for example, Hawley and Zimmer, 1971: 56; Berger, 1960: 59–64; Fischer, 1982b; cf. Gruenberg, 1974). Gans' (1967) study does indicate much joining during the early period of suburban settlement, but this is probably a passing phase (Dobriner, 1963). 2) *Occupational and class groups.* I would speculate here that suburbanism encourages (slightly) the strengthening of class groups at the expense of occupational groups. The argument is twofold: Residential location is

based on income, not job, so that the locality group overlaps more with the *class* group in the suburbs than in the city; at the same time, residential dispersal makes contact among occupational associates more difficult.

22. On suburban resistance to metropolitan government, see Greer (1963), Campbell and Dollenmeyer (1975), and Hawley and Zimmer (1971).

23. At least two studies have found that white suburbanites, though not particularly prejudiced in general, are more resistant to housing integration than are white city-dwellers (Campbell, 1971; Wirt et al., 1972). For general discussions of suburban politics, see Wirt et al. (1972), Wood (1958), Gans (1967), Greer and Orleans (1962), and Greer and Greer (1976).

24. A list of studies on neighboring, as well as further data, appears in Fischer and Jackson (1977). Most notable in that list are Michelson (1973a), Tomeh (1964), Fava (1959), Tallman and Morgner (1970), Berger (1960), and Gans (1967). More recent evidence include Warren (1977), Michelson (1977: 153–159), and Fischer (1982a, 1982b).

25. Hawley and Zimmer (1971: 58–64) examine the "scope" of daily activity engaged in by respondents to their survey, including distance to work, stores, friends, and the like. Not surprisingly, suburbanites travel farther, on the average, than city dwellers do (see n. 11). After all, suburbs are more dispersed. But the differences are not great. And among residents in the larger metropolitan areas who had not moved from the adjacent city (i.e., had not left behind social ties), the differences were reversed; their lives were more spatially circumscribed than those of comparable city-dwellers.

26. Tomeh (1964) found in a Detroit study that suburbanites reported seeing friends (and neighbors) slightly more often than did city-dwellers, and had just as frequent contact as the latter did with kin and coworkers. But in analyses I and my associates did on a 1965 survey of Detroit men, we found no association between suburbanism and either reported number of friends or friendship intimacy (Fischer and Jackson, 1977; Baldassare and Fischer, 1975). In the Northern California Community Study, suburbanites reported more kin than did city-dwellers, but no more nonkin associates. Exclusive of kin and of neighbors, and holding constant background characteristics, suburbanites may have actually had slightly fewer nonkin associates (Fischer, 1982b). See, also, Sutcliffe and Crabbe (1963).

27. Michelson (1973a), Gans (1967), Clark (1966), Berger (1960), Young and Willmott (1957), Smith et al. (1954), Fischer and Jackson (1977), and Fischer (1982a, 1982b).

28. Veroff et al. (1981a: 431) claim to see signs of insecurity in suburbanites' feelings about family roles, but the data are slim. One must keep in mind that suburban families are somewhat self-selected—by wealth and by familistic interest (Michelson, 1977; Bell, 1959, 1968)—which would lead us to expect, if for that reason alone, more cohesive family life in the suburbs.

29. This has been reported by Tallman (1969), Gans (1967), Clark (1966), and Michelson (1973a). On the other hand, the Northern California data show that suburbanites were involved with more kin than were city-dwellers—in large part because of self-selection by age and marital status and in part because suburbanites lived in single-family houses (Fischer, 1982b). The connection between the house and kin ties probably reflects self-selection, too, in that house-buying is part of a commitment to familism (see Fischer, 1982a: 369, n. 10).

30. Studies that have failed to establish notable, general effects of city-versus-suburban residence on psychological states include Berger (1960), Pahl (1970: 125–227), Baldassare and Fischer (1975), Veroff et al. (1981), and Fischer (1982a, 1982b). James (1968) found that "anomia" scores were higher among low-status people in St.

Louis than among low-status people in the suburbs. Critically, however, he did not control for race.

31. Studies have linked suburban women's distress to unemployment (which other research has shown impairs mental health), to uprooting from kin and friends, and to simple boredom, especially for those without personal cars. See Tallman (1969), Gans (1967), Young and Willmott (1957), Clark (1966), Michelson (1973a), Foote et al. (1960: 186), Gillespie (1971), and Fava (1975). Berger notes this problem in passing. He also remarks that the rate of employment among the wives of the newly suburbanized auto workers whom he studied dropped precipitously after the move. In fact, 2 of Berger's 50 male respondents had been deserted by their wives because of the women's inability to adjust to suburbia (1960: 70, n. 31)! L. M. Jones (1974) has documented suburban women's low access to jobs and supportive services, which probably reduces their chances for employment. In preparing Fischer and Jackson (1976), we found, while analyzing a national survey, that the suburban–city distinction was significantly related to men's responses to the question of whether they would be unhappy if they had to move (suburban men less happy), but only marginally related to women's responses. In the Northern California study, we found suburban women to be the only distinctly distressed residential group (Fischer, 1982a: 129). For general reviews of women in suburbia, see Fava (1978), *Signs* (1980), and Harkess (1978).

32. For example, Gallup Polls report attitude differences by metropolitan size, but rarely distinguish center cities from suburbs. Studies in foreign nations are, because of population distributions, largely concentrated on urban–rural rather than city–suburban contrasts. And for historical research, suburbs are relatively new.

33. Carlos (1970), Tallman and Morgner (1970), Fischer (1975c), and Berger (1960). Contrary data are reported by Zimmer and Hawley (1959). See also W. Newman (1976).

34. The application of Wirthian theory to differences within an urbanized area is hindered by one major difficulty: The primary process in the theory is the structural differentiation that results from urbanism. Suburbs are a part of that structural differentiation. That is, suburban communities are specialized territorial units within the greater metropolitan area, emphasizing residence, or in some cases, industry, and housing a selected subsection of the population (Obgurn, 1937). In this sense, the determinist theory of urban anomie is about a whole metropolis and thus cannot be applied to differences within it. But the secondary process in the Wirthian theory might be applicable. This is the argument concerning direct psychological experiences—the "psychic overload" analysis (see Chapter 2).

Chapter 10
The Urban Future: Conclusions, Projections, and Policies

1. One of the more important of these questions concerns the term "community" to refer to human settlements. Are towns and cities, particularly in modern societies, socially significant social forms or are they just differentiated pieces of a national social structure, their cultures simply local manifestations of a national one? More broadly, to what degree is "community"—rural, urban, or suburban—a useful concept in sociology (Greer, 1962; Castells, 1968, 1969; Pickvance, 1974). Similarly, what is the significance of a particular geographical location for a person, particularly in an age of telephones, television, and supersonic airliners? Phrased another way, what is the essential role of space in human relationships? (Webber, 1963,

1970; Bernard, 1973). Another issue concerns the urban–rural distinction. Urban sociology has long used the rural–urban continuum as a basic conceptual scheme for sorting communities. And this book has followed that tradition. But perhaps there is a quite different and more revealing conceptual scheme that could be used. Several have been casually suggested—for example, schemes based on economics or political structure—but no alternative to the variable of urbanism has been fully developed yet (Fischer, 1975a).

2. In the first chapter, we pointed out that one motive for sociologists to study the city is their impression that the processes set into motion by urbanization at the local level parallel and forecast processes accompanying modernization at the societal level. In particular, the joining together of a nation by modern communication and transport has been regarded as similar to the coming together of people in cities. Assuming that the parallelism is valid, our conclusions have direct implications for certain theories about the direction of modern society, in particular, for those about "mass society"—the thesis that modernization erases cultural differences among social units, such as ethnicity, regions, and classes, and results in an atomized mass of individuals who are spoon-fed a cultural pabulum by the media. The conclusion that follows from our analysis holds quite the opposite: that the development of communications and transportation leads to the differentiation of cultural groups, including the appearance of groups founded on new bases of association (hobbies, politics, life-styles, and the like) and to an increased freedom of choice for persons in the society; in short, to a pluralist society rather than a mass society (Shils, 1962; Wilensky, 1964; Webber, 1968a: 189).

3. To avoid leaving the impression that, in this passage, I have endorsed the canard that sociology merely ratifies common sense, I will continue: An analogy can be made to folk astronomy. Primitive beliefs about celestial processes are fairly accurate descriptors and predictors of, for example, sunrises and seasonal changes, in spite of the fact that they are greatly mistaken in their explanations of those events. Scientific astronomy is, in practical terms, not so much better in predicting our common folk experience, though it provides a much improved explanation of those experiences. In that sense, sociology should not be expected, in most cases, to find popular *descriptions* of events to be altogether mistaken but only to provide better *explanations* of those phenomena.

4. Urban violence provides a major impetus for national programs that would redistribute population away from the large metropolises (Sundquist, 1975: Chapter 1).

5. One concern is the possibility of a catastrophic energy shortage. Even were this to become a drastic reality, it is still unlikely that "supercity" would result. Large cities are highly dependent on cheap energy to bring resources to their residents from the hinterland. The more likely consequence of an "eco-catastrophe" would be dense but small and scattered communities.

6. For similar speculations, see Willbern (1964), Friedman and Miller (1965), Greer (1962), Abu-Lughod (1966), and J. Ward (1972).

7. There is some consistency among speculators in preferring the 50,000-to-200,000 range (Sale, 1978), but that is not the same thing as consistent evidence.

8. This does not stop people from trying to come up with summary "quality of life" measures and then ranking communities accordingly, a procedure that ignores the fact that one man's quality of life is another man's poison (Park, 1952). Unlike combining different indicators of similar phenomena—say, measures of health, or wealth—this procedure sums indicators of quite disparate phenomena, largely on the basis of the researcher's values concerning what is "good" or "bad." On the topic of the optimal city size, see H. L. Richardson (1973), Duncan (1957), Alonso

(1971, 1975), Edel et al. (1974), Hoover (1972), Dahl and Tufte (1973), Gilbert (1976) and its following debate, Richardson (1976) versus Gilbert (1977).

9. In one survey, a majority of Americans agreed that the "Federal government should discourage further growth of large metropolitan areas" (52 percent) and that it should "encourage people and industry to move to smaller cities and towns" [58 percent (Mazie and Rawlings, 1972; Sundquist, 1975)]. On the other hand, most people also support spending money to rebuild the cities (Field, 1978).

10. The theory economists have developed to explain how a city could get larger than it "should" is based on the notion of "externalities." Each extra resident of a city does not have to pay the full cost his or her presence brings in pollution, congestion, and so on. Instead, that cost is shared by all the residents of the city. Consequently, each individual is encouraged to come and stay, even though for the city as a whole the resulting costs outweigh the benefits. (This is one variation on the general problem of "collective irrationality.") For a discussion of this thesis, see Alonso (1975).

11. There are apparently few, if any, objective summary assessments of British New Towns. The comments in the text are based largely upon Thomas (1969), Eldridge (1967), Gutheim (1967), Willmott (1967), Johnston (1977), Hall (1977: 41–42), and Popenoe (1980). There are several studies of specific New Towns, e.g., Willmott (1963), and Mogey (1956).

12. The New Deal plan for "greenbelt" towns resulted in only three, notably Radburn, New Jersey. In the 1970s, escalating start-up costs and confusions about political jurisdiction led to abandoning New Town subsidies. (See "HUD Revaluating 'New Towns' Program," *New York Times*, 23 July 1976; "HUD Gives Up on New Towns," *Boston Globe*, 28 September 1978).

13. A number of these direct solutions involve changing "externalities" to "internalities." For general discussions, see Alonso (1971, 1972, 1975).

14. This view is generally one held by many urban ecologists (Kasarda, 1980; Hawley, 1981) and by conservative economists influential in the Reagan Administration. The report has stirred much debate. See, for example, "Help Old Cities or Encourage the Crowd to Escape Them," (*New York Times*, 15 March 1981) and Glickman (1981).

15. For estimates on the spatial effects of federal policy, see Peterson (1980), Vaughan (1980), and Glickman (1980). For more general and "radical" critiques of government's antiurban role, see, for example, essays in Dear and Scott (1981), and Walker (1978), Molotch (1976), Bender (1983), and Yago (1983).

16. See Laquian and Simmons (1979), Sawers (1977), Chen (1972), Bernstein (1977), and Frolic (1978).

17. See Logan and Schneider (1979), Schneider and Logan (1981), Popenoe (1979), Shlay and Rossi (1981), and Hill (1975).

REFERENCES

The page of the text on which a particular study is discussed is indicated by a bold-face number at the end of the entry.

Abbott, W. F. 1974. "Moscow in 1897 as a pre-industrial city." *American Sociological Review* 39: 542–550. **247, 252, 298**

Abler, R. 1975. "Effects of space-adjusting technologies on the human geography of the future," pp. 35–56 in R. Abler et al. (eds.) *Human Geography in a Changing World.* Belmont, CA: Duxbury. **280**

Abrahamson, M. 1974. "The social dimensions of urbanism." *Social Forces 52:* 376–383. **299**

——— and M. A. Du Bick. 1977. "Patterns of urban dominance: the U.S. in 1890." *American Sociological Review* 42: 756–768. **299**

Abu-Lughod, J. A. 1966. "The city is dead—long live the city: some thoughts on urbanity," Monograph 12. Berkeley, CA: Center for Planning and Research. **294, 298, 322**

———. 1971. *Cairo.* Princeton, NJ: Princeton University Press. **46, 53, 132**

——— and R. Hay, Jr. (eds.) 1980. *Third World Urbanization.* New York: Methuen. **301**

Adams, B. 1966. *Kinship in an Urban Setting.* Chicago: Markham. **311**

Aiello, J. R., and A. Baum. 1979. *Residential Crowding and Design.* New York: Plenum. **311, 312**

Aiello, J. R., Y. M. Epstein, and R. A. Karlin. 1975. "Effects of crowding on electrodermal activity." *Sociological Symposium* 14: 43–58. **311**

Aiken, M., and R. R. Alford. 1974. "Community structure and innovation: the case of urban renewal." *American Sociological Review* 39: 19–28. **116**

Aksoy, S. 1969. "The impact of urbanization on change." Mimeographed. Cambridge, MA: Harvard University Center for International Affairs (January). [Findings reported in Inkeles (1969).] **207**

Alba, R. 1976. "Social assimilation among American Catholic national-origin groups." *American Sociological Review* 41: 1030–1047. **148**

——— and M. B. Chamlin. 1983. "Ethnic identification among whites." *American Sociological Review* 48: 240–248. **254**

Alden, A. 1887. *Poems.* Wilton, ME. **17**

Aldous, J. 1962. "Urbanization, the extended family, and kinship ties in West Africa." *Social Forces* 61: 6–12. **310**

Alexander, C. 1967. "The city as a mechanism for sustaining human contact." Reprinted in J. Helmer and N. A. Eddington (eds.) *Urbanman.* New York: Free Press, 1973: 239–274. **6, 157, 192, 202, 306**

Alford, R. R. 1972. "Critical evaluation of the principles of city classification," pp. 331–359 in B.J.L. Berry (ed.) *City Classification Handbook.* New York: John Wiley. **212, 304**

——— and E. C. Lee. 1968. "Voting turnout in American cities." *American Political Science Review* 62: 796–813. **304**

——— and H. M. Scoble. 1968. "Sources of local political involvement." *American Political Science Review* 62: 1192–1206.

Allan, G. A. 1979. *A Sociology of Friendship and Kinship.* London: Allen and Unwin. **156**

Alland, A. 1972. *The Human Imperative.* New York: Columbia University Press. **311**

Allen, I. L. 1968. "Community size, population composition, and cultural activity in smaller communities." *Rural Sociology* 33: 328–338. **300**

Alonso, W. 1964. "The historic and structural theories of urban form." *Land Economics* 60: 227–231. **49**

———. 1970. "What are new towns for?" *Urban Studies* 7: 30–55. **287**

———. 1971. "The economics of urban size." *Papers of the Regional Science Association* 26: 67–83. **71, 85, 322, 323**

———. 1972. "Problems, purposes, and implicit policies for a national strategy of urbanization," pp. 631–648 in S. M. Mazie (ed.) *Population, Distribution, and Policy,* Vol. V. Research Reports. Washington, DC: U.S. Commission of Population and the Future. **323**

———. 1975. "City sizes and quality of life: some observations." Paper presented to the American Association for the Advancement of Science (January), New York. **85, 287, 323**

———. 1978. "Metropolis without growth." *The Public Interest* 53: 68–86. **92, 93, 301**

———. 1980. "The population factor and urban structure," pp. 32–51 in A. P. Solomon (ed.) *The Prospective City.* Cambridge, MA: MIT Press. **279**

——— and M. Fajans. 1970. "Cost of living and income by urban size," Working Paper No. 128. Berkeley, CA: Institute of Urban and Regional Development.

Altman, I. 1978. "Crowding: historical and contemporary trends in crowding research," pp. 3–31 in A. Baum and M. Epstein (eds.) *Human Response to Crowding.* Hillsdale, NJ: Lawrence Erlbaum. **311**

American Public Health Association (APHA). 1970. *Proceedings of the First Invitational Conference on Health Research in Housing and Its Environment.* Washington, DC: American Public Health Association. **299, 310**

Anderson, B. A. 1977. "Who chose cities: migrants to Moscow and St. Petersburg cities in the late nineteenth century," pp. 277–295 in R. D. Lee (ed.) *Population Patterns in the Past.* New York: Academic Press. **301**

Anderson, E. 1978. *A Place on the Corner.* Chicago: University of Chicago Press. **157**

Anderson, E. N., Jr. 1972. "Some Chinese methods of dealing with crowding." *Urban Anthropology* 1: 141–150. **183**

Anderson, M. 1971. *Family Structure in Nineteenth Century Lancashire.* Cambridge, England: Cambridge University Press. **163, 168, 310**

———. 1973. "Family, household, and industrial revolution." Reprinted in M. Gordon (ed.) *The American Family in Historical Perspective.* New York: St. Martin's, 1975: 34–58. **310**

Anderson, T. R., and J. A. Egeland. 1961. "Spatial aspects of social area analysis." *American Sociological Review* 26: 392–399. **247, 318**

Applebaum, R. P., and R. Follett. 1978. "Size, growth, and urban life: a study of medium-sized American cities." *Urban Affairs Quarterly* 14: 139–168. **316**

Archer, D., R. Gartner, and R. Akert et al. 1978. "Cities and homicide: a new look at an old paradox." *Comparative Studies in Sociology* 1: 73–95. **302, 303**

Ardrey, R. 1961. *African Genesis.* New York: Atheneum. **294**

———. 1966. *The Territorial Imperative.* New York: Atheneum. **294**

Arensberg, C. M. 1965. "The community as object and as sample," pp. 7–27 in C. M. Arensberg and S. T. Kimball (eds.) *Culture and Community.* New York: Harcourt Brace Jovanovich. **4, 294**

———. 1968a. *The Irish Countryman.* Rev. ed. Garden City, NY: Natural History Press. **133, 205**

———. 1968b. "The urban in crosscultural perspective," pp. 3–15 in E. M. Eddy (ed.) *Urban Anthropology.* Athens: University of Georgia Press. **295**

Arensen, K. W. 1981. "Housing: After 50 Years, the Heyday Is Over." *New York Times,* 29 March. **65**

Argyle, M. 1968. "Religious observance," vol. 13, pp. 1–38 in D. L. Sills (ed.) *International Encyclopedia of the Social Sciences.* New York: Macmillan and Free Press. **315**

Arkes, H. 1981. *The Philosopher in the City: The Moral Dimensions of Urban Politics.* Princeton, NJ: Princeton University Press. **231**

Axelrod, M. 1956. "Urban structure and social participation." *American Sociological Review* 21: 14–18. **305, 310, 311**

Babchuck, N., and A. Booth. 1969. "Voluntary association membership: a longitudinal analysis." *American Sociological Review* 34: 31–45. **305**

Bach, W. 1972. "Urban climate, air pollution and planning," pp. 69–96 in T. R. Detwyler and M. G. Marcus (eds.) *Urbanization and the Environment.* Belmont, CA: Duxbury. **54**

Bagley, C. 1968. "Migration, race and mental health: a review of some recent research." *Race* 3: 343–356. **301**

Bahr, H. M. 1973. *Skid Row: An Introduction to Disaffiliation.* New York: Oxford University Press. **125, 157**

Balazs, E. 1964. "Chinese towns," pp. 66–78 in E. Balazs (ed.) *Chinese Civilization and Bureaucracy.* New Haven, CT: Yale University Press. **217, 218**

Baldassare, M. 1975. "The effects of density on social behavior and attitudes." *American Behavioral Scientist* 18: 815–825.

———. 1977. "Residential density, household crowding, and social networks," pp. 101–116 in C. S. Fischer et al. (eds.) *Networks and Places.* New York: Free Press. **312**

————. 1978. "Human spatial behavior." *Annual Review of Sociology* 4: 29–56. **311**

————. 1979. *Residential Crowding in Urban America*. Berkeley: University of California Press. **176, 178, 183, 312**

————. 1981. "The effects of household density on subgroups." *American Sociological Review* 46: 110–118. **312**

————. 1982a. "The effects of neighborhood density and social control on resident satisfaction." *Sociological Quarterly* 23: 95–105. **312**

————. 1982b. *The Growth Dilemma*. Berkeley: University of California Press. **94, 295**

———— and S. Feller. 1976. "Cultural variation in personal space: theory, methods and evidence." *Ethos* 3: 481–503. **179, 181, 311**

Baldassare, M., and C. S. Fischer. 1975. "Suburban life: powerlessness and need for affiliation." *Urban Affairs Quarterly* 11: 314–326. **256, 299, 320**

————. 1976. "The relevance of crowding experiments to urban studies," pp. 273–284 in D. Stokols (ed.) *Psychological Perspectives on Environment and Behavior*. New York: Plenum. **185, 312**

Ball-Rokeach, S. J. 1973. "Values and violence: a test of the subculture of violence thesis." *American Sociological Review* 38: 736–749. **317**

Balzac, H. de. 1835. *Père Goriot*. Translated by H. Reed. Reprint ed., 1964. New York: New American Library. **110**

Bane, M. J. 1976. *Here to Stay: American Families in the Twentieth Century*. New York: Basic Books. **168**

Banfield, E. C. 1958. *The Moral Basis of a Backward Society*. New York: Free Press. **192, 310**

Banks, J. A. 1968. "Population change and the Victorian city." Reprinted in C. Tilly (ed.) *An Urban World*. Boston: Little, Brown, 1974: 358–368.

Barker, R. G., and P. V. Gump. 1964. *Big School, Small School*. Stanford, CA: Stanford University Press. **156, 204, 304**

Barnes, S. T., and M. Peil. 1977. "Voluntary association membership in five West African cities." *Urban Anthropology* 6: 83–106. **305**

Barnett, S. 1973. "Urban is as urban does." *Urban Anthropology* 2: 129–160. **154**

Baroja, J. C. 1963. "The city and the country: reflexions on some ancient commonplaces," pp. 473–485 in C. Tilly (ed.) *An Urban World*. Boston: Little, Brown. **14**

Baron, R. A., and P. A. Bell. 1976. "Physical distance and helping." *Journal of Applied Social Psychology* 6: 95–104. **181, 312**

Barringer, F. 1977. "Montgomery's New Frontier Beckons." *Washington Post,* 18 September. **238**

Barth, F. 1969. "Introduction," pp. 1–38 in F. Barth (ed.) *Ethnic Groups and Boundaries*. Boston: Little, Brown. **308**

Barton, J. J. 1975. *Peasants and Strangers: Italians, Rumanians, and Slovaks in an American City, 1890–1950*. Cambridge, MA: Harvard University Press. **49, 71, 305, 308**

Bascom, W. 1963. "The urban African and his world." Reprinted in S. F. Fava (ed.) *Urbanism in World Perspective*. New York: Crowell, 1968: 81–92. **86, 308**

Baskauskas, L. 1977. "Multiple identities: adjusted Lithuanian refugees in Los Angeles." *Urban Anthropology* 6: 141–154. **153, 204**

Bastide, H., and A. Girard. 1974a. "Mobilité de la population et motivations des personnes." *Population* 29: 579–607. **301**

————. 1974b. "Mobilité de la population et motivations des personnes, II: les motifs de la mobilité." *Population* 29: 743–769. **311**

Baum, A., and Y. M. Epstein (eds.) 1978. *Human Responses to Crowding*. Hillsdale, NJ: Lawrence Erlbaum. **311**

————, J. E. Singer, and S. Valins. 1978. *Advances in Environmental Psychology*. Hillsdale, NJ: Lawrence Erlbaum. **311, 312**

Baum, R. 1971. "The cultural revolution in the countryside," pp. 367–376 in T. W. Robinson (ed.) *The Cultural Revolution in China*. Berkeley: University of California Press. **218**

Beale, C. L. 1978. "People on the land," pp. 37–54 in T. R. Ford (ed.) *Rural U.S.A.: Persistence and Change*. Ames: Iowa State University Press. **92**

————. 1980. "The changing nature of rural employment," pp. 37–49 in D. L. Brown and J. M. Wardwell (eds.) *New Directions in Urban–Rural Migration*. New York: Academic Press. **93**

Bell, W. 1959. "Social choice, life styles, and suburban residence," pp. 225–247 in W. M. Dobriner (ed.) *The Suburban Community*. New York: G. P. Putnam's Sons. **243, 255, 265, 295, 320**

———. 1968. "The city, the suburb, and a theory of social choice," pp. 132–169 in S. Greer et al. (eds.) *The New Urbanization.* New York: St. Martin's. **243, 251, 255, 260, 265, 295, 320**

——— and M. Boat. 1957. "Urban neighborhoods and informal social relations." *American Journal of Sociology* 62: 391–398. **157, 164, 305, 307**

Bender, T. 1978. *Community and Social Change in America.* New Brunswick, NJ: Rutgers University Press. **295, 297**

———. 1983. "The end of the city?" *democracy* 3: 8–20. **323**

Bennett, S., and C. Earle. 1982. "The geography of strikes in the United States, 1881–1894." *Journal of Interdisciplinary History* 13: 63–84. **123**

Beranek, L. L. 1966. "Noise." *Scientific American.* **54**

Berger, B. 1960. *Working-Class Suburb.* Berkeley: University of California Press. **243, 245, 255, 259, 262, 266, 318, 319, 320, 321**

Berger, M. L. 1979. *The Devil Wagon in God's Country: The Automobile and Social Change in Rural America, 1893–1929.* Hamden, CT: Archon.

Berger, P., and R. J. Neuhaus. 1977. *To Empower People: The Role of Mediating Structures in Public Policy.* Washington, DC: American Enterprise Institute. **139**

Berkowitz, L., and B. McCaully. 1972. *Altruism and Helping Behavior.* New York: Academic Press. **210**

Bernard, J. 1973. *The Sociology of Community.* San Francisco: Scott Foresman. **321**

Bernstein, T. P. 1977. *Up to the Mountains and Down to the Villages.* New Haven, CT: Yale University Press. **323**

Berreman, G. D. 1978. "Scale and social relations," pp. 41–77 in F. Barth (ed.) *Scale and Social Organization.* Oslo, Sweden: Universitetsforlaget. **309**

Berry, B.J.L. 1967. *Geography of Market Centers and Retail Distribution.* Englewood Cliffs, NJ: Prentice-Hall. **66, 100, 300**

——— (ed.) 1972. *City Classification Handbook: Methods and Applications.* New York: John Wiley. **99**

———. 1976a. "Comparative urbanization strategies." Reprinted in L. Bourne and W. J. Simmons (eds.) *Systems of Cities.* New York: Oxford University Press, 1978: 502–510. **91, 292**

——— (ed.) 1976b. *Urbanization and Counter-Urbanization.* Urban Affairs Annual Reviews, Vol. 11. Beverly Hills, CA: Sage. **91**

——— and D. C. Dahmen. 1977. *Population Redistribution in the United States in the 1970s.* Washington, DC: National Academy of Sciences. **301**

———, C. A. Goodwin, and R. W. Lake et al. 1976. "Opposition to integration," pp. 221–265 in B. Schwartz (ed.) *The Changing Face of the Suburbs.* Chicago: University of Chicago Press. **318**

——— and J. D. Kasarda. 1977. *Contemporary Urban Ecology.* New York: Macmillan. **48, 298**

Betz, D. M. 1972. "The city as a system generating income inequality." *Social Forces* 51: 192–199. **301**

Bibb, R., and W. H. Form. 1977. "The effects of industrial, occupational, and sex stratification on wages in blue-collar markets." *Social Forces* 55: 974–996. **84**

Black, D. 1983. "Crime as social control." *American Sociological Review* 48: 34–45. **229**

Black, G. S. 1974. "Conflict in the community: a theory of the effects of community size." *American Political Science Review* 68: 1245–1261. **254, 304**

Blackwood, L. G., and E. H. Carpenter. 1978. "The importance of anti-urbanism in determining residential preferences and migration patterns." *Rural Sociology* 43: 31–47. **23, 295, 302**

Blake, G. H., and R. I. Lawless (eds.) 1980. *The Changing Middle Eastern City.* London: Croom Helm. **294**

Blau, J. R., and P. M. Blau. 1982. "The cost of inequality: metropolitan structure and violent crime." *American Sociological Review* 47: 114–129. **226, 316**

Blau, P. M., T. C. Blum, and J. C. Schwartz. 1982. "Heterogeneity and marriage." *American Sociological Review* 47: 45–62. **149**

Blau, P. M., and O. D. Duncan. 1967. *The American Occupational Structure.* New York: John Wiley. **83**

Blumenfeld, H. 1971. "Transportation in the modern metropolis," pp. 231–240 in L. S. Bourne (ed.) *Internal Structure of the City.* New York: Oxford University Press. **51**

Blumenthal, M. D., R. L. Kahn, and F. M. Andrews et al. 1972. *Justifying Violence: Attitudes of American Men.* Ann Arbor, MI: Institute for Social Research.   **217, 314**

Blumin, S. M. 1976. *The Urban Threshold: Growth and Change in a Nineteenth-Century American Community.* Chicago: University of Chicago Press.   **116, 305**

Bodnar, J., M. Weber, and R. Simon. 1979. "Migration, kinship, and adjustment: blacks and Poles in Pittsburgh, 1900–1930." *Journal of American History* 66: 548–565.   **87, 168**

Boissevain, J. 1973. *Friends of Friends.* London: Basil Blackwell.   **205, 303, 310**

Bonjean, C. M., and R. L. Lineberry. 1970. "The urbanization-party competition hypothesis: a comparison of all United States counties." *Journal of Politics* 32: 305–321.   **304**

Boorstin, D. J. 1973. *The Americans: The Democratic Experience.* New York: Random House.   **306**

Booth, A., and J. Cowell. 1976. "The effects of crowding upon health." *Journal of Health and Social Behavior* 17: 204–220.   **183**

―――― and J. N. Edwards. 1976. "Crowding and family relations." *American Sociological Review* 41: 308–321.   **183, 299**

Borchert, J. 1981. "Urban neighborhood and community: informal group life, 1850–1970." *Journal of Interdisciplinary History* 11: 607–632.   **301, 305**

Borhek, J. T. 1970. "Ethnic-group cohesion." *American Journal of Sociology* 76: 33–46.   **148, 151**

Bornstein, M. H., and H. G. Bornstein. 1976. "The pace of life." *Nature* (February 19): 557–559.   **314**

Bose, N. K. 1965. "Calcutta: a premature metropolis." Reprinted in K. Davis (ed.) *Cities.* San Francisco: W. H. Freeman, 1973: 251–262.   **76**

Bourg, C. J. 1975. "Elderly in a southern metropolitan area." *Gerontologist* 15: 15–22.   **259, 318**

Bourne, L. S. (ed.) 1971. *Internal Structure of the City.* New York: Oxford University Press.

―――. 1977–1978. "Some myths of Canadian urbanization." *Urbanism Past and Present* 5: 1–11.   **91, 298**

Boyer, P. 1978. *Urban Masses and Moral Order in America: 1820–1920.* Cambridge, MA: Harvard University Press.   **15, 89, 120**

Boyte, H. C. 1981. *The Backyard Revolution: Understanding the New Citizen Movement.* Philadelphia: Temple University Press.   **138, 307**

Bradburn, N. M., S. Sudman, and G. Glockel. 1970. *Racial Integration in American Neighborhoods.* Chicago: National Opinion Research Center.   **81, 306, 319**

Bradfield, S. 1973. "Selectivity in rural–urban migration: the case of Huaylas, Peru," pp. 351–372 in A. Southall (ed.) *Urban Anthropology.* New York: Oxford University Press.   **88, 301**

Bradley, D. S. 1977. "Neighborhood transition: middle-class home buying in an inner-city deteriorating community." Paper presented to the American Sociological Association (August), Chicago.   **319**

Brail, R. K., and F. S. Chapin, Jr. 1973. "Activity patterns of urban residents." *Environment & Behavior* 5: 163–190.   **98, 204**

Breese, G. (ed.) 1969. *The City in Newly Developing Countries.* Englewood Cliffs, NJ: Prentice-Hall.   **282**

Breton, R. 1964. "Institutional completeness of ethnic communities and the personal relations of immigrants." *American Journal of Sociology* 70: 193–205.   **71, 149**

Brown, D. L., and C. L. Beale. 1981. "Sociodemographic diversity," pp. 27–71 in A. Hawley and S. M. Mazie (eds.) *Nonmetropolitan America in Transition.* Chapel Hill: University of North Carolina Press.   **92**

Brown, D. L., and J. M. Wardwell (eds.) 1980. *New Directions in Urban–Rural Migration.* New York: Academic Press.   **301**

Bruner, E. M. 1961. "Urbanization and ethnic identity in North Sumatra." *American Anthropologist* 63: 508–521.   **148**

―――. 1962. "Medan: the role of kinship in an Indonesian city." Reprinted in W. Magnin (ed.) *Peasants in Cities.* Boston: Houghton Mifflin, 1970: 123–124.   **165**

―――. 1973a. "The expression of ethnicity in Indonesia," pp. 251–280 in A. Cohen (ed.) *Urban Ethnicity.* London: Tavistock.   **148, 151, 154**

―――. 1973b. "Kin and non-kin," pp. 373–392 in A. Southall (ed.) *Urban Anthropology.* New York: Oxford University Press.   **97, 163, 171**

Bryson, R. A., and J. E. Ross. 1972. "The climate of the city," pp. 51–68 in T. R. Detwyler and M. G. Marcus (eds.) *Urbanization and the Environment.* Belmont, CA: Duxbury. **54**

Buder, L. 1977. "Half of 1976 Murder Victims Had Criminal Records." *New York Times,* 28 August. **229**

————. 1978. "Murders by Friends and Relatives Found Rising in New York." *New York Times,* 25 June. **229**

Bultena, G. L. 1969. "Rural–urban differences in familial interaction." *Rural Sociology* 34: 5–15. **165, 311**

Burgess, A. 1972. "Cucarachas and Exiles, Potential Death and Life Enhancement." *New York Times Magazine,* 29 October.

Burgess, E. W., and D. J. Bogue (eds.) 1964. *Contributions to Urban Sociology.* Chicago: University of Chicago Press. **28**

Burgess, E. W., and H. J. Locke. 1953. *The Family.* 2nd ed. New York: American Book Company. **260, 310**

Burstein, A. N. 1981. "Immigrants and residential mobility," pp. 174–203 in T. Hershberg (ed.) *Philadelphia.* New York: Oxford University Press. **309**

Burstein, P. 1972. "Social structure and political participation in five countries." *American Journal of Sociology* 77: 1087–1111. **304**

Butler, E. W., F. S. Chapin, Jr., and G. C. Hemmens et al. 1968. *Moving Behavior and Residential Choice.* Chapel Hill, NC: Center for Urban and Regional Studies. **241, 245, 300, 318**

Butterworth, D. S. 1962. "A study of the urbanization process among Mixtec migrants from Tilantongo to Mexico City." Reprinted in W. Magnin (ed.) *Peasants in Cities.* Boston: Houghton Mifflin. 1970: 98–113. **165, 192, 308**

Butterworth, D. 1977. "Selectivity of out-migration from a Mixtec community." *Urban Anthropology* 6: 129–140. **301**

———— and J. K. Chance. 1981. *Latin American Urbanization.* New York: Cambridge University Press. **88, 163, 301, 308**

Calhoun, J. B. 1962. "Population density and social pathology." *Scientific American* 206: 139–148. **174, 311**

Campbell, A. 1971. *White Attitudes toward Black People.* Ann Arbor, MI: Institute for Social Research. **320**

————. 1981. *The Sense of Well-Being in America.* New York: McGraw-Hill. **306, 313**

————, P. E. Converse, and W. E. Miller et al. 1964. *The American Voter.* Abr. ed. New York: John Wiley. **123**

————, P. E. Converse, and W. Rodgers. 1976. *The Quality of American Life.* New York: Russell Sage. **313**

Campbell, A. K., and J. Dallenmyer. 1975. "Governance in a metropolitan society," pp. 355–396 in A. Hawley and V. Rock (eds.) *Metropolitan America in a Contemporary Perspective.* New York: Halstead. **320**

Canada. Statistics Canada. 1980. *Crime and Traffic Enforcement Statistics.* Ottawa: Information Canada. **106, 302**

Canby, V. 1974. "New York's Woes Are Good Box Office." *New York Times,* 10 November. **295**

Canter, D. 1974. "The Menace of Suburbia." *San Francisco Examiner,* 8 December. **241**

Cantor, M. H. 1975. "Life space and the social support system of the inner city elderly of New York." *Gerontologist* 15: 23–26. **259, 311**

Cantril, H. 1965. *The Pattern of Human Concerns.* New Brunswick, NJ: Rutgers University Press. **196, 310**

Cardona, R., and A. Simmons. 1975. "Toward a model of migration in Latin America," pp. 19–48 in B. M. du Toit and H. I. Safa (eds.) *Migration and Urbanization.* The Hague, Netherlands: Mouton. **88**

Carlos, S. 1970. "Suburban–urban religious participation." *American Journal of Sociology* 75: 742–759. **321**

Carnahan, D., W. Gove, and O. R. Galle. 1974. "Urbanization, population density and overcrowding." *Social Forces* 53: 62–72. **52**

Carp, F. M. 1975. "Life-style and location within the city." *Gerontologist* 75: 27–33. **259**

Carpenter, D. B. 1960. "Urbanization and social change in Japan." *Sociological Quarterly* (July): 155–166. **298, 310, 313**

Carpenter, E. H., 1977a. "The importance of anti-urbanism in determining residential preferences and migration patterns." Working paper, University of Arizona, Tucson. **23, 187, 295, 296, 302**

———. 1977b. "The potential for population dispersal." *Rural Sociology* 42: 352–370. **288**

Carr, G. 1975. "Explaining urban form." Paper presented to the American Sociological Association (August), San Francisco. **298**

Carrothers, G. A. 1956. "An historical review of the gravity and potential concepts of human interaction." *Journal of the American Institute of Planners* 22: 94–102. **296**

Carstairs, G. M. 1969. "Overcrowding and human aggression," pp. 751–764 in H. D. Graham and T. R. Gurr (eds.) *Violence in America.* New York: Bantam. **311**

Cassel, J. 1972. "Health consequences of population density and crowding," pp. 249–270 in R. Gutman (ed.) *People and Buildings.* New York: Basic Books. **57, 312**

Castells, M. 1968. "Is there an urban sociology?" Reprinted in C. G. Pickvance (ed.) *Urban Sociology: Critical Essays.* London: Tavistock, 1976: 33–59. **294, 296, 297, 321**

———. 1969. "Theory and ideology in urban sociology." Reprinted in C. G. Pickvance (ed.) *Urban Sociology: Critical Essays.* London: Tavistock, 1976: 60–84. **297, 321**

———. 1977. *The Urban Question.* Translated by Alan Sheridan. Cambridge, MA: MIT Press. **297, 305**

———. 1978. *City, Class and Power.* Translated by E. Lebas. London: Macmillan. **49, 139**

———. 1983. *The City and the Grass Roots.* Berkeley: University of California Press. **117, 139, 305, 307**

Chen, P. -C. 1972. "Overurbanization, rustication of urban-educated youth, and the politics of rural transformation: the case of China." *Comparative Politics* 4: 361–386. **323**

Chernin, A. J. 1981. *Marriage, Divorce, Remarriage.* Cambridge, MA: Harvard University Press. **168, 169**

Childe, V. G. 1951. *Man Makes Himself.* New York: New American Library. **294**

Chilsom, J. J., Jr. 1971. "Lead poisoning." *Scientific American.* **56**

Chinoy, E. (ed.) 1973. *The Urban Future.* New York: Lieber-Atherton. **278, 279**

Choldin, H. M. 1978. "Urban density and pathology." *Annual Review of Sociology* 4: 91–114. **182, 311**

Christian, J. J., J. A. Lloyd, and D. E. Davis. 1960. "Factors in the mass mortality of a herd of Sina deer, *Cervus nippon.*" *Chesapeake Science* 1: 79–95. **179**

Christie, R., and F. L. Geis. 1970. *Studies in Machiavellianism.* New York: Academic Press. **314**

Christman, K., and R. J. Ofshe. In press. "Social behavior: a two-process analysis" Unpublished. University of California, Berkeley. **210**

Chudacoff, H. P. 1975. *The Evolution of American Urban Society.* Englewood Cliffs, NJ: Prentice-Hall. **30, 46, 309**

Clark, P., and P. Slack. 1976. *English Towns in Transition, 1500–1700.* London: Oxford University Press. **220, 298**

Clark, S. D. 1966. *The Suburban Society.* Toronto: University of Toronto Press. **251, 255, 256, 267, 320, 321**

Clarke, M. 1974. "On the concept of 'sub-culture.'" *British Journal of Sociology* 25: 428–441. **297**

Clay, P. L. 1980. "The rediscovery of city neighborhoods: reinvestment by long-time residents and newcomers," pp. 13–26 in S. B. Laska and D. Spain (eds.) *Back to the City.* New York: Pergamon. **249**

Clemente, F., and M. B. Kleiman. 1977. "Fear of crime in the United States." *Social Forces* 56: 519–531. **302**

Clemente, F., and R. B. Sturgis. 1972. "The division of labor in America." *Social Forces* 51: 176–181. **301**

Clinard, M. B. 1964. "Deviant behavior: Urban–rural contrasts," pp. 237–244 in C. E. Elias, Jr., J. Gillies, and S. Reimer (eds.) *Metropolis: Values in Conflict.* Belmont, CA: Wadsworth. **188, 192, 220, 310**

———. 1978. *Cities with Little Crime: The Case of Switzerland.* New York: Cambridge University Press. **227, 287, 302**

——— and D. J. Abbott. 1973. *Crime in Developing Countries.* New York: John Wiley. **208, 302**

Cloward, R. A., and L. A. Ohlin. 1961. *Delinquency and Opportunity.* Glencoe, IL: Free Press. **228, 316**

Cohen, A. 1969. *Custom and Politics in Urban Africa.* Berkeley: University of California Press. **81, 154, 307**

Cohen, D., and E. A. Johnson. 1982. "French criminality: urban–rural differences in the nineteenth century." *Journal of Interdisciplinary History* 12: 477–501. **303, 316**

Cohen, L. E., and M. Felson. 1979. "Social change and crime rates: a routine activity approach." *American Sociological Review* 44: 588–607. **302**

—— and K. C. Land. 1980. "Property crime rates in the United States." *American Journal of Sociology* 86: 90–118. **316**

Cohen, L. E., J. R. Kluegel, and K. C. Land. 1981. "Social inequality and predatory criminal victimization." *American Sociological Review* 46: 505–524. **302**

Cohen, S. D. 1978. "Environmental load and the allocation of attention," pp. 1–30 in A. Baum et al. (eds.), *Advances in Environmental Psychology 1: The Urban Environment.* Hillsdale, NJ: Lawrence Erlbaum. **177**

——, D. C. Glass, and J. E. Singer. 1973. "Apartment noise, auditory discrimination, and reading ability in children." *Journal of Experimental Social Psychology* 9: 407–422. **55**

Cohen, S. M. 1977. "Socioeconomic determinants of intraethnic marriage and friendship." *Social Forces* 55: 997–1010. **308**

—— and R. E. Kapsis. 1977. "Religion, ethnicity and party affiliation." *Social Forces* 56: 637–653. **308**

Coleman, J. S. 1957. *Community Conflict.* New York: Free Press. **304**

——. 1971. "Community disorganization and social conflict," pp. 657–708 in R. Merton and R. Nisbet (eds.) *Contemporary Social Problems.* 3rd ed. New York: Harcourt Brace Jovanovich. **132**

Colson, E. 1974. *Tradition and Contract: The Problem of Order.* Chicago: Aldine. **231**

Commission on Population Growth and the American Future (CPG). 1972. *Population and the American Future.* New York: New American Library. **20**

Connell, J., B. Dasgupta, and R. Laishley et al. 1976. *Migration from Rural Areas: The Evidence from Village Studies.* Delhi: Oxford University Press. **301**

Conzen, K. N. 1975. "Patterns of residence in early Milwaukee," pp. 145–183 in L. F. Schnore (ed.) *The New Urban History.* Princeton, NJ: Princeton University Press. **247, 298**

——. 1976. *Immigrant Milwaukee.* Cambridge, MA: Harvard University Press. **120**

Cook, W. L. 1893. "Murders in Massachusetts." *Journal of the American Statistical Association:* (September) 357–378. **302, 303**

Coombs, L. C., and T. H. Sun. 1981. "Familial values in a developing society: a decade of change in Taiwan." *Social Forces* 59: 1229–1255. **221, 300**

Cooper, C. C. 1972. "Resident dissatisfaction in multi-family housing," pp. 119–144 in W. M. Smith (ed.) *Behavior, Design, and Policy Aspects.* Green Bay: University of Wisconsin Press. **63**

Cornelius, W. A., Jr. 1971. "The political sociology of cityward migration in Latin America: toward empirical theory," pp. 95–147 in F. F. Rabinovitz and F. M. Trueblood (eds.) *Latin American Urban Research,* Vol. 1. Beverly Hills, CA: Sage. **91, 148, 301**

——. 1973. *Political Learning among the Migrant Poor: The Impact of Residential Context.* Beverly Hills, CA: Sage. **132**

Craven, S., and B. Wellman. 1973. "The network city." *Sociological Inquiry* 43: 57–88. **203, 205**

Crowe, P. 1978. "Good fences make good neighbors: social networks at three levels of urbanization in Tirol, Austria." Ph.D. dissertation, Stanford University. **159, 310**

——. 1979. "Social networks in an urban context," pp. 67–80 in M. C. Romanos (ed.) *Western European Cities in Crisis.* Lexington, MA: Lexington Press. **133, 158, 159, 165, 310**

Crowley, R. W. 1973. "Reflection and further evidence on population size and industrial diversification." *Urban Studies* 19: 91–94. **301**

Cummings, J. 1981. "Transit Decline Found to Peril New York Jobs." *New York Times,* 5 April. **291**

Cuomo, M. 1974. *Forest Hills Diary: The Crisis of Low-Income Housing.* New York: Random House. **215**

Curtis, J. 1971. "Voluntary association joining: a cross-cultural comparative note." *American Sociological Review* 36: 872–880. **305**

—— and S. Hawkins. 1975. "Community size, social status and tolerance." Unpublished. University of Waterloo. **314**

Dahl, R. A. 1967. "The city in the future of democracy." *American Political Science Review* 61: 953–970. **284**
—— and E. R. Tufte. 1973. *Size and Democracy*. Stanford, CA: Stanford University Press. **116, 304, 323**
Dailey, G. H., Jr., and R. R. Campbell. 1980. "The Ozark–Ouachita Uplands," pp. 233–265 in D. L. Brown and J. M. Wardwell (eds.) *New Directions in Urban–Rural Migration*. New York: Academic Press. **94**
Danzger, M. H. 1970. "Critical mass and historical process as factors in community conflict." Paper presented to the American Sociological Association (September), Washington, DC. **217**
——. 1975. "Validating conflict data." *American Sociological Review* 40: 570–584. **152, 217**
Danzinger, S. 1976. "Determinants of the level and distribution of family income in metropolitan areas, 1969." *Land Economics* 52: 467–478. **84**
Darley, J. M., A. J. Teger, and L. D. Lewis. 1973. "Do groups always inhibit individuals' responses to potential emergencies?" *Journal of Personality and Social Psychology* 26: 395–399. **210**
Darroch, A. G. 1981. "Migrants in the nineteenth century." *Journal of Family History* 6: 254–277. **304**
Davis, K. A. 1955. "The origin and growth of urbanization in the world." *American Journal of Sociology* 60: 429–437. **3**
——. 1966. "The urbanization of the human population," pp. 3–24 in *Cities*. New York: Knopf–Scientific American. **3, 22, 282**
——. 1972. *World Urbanization 1950–1970*, Vol. II. Berkeley, CA: Institute of International Studies. **3, 282**
——. 1973. "Introduction," pp. 9–18 in K. Davis (ed.) *Cities*. San Francisco: W. H. Freeman. **294, 295**
Dear, M., and A. J. Scott (eds.) 1981. *Urbanization and Urban Planning in Capitalist Society*. New York: Methuen. **305, 323**
DeGrazia, S. 1962. *Of Time, Work and Leisure*. New York: Twentieth Century Fund. **98, 310**
DeJong, G. F., and R. R. Sell. 1977. "Population redistribution, migration, and residential preference." *Annals* 429: 130–144. **23, 295, 302**
de Jonge, D. 1962. "Images of urban areas." *Journal of the American Institute of Planners* 28: 266–277. **311**
Desor, J. A. 1971. "Toward a psychological theory of crowding." *Journal of Applied Social Psychology* 33: 444–456. **311**
Deutsch, K. 1961. "On social communication and the metropolis." *Daedalus* 90: 99–109. **29**
Dietz, H. A. 1979. "Some local-level structural determinants among the migrant poor in Lima, Peru," pp. 76–96 in J. W. White (ed.) *The Urban Impact of Internal Migration*. Chapel Hill: University of North Carolina Press. **132, 301**
Dionne, E. J., Jr. 1977. "What New Yorkers Think of City: Blacks Are Least Pessimistic." *New York Times*, 28 August. **295**
Dobriner, W. M. 1963. *Class in Suburbia*. Englewood Cliffs, NJ: Prentice-Hall. **243, 256, 265, 319**
Dohrenwend, Bruce, and Barbara Dohrenwend. 1974. "Psychiatric disorders in urban settings," pp. 424–447 in *American Handbook of Psychiatry*. New York: Basic Books. **313**
Dollard, J. 1957. *Caste and Class in a Southern Town*. 3rd ed. New York: Doubleday. **305**
Donaldson, S. 1969. *The Suburban Myth*. New York: Columbia University Press. **23, 253, 256, 259, 260, 262, 265**
Dotson, F. 1951. "Patterns of voluntary association among working-class families." *American Sociological Review* 16: 687–693. **305**
Doughty, P. L. 1970. "Behind the back of the city: 'provincial' life in Lima, Peru," pp. 30–46 in W. Magnin (ed.) *Peasants in Cities*. Boston: Houghton Mifflin. **308**
——. 1972. "Peruvian migrant identity in the urban milieu," pp. 39–50 in T. Weaver and D. White (eds.) *The Anthropology of Urban Environments*, Monograph 11. Washington, DC: Society for Applied Anthropology. **309**
Douvan, E., and J. Adelson. 1966. *The Adolescent Experience*. New York: John Wiley. **221**
Downs, A. 1973. *Opening Up the Suburbs*. New Haven, CT: Yale University Press. **241**
Dublin, L. 1963. *Suicide*. New York: Ronald. **188**

Dubos, R. 1970. "The social environment," pp. 202–208 in H. Proshansky and W. Ittelson (eds.) *Environmental Psychology*. New York: Holt, Rinehart & Winston.   **311**

Duncan, O. D. 1957. "Optimum size of cities," pp. 759–772 in P. K. Hatt and A. H. Reiss, Jr. (eds.) *Cities and Society*. New York: Free Press.   **322**

Durkheim, E. 1893. *The Division of Labor in Society*. Translated by G. Simpson. Reprint ed., 1933. New York: Macmillan.   **128, 192, 305, 306, 307**

————. 1897. *Suicide*. Translated by J. A. Spaulding and G. Simpson. Reprint ed., 1951. New York: Free Press.   **71, 188, 296**

du Toit, B. M., and H. I. Safa (eds.) 1976. *Migration and Urbanization*. Paris: Mouton.   **301**

Edel, M., J. R. Harris, and J. Rothenberg. 1975. "Urban concentration and deconcentration," pp. 123–156 in A. Hawley and V. Rock (eds.) *Metropolitan America in Contemporary Perspective*. New York: Halstead.   **323**

Edgerton, R. B. 1979. *Alone Together: Social Order on an Urban Beach*. Berkeley: University of California Press.   **232**

Edwards, J. N., A. Booth, and P. K. Edwards. 1982. "Housing type, stress, and family relations." *Social Forces* 61: 241–258.   **183, 299**

Einstadter, W. J. 1969. "The social organization of armed robbery." *Social Forces* 17: 64–83.   **316**

Eisinger, P. K. 1973. "The urban crisis as a failure of 'community'." Paper presented to the American Political Science Association (August), New Orleans.   **96**

Eldridge, H. W. 1967. "Lessons learned from the British New Towns program," pp. 823–827 in H. W. Eldridge (ed.) *Taming Megalopolis, Volume II*. New York: Doubleday.   **323**

Elgin, D., T. Thomas, and T. Logothetti et al. 1974. *City Size and the Quality of Life*. Washington, DC: National Science Foundation (RANN).   **54, 191, 287**

Elwood, R. (ed.) 1974. *Future City*. New York: Pocket Books.   **15**

Ennis, P. H. 1962. "The contextual dimension in voting," pp. 180–211 in W. M. McPhee and W. A. Glaser (eds.), *Public Opinions and Congressional Elections*. New York: Free Press.   **123**

————. 1967. *Criminal Victimization in the United States: A Report of a National Survey*. Chicago: National Opinion Research Center.   **302**

Epstein, A. L. 1967. "Urbanization and social change in Africa." *Current Anthropology* 8: 275–296.   **155, 305, 308**

Erickson, M. L. 1971. "The group context of delinquent behavior." *Social Problems* 19: 114–128.   **316**

Erlanger, H. S. 1974. "Social class and corporal punishment in childrearing: a reassessment." *American Sociological Review* 39: 68–85.   **317**

Ernst, R. 1949. "The living conditions of the immigrant." Reprinted in A. M. Wakestein (ed.) *The Urbanization of America*. Boston: Houghton Mifflin, 1970: 257–268.   **60**

Evans, A. W. 1973. *The Economics of Residential Location*. London: Macmillan.   **318**

Evans, G. W., and R. B. Howard. 1973. "Personal space." *Psychological Bulletin* 80: 334–344.   **244, 311, 319**

Farberow, N. L. 1975. *Suicide in Different Cultures*. Baltimore: University Park Press.   **313**

Farley, R. 1976. "Components of suburban population growth," pp. 3–38 in B. Schwarz (ed.) *Changing Face of the Suburbs*. Chicago: University of Chicago Press.   **247, 248, 318, 319**

————. 1977. "Residential segregation in urbanized areas of the United States in 1970." *Demography* 14: 497–517.   **298**

————. 1980. "Homicide trends in the United States." *Demography* 17: 177–188.   **302, 316, 317**

Fava, S. F. 1959. "Contrasts in neighboring: New York City and a suburban county," pp. 122–130 in W. M. Dobringer (ed.) *The Suburban Community*. New York: G.P. Putnam's Sons.   **255, 306, 320**

————. 1975. "Beyond suburbia." *Annals* 422: 10–24.   **261, 321**

————. 1978. "Women's place in suburbia." Paper presented to the American Sociological Association (August), San Francisco.   **321**

Feiffer, J. 1968. *Little Murders*. New York: Random House.   **100**

Feller, I. 1973. "Determinants of the composition of urban invention." *Economic Geography* 49: 47–58.   **316**

Fellin, P., and E. Litwak. 1963. "Neighborhood cohesion under conditions of mobility." *American Sociological Review* 28: 364–376.   **306**

Ferdinand, T. N. 1967. "The criminal patterns of Boston since 1849." *American Journal of Sociology* 73: 84–99.   **302**

——. 1978. "Criminal justice: from colonial intimacy to bureaucratic formality," pp. 261–287 in D. Street and Associates (eds.) *Handbook of Contemporary Urban Life*. San Francisco: Jossey-Bass.   **302**

Feron, J. 1978. "Suburbs Feeling Impact of Problems from Cities." *New York Times*, 13 November.   **239**

Field, M. D. 1978. "California Poll: 'Urban Spread' Control Favored." *San Francisco Chronicle*, 20 January.   **323**

Findlay, A. M. 1969. "Migration in space: immobility in society," pp. 54–76 in I. M. Lapidus (ed.) *Middle-Eastern Cities*. Berkeley: University of California Press.   **87, 149**

Fine, J., H. D. Glenn, and J. K. Monts. 1971. "The residential segregation of occupational groups in central cities and suburbs." *Demography* 8: 91–101.   **319**

Firey, W. 1945. "Sentiment and symbolism as ecological variables." *American Sociological Review* 10: 140–148.   **49**

——, C. P. Loomis, and J. A. Beegle. 1957. "The fusion of urban and rural," pp. 214–222 in P. K. Hatt and A. J. Reiss, Jr. (eds.) *Cities and Society*. New York: Free Press.   **294**

Fischer, C. S. 1971. "A research note on urbanism and tolerance." *American Journal of Sociology* 76: 847–856.   **315**

——. 1972. "'Urbanism as a way of life': a review and an agenda." *Sociological Methods and Research* 1: 187–242.   **296, 300**

——. 1973a. "On urban alienation and anomie." *American Sociological Review* 38: 311–326.   **192, 194, 310, 313**

——. 1973b. "Urban malaise." *Social Forces* 52: 221–235.   **21, 62, 71, 196, 198, 263, 295, 300, 306**

——. 1975a. "The study of urban community and personality." *Annual Review of Sociology* 1: 67–89.   **4, 27, 294, 296, 297, 322**

——. 1975b. "Toward a subcultural theory of urbanism." *American Journal of Sociology* 80: 1319–1341.   **35, 297**

——. 1975c. "The effects of urban life on traditional values." *Social Forces* 53: 420–432.   **219, 221, 315, 321**

——. 1975d. "The city and political psychology." *American Political Science Review* 69: 559–571.   **254, 304**

——. 1975e. "The myth of 'territoriality' in van der Berghe's 'Bringing beasts back in.'" *American Sociological Review* 40: 674–676.   **311**

——. 1976. "Alienation: trying to bridge the chasm." *British Journal of Sociology* 27: 35–49.   **299, 313**

——. 1978a. "On the Marxian challenge to urban sociology." *Comparative Urban Research* 6: 10–19.   **218, 224, 297, 303, 304**

——. 1978b. "Sociological comments on psychological approaches to urban life," pp. 131–144 in A. Baum et al. (eds.) *Advances in Environmental Psychology, Vol. 1: The Urban Environment*. Hillsdale, NJ: Lawrence Erlbaum.   **178, 312, 314**

——. 1978c. "Urban-to-rural diffusion of opinion in contemporary America." *American Journal of Sociology* 84: 151–159.   **217, 222, 223, 316**

——. 1980. "The spread of violent crime from city to countryside, 1955 to 1975." *Rural Sociology* 45: 416–434. (Extended version appears as Working Paper No. 293, Institute of Urban and Regional Development, Berkeley.)   **103, 217, 222, 223, 302, 316**

——. 1981a. "The public and private worlds of city life." *American Sociological Review* 46: 306–316.   **96, 195**

——. 1981b. "Making friends in the city." *New Society* 20: 301–302.   **109**

——. 1982a. *To Dwell among Friends: Personal Networks in Town and City*. Chicago: University of Chicago Press.   **71, 98, 99, 109, 121, 125, 127, 133, 144, 146, 148, 150, 152, 159, 160, 163, 165, 166, 171, 190, 204, 206, 207, 226, 256, 258, 302, 305, 306, 307, 309, 310, 311, 312, 313, 314, 315, 318, 319, 320, 321**

——. 1982b. Analyses of city–suburban differences in the Bay Area portion of the Northern California Community Study. Unpublished. Berkeley: University of California.   **256, 319, 320**

——. 1982c. "What do we mean by 'friend'?: an inductive study." *Social Networks* 3: 287–307.   **156, 310**

————. 1982d. "Rethinking urban life: order and disorder in urban public life." Paper presented to the American Sociological Association (September), San Francisco. **274**

————. 1982e. "The dispersion of kinship ties in modern society." *Journal of Family History* 7: 353–375.   **163, 311**

————, M. Baldassare, and R. J. Ofshe. 1975. "Crowding studies and urban life: a critical review." *Journal of the American Institute of Planners* 31: 406–416.   **176, 312**

Fischer, C. S., R. M. Jackson, and C. A. Stueve et al. 1977. *Networks and Places: Social Relations in the Urban Setting.* New York: Free Press.   **303, 311, 312**

Fischer, C. S., and R. M. Jackson. 1976. "Suburbs, networks, and attitudes," pp. 279–306 in B. Schwartz (ed.) *The Changing Face of the Suburbs.* Chicago: University of Chicago Press.   **319, 320, 321**

————. 1977. "Suburbanism and localism," pp. 117–138 in C. S. Fischer et al. (eds.) *Networks and Places.* New York: Free Press.   **205, 206, 255, 256, 307, 320**

Flink, J. J. 1976. *The Car Culture.* Cambridge, MA: MIT Press.   **318**

Foley, D. 1975. "Accessibility for residents in the metropolitan environment," pp. 157–200 in A. Hawley and V. Rock (eds.) *Metropolitan America: Papers on State of Knowledge.* New York: Halstead.   **245**

Foley, J. W. 1977. "Community structure and the determinants of health care differentiation." *Social Forces* 56: 654–660.   **66**

Foote, M. N., J. Abu-Lughod, and M. M. Foley et al. 1960. *Housing Choices and Housing Constraints.* New York: McGraw-Hill.   **321**

Forbes, G. B., and H. F. Gromoli. 1971. "The lost-letter technique as a measure of social variables: some exploratory findings." *Social Forces* 50: 113–115.   **315**

Ford, A. B. 1976. *Urban Health in America.* New York: Oxford University Press.   **57, 58, 68, 299**

Ford, T. R. (ed.) 1979. *Rural U.S.A.: Persistence and Change.* Ames: Iowa State University Press.   **222, 301**

————. 1979. "Contemporary rural America: persistence and change," pp. 3–18 in T. R. Ford (ed.) *Rural U.S.A.: Persistence and Change.* Ames: Iowa State University Press.

Form, W. H. 1954. "The place of social structure in the determination of land use." *Social Forces* 32: 317–323.   **49**

Foster, G. M. 1960–1961. "Interpersonal relations in peasant society." *Human Organization* 19: 174–184.   **192, 205, 305**

————. 1961. "The dyadic contact: a model for the social structure of a Mexican peasant village." *American Anthropologist* 63: 1173–1192.

————. 1967. *Tzintzuntzan: Mexican Peasants in a Changing World.* Boston: Little, Brown.   **310, 313**

Foster, L. 1974. "Dimensions of 'urban unease' in ten cities." *Urban Affairs Quarterly* 10: 185–196.   **96**

Frankenburg, R. 1965. *Communities in Britain: Social Life in Town and Country.* Baltimore: Penguin.   **135, 203, 205, 310**

Freedman, J. L. 1973. "The effects of population density on humans," pp. 209–238 in J. T. Fawcett (ed.) *Psychological Perspectives on Population.* New York: Basic Books.   **312**

————. 1975. *Crowding and Behavior.* San Francisco: W. H. Freeman.   **185, 311, 312**

———— and P. Erlich. 1971. "The Impact of Crowding on Human Behavior." *New York Times,* 11 September.   **185, 312**

————, S. Klevansky, and P. R. Ehrlich. 1971. "The effect of crowding on human task performance." *Journal of Applied Social Psychology* 1: 7–25.   **312**

————, A. Levy, and R. Buchanan et al. 1972. "Crowding and human aggressiveness." *Journal of Experimental Social Psychology* 8: 528–547.   **312**

Freeman, H. E., and J. M. Giovannoni. 1969. "Social psychology of mental health," pp. 660–719 in G. Lindzey and A. Aronson (eds.) *The Handbook of Social Psychology,* Vol. V. Reading, MA: Addison-Wesley.   **190**

Freeman, S. T. *Neighbors: The Social Contract in a Castilian Hamlet.* Chicago: University of Chicago Press.   **135, 205**

Frey, W. H. 1979. "Central city white flight: racial and nonracial causes." *American Sociological Review* 44: 425–448.   **318, 319**

Frieden, B. J. 1977. "The new housing-cost problem." *Public Interest* 49: 70–86.   **65**

————. 1979. *The Environmental Protection Hustle.* Cambridge, MA: MIT Press.   **290**

Friedl, E. 1964. "Lagging emulation in post-peasant society." *American Anthropologist* 66: 569–586.   **223**

Friedmann, J., and J. Miller. 1965. "The urban field." *Journal of the American Institute of Planners* 21: 312–320.   **316, 322**

Frisch, M. H. 1972. *Town into City: Springfield, Massachusetts, and the Meaning of Community, 1840–1880.* Cambridge, MA: Harvard University Press.   **116**

Frolic, B. M. 1971. "Soviet urban sociology." *International Journal of Comparative Sociology* 12: 234–51.   **306**

———. 1978. "Reflections on the Chinese model of development." *Social Forces* 57: 385–418.   **84, 323**

Fuguitt, G. V., and D. R. Field. 1972. "Some population characteristics of villages differentiated by size, location and growth." *Demography* 9: 295–308.   **300, 301**

——— and J. J. Zuiches. 1973. "Residential preferences and population distribution: results of a national survey." Paper presented to Rural Sociological Society (August), College Park, MD.   **23, 262, 295**

Furstenberg, F. F., Jr., T. Hershberg, and J. Modell. 1975. "The origins of the female-headed black family: the impact of the urban experience." *Journal of Interdisciplinary History* 6: 211–233.   **168**

Gale, D. E. 1980. "Neighborhood resettlement: Washington DC," pp. 95–114 in S. B. Laska and D. Spain (eds.) *Back to the City.* New York: Pergamon.   **249, 319**

Galle, O. R., and W. R. Gove. 1979. "Crowding and behavior in Chicago, 1940–1970," pp. 23–40 in J. R. Aiello and A. Baum (eds.) *Residential Crowding and Design.* New York: Plenum.   **312**

——— and J. M. McPherson. 1972. "Population density and pathology: what are the relationships for man?" *Science* 176: 23–30. Reprinted in K. Schirwian (ed.) *Comparative Urban Structure.* Lexington, MA: D. C. Heath, 1974: 198–214.   **312**

Gallup Opinion Index. Princeton, NJ: American Institute of Public Opinion.   **21, 54, 98, 99, 102, 105, 189, 197, 217, 219, 221, 295, 300, 301, 309, 310**

Gans, H. J. 1951. "Park Forest: the birth of a Jewish community." *Commentary* 11: 330–339.   **248, 258**

———. 1957. "Progress of a suburban Jewish community: Park Forest revisited." *Commentary* 23: 113–122.   **258**

———. 1962a. "Urbanism and suburbanism as ways of life: a reevaluation of definitions," pp. 625–648 in A. M. Rose (ed.) *Human Behavior and Social Processes.* Boston: Houghton Mifflin.   **32, 49, 243, 266**

———. 1962b. *The Urban Villagers.* New York: Free Press.   **32, 129, 151, 308, 310**

———. 1967. *The Levittowners.* New York: Random House.   **32, 243, 245, 248, 251, 256, 257, 258, 259, 260, 262, 263, 264, 265, 266, 318, 319, 320, 321**

———. 1969. "Negro–Jewish conflict in New York City." *Midstream* 15: 3–15.   **215**

Gardner, J. 1971. "Educated youth and urban–rural inequalities," pp. 235–286 in J. W. Lewis (ed.) *The City in Communist China.* Stanford, CA: Stanford University Press.   **84**

Garigue, P. 1956. "French-Canadian kinship and urban life." *American Anthropologist* 58: 1091–1101.   **310**

Gates, A. S., H. Stevens, and B. Wellman. 1973. "What makes a good neighbor?" Paper presented to the American Sociological Association (August), New York.   **64, 306**

Gelfant, B. H. 1954. *The American City Novel.* Norman: University of Oklahoma Press.   **18**

Gellen, M. 1982. "Migration and urban revitalization: the case of San Francisco," Working Paper No. 394. Berkeley, CA: Institute of Urban and Regional Development.   **249, 250**

Geller, D. M. 1980. "Response to urban stimuli: a behavioral approach." *Journal of Social Issues* 36: 86–100.   **29, 178**

George, M. D. 1964. *London Life in the Eighteenth Century.* New York: Harper & Row.   **9**

Gergen, K. J. 1972. "Multiple identity." *Psychology Today* (May): 31ff.   **203, 206**

Germani, G. 1966. "Mass immigration and modernization in Argentina." *Studies in Comparative International Development II,* No. 11. St. Louis: Washington University.   **81**

Gernet, J. 1962. *Daily Life in China on the Eve of the Mongol Invasion, 1250–1276.* Translated by H. M. Wright. Stanford, CA: Stanford University Press.   **9, 107, 126**

Gibbs, J. P. 1971. "Suicide," pp. 271–312 in R. K. Merton and R. A. Nisbet (eds.) *Contemporary Social Problems.* 3rd ed. New York: Harcourt Brace Jovanovich.   **188**

Gilbert, A. 1976. "The argument for very large cities reconsidered." *Urban Studies* 13: 27–34.   **323**

———. 1977. "The argument for very large cities reconsidered: a *Urban Studies* 14: 225–227. **323**

Gillespie, C. L. 1971. "Who has the power? The marital struggle." *Journal of Marriage and the Family* 33: 445–458. **321**

Gillis, A. R. 1974. "Population density and social pathology." *Social Forces* 53: 306–314. **64**

Ginsberg, Y. 1975. *Jews in a Changing Neighborhood.* New York: Free Press. **215**

———. 1979. "After the change in a changing neighborhood." Unpublished. Tel-Aviv University, Israel. **215**

———. 1980. "Attachment to a neighborhood: a research note," Working Paper No. 64. Tel-Aviv University, Israel: Center for Urban and Regional Studies. **307**

———. 1981. "Jewish attitudes toward black neighbors in Boston and London." *Ethnicity* 8: 206–218.

——— and A. Churchman. 1981. "The future of housing quality: satisfaction with living quality in multi-storey housing." Unpublished. Tel-Aviv University, Israel. **65, 183, 299**

Girard, A., H. Bastide, and G. Pourcher. 1966. "Geographic mobility and urban concentration in France." Reprinted in C. J. Jansen (ed.) *Readings in the Sociology of Migration.* Oxford: Pergamon, 1970: 179–202. **21, 301**

Girdner, J. H. 1896. "To abate the plague of city noises." Reprinted in A. Cook, M. Gittell, and H. Mack (eds.) *City Life, 1865–1900: Views of Urban America.* New York: Praeger, 1973: 158–159. **9**

Given, J. B. 1977. *Society and Homicide in 13th Century England.* Stanford, CA: Stanford University Press. **107, 302**

Glaab, C. N., and A. T. Brown. 1967. *A History of Urban America.* New York: Macmillan. **227**

Glass, D. C., and J. E. Singer. 1972. *Urban Stress.* New York: Academic Press. **55**

Glazer, N., and D. P. Moynihan. 1970. *Beyond the Melting Pot.* Rev. ed. Cambridge, MA: MIT Press. **49, 199, 232, 308**

Glenn, N. K., and J. Alston. 1967. "Rural–urban differences in reported attitudes and behavior." *Southwestern Social Science Quarterly* 47: 381–406. **218, 222, 315**

Glenn, N. D., and L. Hill, Jr. 1977. "Rural–urban differences in attitudes and behavior in the United States." *Annals* 429: 36–50. **218, 315**

Glickman, N. J. (ed.) 1980. *The Urban Impacts of Federal Policies.* Baltimore: Johns Hopkins University Press. **323**

———. 1981. "Emerging urban policies in a slow-growth economy: conservative initiatives and progressive responses," Working Paper No. 353. Berkeley, CA: Institute of Urban and Regional Development. **323**

Goering, J. M. (ed.) 1978. "Marx and the city: a symposium." *Comparative Urban Research* 6. **297**

Goffman, E. 1971. *Relations in Public.* New York: Basic Books. **213, 311**

Goist, P. D. 1977. *From Main Street to State Street.* Port Washington, NY: Kennikat. **15**

Goldfield, D. R. 1980. "Private neighborhood and redevelopment and displacement: the case of Washington, D.C." *Urban Affairs Quarterly* 15: 453–468. **319**

Goldsmith, J. R., and E. Jonsson. 1973. "Health effects of community noise." *American Journal of Public Health* 63: 782–793. **54**

Goldstein, S. 1962. "Some economic consequences of suburbanization in the Copenhagen metropolitan area." *American Journal of Sociology* 68: 551–564. **50**

——— and C. Goldscheider. 1968. *Jewish–Americans.* Englewood Cliffs, NJ: Prentice-Hall. **258**

Gonen, A. 1976. "The suburban mosaic in Israel," pp. 163–186 in D. H. K. Amizan and Y. Ben-Arieh (eds.) *Geography in Israel.* Jerusalem: Israel National Committee of the International Geographical Union. **240**

Goode, W. J. 1963. *World Revolution and Family Patterns.* New York: Free Press. **162, 163, 310, 311**

Goodman, J. L., Jr. 1979. "Reasons for moves out of and into large cities." *Journal of the American Institute of Planners* 45: 407–416. **249, 318**

Gordon, D. N. 1970. "Immigrants and municipal voting turnout." *American Sociological Review* 35: 665–681. **308**

Gordon, M. 1977. "Primary-group differentiation in urban Ireland." *Social Forces* 55: 743–752. **307**

Gottdeiner, M. 1977. *Planned Sprawl.* Beverly Hills, CA: Sage. **49, 132, 292**

Gove, W. R., and M. Hughes. 1980. "Reexamining the ecological fallacy: . . . The pathological effects of living alone." *Social Forces* 58: 1157–1177. **312**

——— and O. Galle. 1979. "Overcrowding in the home: an empirical investigation of possible pathological consequences." *American Sociological Review* 44: 59–80. **183**

Governor's Commission on the Los Angeles Riots. 1965. *Violence in the City—An End or a Beginning?* Sacramento, CA: Governor's Commission on the Los Angeles Riots. **89**

Graham, F. P. 1969. "A contemporary history of American crime rates," pp. 485–504 in H. D. Graham and T. R. Gurr (eds.) *The History of Violence in America.* New York: Bantam.

Grasmick, H. G. 1974. "Rural culture and the Wallace movement in the South." *Rural Sociology* 39: 454–470. **315**

——— and M. K. Grasmick. 1978. "The effect of farm family background on the value orientations of urban residents." *Rural Sociology* 43: 367–385. **315**

Great Britain. Royal Commission on Local Government in England. 1969. *Report, Vol. III: Research Appendices.* London: Her Majesty's Stationer's Office. **116, 304**

Greenberg, S. W.,1981. "Industrial location and ethnic residential pattern in an industrial city: Philadelphia, 1880," pp. 204–232 in T. Hershberg (ed.) *Philadelphia.* New York: Oxford University Press. **309**

Greenshields, T. H. 1969. "'Quarters' and ethnicity," pp. 120–140 in I. M. Lapidus (ed.) *Middle Eastern Cities.* Berkeley: University of California Press. **298**

Greer, S. 1956. "Urbanism reconsidered: a comparative study of local areas in a metropolis." *American Sociological Review* 21: 19–25. **164, 310**

———. 1962. *The Emerging City.* New York: Free Press. **118, 140, 254, 294, 310, 316, 321, 322**

———. 1963. *Metropolitics.* New York: John Wiley. **320**

———. 1972. *The Urbane View.* New York: Oxford University Press. **267**

——— and A. L. Greer. 1976. "Suburban politics," pp. 203–220 in B. Schwarz (ed.) *The Changing Face of the Suburbs.* Chicago: University of Chicago Press. **320**

Greer, S., and P. Orleans. 1962. "The mass society and the parapolitical structure." *American Sociological Review* 27: 643–646. **320**

Greven, P. J. 1970. *Four Generations.* Ithaca, NY: Cornell University Press. **310**

Grier, G., and E. Grier. 1980. "Urban displacement: a reconnaissance," pp. 252–269 in S. B. Laska and D. Spain (eds.) *Back to the City.* New York: Pergamon. **250**

Griffit, W., and R. Veitch. 1971. "Hot and crowded." *Journal of Personality and Social Psychology* 17: 92–98. **185**

Gruenberg, B. 1974. "How free is time?" Ph.D. dissertation. University of Michigan. **251, 319**

Guest, A. M. 1971. "Retesting the Burgess zonal hypothesis." *American Journal of Sociology* 76: 1094–1108. **247, 318**

———. 1972a. "Patterns of family location." *Demography* 9: 159–171. **48, 318, 319**

———. 1972b. "Urban history, population densities, and higher status residential location." *Economic Geography* 48: 375–387. **45, 46**

———. 1974. "Neighborhood life cycles and social status." *Economic Geography* 50: 228–243. **50**

———. 1975. "Journey to work, 1960–1970." *Social Forces* 54: 220–225. **251**

———. 1982. "Fertility variation among the U.S. foreign stock population in 1900." *International Migration Review* 16: 577–594. **300, 308**

Gugler, J., and W. G. Flanagan. 1978. *Urbanization and Social Change in West Africa.* New York: Cambridge University Press. **59, 164, 221, 301, 308**

Gulick, J. 1973. "Urban anthropology," pp. 979–1029 in J. J. Honigman (ed.) *Handbook of Social and Cultural Anthropology.* Chicago: Rand-McNally. **162, 164**

———. 1980. "Village and city: cultural continuities in twentieth century Middle Eastern cultures," pp. 122–153 in G. H. Blake and R. I. Lawless (eds.) *The Changing Middle Eastern City.* London: Croom Helm. **14, 207, 315**

Gurr, T. R. 1971. *Why Men Rebel.* Princeton, NJ: Princeton University Press. **315**

———. 1977. "The comparative analysis of public order," pp. 619–770 in T. R. Gurr, P. N. Grabosky, and R. C. Hula (eds.) *The Politics of Crime and Conflict.* Beverly Hills, CA: Sage. **108, 302**

———. 1980. "Development and decay: their impact on public order in Western history," pp. 31–33 in J. A. Inciardi and C. E. Faupel (eds.) *History and Crime.* Beverly Hills, CA: Sage. **302**

Gusfield, J. R. 1975. *Community: A Critical Response.* Oxford: Basil Blackwell. **295**

Guterbock, T. M. 1976. "The push hypothesis: minority presence, crime, and urban deconcentration," pp. 137–164 in B. Schwartz (ed.) *The Changing Face of the Suburbs.* Chicago: University of Chicago Press. **318, 319**

Guterman, S. S. 1969. "In defense of Wirth's 'Urbanism as a way of life.'" *American Journal of Sociology* 74: 492–499. **310**

Gutheim, F. 1967. "Continental Europe offers new town builders experience," pp. 823–837 in H. W. Eldridge (ed.) *Taming Megalopolis, Volume II.* New York: Doubleday. **323**

Gutkind, P.C.W. 1969. "African urbanism, mobility, and social network." Pp. 389–400 in G. Breese (ed.) *The City in Newly Developing Countries.* Englewood Cliffs, NJ: Prentice-Hall. **121, 309**

Gutkind, P. C. 1974. *Urban Anthropology.* New York: Barnes and Noble. **164, 221**

Hacker, A. 1973. "The City's Comings, Goings." *New York Times,* 2 December. **239**

Hagan, J. 1977. "Criminal justice in rural and urban communities." *Social Forces* 55: 597–612. **207**

Hagerstrand, T. 1967. *Innovation Diffusion as a Spatial Process.* Translated by A. Pred. Chicago: University of Chicago Press. **221**

Hall, E. 1966. *The Hidden Dimension.* New York: Doubleday. **181, 184, 311**

Hall, P. 1977. *The World Cities.* 2nd ed. New York: McGraw-Hill. **50, 240, 290, 292, 323**

Haller, O., and C. E. Wolff. 1962. "Personality orientations of farm, village, and urban boys." *Rural Sociology* 27: 275–293. **313**

Halpern, J. 1965. "Peasant culture and urbanization in Yugoslavia." *Human Organization* 24: 62–174. **91, 308, 310**

Hamilton, R. 1967. *Affluence and the French Worker.* Princeton, NJ: Princeton University Press. **118, 123, 304**

———. 1972. *Class and Politics in the United States.* New York: John Wiley. **123, 304**

Hammett, C., and P. R. Williams. 1980. "Social change in London: a study of gentrification." *Urban Affairs Quarterly* 15: 467–487. **250, 319**

Handlin, O. H. 1951. *The Uprooted.* New York: Grosset & Dunlap. **308**

———. 1969. *Boston's Immigrants.* Rev. ed. New York: Atheneum. **81, 299, 305, 308, 309**

——— and J. Burchard (eds.) 1963. *The Historian and the City.* Cambridge, MA: MIT Press. **295**

Hanna, J. L. 1982. "Public policy and the children's world," pp. 316–355 in G. S. Spindler (ed.) *Doing the Ethnography of Schooling.* New York: Holt, Rinehart & Winston. **82, 317**

Hanna, W. J., and J. L. Hanna. 1971. *Urban Dynamics in Black Africa.* Chicago: Aldine–Atherton. **21, 22, 77, 81, 301, 303, 305, 308, 309**

Hannerz, U. 1969. *Soulside.* New York: Columbia University Press. **157**

Harden, W. R. 1961. "Social and economic effects of community size." *Rural Sociology* 26: 204–211. **300**

Hardy, C. C. 1983. "Segregation Continues in Area Schools." *San Francisco Examiner,* 30 January. **309**

Harkess, S. 1978. "Family and sex roles in urban society," pp. 163–201 in D. Street et al. (eds.) *Handbook of Contemporary Urban Life.* San Francisco: Jossey-Bass. **321**

Harris, M. 1956. *Town and Country in Brazil.* New York: Columbia University Press. **21**

Harry, J. 1974. "Urbanization and the gay life." *Journal of Sex Research* 10: 238–247. **66, 220, 305**

Harvey, D. 1973. *Social Justice in the City.* Baltimore: Johns Hopkins Press. **85, 297**

Hauser, P. H. (ed.) 1957. *Urbanization in Asia and the Far East.* Calcutta: UNESCO. **303**

Hawley, A. 1981. *Urban Society.* 2nd ed. New York: John Wiley. **238, 240, 282, 294, 323**

——— and B. Zimmer. 1971. *The Metropolitan Community.* Beverly Hills, CA: Sage. **196, 244, 247, 254, 261, 298, 300, 307, 318, 319, 320**

Hawley, A. H., and S. Mazie (eds.) 1981. *Understanding Nonmetropolitan America.* Chapel Hill: University of North Carolina Press. **248, 298, 301**

Hayduk, L. A. 1978. "Personal space: an evaluative and orienting overview." *Psychological Bulletin* 85: 117–134. **311**

Heberle, R. 1960. "The normative element in neighborhood relations." *Pacific Sociological Review* 3: 3–11. **132, 134, 307**

Hebers, J. 1983a. "Census Data Reveal 70s Legacy: Poorer Cities and Richer Suburbs." *New York Times,* 27 February. **51, 246, 247, 318**

———. 1983b. "America's Newer Immigrants Choosing Suburbs over Cities." *New York Times,*
1 March.

———. 1983c. "New Mass Transit Data Rekindle Urban Issue." *New York Times,* 31
March. **246, 318**

Hechter, M. 1974. "The political economy of ethnic change." *American Journal of Sociology*
79: 1151–1178. **307**

Henry, A. P. 1978. "To These Kids, the City Is Poison." *Boston Globe,* 27 September. **242**

Herbert, D. 1972. *Urban Geography.* New York: Praeger. **99, 252, 298**

Hershberg, T., A. N. Burstein, and E. P. Ericksen et al. 1981a. "A tale of three cities: blacks,
immigrants, and opportunity in Philadelphia, 1850–1880, 1930, 1970," pp. 461–491 in
T. Hershberg (ed.) *Philadelphia.* New York: Oxford University Press. **298, 308, 317**

Hershberg, T., H. E. Cox, and D. Light, Jr., et al. 1981b. "The journey to work," pp. 128–173 in
T. Hershberg (ed.) *Philadelphia.* New York: Oxford University Press. **298**

Hertz, E., and O. Hutheesing. 1975. "At the edge of society: the nominal culture of urban hotel
isolates." *Urban Anthropology* 4: 317–332. **157**

Heshka, S., and Y. Nelson. 1972. "Interpersonal speaking distance as a function of age, sex,
and relationship." *Sociometry* 35: 491–499. **180**

Higgs, R. 1975. "Urbanization and inventiveness in the United States 1870–1920,"
pp. 247–259 in L. F. Schnore (ed.) *The New Urban History.* Princeton, NJ: Princeton
University Press. **316**

Hill, R. C. 1975. "Fiscal collapse and political struggle in decaying central cities in the United
States." Reprinted in W. K. Tabb and L. Sawers (eds.) *Marxism and the Metropolis.* New
York: Oxford University Press, 1978: 213–240. **323**

Hindelang, M. J. 1978. "Race and involvement in crimes." *American Sociological Review*
43: 93–109. **316**

———, T. Hirschi, and J. G. Weis. 1979. "Correlates of delinquency: discrepancy between
self-report and official measures." *American Sociological Review* 44: 995–1014. **227**

Hine, R. V. 1980. *Community on the American Frontier.* Norman: University of Oklahoma
Press. **147**

Hirabayashi, J., W. Willard, and L. Kemnitzer. 1972. "Pan-Indianism in the urban setting,"
pp. 77–87 in T. Weaver and D. White (eds.) *The Anthropology of Urban Environments,*
Monograph 11. Washington, DC: Society for Applied Anthropology. **150**

Hobsbawm, E. 1959. *Primitive Rebels.* New York: W. W. Norton. **315**

Hoch, I. 1972. "Income and city size." *Urban Studies* 9: 299–328. **85, 197, 315**

———. 1974. "Factors in urban crime." *Journal of Urban Economics* 1: 184–229. **316**

———. 1976. "City size effects, trends, and policies." *Science* 193: 856–863. **84, 85, 314**

Hochstadt, S. 1981. "Migration and industrialization in Germany, 1815–1977." *Social Science
History* 5: 445–468. **314**

Hoffman, M. 1968. *The Gay World.* New York: Basic Books. **220, 305**

Holahan, C. J. 1977. "Effects of urban size and heterogeneity on judged appropriateness of
altruistic responses: situational versus subject variables." *Sociometry* 40: 378–382.
211, 212

Hollingshead, A. B. 1939. "Behavior systems as a field for research." Reprinted in D. O. Arnold
(ed.) *Subcultures.* Berkeley, CA: Glendessary, 1970: 21–30. **297**

Homans, G. C. 1974. *Social Behavior: Its Elementary Forms.* New York: Harcourt Brace
Jovanovich. **271**

Hoover, E. M. 1972. "Policy objectives for population redistribution," pp. 649–664 in S. M.
Mazie (ed.) *Population, Distribution, and Policy,* Vol. V, Research Reports of the U.S.
Commission on Population and the American Future. Washington, DC: Government Printing
Office. **323**

——— and R. Vernon. 1959. *Anatomy of a Metropolis.* New York: Doubleday. **239**

Horowitz, D. L. 1975. "Ethnic identity," pp. 111–140 in N. Glazer and D. P. Moynihan (eds.)
Ethnicity. Cambridge, MA: Harvard University Press. **307**

———. 1977. "Cultural movements and ethnic change." *Annals* 433: 6–18. **154**

Horowitz, H., and G. Schwartz. 1974. "Honor, normative ambiguity and gang violence."
American Sociological Review 39: 224—237. **317**

Horton, F. E., and D. R. Reynolds. 1971. "Effects of urban spatial structure on individual
behavior." *Economic Geography* 47: 36–48. **311**

House, J. S., and S. Wolf. 1978. "Effects of urban residence on interpersonal trust and helping behavior." *Journal of Personality and Social Psychology* 9: 1029–1043. **109, 195, 198, 211, 313**

Howe, I. 1971. "The city in literature." *Commentary* 57(5): 61–68. **14**

———. 1976. *World of Our Fathers*. New York: Harcourt Brace Jovanovich. **308**

Hoyt, H. 1969. "Growth and structure of twenty-one great world cities," pp. 205–218 in G. Breese (ed.) *The City in Newly Developing Countries*. Englewood Cliffs, NJ: Prentice-Hall. **50, 240, 248**

Hughes, D. O. 1975. "Urban growth and family structure in medieval Genoa." *Past and Present* 66: 3–28. **162, 300**

Hull, R. W. 1976. *African Cities and Towns Before the European Conquest*. New York: W. W. Norton. **86, 295, 300**

Hummon, D. 1980. "Community Ideology." Ph.D. dissertation. University of California, Berkeley. **240, 294, 295**

Hunter, A. 1974. "Community change: a stochastic analysis of Chicago's local communities." *American Journal of Sociology* 79: 923–947. **50**

———. 1975. "The loss of community: an empirical test through replication." *American Sociological Review* 40: 537–552. **139**

———. 1979. "The persistence of local sentiments in mass society," pp. 133–162 in D. Street et al. (eds.) *The Handbook of Contemporary Urban Life*. San Francisco: Jossey-Bass.

———. 1980. "Why Chicago." *American Behavioral Scientist* 24: 215–227. **28**

——— and T. L. Baumer. 1982. "Street traffic, social integration, and fear of crime." *Sociological Inquiry* 52: 122–131. **303**

Husain, A. F. A. 1956. "Dacca," pp. 107–142 in R. B. Textor et al. (eds.) *Social Implications of Industrialization and Urbanization: Five Studies in Asia*. Calcutta: UNESCO. **153, 308**

Iga, M., and K. Tatai. 1975. "Characteristics of suicide and attitudes toward suicide in Japan," in N. L. Farberow (ed.) *Suicide in Different Cultures*. Baltimore, Maryland: University Park Press. **313**

Inkeles, A. 1969. "Making men modern: on the causes and consequences of individual change in six developing countries." *American Journal of Sociology* 75: 208–225. **187**

Jackson, K. T. 1975. "Urban deconcentration in the nineteenth century," pp. 110–144 in L. F. Schnore (ed.) *The New Urban History*. Princeton, NJ: Princeton University Press. **298**

Jackson, R. M. 1977. "Social structure and process in friendship choice," pp. 59–78 in C. S. Fischer et al. (eds.) *Networks and Places*. New York: Free Press. **258, 305**

Jacobs, J. 1961. *The Death and Life of Great American Cities*. New York: Random House. **130**

Jacoby, S. 1974. "49 Million Singles Can't All Be Right." *New York Times Magazine,* 17 February. **80**

James, G. 1968. "Community structure and anomie," pp. 189–197 in S. Greer et al. (eds.) *The New Urbanization*. New York: St. Martin's. **320**

Janowitz, M. 1967. *The Community Press in an Urban Setting*. 2nd ed. Chicago: University of Chicago Press. **140**

Janson, C.-G. 1980. "Factorial social ecology: an attempt at summary and evaluation." *Annual Review of Sociology* 6: 433–456. **48, 298**

Japan Statistical Yearbook. Japan. 1967–1975. Tokyo: Office of the Prime Minister. **303**

Jenkins, G. 1968. "Urban violence in Africa." *American Behavioral Scientist* 11: 37–39. **305**

Johansen, N. E., and G. V. Fuguitt. 1973. "Changing retail activity in Wisconsin villages: 1939–1954–1970." *Rural Sociology* 38: 207–218. **67, 300**

Johnston, F. J. 1971. *Urban Residential Patterns*. New York: Praeger. **298**

Johnston, L. 1973. *Drugs and American Youth*. Ann Arbor, MI: Institute for Social Research. **216**

Johnston, M. 1977. "Public policies, private choices: new-town planning and lifestyles in three nations." *Urban Affairs Quarterly* 13: 3–32. **323**

Jones, E. 1966. *Towns and Cities*. New York: Oxford University Press. **77, 300**

Jones, E. E., and R. E. Nisbett. 1972. "The actor and the observer: divergent perceptions of the causes of behavior," pp. 79–94 in E. E. Jones et al. (eds.) *Attribution: Perceiving the Cause of Behavior*. Morriston, NJ: General Learning Press. **315**

Jones, L. M. 1974. "The labor force participation of married women." Master's thesis. University of California, Berkeley. **321**

Juvenal. 1958. *The Satires of Juvenal*. Translated by R. Humphries. Bloomington: Indiana University Press. **14**

Kamman, R., R. Thomson, and R. Irwin. 1979. "Unhelpful behavior in the street." *Environment & Behavior* 11: 245–250. **210, 315**

Kandell, J. 1978. "Amsterdam Halts Decay in Center but Prices Workers Out of the Area." *New York Times*, 11 June. **250**

Kantrowitz, N. 1979. "Racial and ethnic residential segregation: Boston, 1830–1970." *Annals* 441: 41–54. **298**

Karnig, A. A. 1979. "Black economic, political, and cultural development: does city size make a difference? *Social Forces* 57: 1194–1211. **150, 152**

Kasarda, J. D. 1972. "The impact of suburban population growth on central city service functions." *American Journal of Sociology* 77: 1111–1124. **248**

———. 1976. "The changing structure of metropolitan America," pp. 113–136 in B. Schwartz (ed.) *The Changing Face of the Suburbs*. Chicago: University of Chicago Press. **238, 245**

———. 1978. "Industry, community, and the metropolitan problem," pp. 27–57 in D. Street et al. (eds.) *The Handbook of Contemporary Urban Life*. San Francisco: Jossey-Bass. **251**

———. 1980. "The implications of contemporary redistribution trends for national urban policy." *Social Science Quarterly* 61: 373–400. **323**

——— and M. Janowitz. 1974. "Community attachment in mass society." *American Sociological Review* 39: 328–339. **296, 305, 306, 310**

Kasarda, J. D., and G. V. Redfearn. 1975. "Differential patterns of city and suburban growth." *Journal of Urban History* 2: 43–66. **52, 317**

Katznelson, I. 1981. *City Trenches*. New York: Pantheon. **138**

Keller, S. 1968. *The Urban Neighborhood*. New York: Random House. **130, 133, 135, 141, 306, 307**

Kemper, R. V. 1975. "Social factors in migration: the case of Tzintzuntzeños in Mexico City," pp. 225–244 in B. D. du Toit and H. J. Safa (eds.) *Migration and Urbanization*. The Hague, Netherlands: Mouton. **90, 259, 301**

Kentor, J. 1981. "Structural determinants of peripheral urbanization." *American Sociological Review* 46: 201–211. **290**

Kerner Commission. 1968. *Report of the National Advisory Commission on Civil Disorders*. Washington, DC: Government Printing Office. **301**

Kertzer, D. I. 1978. "The impact of urbanization on household composition: implications from an Italian parish: 1880–1919." *Urban Anthropology* 7: 1–25. **310**

Kesselman, M. 1966. "French local politics: a statistical examination of grass roots consensus." *American Political Science Review* 60: 963–974. **118, 304**

Key, W. H. 1968. "Rural–urban social participation," pp. 305–312 in S. F. Fava (ed.) *Urbanism in World Perspective*. New York: Crowell. **165, 306, 307, 310**

Keyes, F. 1958. "The correlation of social phenomena with community size." *Social Forces* 36: 311–315. **67, 299**

Kimball, T. 1965. "The rural community," pp. 117–134 in C. M. Arensberg and S. T. Kimball (eds.) *Culture and Community*. New York: Harcourt Brace Jovanovich. **122**

King, S. S. 1971. "Supermarkets Hub of Suburbs." *New York Times*, 7 February. **245**

Kish, L. 1954. "Differentiation in metropolitan areas." *American Sociological Review* 19: 388–398. **319**

Klatzky, S. R. 1971. *Patterns of Contact with Relatives*. Washington, DC: American Sociological Association. **163, 165, 166**

Klein, K., and B. Harris. 1979. "Disruptive effects of disconfirmed expectancies about crowding." *Journal of Personality and Social Psychology* 37: 769–777. **182**

Kleiner, R. J., and S. Parker. 1976. "Network participation and psychological impairment in an urban environment," pp. 322–326 in P. Meadows and E. Mizruchi (eds.) *Urbanism, Urbanization, and Change*. 2nd ed. Reading, MA: Addison-Wesley. **310**

Kleinfeld, N. R. 1972. "How Do You Get Rid of a Dead Elephant? Move It to New York: City's Offal Truck Will Take Expired Rhinoceroses, Yaks or Mules Offal Your Hands." *Wall Street Journal*, 3 October. **66**

Kleinman, J. C. 1981. "Medical care use in nonmetropolitan areas," pp. 55–61 in *Health—United States*, DHHS (PHS) 82-1232. Washington, DC: Department of Health and Human Services. **57, 58**

Kneeland, D. E. 1978. "Croats and Serbs in Chicago: Pride and Fear over Growing Violence." *New York Times*, 9 December. **147**

Knodel, J. 1977. "Town and country in nineteenth-century Germany." *Social Science History* 1: 356–382. **220, 221, 300**

———— and S. Hochstadt. 1981. "Urban and rural illegitimacy in Imperial Germany," Ch. 12 in P. Laslett et al. (eds.) *Bastardy and Its Comparative History.* London: Edward Arnold.   **220**

Komarovsky, M. 1946. "The voluntary associations of urban dwellers." *American Sociological Review* 11: 686–698.   **305**

Konig, R. 1968. *Community.* London: Routledge and Kegan Paul.   **117**

Kornblum, W. 1974. *Blue Collar Community.* Chicago: University of Chicago Press.   **36, 119, 136, 147**

Korte, C. 1978. "Helpfulness in the urban environment," pp. 85–110 in A. Baum et al. (eds.) *Advances in Environmental Psychology, Volume I: The Urban Environment.* Hillsdale, NJ: Lawrence Erlbaum.   **64, 109, 210, 211, 315**

————. 1980. "Urban–nonurban differences in social behavior and social psychological models of urban impact." *Journal of Social Issues* 36: 29–51.   **211, 315**

———— and N. Kerr. 1975. "Response to altruistic opportunities in urban and nonurban settings." *Journal of Personality and Social Psychology* 95: 183–184.   **315**

Korte, C., I. Ypma, and A. Toppen. 1975. "Helpfulness in Dutch society as a function of urbanization and environmental input level." *Journal of Personality and Social Psychology* 32: 996–1003.   **315**

Koyama, T. 1970. "Rural–urban comparisons of kinship relations in Japan," pp. 318–337 in R. Hill and R. Konig (eds.) *Families in East and West.* Paris: Mouton.   **163, 165, 307, 310, 311**

Krapf-Askari, E. 1969. *Yoruba Towns and Cities.* Oxford, England: Oxford University Press.   **86, 300**

LaFrance, M., and C. Mayo. 1976. "Racial differences in gaze behavior during conversations." *Journal of Personality and Social Psychology* 33: 547–552.   **151**

Lane, R. 1969. "Urbanization and criminal violence in the 19th century: Massachusetts as a test case," pp. 468–484 in H. D. Graham and T. R. Gurr (eds.) *The History of Violence in America.* New York: Bantam.   **302**

————. 1979. *Violent Death in the City.* Cambridge, MA: Harvard University Press.   **302, 313, 316**

Langer, W. L. 1954. "The black death." *Scientific American* 210: 114–121. Reprinted in K. Davis (ed.) *Cities.* San Francisco: W. H. Freeman, 1973: 106–112.   **298**

Lansing, J. B. 1966. *Residential Relocation and Urban Mobility.* Ann Arbor: University of Michigan Survey Research Center.   **55**

———— and G. Hendricks. 1967. *Living Patterns and Attitudes in the Detroit Region.* Detroit: Southeast Michigan Council of Governments.   **65, 239, 241, 251, 299**

Lansing, J. B., and W. Ladd. 1964. *The Propensity to Move.* Washington, DC: Government Printing Office.   **241**

Lantz, H. R. 1971. *Coaltown.* 2nd ed. Carbondale: Southern Illinois University Press.   **122, 207, 313**

Lapidus, I. M. 1966. *Muslim Cities in the Later Middle Ages.* Cambridge, MA: Harvard University Press.   **102, 132, 294**

————. (ed.) 1969. *Middle Eastern Cities.* Berkeley: University of California Press.   **294**

Laquian, A. A., and A. B. Simmons. 1979. "Public policy and migratory behavior in selected cities," pp. 97–121 in J. W. White (ed.) *The Urban Impact of Internal Migration.* Chapel Hill, NC: Institute for Research in Social Science.   **301, 323**

Larson, O. F. 1979. "Values and beliefs of rural people," pp. 91–114 in T. R. Ford (ed.) *Rural U.S.A.: Persistence and Change.* Ames: Iowa State University Press.   **218, 314**

Laska, S., and D. Spain (eds.) 1980. *Back to the City.* New York: Pergamon.   **249, 319**

Laslett, P. 1973. "The comparative history of household and family," pp. 19–33 in M. Gordon (ed.) *The American Family in Historical Perspective.* New York: St. Martin's.   **162**

————. 1977. *Family Life and Illicit Love in Earlier Generations.* New York: Cambridge University Press.

Lasswell, T. E. 1959. "Social class and size of community." *American Journal of Sociology* 64: 505–508.   **301**

Latané, B., and J. M. Dabbs, Jr. 1975. "Sex, group size and helping in three cities." *Sociometry* 38: 180–194.

Latané, B., and J. M. Darley. 1969. "Bystander 'apathy.'" *American Scientist* 57: 244–268.   **210**

Laumann, E. O. 1966. *Prestige and Association in an Urban Community.* Indianapolis: Bobbs-Merrill.   **122**

————. 1973. *Bonds of Pluralism.* New York: John Wiley.   **305, 310**

Lawrence, J.E.S. 1974. "Science and sentiment: overview of research on crowding and human behavior." *Psychological Bulletin* 81: 712–720.

Lazerwitz, B. 1977. "The Community variable in Jewish identification." *Journal of the Scientific Study of Religion* 16: 361–369.   **146, 312**

Le Comité d'Études sur la Violence, la Criminalité et la Délinquance. 1977. *Réponses a la Violence* [Responses to violence]. Several volumes. Paris: La Documentation Française.   **35**

Lech, J. M., and J. Labrousse. 1977. "L'opinion public française et la violence," pp. 215–288 in *Réponses a la Violence*, Annexes au Rapport du Comité d'Études sur la Violence, Vol. 3: Recherches sur l'Urbanisation, l'Habitat, et la Violence. Paris: La Documentation Française.   **102, 208, 211, 217, 303**

Lee, B. A., R. S. Oropesa, and B. Metch et al. In press. "Testing the decline of community thesis: neighborhood organizations in Seattle, 1929 and 1979." *American Journal of Sociology*.   **133, 138**

Lee, T. R. 1980. "The resilience of social networks to changes in mobility and propinquity." *Social Networks* 2: 423–437.   **134**

Leeds, A. 1973. "Locality power in relation to supralocal power institutions," pp. 15–42 in A. Southall (ed.) *Urban Anthropology*. New York: Oxford University Press.   **132**

Lees, L. H. 1969. "Patterns of lower-class life: Irish slum communities in nineteenth-century London," pp. 359–385 in S. Thernstrom and R. Sennett (eds.) *Nineteenth-Century Cities*. New Haven, CT: Yale University Press.   **311**

Leevey, J. R. 1950. "Leisure time of the American housewife." *Sociology and Social Research* 35: 99–105.   **98, 163**

Levine, D. N. 1975. "Simmel at a distance: on the history and systematics of the sociology of the stranger." Paper presented to the American Sociological Association (August), San Francisco.   **95**

———, E. B. Carter, and E. M. Gorman. 1976. "Simmel's influence on American sociology: II." *American Journal of Sociology* 81: 000–000.   **29**

Levine, M. P. 1979. "Gay ghetto," pp. 182–204 in M. P. Levine (ed.) *Gay Men*. New York: Harper & Row.   **305**

Lewis, O. 1952. "Urbanization without breakdown." *Scientific Monthly* 75: 31–41.   **32, 165, 301, 310**

———. 1965. "Further observations on the folk–urban continuum and urbanization," pp. 491–503 in P. H. Hauser and L. Schnore (eds.) *The Study of Urbanization*. New York: John Wiley.   **161, 165**

Leyhausen, P. 1965. "The communal organization of solitary mammals." *Symposium of the Zoological Society of London* 14: 249–263.   **311**

Lichtenberger, E. 1976. "The changing nature of European urbanization," pp. 81–108 in B.J.L. Berry (ed.) *Urbanization and Counterurbanization*. Beverly Hills, CA: Sage.   **286, 299**

Lieberson, S. 1962. "Suburbs and ethnic residential patterns." *American Journal of Sociology* 67: 673–681.   **258**

———. 1970. *Language and Ethnic Relations in Canada*. New York: John Wiley.   **150, 154**

———. 1980. *A Piece of the Pie: Black and White Immigrants Since 1880*. Berkeley: University of California Press.   **168, 309**

———, G. Dalto, and M. E. Johnston. 1975. "The course of mother-tongue diversity in nations." *American Journal of Sociology* 81: 34–62.   **309**

Liebow, E. 1967. *Tally's Corner*. Boston: Little, Brown.   **157**

Lieske, J. A. 1978. "Group disorders in urban schools." *Urban Affairs Quarterly* 14: 79–101.   **309**

Lincoln, J. R. 1978. "Community structure and industrial conflict." *American Sociological Review* 43: 199–219.   **123**

——— and R. Friedland. 1978. "Metropolitan accessibility and socioeconomic differentiation." *Social Forces* 57: 688–696.   **300, 301**

Lipowski, Z. J. 1975. "Sensory information and inputs overload: behavior effects." *Comprehensive Psychiatry* 16: 199–221.   **175**

Lipset, S. M. 1963. *Political Man*. New York: Doubleday.   **217**

———, M. Trow, and J. S. Coleman. 1956. *Union Democracy*. New York: Doubleday.   **125**

Liska, A. E., J. J. Lawrence, and A. Sanchiriko. 1982. "Fear of crime as a social fact." *Social Forces* 60: 760–770.   **302, 303**

Little, K. L. 1965. *West African Urbanization: A Study of Voluntary Associations in Social Change*. Cambridge, England: Cambridge University Press.   **305, 308**

———. 1973. *African Women in Towns*. London: Cambridge University Press.   **21, 76, 77, 153, 301**

Litwak, E. 1960. "Geographical mobility and extended family cohesion." *American Sociological Review* 25: 385–394.   **311**

——— and A. Szelenyi. 1969. "Primary group structures and their functions: kin, neighbors, and friends." *American Sociological Review* 34: 465–481.   **163, 305, 310**

Lizote, A. J., and B. J. Bordua. 1980. "Firearms ownership for sport and protection." *American Sociological Review* 45: 229–243. [See, also, corrections in supra, 46 (1981): 499–503.]   **127**

Lodhi, A. Q., and C. Tilly, 1973. "Urbanization, crime and collective violence in 19th century France." *American Journal of Sociology* 79: 296–318.   **217, 303**

Lofland, L. 1972. "Self-management in public settings: Part I." *Urban Life and Culture* 1: 93–108.   **95**

———.1973. *A World of Strangers*. New York: Basic Books.   **12, 93, 213, 232**

Loftin, C., and S. K. Ward. 1983. "A spatial autocorrelation model of the effects of population density on fertility." *American Sociological Review* 48: 121–128.   **312**

Logan, J. R. 1978. "Rural–urban migration and working class consciousness: the Spanish case." *Social Forces* 56: 1159–1178.   **301, 305**

——— and M. Schneider. 1979. "Governmental organization and city–suburb income inequality, 1960–70." Paper presented to the American Sociological Association (August), Boston.   **323**

Lomnitz, L. A. 1977. *Networks and Marginality: Life in a Mexican Shantytown*. New York: Academic Press.   **90, 133, 301**

London, B. 1980. "Gentrification as urban reinvasion," pp. 77–94 in S. B. Laska and D. Spain (eds.) *Back to the City*. New York: Pergamon.   **249**

——— and W. G. Flanagan. 1976. "Comparative urban ecology," pp. 41–66 in J. Walton and L. Masotti (eds.) *The City in Comparative Perspective*. Beverly Hills, CA: Sage.   **240, 248**

Long, L. H. 1976. "The geographical mobility of Americans." *Current Population Reports, Special Studies*, Ser. P-23, No. 64. Washington, DC: U.S. Bureau of the Census.

———. 1980. "Back to the city and back to the countryside in the same decade," pp. 61–76 in S. B. Laska and D. Spain (eds.) *Back to the City*. New York: Pergamon.   **250**

——— and C. G. Boertlein. 1978a. "Urban residential mobility in comparative perspective." Paper presented to the International Sociological Association (August), Uppsala, Sweden.   **248, 301, 314**

———. 1978b. "The geographical mobility of Americans: An international comparison," *Current Population Reports, Special Studies*, Ser. P-23, No. 64. Washington, DC: U.S. Bureau of the Census.   **301, 304**

Long, L., and D. C. Dahman. 1980. "The city–suburban income gap." *Special Demographic Analyses*, CDS-80-1 (March). Washington, DC: U.S. Department of Commerce.   **318**

Long, L. H., and D. DeAre. 1980. "Migration to nonmetropolitan areas," *Special Demographic Analyses*, CDS 80-2. Washington, DC: U.S. Bureau of the Census.   **84, 92, 302**

———. 1981. "The suburbanization of blacks." *American Demographics* (September): 16–21, 44.

———. 1982a. "Repopulating the countryside: a 1980 census trend." *Science* 217: 1111–1116.   **91, 278**

———. 1982b. "The economic base of recent population growth in nonmetropolitan settings." Mimeo. Washington, DC: U.S. Bureau of the Census, Center for Demographic Studies.   **83, 91, 100, 278**

Long, L. H., and P. C. Glick. 1976. "Family patterns in suburban areas," pp. 39–68 in B. Schwartz (ed.) *The Changing Face of the Suburbs*. Chicago: University of Chicago Press.

Lopata, H. Z. 1964. "The function of voluntary associations in an ethnic community." Reprinted in E. W. Burgess and D. J. Bogue (eds.) *Urban Sociology*. Chicago: University of Chicago Press, 1967: 117–137.   **150**

———. 1972. *Occupation: Housewife*. New York: Oxford University Press.   **299**

Lopez, D. E. 1978. "Chicano language loyalty in an urban setting." *Sociology and Social Research* 42: 267–278.   **308**

Lorenz, K. 1966. *On Aggression*. Translated by M. K. Wilson. New York: Bantam.   **185, 311**

Lorinskas, R. A., B. W. Hawkins, and S. D. Edwards. 1969. "The persistence of ethnic voting in urban and rural areas." *Social Science Quarterly* 49: 891–899.   **148**

346 *References*

Louis Harris Assoc. 1976. *The Harris Survey Yearbook 1972.* New York: Louis Harris. **190**
————. 1979. *A Survey of Citizen Views and Concerns about Urban Life.* Washington, DC: U.S. Department of Housing and Urban Development, Office of Policy Development and Research. **20, 21, 55, 62, 67, 98, 101, 116, 118, 157, 242, 244, 245, 249, 252, 254, 255, 259, 260, 295, 296, 300, 302, 306, 318, 319**
Lowe, G. D., and C. W. Peek. 1974. "Location and lifestyle." *Rural Sociology* 39: 392–420. **315**
Lowry, W. P. 1967. "The climate of cities." *Scientific American* 217: 15–23. Reprinted in K. Davis (ed.) *Cities.* San Francisco: W. H. Freeman, 1973: 141–150. **54**
————. 1979. "Interactions between cities and their local regional weather and climate," pp. 83–102 in M. C. Romanos (ed.) *Western European Cities in Crisis.* Lexington, MA: Lexington Press.
Lynch, K. 1960. *The Image of the City.* Cambridge, MA: MIT Press. **311**
Lynn, F. 1974. "Survey Finds New Yorkers Optimistic about City's Future." *New York Times,* 14 January. **296**
Madden, R. L. 1978. "Poll of Suburbanites Shows a Growing Sense of a Separate World." *New York Times,* 14 November. **252, 261**
Madsen, M. C. 1967. "Cooperative and competitive motivation of children in three Mexican sub-cultures." *Psychological Reports* 20: 1307–1320. **314**
———— and S. Yi. 1975. "Cooperation and competition of urban and rural children in the Republic of South Korea." *International Journal of Psychology* 10: 269–274. **314**
Malcolm, A. H. 1974. "Crime Follows Population from Cities to Suburbs." *New York Times,* 21 April. **252**
Mangin, W. 1967. "Squatter settlements." Reprinted in K. Davis (ed.) *Cities.* San Francisco: W. H. Freeman, 1973: 233–240. **88**
———— (ed.) 1970. *Peasants in Cities.* Boston: Houghton Mifflin. **305**
Mann, P. H. 1964. *An Approach to Urban Sociology.* London: Routledge and Kegan Paul. **20, 58, 188, 300, 302, 306, 310, 313**
Marans, R. W., and W. Rodgers. 1975. "Toward an understanding of community satisfaction," pp. 299–324 in A. Hawley and V. Rock (eds.) *Metropolitan America in Contemporary Perspective.* New York: Halstead. **21, 62, 65, 102, 196, 244, 252, 263, 299**
Marden, D. G. 1966. "A demographic and ecological analysis of the distribution of physicians in metropolitan America." *American Journal of Sociology* 72: 290–300. **67, 299**
Marshall, H. 1973. "Suburban life styles: a contribution to the debate," pp. 123–148 in C. H. Masotti and J. K. Hadden (eds.) *The Urbanization of the Suburbs,* Urban Affairs Annual Review No. 7. Beverly Hills, CA: Sage. **256**
————. 1979. "White movement to the suburbs." *American Sociological Review* 44: 975–994. **317, 318, 319**
Martin, E. P., and J. M. Martin. 1978. *The Black Extended Family.* Chicago: University of Chicago Press. **168**
Martin, R. D. 1972. "Concepts of human territoriality," pp. 427–445 in P. J. Veko, R. Tringham, and G. W. Dimbelby (eds.) *Man, Settlement and Urbanism.* Cambridge, MA: Schenkman. **311, 319**
Martin, W. T. 1959. "The structuring of social relationships engendered by suburban residence," pp. 95–103 in W. M. Dobriner (ed.) *The Suburban Community.* New York: G. P. Putnam's Sons. **254**
Marx, G. 1964. *Protest and Prejudice.* New York: Harper & Row. **309**
Mathiasson, C. J. 1974. "Coping in a new urban environment: Mexican–Americans in Milwaukee." *Urban Anthropology* 3: 262–277. **150**
Mawby, R. I. 1977. "Defensible space: a theoretical and empirical appraisal." *Urban Studies* 14: 169–179. **64**
Mazie, S. M., and S. Rawlings. 1972. "Public attitude towards population distribution," pp. 599–616 in S. M. Mazie (ed.) *Population, Distribution and Policy,* Research Report V. Washington, DC: U.S. Commission on Population Growth. **287, 295, 296, 323**
McCarthy, D. P., and S. Saegert. 1979. "Residential density, social overload, and social withdrawal," pp. 57–76 in J. R. Aiello and A. Baum (eds.) *Residential Crowding and Design.* New York: Plenum. **64, 183, 299**
McCausland, J. L. 1972. "Crime in the suburbs," pp. 61–64 in C. M. Haar (ed.) *The End of Innocence: A Suburban Reader.* Glenview, IL: Scott, Foresman. **252**

McDermott, W. 1961. "Air pollution and public health." *Scientific American* 205: 49–57. Reprinted in K. Davis (ed.) *Cities.* San Francisco: W. H. Freeman, 1973: 132–140. **56, 57**

McDonald, J. S., and L. D. McDonald. 1964. "Chain migration, ethnic neighborhood formation, and social networks." Reprinted in C. Tilly (ed.) *An Urban World.* Boston: Little, Brown, 1973: 226–235. **301**

McGee, T. G. 1975. "An aspect of urbanization in Southeast Asia," pp. 224–239 in E. Jones (ed.) *Readings in Social Geography.* London: Oxford University Press. **77**

McHale, V. E., and E. A. Johnson. 1976. "Urbanization, industrialization, and crime in imperial Germany," Part I. *Social Science History* 1: 45–48. **303, 316**

———. 1977. "Urbanization, industrialization, and crime in imperial Germany," Part II. *Social Science History* 1: 210–247. **303**

McPherson, J. M. 1975. "Population density and social pathology: a reexamination." *Sociological Symposium* 14: 77–92. **312**

Mead, G. H. 1934. *Mind, Self, and Society.* Chicago: University of Chicago Press. **203**

Meier, R. L. 1962. *A Communications Theory of Urban Growth.* Cambridge, MA: MIT Press. **29, 70, 203, 280, 311**

Mellor, R. 1975. "Urban sociology in an urbanized society." *British Journal of Sociology* 26: 276–293. **297**

Menchik, M. D. 1981. "The service sector," pp. 231–254 in A. M. Hawley and S. M. Mazie (eds.) *Nonmetropolitan America in Transition.* Chapel Hill: University of North Carolina Press. **100**

Merry, S. E. 1981. *Urban Danger: Life in a Neighborhood of Strangers.* Philadelphia: Temple University Press. **97, 101, 108, 151, 317**

Merton, R. K. 1938a. "Social structure and anomie." Reprinted in R. Merton (ed.) *Social Theory and Social Structure.* Rev. ed. New York: Free Press, 1980: 185–214. **71, 192**

———. 1938b. "Science, technology and society in seventeenth century England." *Osiris* 4: 360–632. Reprint; New York: Howard Fertig, 1970. **297, 316**

———. 1964. "Anomie, anomia, and social interaction: contexts of deviant behavior," pp. 213–242 in M. B. Clinard (ed.) *Anomie and Deviant Behavior.* New York: Free Press. **71**

Michelson, W. 1970. *Man and His Urban Environment.* Reading, MA: Addison-Wesley. **63, 299, 302, 306**

———. 1973a. "Environmental change," Research Paper No. 60. University of Toronto: Centre for Urban and Community Studies. **64, 245, 251, 255, 256, 262, 264, 265, 267, 318, 320, 321**

———. 1973b. "The reconciliation of 'subjective' and 'objective' data on physical environment in the community." *Sociological Inquiry* 43: 147–173.

———. 1977. *Environmental Choice, Human Behavior, and Residential Satisfaction.* New York: Oxford University Press. **64, 65, 183, 245, 255, 260, 261, 299, 300, 318, 320**

———, D. Belgue, and J. Stewart. 1973. "Intentions and expectations in differential residential selection." *Journal of Marriage and the Family* 35: 189–196. **256, 317**

Michelson, W., and E. Roberts. 1979. "Children and the urban physical environment," pp. 410–477 in W. Michelson et al. (eds.) *The Child in the City: Changes and Challenges.* Toronto: University of Toronto Press. **55, 64, 176, 183**

Midlarsky, M. I. 1977. "Size effects and the diffusion of violence in American cities." *Papers of the Peace Science Society* 27. **217**

Mileski, M., and D. Black. 1972. "The social organization of homosexuality." *Urban Life and Culture* 1: 187–202. **305**

Milgram, S. 1970. "The experience of living in cities." *Science* 167: 1461–1468. **29, 70, 177, 209, 311, 315**

———, J. Greenwald, and S. Kessler et al. 1972. "A psychological map of New York City." *American Scientist* 60: 194–200. **174**

Millon, R. 1967. "Teotihuacan." *Scientific American* 216: 38–48. Reprinted in K. Davis (ed.) *Cities.* San Francisco: W. H. Freeman, 1973: W. H. 82–92. **298, 313**

Miner, H., and G. DeVos. 1960. *Oasis and Casbah.* Ann Arbor: University of Michigan Museum of Anthropology.

Mitchell, J. C. (ed.) 1969. *Social Networks in Urban Situations.* Manchester, England: Manchester University Press. **303**

———. 1970. "Africans in industrial towns in Northern Rhodesia," pp. 160–169 in W. Mangin (ed.) *Peasants in Cities*. Boston: Houghton Mifflin.   **308**

Mitchell, R. E. 1971. "Some social implications of high density housing." *American Sociological Review* 36: 18–29.   **63, 183, 299**

———. 1974. "Misperceptions about man-made space." *Family Coordinator* (January): 51–56.   **176, 299**

———. 1975. "Ethnographic and historical perspectives on relationships between physical and socio-spatial environments." *Sociological Symposium* 14: 25–42.   **179**

Modell, J. 1979. "Suburbanization and change in the American family." *Journal of Interdisciplinary History* (Spring): 621–646.   **31**

Mogey, J. M. 1956. *Family and Neighborhood*. London: Oxford University Press.   **323**

Mollenkopf, J. 1981. "Community and accumulation," pp. 319–338 in M. Dear and A. J. Scott (eds.) *Urbanization and Urban Planning in Capitalist Society*. New York: Methuen.   **292**

Molotch, H. 1969. "Racial integration in a transition community." *American Sociological Review* 34: 878–893.   **97, 208**

———. 1976. "The city as a growth machine." *American Journal of Sociology* 82: 309–332.   **49, 323**

———. 1979. "Capital and neighborhood in the United States." *Urban Affairs Quarterly* 14: 289–312.   **297**

Monkkonen, E. H. 1975. *The Dangerous Class*. Cambridge, MA: Harvard University Press.   **302**

Montagu, A. (ed.) 1973. *Man and Aggression*. 2nd ed. New York: Oxford University Press.   **311**

Montero, D. 1981. "The Japanese–Americans: changing patterns of assimilation over three generations." *American Sociological Review* 46: 829–839.   **148**

Morgan, D. L., and D. F. Alwin. 1980. "When less is more: school size and student participation." *Social Psychology Quarterly* 43: 241–245.   **204, 304, 314**

Morgan, N. R., and T. R. Clark. 1973. "The causes of racial disorders." *American Sociological Review* 38: 611–624.   **82, 152, 217**

Moots, B. L. 1976. "Migration, community of origin, and status attainment." *Social Forces* 54: 816–832.   **301**

Morris, D. 1968. *The Naked Ape*. New York: McGraw-Hill.   **311**

———. 1969. *The Human Zoo*. New York: McGraw-Hill.   **35, 294**

——— and K. Hess. 1975. *Neighborhood Power*. Boston: Beacon.   **307**

Morris, R. N. 1968. *Urban Sociology*. New York: Praeger.   **296, 311**

Morton, J. 1972. "Urban entrapment." Unpublished. Hunter College, New York.   **312**

Mosk, C. 1980. "Rural–urban fertility differences and the fertility transition." *Population Studies* 34: 77–90.   **300**

Muller, P. O. 1974. "Towards a geography of the suburbs." *Proceedings of the Association of American Geographers* 6: 36–40.   **245, 318**

———. 1981. *Contemporary Suburban America*. Englewood Cliffs, NJ: Prentice-Hall.   **238, 243, 245, 251, 281**

Murdie, R. A. 1976. "Spatial form in the residential mosaic," pp. 237–272 in D. T. Herbert and R. J. Johnston (eds.) *Spatial Processes and Form*, Vol. 1. New York: John Wiley.   **298**

Mulvihill, D. J., and M. M. Tumin. 1969. *Crimes of Violence: A Staff Report to the National Commission on the Causes and Prevention of Violence*, Vol. 12. Washington, DC: Government Printing Office.   **107, 302**

Mumford, L. 1961. *The City in History*. New York: Harcourt Brace & World.   **85, 86, 87, 192, 294, 295**

Murphey, R. 1954. "The city as a center of change: Western Europe and China." *Annals of the American Association of Geographers* 44: 349–362.   **54, 217**

———. 1972. "City and countryside as ideological issues: India and China." *Comparative Studies in Society and History* 14: 250–267.   **14, 217**

———. 1976. "Chinese urbanization under Mao," pp. 311–330 in B.J.L. Berry (ed.) *Urbanization and Counterurbanization*. Beverly Hills, CA: Sage.   **84**

National Urban Coalition (NUC). 1978. *Displacement: City Neighborhoods in Transition*. Washington, DC: National Urban Coalition.   **249, 250**

Nayacakalov, R. R., and A. Southall. 1973. "Urbanization and Fijian cultural traditions in the context of Pacific port cities," pp. 393–406 in A. Southall (ed.) *Urban Anthropology*. New York: Oxford University Press.

Nelli, H. M. 1970. *The Italians in Chicago 1890–1930.* New York: Oxford University Press. **148, 151**

Nelsen, H. M., and R. H. Potkin. 1977. "The rural church and rural religion: analysis of data from children and youth." *Annals* 429: 103–114. **315**

Nelsen, H. M., and S. E. Storey. 1969. "Personality and adjustment of rural and urban youth." *Rural Sociology* 35: 43–55. **312**

Nelsen, H. M., R. L. Yokley, and T. W. Madron. 1971. "Rural–urban differences in religiosity." *Rural Sociology* 36: 389–396. **315**

Nelson, J. 1973. "Participation and college aspirations: complex effects of community size." *Rural Sociology* 38: 7–16. **304**

Nelson, J. M. 1981. *Access to Power: Politics and the Urban Poor in Developing Nations.* Princeton, NJ: Princeton University Press. **90, 146, 196, 301, 308**

Nelson, S. D. 1974. "Nature/nurture revisited I: a review of the biological bases of conflict." *Journal of Conflict Resolution* 18: 285–335. **311**

Newman, O. 1973. *Defensible Space.* New York: Collier. **64**

———. 1980. *Community of Interest.* New York: Doubleday. **64**

Newman, W. 1976. "Religion in suburbia," pp. 265–278 in B. Schwartz (ed.) *The Changing Face of the Suburbs.* Chicago: University of Chicago Press. **320**

Nie, N. H., G. G. Powell, and K. Prewitt. 1969. "Social structure and political participation: developmental relationships, Part I." *American Political Science Review* 63: 361–378. **304**

Nisbet, R. 1967. *Community and Power* (original title: *The Quest for Community*). New York: Oxford University Press. **128, 141, 306**

Nogami, G. Y. 1976. "Crowding: effects of group size, room size, or density?" *Journal of Applied Social Psychology* 6: 105–125. **312**

Nossiter, B. D. 1980. "World Population Explosion Is Slowing." *New York Times,* 15 June. **278**

Nugent, W. 1981. *Structures of American Social History.* Bloomington: Indiana University Press. **297**

O'Brien, D. J. 1975. *Neighborhood Organization and Interest-Group Processes.* Princeton, NJ: Princeton University Press. **307**

Oelsner, L. 1971. "The World of the City Prostitute Is a Tough and Lonely One." *New York Times* 9 August. **125**

Ogburn, W. F. 1937. *Social Characteristics of Cities.* Chicago: International City Managers' Association. **321**

———. 1954. "Why the family is changing," pp. 174–186 in O. D. Duncan (ed.) *William F. Ogburn on Culture and Social Change.* Chicago: University of Chicago Press (1964). **163, 310**

——— and O. D. Duncan. 1964. "City size as a sociological variable," pp. 56–78 in E. W. Burgess and D. F. Bogue (eds.) *Urban Sociology.* Chicago: University of Chicago Press. **299, 301, 316**

Oi, N. Y., and P. W. Shuldiner. 1962. *An Analysis of Urban Travel Demands.* Evanston, IL: Northwestern University Press. **317**

Olsen, R. A., and A. M. Guest. 1977. "Migration and city–suburb differences." *Urban Affairs Quarterly* 12: 523–532. **247**

O'Reilly, J. M. 1981. "A demographic analysis of white 'flight' . . . in metropolitan America: 1973–1977 [Abstract]." Ph.D. dissertation, Duke University. **303**

Packard, V. 1972. *A Nation of Strangers.* New York: McKay. **306**

Pahl, R. E. 1970. *Patterns of Urban Life.* London: Longmans, Green. **320**

Palen, J. J. 1979. "The urban nexus: toward the year 2000," pp. 141–156 in A. Hawley (ed.) *Societal Growth.* New York: Free Press. **35, 316**

Palmore, J. A., R. E. Klein, and A. Bin Marzuki. 1970. "Class and family in a modernizing society." *American Journal of Sociology* 76: 375–396. **165, 166, 311**

Park, R. E. 1916. "The city: suggestions for investigation of human behavior in the urban environment." Reprinted in R. Sennet (ed.) *Classic Essays on the Culture of Cities.* New York: Appleton-Century-Crofts, 1969: 91–130. **22, 124, 125, 127, 129, 135, 156, 203, 206, 225, 296, 303, 305, 306**

———. 1952. "The city as a natural phenomenon," pp. 118–127 in R. E. Park (ed.) *Human Communities.* Glencoe, IL: Free Press. **322**

——— and H. A. Miller. 1921. *Old World Traits Transplanted.* New York: Harper & Row. **145**

Parker, R. N., and M. D. Smith. 1979. "Deterrence, poverty, and type of homicide." *American Journal of Sociology* 85: 614–624. **229**

Pedersen, D. M., and L. M. Shears. 1973. "A review of personal space research in the framework of general systems theory." *Psychological Bulletin* 80: 367–388. **311**

Pedersen, P. O. 1970. "Innovation diffusion between and within national urban systems." *Geographical Analysis* 3: 203–254. **221**

Peil, M. 1981. *Cities and Suburbs: Urban Life in West Africa.* New York: Africana Publishing. **146, 318**

Perlman, J. E. 1975. *Myths of Marginality.* Berkeley: University of California Press. **22, 88, 90, 259, 301, 310, 315**

Petersen, K. K. 1971. "Villages in Cairo: Hypotheses versus data." *American Journal of Sociology* 77: 560–573. **306, 307**

Petersen, W. 1961. *Population.* New York: Macmillan. **300**

Peterson, G. E. 1980. "Federal tax policy and the shaping of urban development," pp. 399–425 in A. P. Solomon (ed.) *The Prospective City.* Cambridge, MA: MIT Press. **323**

Pettigrew, T. F. 1967. "Social comparison theory," pp. 241–315 in *Nebraska Symposium on Motivation.* Lincoln: University of Nebraska Press. **71**

Photiadis, J. D. 1967. "Social integration of businessmen in varied size communities." *Social Forces* 46: 229–236. **192**

Pickard, J. P. 1972. "U.S. metropolitan growth and expansion, 1970–2000," pp. 127–182 in S. M. Mazie (ed.) *Population, Distribution, and Policy,* Vol. V, Research Reports. Washington, DC: U.S. Commission on Population Growth and the American Future. **277**

Pickvance, C. G. 1974. "On a materialist critique of urban sociology." *Sociological Review* 22: 203–220. **297, 320**

—— (ed.) 1976. *Urban Sociology: Critical Essays.* New York: St. Martin's.

Pilcher, W. W. 1972. *The Portland Longshoremen: A Dispersed Urban Community.* New York: Holt, Rinehart & Winston. **125**

Piliavin, J., J. Rodin, and J. A. Piliavin. 1969. "Good Samaritanism: an underground phenomenon?" *Journal of Personality and Social Psychology* 13: 289–330. **210**

Pirenne, H. 1925. *Medieval Cities.* Princeton, NJ: Princeton University Press. **298**

Plateris, A. A. 1978. "Divorces and Divorce Rates, United States." *Vital and Health Statistics,* Ser. 21, No. 29. Washington, DC: U.S. Department of Health, Education and Welfare. **78, 161**

Ploch, L. A. 1980. "Effects of turnaround migration on community structure in Maine," pp. 291–312 in D. L. Brown and J. M. Wardwell (eds.) *New Directions in Urban–Rural Migration.* New York: Academic Press. **94**

Plotnicov, L. 1967. *Strangers to the City.* Pittsburgh: University of Pittsburgh Press. **205**

Polanyi, K. 1944. *The Great Transformation.* Boston: Beacon. **26**

Polls. 1967. 2 (Summer). **20**

Pons, V. 1969. *Stanleyville.* London: Oxford University Press. **205, 309**

Popenoe, D. 1977. *The Suburban Environment: Sweden and the United States.* Chicago: University of Chicago Press. **240, 243, 257, 267, 309, 317**

——. 1979. "Urban sprawl: some neglected considerations." *Sociology and Social Research* 63: 255–268. **292, 323**

——. 1980. "Urban form in advanced societies: A national inquiry," in U. Karn and C. Ungerson (eds.) *The Consumer Experience of Housing.* London: Gower. **50, 267, 280, 292, 323**

Prabhu, P. N. 1956. "Bombay," pp. 49–106 in R. B. Textor et al. (eds.) *The Social Implications of Industrialization and Urbanization: Five Studies of Asia.* Calcutta: UNESCO. **153**

President's Commission for a National Agenda for the Eighties. 1980. *Urban America in the Eighties,* Report of the Panel of Policies and Prospects for Metropolitan and Nonmetropolitan America. Washington, DC: Government Printing Office. **288, 292**

Preston, S. H. 1977. "Mortality trends." *Annual Review of Sociology* 3: 163–178. **57**

—— and A. T. Richards. 1975. "The influence of women's work on marriage rates." *Demography* 12: 209–221. **78**

Prewitt, K., and H. Eulau. 1969. "Political matrix and political representation." *American Political Science Review* 63: 427–461. **116, 254, 304**

Price, C. 1978. "Individual preference and optimal city size." *Urban Studies* 15: 75–81. **285**

Price, J. A. 1975. "U.S. and Canadian Indian urban ethnic institutions." *Urban Anthropology* 4: 35–52. **309**

Provencher, R. 1972. "Comparisons of social interaction styles: urban and rural Malay culture," pp. 69–76 in T. Weaver and D. White (eds.) *The Anthropology of Urban Environments,* Monograph 11. Washington, DC: Society for Applied Anthropology. **214**

Ramsøy, N. R. 1966. "Assortative mating and the structure of cities." *American Sociological Review* 31: 773–786. **137**

Redfield, R., and M. Singer. 1954. "The cultural role of cities." *Economic Development and Cultural Change* 3: 53–77. **34, 295**

Rees, P. H. 1972. "Problems of classifying subareas within cities," pp. 265–330 in B.J.L. Berry (ed.) *City Classification Handbook.* New York: John Wiley. **50, 298**

Reinhold, R. 1979. "Census Finds Unmarried Couples Doubled from 1970 to 1978." *New York Times,* 27 June. **78, 220**

Reiss, A. J. 1955. "An analysis of urban phenomena," pp. 41–51 in R. M. Fisher (ed.) *The Metropolis in Modern Life.* New York: Doubleday. **32, 69, 114**

———. 1959a. "The sociological study of community." *Rural Sociology* 24: 118–130. **4, 294**

———. 1959b. "Rural–urban and status differences in interpersonal contacts." *American Journal of Sociology* 65: 182–195. **98, 158, 165, 166, 204**

Reiss, I. 1967. *The Social Context of Premarital Sexual Permissiveness.* New York: Holt, Rinehart & Winston. **220**

Reissman, L. 1964. *The Urban Process.* New York: Free Press. **294**

Reskin, B., and F. L. Campbell. 1974. "Physician distribution across metropolitan areas." *American Journal of Sociology* 79: 981–998. **67, 299**

Revelle, R. 1970. "Pollution and cities," pp. 96–143 in J. Q. Wilson (ed.) *The Metropolitan Enigma.* New York: Doubleday. **57**

Reynolds, P. D., and D. A. Blyth. 1974. "Sources of variation affecting the relationship between police and survey based estimates of crime rates." Paper presented to the American Sociological Association (August), Montreal. **302**

Richardson, B. M. 1973. "Urbanization and political participation: the case of Japan." *American Political Science Review* 67: 433–452. **118, 304, 306**

Richardson, H. L. 1973. *The Economics of City Size.* London: Saxon House. **66, 85, 284, 303, 316, 322**

———. 1976. "The argument for very large cities reconsidered: a comment." *Urban Studies* 13: 307–310. **323**

Riemer, S., and J. McNamara. 1957. "Contact patterns in the city." *Social Forces* 36: 137–140. **307**

Riesman, D. 1952. *The Lonely Crowd.* New Haven, CT: Yale University Press. **193**

———. 1959. "The suburban sadness," pp. 375–408 in W. M. Dobriner (ed.) *The Suburban Community.* New York: G. P. Putnam's Sons. **265, 269**

Riley, M. W., and A. Foner. 1968. *Aging and Society.* New York: Russell Sage. **68**

Rindfuss, R. R., and J. A. Sweet. 1977. *Postwar Fertility Trends and Differentials in the United States.* New York: Academic Press. **78**

Rischlin, M. 1977. *The Promised City: New York's Jews: 1870–1914.* Cambridge, MA: Harvard University Press. **149, 309**

Ritchey, P. N. 1976. "Explanations of migration." *Annual Review of Sociology* 2: 364–404. **301**

Roberts, B. 1973. *Organizing Strangers.* Austin: University of Texas Press. **163, 205, 259, 301, 309**

Robinson, W. C. 1963. "Urbanization and fertility: the non-western experience." *Millbank Memorial Fund Quarterly* 41: 291–308. **300**

Rodgers, W. 1980. "Residential satisfaction in relationship to size of place." *Social Psychology Quarterly* 43: 436–441. **21, 123, 196, 314**

———. 1982. "Trends in reported happiness within demographically defined subgroups." *Social Forces* 60: 826–843. **197, 314**

Rodin, J. 1979. "Density, perceived choice, and response to controllable and uncontrollable outcomes," pp. 77–94 in J. R. Aiello and A. Baum (eds.) *Residential Crowding and Design.* New York: Plenum. **176**

———, S. K. Solomon, and J. Metcalf. 1978. "Role of control in mediating perceptions of density." *Journal of Personality and Social Psychology* 36: 988–999. **182**

Rogers, E. M. 1962. *Diffusion of Innovations.* New York: Free Press. **316**

Romanos, M. C. 1979. "Forsaken farms: the village-to-city movement in Europe," pp. 3–19 in M. C. Romanos (ed.) *Western European Cities in Crisis.* Lexington, MA: Lexington Press. **88**

Roncek, D. 1981. "Dangerous places: crime and residential environment." *Social Forces* 60: 74–96. **138, 316**

Roof, W. C. 1976. "Traditional religion in contemporary society." *American Sociological Review* 41: 195–208. **315**

———— and D. Spain. 1977. "A research note on city–suburban socioeconomic differences among American blacks." *Social Forces* 56: 15–20. **317**

Roof, W. C., and R. C. van Valley. 1972. "Residential segregation and social differentiation in American urban areas." *Social Forces* 51: 87–91. **317**

Rose, P. I., with L. O. Pertzoff. 1977. *Strangers in Their Midst: Small-Town Jews and Their Neighbors.* Merrick, NY: Richwood. **309**

Rosenblatt, R. A. 1981. "Health and health services," pp. 614–644 in A. Hawley and S. M. Mazie (eds.), *Nonmetropolitan America in Transition.* Chapel Hill: University of North Caroline Press. **58, 67, 68**

Rosenthal, E. 1967. "Jewish inter-marriage in Indiana." *American Jewish Yearbook* 68: 243–64. **149**

Ross, M., B. Layton, and B. Erickson et al. 1973. "Affect, facial regard and reactions to crowding." *Journal of Personality and Social Psychology* 28: 69–76. **312**

Rossi, P. H. 1955. *Why Families Move.* Glencoe, IL: Free Press. **318**

————, E. Waite, and C. E. Bose et al. 1974. "The seriousness of crimes: Normative structure and individual differences." *American Sociological Review* 39: 224–237. **317**

Rotondo, H. 1962. "Problèmes psychologiques et de santé mentale resultant de l'urbanisation d'après des cas études au Perou," pp. 249–257 in P. H. Hauser (ed.) *L'urbanisation en Amerique Latine.* Liège, Belgium: UNESCO. **313**

Rotter, J. B. 1966. "Generalized expectancies for internal versus external control of reinforcements." *Psychological Monographs,* Whole No. 609. **191**

Rourke, F. E. 1964. "Urbanism and American democracy." *Ethics* 74: 251–268. **15**

Rowe, W. L. 1973. "Caste, kinship and association in urban India," pp. 211–250 in A. Southall (ed.) *Urban Anthropology.* New York: Oxford University Press. **86, 308**

Rushforth, N. B., A. B. Ford, and C. S. Hirsch et al. 1977. "Violent death in a metropolitan community." *New England Journal of Medicine* 297: 531–538. **302**

Sale, K. 1978. "The polis perplexity: an inquiry into the size of cities." *Working Papers for a New Society* 6: 64–77. **284, 322**

————. 1980. *Human Scale.* New York: Coward, McCann & Geoghegan. **35**

Saltzman, A., and L. Newlin. 1981. "The availability of passenger transportation," pp. 255–284 in A. Hawley and S. M. Mazie (eds.) *Nonmetropolitan America in Transition.* Chapel Hill: University of North Carolina. **68**

Sandburg, C. 1926. "Chicago" and "The Windy City," in *Selected Poems of Carl Sandburg.* Edited by Rebecca West. New York: Harcourt Brace. **15**

Sauer, H. I. 1980. "Geographic patterns in the risk of dying and associated factors, ages 35–74 years, United States, 1968–72." *Vital and Health Statistics,* Series 3, Analytical Studies No. 18. Washington, DC: Government Printing Office. **57, 189, 299, 313**

Sawers, L. 1977. "Cities and countryside in the Soviet Union and China." Reprinted in W. Tabb and L. Sawers (eds.) *Marxism and the Metropolis.* New York: Oxford University Press, 1978: 338–364. **323**

Schacht, R. 1971. *Alienation.* New York: Doubleday. **312**

Scherer, K. R., R. P. Abeles, and C. S. Fischer. 1975. *Human Aggression and Conflict.* Englewood Cliffs, NJ: Prentice-Hall. **316**

Schiffenbauer, A. I., J. E. Brown, and P. L. Perry et al. 1977. "The relationship between density and crowding: some architectural modifiers." *Environment & Behavior* 9: 3–14. **181**

Schildkrout, E. 1974. "Ethnicity and generational differences among urban immigrants," pp. 187–222 in A. Cohen (ed.) *Urban Ethnicity.* London: Tavistock. **307**

Schiltz, T., and W. Moffitt. 1971. "Inner-city/outer-city relationships in metropolitan areas: a bibliographic essay." *Urban Affairs Quarterly* 7: 75–108. **247**

Schnaiberg, A. 1970. "Rural–urban residence and modernism: a study of Ankara province, Turkey." *Demography* 7: 7–85. **163, 165, 166**

————. 1971. "The modernizing impact of urbanization: a causal analysis." *Economic Development and Cultural Change* 20: 80–104. **315**

Schneider, J. C. 1980. *Detroit and the Problem of Order, 1830–1880.* Lincoln: University of Nebraska Press. **49, 138, 247, 302**

Schneider, M., and J. R. Logan. 1981. "The fiscal implications of class segregation for suburban municipalities." *Urban Affairs Quarterly* 17(1): 23–36. **254, 323**

Schnore, L. F. 1963. "Some correlates of urban size." *American Journal of Sociology* 69: 185–193. **51**

———. 1965. "On the spatial structure of cities in the two Americas," pp. 347–398 in P. H. Hauser and L. F. Schnore (eds.) *The Study of Urbanization.* New York: John Wiley. **50, 247, 248**

———. 1967. "Community," pp. 79–150 in N. Smelser (ed.) *Sociology.* New York: John Wiley. **100**

———. 1972. *Class and Race in Cities and Suburbs.* Chicago: Markham. **247, 319**

——— and H. H. Winsborough. 1972. "Functional classification and the residential location of social class," pp. 124–151 in B.J.L. Berry (ed.) *City Classification Handbook.* New York: John Wiley. **319**

Schooler, C. 1972. "Social antecedents of adult psychological functioning." *American Journal of Sociology* 78: 299–322. **192, 312**

Schorr, A. L. n.d. *Slums and Social Insecurity,* Social Security Administration, Division of Research and Statistics, Report 1. Washington, DC: Government Printing Office. **63**

Schorske, C. E. 1963. "The idea of the city in European thought: Voltaire to Spengler," pp. 95–115 in O. Handlin and J. Burchard (eds.) *The Historian and the City.* Cambridge, MA: MIT Press. **14, 295**

Schwab, J. J., G. J. Warheit, and C. E. Holzer III. 1972. "Mental health: rural–urban comparisons." Paper presented to the Fourth International Congress of Social Psychiatry (May), Jerusalem. **190, 312**

Schwab, W. A. 1968. "Oshogbo: an urban community?" pp. 85–109 in H. Kuper (ed.) *Urbanization and Migration in West Africa.* Berkeley: University of California Press. **310**

Schwartz, B. 1976a. "Images of suburbia," pp. 325–342 in B. Schwartz (ed.) *The Changing Face of the Suburbs.* Chicago: University of Chicago Press. **317**

——— (ed.) 1976b. *The Changing Face of the Suburbs.* Chicago: University of Chicago Press. **239**

———. 1980. "The suburban landscape." *Contemporary Sociology* 9: 640–649. **241, 317**

Schwirian, K. (ed.) 1974. *Comparative Urban Structure.* Lexington, MA: D. C. Heath. **298**

Seeman, M. 1959. "On the meaning of alienation." *American Sociological Review* 24: 783–791. **313**

———. 1971. "The urban alienations: some dubious theses from Marx to Marcuse." *Journal of Personality and Social Psychology* 19: 135–143. **191**

———. 1972. "Alienation and engagement," pp. 441–446 in A. Campbell and P. Converse (eds.) *The Human Meaning of Social Change.* New York: Russell Sage. **191, 313**

———. 1975. "Alienation studies." *Annual Review of Sociology* 1: 91–124. **313**

Seligson, M. A. 1972. "The 'dual society' thesis in Latin America: a reexamination of the Costa Rican case." *Social Forces* 51: 91–98. **315**

Selznik, G. J., and S. Steinberg. 1969. *The Tenacity of Prejudice.* New York: Harper & Row. **314**

Sengstock, M. C. 1969. "Differential rates of assimilation in an ethnic group: in ritual, social interaction, and normative culture." *International Migration Review* 3: 18–32. **308**

Seninger, S. F., and T. H. Smeeding. 1981. "Poverty: a human capital perspective," pp. 382–436 in A. Hawley and S. M. Mazie (eds.) *Understanding Nonmetropolitan America.* Chapel Hill: University of North Carolina Press. **83**

Sennett, R. 1969. "Introduction," pp. 3–22. in R. Sennett (ed.) *Classic Essays on the Culture of Cities.* Englewood Cliffs, NJ: Prentice-Hall.

———. 1977. *The Fall of Public Man.* New York: Knopf. **35, 173**

Sewell, W. H., and E. E. Amend. 1943. "The influence of size of home community on attitudes and personality traits." *American Sociological Review* 8: 180–184. **313**

Shack, W. A. 1973. "Urban ethnicity and the cultural process of urbanization in Ethiopia," pp. 251–287 in A. Southall (ed.) *Urban Anthropology.* New York: Oxford University Press. **308**

Sharlin, A. 1978. "Natural decrease in early modern cities: A reconsideration." *Past and Present* 79: 126–138. **87, 165**

———. 1980. "Urban–rural differences in fertility in Europe during the demographic transition," Working Paper No. 329. Berkeley, CA: Institute of Urban and Regional Development. **221, 300**

———. 1981. "Debate: natural decrease in early modern cities: a rejoinder." *Past and Present*
92: 175–180.   **87**

Sheerin, I. G., and J. R. Barnett. 1978. "Crime rates and city size in New Zealand." *New
Zealand Geographer* 34: 75–84.   **303**

Shelley, L. I. 1980. "The geography of Soviet criminality." *American Sociological Review*
45: 111–122.   **227, 303**

———. 1981. *Crime and Modernization.* Carbondale: Southern Illinois University Press.   **226,
227, 302, 303, 316**

Sherrod, D. R., and R. Downs. 1974. "Environmental determinants of altruism." *Journal of
Experimental Social Psychology* 10: 468–479.   **185**

Shils, E. 1962. "The theory of mass society." *Diogenes* 39: 45–66.   **322**

Shipler, D. K. 1978. "Rising Youth Crime in Soviet Union Troubles Regime and Public." *New
York Times,* 5 March.   **108**

Shlay, A. B., and P. H. Rossi. 1981. "Keeping up the neighborhood: estimating net effects of
zoning." *American Sociological Review* 46: 703–720.   **49, 323**

Short, J. F., Jr. 1971. "Introduction," pp. xi–xlvi in J. F. Short (ed.) *The Social Fabric of the
Metropolis.* Chicago: University of Chicago Press.   **28, 303**

Shorter, E. 1971. "Illegitimacy, sexual revolution and social change in modern Europe." *Journal
of Interdisciplinary History* 2: 237–272.   **220**

———. 1975. *The Making of the Modern Family.* New York: Basic Books.   **165**

Shulman, N. 1972. "Urban social networks." Ph.D. dissertation. University of Toronto.   **156**

———. 1976. "Race differentiation in networks." *Sociological Focus* 9: 149–156.   **310**

Sieber, S. D. 1974. "Toward a theory of role accumulation." *American Sociological Review*
39: 567–578.   **206**

Signs. 1980. "Women and the American city." Special issue. 5 (Spring).

Silberman, C. E. 1978. *Criminal Violence, Criminal Justice.* New York: Random House.   **302**

Silverman, C. J. 1982. "Place types as social constructions," Working Paper No. 381. Berkeley,
CA: Institute of Urban and Regional Development.   **101, 240, 288, 295**

———. 1983. "Negotiated claim." Ph.D. dissertation. University of California, Berkeley.   **64,
65, 255, 299, 306**

Simic, A. 1973. "Kinship reciprocity and rural–urban integration in Serbia." *Urban
Anthropology* 2: 205–213.   **311**

Simmel, G. 1905. "The metropolis and mental life." Reprinted in R. Sennett (ed.) *Classic Essays
on the Culture of Cities.* New York: Appleton-Century-Crofts, 1969: 47–60.   **28, 156, 206,
208, 209, 296, 305, 306**

———. 1922. "The web of group affiliations." Translated by R. Bendix. Reprinted in G. Simmel
(ed.) *Conflict and the Web of Group Affiliations.* New York: Free Press, 1955:
125–195.   **203, 204**

———. 1950. "The stranger," pp. 402–408 in *The Sociology of Georg Simmel.* Translated by
K. H. Wolff. Glencoe, IL: Free Press.   **17, 95**

Sjoberg, G. 1960. *The Preindustrial City.* New York: Free Press.   **44, 294, 295, 296, 298, 300**

———. 1964. "The rural–urban dimension in preindustrial, transitional and industrial
societies," pp. 127–160. in R.E.L. Faris (ed.) *The Handbook of Modern Sociology.* Chicago:
Rand-McNally.   **316**

———. 1965a. "Cities in developing and in industrialized societies: a cross-cultural analysis,"
pp. 213–263 in P. H. Hauser and L. F. Schnore (eds.) *The Study of Urbanization.* New
York: John Wiley.   **295, 316**

———. 1965b. "Theory and research in urban sociology," pp. 157–190. in P. H. Hauser and
L. F. Schnore (eds.) *The Study of Urbanization.* New York: John Wiley.   **296**

Skeldon, R. 1976. "Regional associations and population migration in Peru: an interpretation."
Urban Anthropology 5: 233–252.   **90**

Sklare, M., and J. Greenblum. 1967. *Jewish Identity on the Suburban Frontier.* New York:
Basic Books.   **258**

Skogan, W. G. 1977. "The changing distribution of big-city crime." *Urban Affairs Quarterly*
13: 33–49.   **103**

Slesinger, D. P. 1974. "The relationship of fertility to measures of metropolitan dominance: a
new look." *Rural Sociology* 39: 350–361.   **300**

Smith, J., W. H. Form, and G. P. Stone. 1954. "Local intimacy in a middle-sized city."
American Journal of Sociology 60: 276–284.   **157, 307, 320**

Smith, N. 1979. "Toward a theory of gentrification." *Journal of the American Institute of Planners* 8: 538–548. **319**

Smith, P. 1968. *As a City upon a Hill: The Town in American History.* New York: Knopf. **310**

Smith, R. J. 1961. "The Japanese rural community: norms, sanctions, and ostracism." Reprinted in J. Potter, M. Diaz, and G. Foster (eds.) *Peasant Society.* Boston: Little, Brown, 1967: 246–254. **231**

———. 1973. "Town and city in pre-modern Japan: small families, small households, and residential instability," pp. 163–210 in A. Southall, (ed.) *Urban Anthropology.* New York: Oxford University Press. **301**

Smith, S. R. 1973. "The London apprentices as seventeenth-century adolescents." *Past and Present* 61: 149–161. **126**

Smith, T. W. 1979. "Happiness." *Social Psychology Quarterly* 42: 18–30. **197, 319**

Snyder, P. Z. 1971. "The social environment of the urban Indian," pp. 206–243 in J. O. Waddell and O. M. Watson (eds.) *The American Indian in Urban Society.* Boston: Little, Brown. **301, 308**

Sokolow, A. D. 1981. "Local governments: capacity and will," pp. 704–735 in A. Hawley and S. M. Mazie (eds.) *Nonmetropolitan America in Transition.* Chapel Hill: University of North Carolina Press. **116**

Somer, R. 1969. *Personal Space.* Englewood Cliffs, NJ: Prentice-Hall. **178, 180, 311**

Sorokin, P. A., C. C. Zimmerman, and C. J. Galpin. 1930. *A Systematic Source Book in Rural Sociology.* Minneapolis: University of Minnesota Press. **295**

Southall, A. (ed.) 1973a. *Urban Anthropology.* New York: Oxford University Press. **295, 308, 310**

———. 1973b. "The density of role-relationships as a universal index of urbanization," pp. 71–106 in A. Southall (ed.) *Urban Anthropology.* New York: Oxford University Press. **205**

Spain, D. 1980. "Black to white succession in central city housing: limited evidence of urban revitalization." *Urban Affairs Quarterly* 15: 381–396. **250**

Spengler, J. J. 1967. "Africa and the theory of optimum city size," pp. 55–90 in H. Miner (ed.) *The City in Modern Africa.* New York: Praeger. **284**

Spiegel, I. 1973. "Jews Assay Life in Small Towns." *New York Times,* 25 November. **309**

Spilerman, S. 1971. "The causes of racial disturbances: tests of an explanation." *American Sociological Review* 36: 427–442. **152, 217, 304**

Srole, L. 1972. "Urbanization and mental health: some reformulations." *American Scientist* 60: 576–583. **188, 189, 313**

———. 1978a. "The city versus town and country: new evidence on an ancient bias, 1975," pp. 433–459 in L. Srole and A. K. Fischer (eds.) *Mental Health in the Metropolis.* Rev. ed. New York: New York University Press. **187**

———. 1978b. "Rural–urban diagnostic issues," pp. 519–523 in L. Srole and A. K. Fischer (eds.) *Mental Health in the Metropolis.* Rev. ed. New York: New York University Press. **188, 313**

———. 1980. "Mental health in New York." *Sciences* 20: 16–29. **189**

Stack, C. 1974. *All Our Kin.* New York: Harper & Row. **168**

Stahura, J. M. 1979. "Suburban status evolution/persistence." *American Sociological Review* 44: 914–924. **298**

Stegman, M. A. 1969. "Accessibility models and residential location." *Journal of the American Institute of Planners* 35: 22–29.

Stein, M. R. 1960. *The Eclipse of Community.* New York: Harper & Row. **115, 262, 316**

Stephan, G. E., and D. R. McMullin. 1982. "Tolerance of sexual nonconformity: city size as a situational and early learning determinant." *American Sociological Review* 47: 411–415. **218, 220, 315**

Stephan, W. G. 1975. "Actor vs. observer: attributions of behavior with positive or negative outcomes and empathy for the other role." *Journal of Experimental Social Psychology* 11: 205–214. **315**

Stephens, S. 1979. "Ethnic identity in an urban community." Paper presented to the American Sociological Association (August), Boston. **150**

Stevenson, G. M., Jr. 1972. "Noise and the urban environment," pp. 195–228 in T. R. Detwyler and M. G. Marcus (eds.) *Urbanization and Environment.* Belmont, CA: Duxbury. **54**

Stinchcombe, A. L. 1963. "Institutions of privacy in the determination of police administrative practice." *American Journal of Sociology* 69: 150–160. **302**

————, R. Adams, and C. A. Heimer et al. 1980. *Crime and Punishment: Changing Attitudes in America*. San Francisco: Jossey-Bass. **109, 302**

Stokols, D. 1972a. "A social-psychological model of human crowding phenomena." *Journal of the American Institute of Planners* 38: 72–83. **179**

————. 1972b. "On the distinction between density and crowding." *Psychological Review* 79: 275–278.

————. 1974. "The experience of crowding in primary and secondary environments." Paper presented to the American Psychological Association (September), New Orleans. **176**

———— (ed.) 1977. *Psychological Perspectives on Environment and Behavior*. New York: Plenum. **311, 312**

————. 1978. "Environmental psychology." *Annual Review of Psychology* 29: 253–295. **311**

————, W. Ohlig, and S. M. Resnick. 1979. "Perception of residential crowding, classroom experiences, and student health," pp. 107–126 in J. R. Aiello and A. Baum (ed.) *Residential Crowding and Design*. New York: Plenum. **182**

Stokols, D., M. Rall, and B. Pinner et al. 1973. "Physical, social, and personal determinants of the perception of crowding." *Environment & Behavior* 5: 87–116. **312**

Stone, L. 1977. *The Family, Sex and Marriage in England, 1500–1800*. New York: Harper & Row. **165**

Storr, A. 1968. *Human Aggression*. New York: Atheneum. **175**

Strauss, A. L. 1961. *Images of the American City*. New York: Free Press. **16, 295**

Stueve, C. A., K. Gerson, and C. S. Fischer. 1975. "The structure and determinants of attachment to place." Paper presented to the American Sociological Association (August), San Francisco.

Sundquist, J. L. 1975. *Dispersing Population*. Washington, DC: Brookings Institution. **175, 286, 287, 320, 322, 323**

Sundstrom, E. 1978. "Crowding as a sequential process: review of research on the effects of population density on humans," pp. 32–116 in A. Baum and Y. M. Epstein (eds.) *Human Responses to Crowding*. Hillsdale, NJ: Lawrence Erlbaum. **184, 311**

Sutcliffe, J. P., and B. D. Crabbe. 1963. "Incidence and degrees of friendship in urban and rural areas." *Social Forces* 42: 60–67. **310, 320**

Suttles, G. D. 1968. *The Social Order of the Slum: Ethnicity and Territory in the Inner City*. Chicago: University of Chicago Press. **97, 119, 130, 151, 208, 309, 310**

————. 1970. "Friendship as a social institution," pp. 95–135 in G. J. McCall et al. (eds.) *Social Relationships*. Chicago: Aldine. **156**

————. 1972. *The Social Construction of Communities*. Chicago: University of Chicago Press. **49, 307**

Swanson, L. L. 1983. "SMSA characteristics and nonmetropolitan-destined outmigration." Paper presented to the Population Association of America, Pittsburgh. **93, 303**

Swedner, H. 1960. *Ecological Differentiation of Habits and Attitudes*. Lund, Sweden: GWK Gleerup. **98, 163, 165, 299, 306, 310, 313, 315**

Szabo, D. 1960. *Crimes et Villes*. Paris: Cujas. **189, 303, 313**

Tabb, W. K., and L. Sawers (eds.) 1978. *Marxism and the Metropolis*. New York: Oxford University Press. **305**

Taeuber, I. B. 1972. "The changing distribution of the population of the United States in the twentieth century," pp. 31–108 in S. M. Mazie (ed.) *Population, Distribution and Policy*, Vol. V, Research Reports. Washington, DC: U.S. Commission on Population Growth and the American Future. **80, 300**

Tallman, I. 1969. "Working-class wives in suburbia: fulfillment or crisis?" *Journal of Marriage and the Family* 31: 65–72. **320, 321**

———— and R. Morgner. 1970. "Life-style differences among urban and suburban blue collar families." *Social Forces* 48: 334–348. **255, 320, 321**

Tarr, J. A. 1971. "Urban pollution—many years ago." *American Heritage* 22: 65–69. **53**

————. 1973. "From city to suburb: the 'moral' influence of transportation and technology," pp. 202–212 in A. B. Callow, Jr. (ed.) *American Urban History*. 2nd ed. New York: Oxford University Press. **23, 241, 242**

Tarrow, S. 1971. "Political involvement in rural France." *American Political Science Review* 65: 341–357. **304**

Taub, R. P., and D. G. Taylor. 1982. "Crime, fear of crime, and the deterioration of urban neighborhoods." Washington, DC: U.S. Department of Justice, National Institute of Justice. **109, 303**

Taub, R. P., G. P. Surgeon, and S. Lindholm et al. 1977. "Urban voluntary associations, locality based and externally induced." *American Journal of Sociology* 83: 425–442. **132**

Tedesco, J. F., and D. K. Fromme. 1974. "Cooperation, competition, and personal space." *Sociometry* 37: 116–121. **174**

Terrill, R. 1975. *Flowers on the Iron Tree: Five Cities of China.* Boston: Little, Brown. **221**

Thernstrom, S. 1968. "Urbanization, migration and social mobility in the late nineteenth-century America," pp. 158–175 in B. J. Bernstein (ed.) *Towards a New Past: Dissenting Essays in American History.* New York: Pantheon. **87**

———. 1973. *The Other Bostonians: Poverty and Progress in the American Metropolis, 1880–1970.* Cambridge, MA: Harvard University Press. **87, 301, 304**

Thoits, P. 1983. "Multiple identities and psychological well-being." *American Sociological Review* 48: 174–188. **206**

Thomas, J. L. 1951. "The factor of religion in the selection of marriage mates." *American Sociological Review* 16: 487–491. **149**

Thomas, R. 1969. *London's New Towns,* PEP Vol. 35, Broadsheet S10. London: Political and Economic Planning. **323**

Thomas, W. I., and F. Znaniecki. 1918. *The Polish Peasant in Europe and America.* New York: Knopf.

Thompson, R. W. 1974. "Rural–urban differences in individual modernization in Buganda." *Urban Anthropology* 3: 64–78. **313**

Thompson, S. I. 1974. "The survival of ethnicity in the Japanese community of Lima, Peru." *Urban Anthropology* 3: 243–261. **308**

Thompson, W. R. 1965. *A Preface to Urban Economics.* Baltimore: Johns Hopkins University Press. **100, 299**

Thrupp, S. L. 1963. "The city as the idea of social order," pp. 121–132 in O. Handlin and J. Burchard (eds.) *The Historian and the City.* Cambridge, MA: MIT Press. **17**

Tienda, M. 1978. "Dependency, extension, and the 'family life-cycle squeeze,'" Working Paper 78-28. Madison: University of Wisconsin, Center for Demography and Ecology. **162**

Till, T. E. 1981. "Manufacturing industry," pp. 194–230 in A. Hawley and S. Mazie (eds.) *Understanding Nonmetropolitan America.* Chapel Hill: University of North Carolina Press. **93**

Tilly, C. 1965. *Migration to an American City.* Wilmington: University of Delaware Press. **301**

———. 1969. "Collective violence in European perspective," pp. 4–44 in H. Graham and H. Gurr (eds.) *The History of Violence in America.* New York: Bantam. **301**

———. 1970a. "Migration to American cities," pp. 171–186 in D. P. Moynihan (ed.) *Urban America: The Expert Looks at the City.* Washington, DC: Voice of America Forum Lectures. **301**

———. 1970b. "Race and migration to the American city," pp. 144–169 in J. Q. Wilson, Jr. (ed.) *The Metropolitan Enigma.* New York: Doubleday. **301**

———. 1973. "Do communities act?" *Sociological Inquiry* 43: 209–240. **304**

———. 1974. "The chaos of the living city," pp. 86–107 in C. Tilly (ed.) *An Urban World.* Boston: Little, Brown. **123, 217, 304**

———, L. Tilly, and R. Tilly. 1975. *The Rebellious Century.* Cambridge, MA: Harvard University Press. **123, 301, 304, 315**

Tisdale, H. 1942. "The process of urbanization." *Social Forces* 20: 311–316. **24**

Tobias, J. J. 1972. *Urban Crime in Victorian England.* New York: Schocken. **9, 102, 228, 302**

Tomeh, A. K. 1964. "Informal group participation and residential pattern." *American Journal of Sociology* 70: 28–35. **255, 259, 320**

———. 1967. "Informal participation in a metropolitan community." *Sociological Quarterly* 8: 85–102. **307**

Tönnies, F. 1887. *Community and Society.* Translated by C. P. Loomis. Reprint ed., New York: Harper & Row, 1957. **304, 306, 310**

Treadway, R. 1969. "Social components of metropolitan population densities." *Demography* 6: 55–74. **244**

———. 1983. "Suburbs and center cities: misleading dichotomy?" Paper presented to the Population Association of America, Pittsburgh. **240**

Trembly, K. R., D. A. Dillman, and K. D. Van Liere. 1980. "An examination of the relationship between housing preference and community size preference." *Rural Sociology* 45: 509–519. **299**

Trice, H. M. 1966. *Alcoholism in America.* New York: McGraw-Hill. **189**

Trovato, F., and C. F. Grindstaff. 1980. "Decomposing the urban–rural fertility differential: Canada, 1971." *Rural Sociology* 45: 448–468.   **300**

Tsai, Y -M., and L. Sigelman. 1982. "The community question: a perspective from national survey data — the case of the USA." *British Journal of Sociology* 33: 579–588.   **165, 306, 310**

Tucker, C. J. 1976. "Changing patterns of migration between metropolitan and nonmetropolitan areas in the United States." *Demography* 13: 435–443.   **92**

Turner, R. E. 1940. "The industrial city: center of cultural change," pp. 228–242 in C. F. Ware (ed.) *The Cultural Approach to History.* New York: Columbia University Press.   **316**

U.S. Department of Commerce. Bureau of the Census (BOC). 1968. "Lifetime migration histories of the American people," *Current Population Reports,* Ser. P-23, No. 25. Washington, DC: Government Printing Office.   **301**

————. 1971. "General demographic trends for metropolitan areas, 1960 to 1970, final report PHC (2)-1 United States," *Census of Population and Housing: 1970.* Washington, DC: Government Printing Office.   **52**

————. 1973. *We the Americans: Our Cities and Suburbs.* Washington, DC: Government Printing Office.   **98**

————. 1977a. *Annual Housing Survey. A: General Housing Characteristics,* Current Housing Reports, Ser. H-150-77. Washington, DC: Government Printing Office.   **61, 65, 83, 248, 317**

————. 1977b. *Annual Housing Survey. B: Indicators of Housing and Neighborhood Quality,* Current Housing Reports, Ser. H-150-77. Washington, DC: Government Printing Office.   **56, 61, 67, 302, 319**

————. 1977c. *Annual Housing Survey. C: Financial Characteristics of the Housing Inventory for the United States and Regions,* Current Housing Reports, Ser. H-150-77. Washington, DC: Government Printing Office.

————. 1980. "Money income of households in the United States, 1978." *Current Population Reports.* Ser. P-60, No. 126. Washington, DC: Government Printing Office.   **61, 84**

————. 1982a. *Statistical Abstract of the United States, 1982–83.* Washington, DC: Government Printing Office.   **23, 161, 278, 289, 301, 302, 316**

————. 1982b. *State and Metropolitan Area Data Book.* Washington, DC: Government Printing Office.   **78, 79, 80**

U.S. Department of Health and Human Services (DHHS) 1981. *Health: United States, 1981,* DHHS Publication No. (PHS)82-1232. Washington, DC: Government Printing Office.   **58**

U.S. Environmental Protection Agency (EPA) 1971. "The social impact of noise." Washington, DC: Government Printing Office.   **54**

U.S. Public Health Department. National Center for Health Statistics (NCHS) 1967a. "Health characteristics . . . July 1963–June 1965," *Vital and Health Statistics,* Ser. 21, No. 15. Washington, DC: Government Printing Office.   **58**

————. 1967b. "Suicide in the United States 1950–1964," *Vital and Health Statistics,* Ser. 21, No. 5. Washington, DC: Government Printing Office.   **313**

————. 1968. "Trends in illegitimacy, United States—1940–1965," *Vital and Health Statistics,* Ser. 21, No. 15. Washington, DC: Government Printing Office.   **220**

————. 1969a. "Chronic conditions causing activity limitations, United States—July 1963–June 1965," *Vital and Health Statistics,* Ser. 10, No. 51: Tables 2, 14. Washington, DC: Government Printing Office.   **55, 58**

————. 1969b. "Divorce statistics analysis," *Vital and Health Statistics,* Ser. 21, No. 17. Washington, DC: Government Printing Office.   **68**

————. 1971. "Health characteristics . . . 1969–1970," *Vital and Health Statistics,* Ser. 10, No. 86. Washington, DC: Government Printing Office.   **58**

————. 1972. "Hearing levels of children by demographic and socioeconomic characteristics," *Vital and Health Statistics,* Ser. 11, No. 111. Washington, DC: Government Printing Office.   **55**

————. 1973. "Hypertension and hypertensive heart disease in adults," *Vital and Health Statistics,* Ser. 11, No. 13. Washington, DC: Government Printing Office.   **187**

Useem, R. H., J. Useem, and D. L. Gibson. 1960. "The function of neighboring for the middle-class male." *Human Organization* 19: 69.   **307**

Valentine, C. A. 1968. *Culture and Poverty.* Chicago: University of Chicago Press.   **297**

van den Berghe, P. 1974. "Bringing beasts back in: toward a biosocial theory of aggression." *American Sociological Review* 39: 777–788.   **176, 185, 311** van Es, J. C., and J. E. Brown, Jr. 1974. "The rural–urban variable once more." *Rural Sociology* 39: 373–391. **304, 305, 316**

Van Valey, T. L., W. C. Roof, and J. E. Wilcox. 1977. "Trend in residential segregation, 1960–1970." *American Journal of Sociology* 82: 826–844. **298**

Vatuk, S. 1972. *Kinship and Urbanization.* Berkeley: University of California Press. **310, 311**

Vaughan, R. J. 1980. "The impact of federal policies on urban economic development," pp. 348–398 in A. P. Solomon (ed.) *The Prospective City.* Cambridge, MA: MIT Press. **323**

Verba, S., and N. H. Nie. 1972. *Participation in American Life: Political Democracy and Social Equality.* New York: Harper & Row. **254, 304**

———— and J. -O. Kim. 1978. *Participation and Political Equality: A Seven-Nation Comparison.* New York: Cambridge University Press. **304**

Verbrugge, L. 1973. "Adult friendship contact." Ph.D. dissertation. University of Michigan. **310**

———— and R. B. Taylor. 1980. "Consequences of population size and density." *Urban Affairs Quarterly* 16: 135–160. **312**

Veroff, J., E. Douvan, and R. A. Kulka. 1981a. *The Inner American: A Self-Portrait from 1957 to 1976.* New York: Basic Books. **190, 197, 311, 314, 320**

Veroff, J., R. A. Kulka, and E. Douvan. 1981b. *Mental Health in America.* New York: Basic Books. **188, 197, 320**

Vining, D. R., Jr., and T. Kontuly. 1978. "Population dispersal from major metropolitan regions: an international comparison." *International Regional Science Review* 3: 49–73. **91, 301**

Von Rosenbladt, B. 1972. "The outdoor activity system in an urban environment," pp. 335–355 in A. Szalai (ed.) *The Use of Time.* The Hague, Netherlands: Mouton. **251, 317**

Walker, M. 1971. *German Home Towns: Community, State, and General Estate.* Ithaca, NY: Cornell University Press. **34**

Walker, R. A. 1978. "The transformation of urban structure in the nineteenth century and the beginning of suburbanization," pp. 162–213 in K. Cox (ed.) *Urbanization and Conflict in Market Societies.* Chicago: Maaroufa Press. **247, 317, 323**

Walker, R. H. 1962. "The poet and the rise of the city." Reprinted in A. B. Callow, Jr. (ed.) *American Urban History.* New York: Oxford University Press, 1969: 363–372. **15**

Wallace, K. 1975. "A Fond Look at the No. 30." *San Francisco Examiner Sunday Punch,* 29 June. **98**

Wallden, M. 1975. "Activity patterns of urban residents: Part 2: the frequency of activities outside the home." *National Swedish Building Research Summaries* R9: 1975. **251**

Ward, D. 1971. *Cities and Immigrants.* New York: Oxford University Press. **45, 247**

Ward, J. 1972. "Peter Goldmark and the electronic rural society." *Intellectual Digest* (June): 82–84. **322**

Ward, R. A., M. La Gory, and S. Sherman et al. 1982. "Neighborhood age structure and support networks." Mimeo. Albany: State University of New York. **307**

Ward, S. K. 1974. "Overcrowding and social pathology: re-examination of the implications for the human population." Paper presented at the Annual Meeting of the Population Association of America (April), New York. **312**

Ward, Z. A. 1979. "A public antimony: public attitudes versus urban conditions in Western Europe," pp. 47–63 in M. C. Romanos (ed.) *Western European Cities in Crisis.* Lexington, MA: Lexington Press. **217, 314**

Wardwell, J. M. 1980. "Toward a theory of urban–rural migration in the developed world," pp. 71–114 in D. L. Brown and J. M. Wardwell (eds.) *New Directions in Urban–Rural Migration.* New York: Academic Press. **93**

Warner, S. B. 1962. *Streetcar Suburbs.* Cambridge, MA: Harvard University Press. **23, 64, 65, 238, 242, 243, 298, 317**

————. 1968. *The Private City: Philadelphia in Three Periods of Its Growth.* Philadelphia: University of Pennsylvania Press. **120**

Warner, W. L., J. O. Low, and P. S. Lunt et al. 1963. *Yankee City.* Abr. ed. New Haven, CT: Yale University Press. **122**

Warren, D. 1977. "The functional diversity of urban neighborhoods." *Urban Affairs Quarterly* 13: 151–178. **136, 320**

Watson, O. M. 1972. "Symbolic and expressive uses of space: an introduction to proxemic behavior," *McCaleb Module in Anthropology* No. 20. Reading, MA: Addison-Wesley. **178, 311**

Wattell, H. L. 1959. "Levittown: a suburban community," pp. 287–313 in W. M. Dobriner (ed.) *The Suburban Community.* New York: G. P. Putnam's Sons.   **264**

Webb, S. D., and J. Collette. 1977. "Rural–urban differences in the use of stress-alleviative drugs." *American Journal of Sociology* 83: 700–707.   **312**

———. 1979. "Rural–urban stress: New data and new conclusions." *American Journal of Sociology* 84: 1446–1452.   **312**

Webber, M. M. 1963. "The urban place and the nonplace urban realm," pp. 79–153 in M. M. Webber, J. W. Dyckman, and D. L. Foley et al. (eds.) *Explorations into Urban Structure.* Philadelphia: University of Pennsylvania Press.   **280, 321**

———. 1968a. "Planning in an environment of change, I." *The Town Planning Review* 39: 179–195.   **322**

———. 1968b. "The post-city age." *Daedalus* 97: 1091–1110.   **141, 280**

———. 1970. "Order in diversity: community without propinquity," pp. 792–811 in R. Gutman and D. Popenoe (eds.) *Neighborhood, City and Metropolis.* New York: Random House.   **322**

———. 1973. "Urbanization and communications," pp. 293–304 in G. Gardner, L. P. Gross, and W. H. Melody (eds.) *Communications Technology and Social Policy.* New York: John Wiley.   **280**

Weber, D., and R. C. Burt. 1972. *Who's Home When?* Washington, DC: U.S. Bureau of the Census.   **81, 83, 204, 319**

Weber, E. 1976. *Peasants into Frenchmen.* Stanford, CA: Stanford University Press.   **53, 59, 83, 134, 165, 217, 220, 231, 295**

Webster, W. 1981. *Crime in the United States, 1980.* Washington, DC: U.S. Federal Bureau of Investigation.   **104, 227, 229, 252, 316**

Weiner, F. H. 1976. "Altruism, ambiance, and action: the effects of rural and urban rearing on helping behavior." *Journal of Personality and Social Psychology* 34: 112–124.   **210, 212**

Weisner, T. S. 1976. "The structure of sociability: urban migration and urban–rural ties in Kenya." *Urban Anthropology* 5: 199–224.   **301**

Wellman, B. 1972. "Who needs neighborhoods?" pp. 94–100 in A. Powell (ed.) *The City: Attacking Modern Myths.* Toronto: McClelland and Stewart.   **137**

———. 1979. "The community question: the intimate networks of East Yorkers." *American Journal of Sociology* 84: 1201–1231.   **310**

———, P. Craven, M. Whitaker et al. 1972. "Community ties and support systems," Research Report No. 47. University of Toronto: Centre for Urban and Community Studies.   **137, 163, 299, 305, 310, 311**

Westergaard, J. H. 1966. *Scandinavian Urbanism.* London: Centre for Urban Studies.   **303, 313**

White, E. B. 1949. "Here is New York." Reprinted in O. Shoenfeld and H. MacLean (eds.) *City Life.* New York: Grossman, 1969.

White, J. W. 1973. *Political Implications of Cityward Migration: Japan as an Exploratory Case,* Sage Professional Paper in Comparative Politics. Beverly Hills, CA: Sage.   **315**

White, M., and L. White. 1962. *The Intellectual Versus the City.* New York: Mentor.   **15, 191, 295**

Whiteford, M. B. 1976. "A comparison of migrants' satisfaction in two low-income housing settlements of Popayán, Colombia." *Urban Anthropology* 5: 271–284.

Whitt, H. P., and H. M. Nelsen. 1975. "Residence, moral traditionalism, and tolerance of atheists." *Social Forces* 54: 328–340.   **314**

Whyte, M. K., and W. L. Parish. 1983. *Urban Life in Contemporary China.* Chicago: University of Chicago Press.   **134, 306**

Whyte, W. F. 1955. *Street Corner Society.* Enlarged ed. Chicago: University of Chicago Press.   **129, 309**

Whyte, W. H. 1956. *The Organization Man.* New York: Simon & Schuster.   **264, 319**

———. 1968. "The case for crowding," pp. 375–394 in W. H. Whyte (ed.) *The Last Landscape.* New York: Doubleday.   **241, 287**

Wicker, A. W. 1968. "Undermanning, performance, and students' subjective experiences. . . ." *Journal of Personality and Social Psychology* 10: 255–261.   **304**

———. 1969. "Size of church membership and members' support of church behavior settings." *Journal of Personality and Social Psychology* 13: 278–288.   **304**

———. 1973. "Undermanning theory and research." *Representative Research in Social Psychology* 4: 185–206.   **176, 204**

Wilensky, H. 1964. "Mass society and mass culture." *American Sociological Review* 29: 173–197. **305, 322**

Wilkinson, K. P. 1978. "Rural community change," pp. 115–126 in T. R. Ford (ed.) *Rural U.S.A.: Persistence and Change.* Ames: Iowa State University Press. **297**

Wilks, J. A. 1967. "Ecological correlates of crime and delinquency," pp. 138–156 in *Crime and its Impact—An Assessment,* Task Force Report of the President's Commission on Law Enforcement and Administration of Justice. Washington, DC: Government Printing Office. **316**

Willbern, Y. 1964. *The Withering Away of the City.* Tuscaloosa: University of Alabama Press. **322**

Willems, E. 1970. "Peasantry and city: cultural persistence and change in historical perspective, a European case." *American Anthropologist* 72: 528–544. **308, 310**

Williams, J. A., C. S. Nunn, and L. St. Peter. 1976. "Origins of tolerance." *Social Forces* 55: 394–408. **222, 315**

Williams, J. D., and D. McMillen. 1980. "Migration decision-making among nonmetropolitan-bound migrants," pp. 189–211 in D. L. Brown and J. M. Wardwell (eds.) *New Directions in Urban–Rural Migration.* New York: Academic Press. **302**

Williams, R. 1973. *The Country and the City.* New York: Oxford University Press. **14, 17, 295**

Willitis, F. K., R. C. Bealer, and D. M. Crider. 1973. "Leveling of attitudes in mass society: rurality and traditional morality in America." *Rural Sociology* 38: 36–45. **222**

———. 1974. "The ecology of social traditionalism in a rural hinterland." *Rural Sociology* 39: 334–349. **315**

Willmott, P. 1963. *The Evolution of a Community.* London: Routledge and Kegan Paul. **261, 323**

———. 1967. "Social research and new communities." *Journal of the American Institute of Planners* 33(16): 387–397. **323**

Wilson, J. Q. 1968. "The urban unease," *Public Interest* 12: 1125–1139.

———. 1983. "Crime and American culture." *Public Interest* 27: 22–48. **96, 302**

Winch, R. F., and S. A. Greer. 1968. "Urbanism, ethnicity, and extended familism." *Journal of Marriage and the Family* 30: 40–45. **165, 311**

Wirt, F. M., B. Walter, and E. F. Rabinovitz et al. 1972. *On the City's Rim: Politics and Policy in Suburbia.* Lexington, MA: D. C. Heath. **264, 320**

Wirth, L. 1928. *The Ghetto.* Reprint ed., 1956. Chicago: University of Chicago Press. **145, 309**

———. 1938. "Urbanism as a way of life." *American Journal of Sociology* 44: 3–24. Reprinted in R. Sennett (ed.) *Classic Essays on the Culture of Cities.* New York: Appleton-Century-Crofts, 1969: 143–164. **26, 114, 160, 163, 186, 192, 203, 207, 303, 304, 305, 306, 310**

———. 1956. "Rural–urban differences." Reprinted in R. Sennett (ed.) *Classic Essays on the Culture of Cities.* New York: Appleton-Century-Crofts, 1969: 165–169. **5, 6**

Wolf, M. 1975. "Women and suicide in China," pp. 111–141 in M. Wolf and R. White (eds.) *Women in Chinese Society.* Stanford, CA: Stanford University Press. **313**

Wolf, S. G. 1976. *Urban Village: Population, Community, and Family Structure in Germantown, Pennsylvania 1683–1800.* Princeton, NJ: Princeton University Press. **116, 297**

Wolfgang, M. E. 1970. "Urban crime," pp. 270–311 in J. Q. Wilson (ed.) *The Metropolitan Enigma.* New York: Doubleday. **229, 302**

——— and F. Ferracuti. 1967. *The Subculture of Violence.* London: Tavistock. **302, 316**

Wolfinger, R. E. 1965. "The development and persistence of ethnic voting." *American Political Science Review* 59: 896–908. **308**

Wood, R. C. 1958. *Suburbia: Its People and Their Politics.* Boston: Houghton Mifflin. **320**

———. 1961. *1400 Governments.* New York: Doubleday. **290**

Woodrum, E. 1981. "An assessment of Japanese–American assimilation, pluralism, and subordination." *American Sociological Review* 87: 157–169. **148, 308**

Worden, M. A. In press. "Criminogenic correlates of intermetropolitan crime rates," in D. E. Georges and K. D. Harries (eds.) *Crime: A Spatial Perspective.* New York: Columbia University Press. **107, 227, 316**

Wright, R. A. 1970. "Apartment Living Gaining Favor in U.S." *New York Times,* 12 July. **299**

Wurster, C. B. 1963. "The form and structure of the future urban complex," pp. 73–101 in L. Wingo, Jr. (ed.) *Cities and Space.* Baltimore: Johns Hopkins University Press. **278, 279, 281**

Wylie, L. 1964. *Village in the Vaucluse*. New York: Harper & Row. **194, 205, 310**
———. 1973. "The new French village, *hélas*." *New York Times Magazine*, 25 November. **313**
Wynne-Edwards, V. C. 1964. "Population control in animals." *Scientific American* 211: 68–74. Offprint 192. **311**
Yago, G. 1983. "Urban transportation in the eighties." *democracy* 1: 43–55. **323**
Yancey, W. L., and E. P. Ericksen. 1979. "The antecedents of community." *American Sociological Review* 44: 253–261. **303, 317**
Yang, C. K. 1959. *The Chinese Family in the Communist Revolution*. Cambridge, MA: MIT Press. **221**
Yans-McLaughlin, V. 1971. "Patterns of work and family organization: Buffalo's Italians." *Journal of Interdisciplinary History* 2: 293–314. **168, 308**
Yazaki, T. 1973. "The history of urbanization in Japan," pp. 139–162 in A. Southall (ed.) *Urban Anthropology*. New York: Oxford University Press. **298**
Yeates, M. H., and B. J. Garner. 1971. *The North American City*. New York: Harper & Row. **69, 298, 299, 303**
Youmans, E. G. 1977. "The rural aged." *Annals* 429: 81–90. **67, 68, 165, 310, 311**
Young, M., and P. Willmott. 1957. *Family and Kinship in East London*. Baltimore: Penguin. **130, 164, 261, 309, 320, 321**
———. 1973. *The Symmetrical Family*. Baltimore: Penguin. **241**
Zahn, M. A. 1980. "Homicide in twentieth-century United States," pp. 111–133 in J. A. Inciardi and C. E. Faupel (eds.) *History and Crime*. Beverly Hills, CA: Sage. **229, 302**
Zehr, H. 1975. "The modernization of crime in Germany and France, 1830–1913." *Journal of Social History* 8: 117–141. **303, 316**
Zelan, J. 1968. "Does suburbia make a difference?" pp. 401–408 in S. F. Fava (ed.) *Urbanism in World Perspective*. New York: Oxford University Press. **251, 256, 261, 265, 295**
Zikmund, J. II. 1971. "Do suburbanites use the central city?" *Journal of the American Institute of Planners* 37: 192–195. **239, 251**
Zimbardo, P. G. 1969. "The human choice: individuation, reason and order vs. deindividuation, impulse and chaos." Reprinted in J. Helmer and N. A. Eddington (eds.) *Urbanman*. New York: Free Press, 1973: 196–238. **315**
Zimmer, B. G. 1975. "Urban centrifugal drift," pp. 23–92 in A. Hawley and V. Rock (eds.) *Metropolitan America in Contemporary Perspective*. New York: Halstead. **51, 238**
——— and A. H. Hawley. 1959. "Suburbanization and church participation." *Social Forces* 37: 348–354. **321**
Zorbaugh, H. W. 1929. *The Gold Coast and the Slum*. Chicago: University of Chicago Press. **77, 89, 138, 204, 305, 310, 317**
Zuiches, J. J. 1981. "Residential preferences in the United States," pp. 72–115 in A. Hawley and S. Mazie (eds.) *Understanding Nonmetropolitan America*. Chapel Hill: University of North Carolina Press. **20, 92, 295, 302**
——— and D. L. Brown. 1978. "The changing character of the nonmetropolitan population, 1950–1975," pp. 55–79 in T. R. Ford (ed.) *Rural U.S.A.: Persistence and Change*. Ames: Iowa State University Press. **83, 93**
Zuiches, J. J., and G. V. Fuguitt. 1972. "Residential preferences," pp. 617–631 in S. M. Mazie (ed.) *Population, Distribution, and Policy*, Vol. V, Research Reports. Washington, DC: U.S. Commission on Population Growth and the American Future. **295**

Index

This is primarily a subject index. To locate the discussion of a particular study, see the listing in the References section.

A 4
B 5
C 6
D 7
E 8
F 9
G 0
H 1
I 2
J 3

DATE DUE

11 01 '84	
JUN 15 1985	
'A 15 '8?	
5. 13. 8?	
11 04 '87	
ret. 11/25	
AUG 0 8 '90	
JAN 30 92	
MAR 2 0 1998	
JAN 1 5 2003	
APR 1 7 2003	
FEB 2 3 2006	

BRODART, INC.   Cat. No. 23-221